# APARTHEID SPIES AND THE REVOLUTIONARY UNDERGROUND

# APARTHEID SPIES AND THE REVOLUTIONARY UNDERGROUND

BILLY KENISTON

WITS UNIVERSITY PRESS

Published in South Africa by:
Wits University Press
1 Jan Smuts Avenue
Johannesburg 2001

www.witspress.co.za

Copyright © William Keniston 2024
Published edition © Wits University Press 2024
Cover image © André de Wet, Protest at the murder of Jeanette and Katryn Schoon, 1984, courtesy of the AAM Archive, MSS AAM 2413

First published 2024

Accounts of events have been gathered from several sources. The author has captured how people have remembered them, although others may remember these events differently. Any perceived mischaracterisations are therefore not intended.

http://dx.doi.org.10.18772/12024119018

978-1-77614-901-8 (Paperback)
978-1-77614-902-5 (Hardback)
978-1-77614-903-2 (Web PDF)
978-1-77614-904-9 (EPUB)

All rights reserved. No part of this publication may be reproduced, stored in a retrieval system, or transmitted in any form or by any means, electronic, mechanical, photocopying, recording or otherwise, without the written permission of the publisher, except in accordance with the provisions of the Copyright Act, Act 98 of 1978.

This publication is peer reviewed following international best practice standards for academic and scholarly books.

Project manager: Alison Paulin
Copyeditor: Alison Lowry
Proofreader: Alison Paulin
Indexer: Margaret Ramsay
Cover design: Hybrid Creative
Typeset in 11.5 point Crimson

*For Tony Morphet (1940–2021)*

# Contents

| | |
|---|---|
| Preface | ix |
| Acknowledgements | xix |
| Acronyms and abbreviations | xxvii |
| Timeline | xxix |
| Introduction | 1 |
| Prologue: The Assassination, 1984 | 27 |
| **Part 1: From Student Radicals to Post-student People, 1972–1976** | 47 |
| 1 Student Radicals | 49 |
| 2 Post-student People | 61 |
| **Part 2: Cover Stories and Undercover Stories, Botswana and Geneva, 1977–1980** | 85 |
| 3 Cover Stories | 87 |
| 4 Undercover Stories | 111 |
| 5 Exposing Craig Williamson | 137 |
| 6 The Damage is Done | 159 |

## Part 3: Furthering the Aims, 1980–1983     169

  7  Arrests and Detention     171

  8  The Trials     191

## Part 4: Forced Asylum, 1981–1984     223

  9  No Asylum from Her Majesty     225

 10  A Kind of Asylum     245

    Epilogue: Amnesty and Justice, 1995–2007     271

    Notes     293

    Bibliography     319

    Index     327

# Preface

> The shootings at Sharpeville marked a turning point ... broke the belief that a non-violent solution was possible ... the belief was growing that a revolutionary and necessarily violent struggle would have to be waged to break the apartheid state.
>
> — Ben Turok, *The ANC and the Turn to Armed Struggle, 1950–1970*

On 26 and 27 March 2019, almost 60 years since the Sharpeville Massacre, a group of 50 or more veterans from the ANC's armed wing, Umkhonto we Sizwe (MK), came together for a conference at Liliesleaf, which is now a 'space of liberation', a museum and conference centre, but was once the site of a dramatic police raid, in 1963, which led to the imprisonment of most of the African National Congress's (ANC) executive leadership.[1] At this conference, on multiple occasions I witnessed MK members saying, 'we fought against apartheid ... and apartheid ended.' Likewise, younger people in the audience repeatedly congratulated the veterans for having taken up arms, and therefore for ending apartheid. In other words, there was no need to fill in the missing information that is contained within the ellipses. We fought ... we won. Story told.

As the veterans told their personal stories about their time in the military underground, I saw that *all* stories were received as heroic accounts, regardless of the actual details. One veteran spoke of the disastrous failure to bring a large ship down the east coast of Africa, intended to land in the Transkei, to launch a guerrilla uprising, in imitation of the

Cubans. The veteran recounted the way in which 'the boat got sick' and had to turn back again and again, never making it further south than Dar es Salaam. Another veteran recounted, in gripping detail – and with a remarkable sense of humour – being one of a group of soldiers instructed to march through Rhodesia (now Zimbabwe) from the Zambian border in the north and attempt to infiltrate South Africa. Desperate for food and water, the group found themselves wandering through a game reserve, hunting zebra ('the striped quagga') while being hunted down themselves by the Rhodesian special forces. Many of his comrades died, and he spent months in jail.[2]

A third veteran remembered years spent peeling potatoes, playing basketball and putting on theatrical performances for other comrades at a barracks in Tanzania. She remembered that ANC leadership would often visit from London. The soldiers living in the barracks spoke of the London leadership as 'the revolutionary situation', because the endless refrain they heard on these visits was that 'the revolutionary situation is not yet right' to wage war in South Africa.

No matter how little happened in these stories, or how much failure was involved, everything was neatly framed inside a heroic story of having defeated apartheid.

In a political climate such as this, what use is there of having carefully researched accounts of history? According to Janet Cherry, the author of a popular account of MK, *Spear of the Nation* (and herself an ANC member), 'it is hard to find anyone in South Africa today who will argue with conviction that the armed struggle for liberation from apartheid was not justified'.[3] But what does it mean to say that the armed struggle was 'justified'?

One of the central protagonists of this book is Marius Schoon. Schoon, a lifelong supporter of the ANC, participated in the first wave of sabotage attempts in the early 1960s. For his part in attempting to bomb a police station in Hillbrow, Johannesburg, he spent 12 years in Pretoria Central Prison. Not long after the devastating loss of his wife and daughter, who were killed by an apartheid parcel bomb in Lubango, Angola, in 1984, Schoon was asked by writer and film producer Julie Frederikse to explain his reasons for supporting the armed struggle. He offered an incisive account of the question of 'justifying' armed struggle:

> I have no doubt ... whatsoever that the war against Hitler was completely justified ... Now why should it be more difficult to see the justness of the people of South Africa, not at last but again defending themselves against the brutality of the state to establish a sane society in our country – why is it more difficult to see that than to see that it was correct for somebody from Minnesota to go and fight Hitler in Europe?[4]

It is difficult to argue against the moral clarity of Schoon's position. Certainly, this book does not intend, in any form, to question the morality of Schoon's (or anyone else's) engagement in an armed struggle against apartheid. However, there is a critical distinction missing here. For historians it is not enough to simply decide whether using violence against apartheid was 'justified', in a moral or even in a strategic sense. In the telling of histories, there is an ethical component to our work. By marking the boundaries of ethical choices – one hopes – and providing lessons from the past, this may work towards helping prevent the reiteration of crimes against humanity such as apartheid. Beyond our ethical duties, however, historians must also attempt, given the critical limitations of archival sources and memory, to address what happened.

In contrast to the established narrative arc regarding the armed struggle – after Sharpeville and before the release of Mandela – this book exists in the ellipses, in between 'we fought' and 'we won'. Set within a fifteen-year span, it contends that during this period neither armed struggle nor victory were taken for granted.

Because much of the research for this book is grounded in an extensive set of interviews, it is important to outline some of the strengths, limitations and peculiarities of my particular approach to oral history research, so that these issues are clear from the start.

First, it must be noted that the book builds on more than five years of prior research into related topics. My study of this period of the anti-apartheid movement began in 2008, working towards an MA in History from the University of the Western Cape. Then, the MA thesis was expanded into a full-length biography of Rick Turner, a white radical professor who was assassinated in 1978. My work on Rick Turner relied heavily on over 20 interviews with friends, comrades and family of Turner. As that project was explicitly a biography, many of my connections with those who knew Turner were warmer, deeper and more sustained than many academic projects might afford. I have been a guest in most of these people's homes, and we have come to know one another on levels far beyond the specific set of questions that first led me to contact them. By now I have a sustained friendship that has been continuous, over the last decade, with at least a handful of Turner's peers. All of this is relevant to the present study, because many of Turner's contemporaries are the focus of this book.

One factor that influences the dynamic I have developed with the people I've interviewed is that the South African white community is relatively small and is – by necessity, as a result of apartheid – largely an insular group. Among South African white people, the group that opposed apartheid is far smaller. In addition, as the people I've spoken to are generally my parents' age, this also means that many of the younger people with whom I have ended up crossing paths in my daily life in contemporary South Africa are often the children of 1970s activists. This leads to intriguing overlaps between my social life and my research. Many times, during an interview, I will find that the person we're discussing is the mom or dad of a friend of mine. Or, at a dinner party, I'll meet the son of someone I'm hoping to interview. Or, over tea with a friend's parents, I will casually mention the name of a person I hope to speak with, and the parents will respond, 'Oh, I just saw them the other day, buying the newspaper.' When I rented an apartment in Johannesburg for my research year, the woman in charge of the flat was Fiona Lloyd, the widow of Hugh Lewin, whose life story is intensely interwoven with multiple aspects of this book. Furthermore, in the same suburb where I lived, three of the people I interviewed for this project also lived, just a short walk away.

Perhaps all of the above gives the impression that my oral history research process was somehow casual, or 'informal'. This would be missing the point.

My interviews proceeded with the formal backing of the Institutional Review Board for the University of Illinois at Urbana-Champaign,[5] with all participants signing a document that outlines the nature of my project and specifically articulates the terms of their consent to be quoted. Given the intensity of political commitment involved and the intensity of their engagement with narrating their own history, the people I interviewed, in general and on the whole, ardently insisted on having a clean demarcation of their rights and ethical protections in this process. Everyone quoted in this book has had a chance to read the draft, not only to confirm their own quotations, but also offering everything from grammatical advice to political critique and insights. In addition, there are a few people whose assistance I have drawn on repeatedly. This continuing intellectual exchange reflects not only my personal approach as a historian, but also speaks to the particular social position in which many of these individuals now find themselves.

A number of the people interviewed have spent a lifetime as politically engaged intellectuals. They include lawyers, professors, executive directors of NGOs, filmmakers, poets, journalists and even the occasional politician. At this point in South Africa, such intellectuals are directly and actively involved in producing and contesting the nation's history. Therefore, many of the people whom I've relied on for information are themselves busy collecting and analysing archival documents, writing memoirs, testifying before contemporary government commissions regarding apartheid atrocities, and so on. Horst Kleinschmidt, for example, who is quoted in this book, has an archive in his home that is among the most extensive collections of student and Christian anti-apartheid activities in the 1960s and 1970s anywhere existent, and is organised as meticulously as any public archive might be. In this case, it was only natural that I would spend many days in Kleinschmidt's home, consulting his archive extensively, and that our conversations would proceed on the level of two historians studying the same topic. Kleinschmidt's was only one of the multiple personal archives that I consulted for this project.

The fact that my interviewees are intellectually and politically engaged in the production of South African history influences not only the ways in which I utilise the transcripts, but also the specific nature of the interview process. The interviews conducted for this book are not 'oral histories' in the way in which that phrase is often interpreted by historians, and particularly by historians of Africa. While some portion of every interview allowed space for people to narrate their life story – particularly in relation to how they first became politically active – the remainder of our time was far more conversational and dynamic than life histories would be. In many instances, the questions I asked were in relation to specific documents, such as political pamphlets or papers written either by themselves or by their organisations (back in the 1970s). In other words, I asked my interviewees to articulate and reflect on their own political positions, and those of their peers. In addition, as this study looks extensively into the repressive mechanisms of the apartheid state, I also asked questions related to trial transcripts and other documents produced by the state. In making sense of the strategic thinking of the state, I am also concerned with how the *targets* of state repression understand what happened to them, both as it was happening and upon reflection.

A critical aspect of the trust-building that was required for these interviews to proceed with respect and integrity was precisely the fact that I was *not* an impartial researcher. While having been raised in the United States makes me – at the simplest level – a 'foreign' researcher, the specific political tradition I was raised within is very much resonant with the core questions this book addresses. That is, as a young adult I was mentored by older radicals, both Black[6] and white, who taught me that the Black freedom struggle is the engine of historical transformation in the US and that I, as a white person, must do everything I can to understand how to assist that struggle. The depth of my own political commitment – opposition to white supremacy and a desire for socialism – allowed many of the people whom I spoke with to respect me as an individual, as well as to trust the intentions behind my research. On several occasions, up to half of the 'interview' time was spent with the other person 'vetting' me, asking probing questions to understand who I am more precisely. Many requested that I share a draft of my work prior to meeting, and my writing was always carefully analysed to make sure that I had sufficiently studied the subject at hand, as well as to make sure that my political stance was not in some way objectionable. I suspect that without my personally having a commitment to radical politics, some of these people would have refused to be interviewed or would have spoken on much more of a surface level than the deep conversations that constitute the core of the oral histories included here.

None of this description conveys, in any way, the particular complexities and difficulties of interviewing people who were (and often still are) active members of the ANC. From my experience, the political culture that has developed within the ANC is far more secretive, far more suspicious and far more reticent to engage than the independent socialists that I dealt with. More than one ANC member refused to meet with me, and quite bitterly so. The mere fact that my project was focused on white people, and took Black Consciousness seriously, caused one ANC member to refuse to be interviewed. Another was disgusted by the suggestion that the ANC bears any responsibility for the damage caused by Craig Williamson's infiltration of the movement. Other ANC members agreed to meet with me, and spoke cordially, even warmly – as long as the topic at hand had nothing at all to do with the deeper substance of their involvement in the ANC. Among the ANC members who agreed to be interviewed, many of their answers included vague references to internal processes of the ANC, of which I could not possibly have knowledge. One very basic consequence of a sustained period of underground struggle is the fact that people do not actually know very much regarding the activities of their comrades within the ANC. In this sense, my interviewees were not being evasive or wilfully withholding – they genuinely *didn't know* the answers to my questions.

Furthermore, for participants of the ANC's underground and exile structures, the stakes of this history are far higher than for those who participated in the aboveground movement. Therefore, the process of seeking feedback regarding how these individuals' words were quoted was far more animated and – at times – tense. While I made every attempt to confine these conversations to resolving factual errors rather than disagreements based on political interpretation, this distinction is not so easily drawn. From the perspective of an organisation that has played an outsized role in shaping the history of the 'liberation struggle', the correct 'line' on a given issue is largely taken as a matter of fact, rather than something that is open to debate and disagreement. These are the endemic problems that confront anyone doing research into the history of the ANC.

From my time as a guest of the History Workshop at the University of Witwatersrand, I saw that successful research projects into the ANC and MK *can* be done, especially when undertaken by people with a direct connection to the organisation. For example, a young MA student was the daughter of an MK veteran, and her father's comrades were happy to speak with her in her capacity as a family member, rather than in her capacity as a 'researcher'. Likewise, some worthwhile projects have begun at a regional level, with Black South African historians researching the presence of MK in rural areas, based on interviews conducted in people's mother tongues. Such projects are not merely admirable. It may be that, for the foreseeable future at least, the only true histories of the ANC will have to be written by those within 'the family', either literally or figuratively.

At the other end of the spectrum, a critical piece of my oral history research was related to Craig Williamson. I've done interviews with 10 or more different people who knew Williamson during those years. Jonathan Ancer, whose biography of Williamson was inspirational for my own project, also did at least as many interviews with those in the white left who knew Williamson and were damaged by him. These interviews are an important and necessary step, but they are only able to provide a deeply limited perspective, because they rely heavily on what people *think* they understood at the time, or now suspect, with the benefit of hindsight. Since Williamson was successfully operating undercover for nearly a decade, there is very little concrete evidence that people within those infiltrated organisations can provide about what Williamson was doing or thinking at the time.

Even worse are the interviews with Williamson himself, which I and so many others have conducted. Sitting across the table from a man who you know for sure is a liar is a dizzying, bewildering experience. Both during the interview, as well as transcribing it afterwards, I asked myself constantly, is he lying when he says that? The problem with a man like Williamson is that his talent and his training is in saying things that at least sound plausible. Although I did catch him outright lying on a few occasions, more often I found Williamson to be evasive. Williamson's style of evading my questions was to answer them, but to do so in a way that was so superficial and vague that it didn't offer any actual information. There were multiple occasions during our two hours together where Williamson would slow his speech down considerably, carefully choosing his words, and then would tell me something completely trite, as if he were merely an outside observer rather than the most knowledgeable person regarding the question I had asked. In addition, Williamson's way of speaking is riddled with clichés and metaphors related to spy craft, a career that he repeatedly referred to as a 'game', or a 'dance', while rarely offering any details to explain the practical mechanics of playing. The implication that underlies everything Williamson says is that you (the listener) cannot possibly understand what he really did as a spy, because you are not a spy. Therefore, he speaks not to make things more transparent, but rather to erect an even greater air of mystery around himself.

How could all the different voices of the people that I've interviewed be woven together into one coherent narrative? That was a question I thought about endlessly throughout the years of writing this book. Especially because the stories contain so many competing explanations and so many contradictions, how to unify them was not immediately obvious. My answer to this predicament may confuse or upset some readers, but it is worth explaining, because it is critical to understanding the structure and argument that the book is making.

Quite simply, I didn't try to unify them. That is, rather than attempt to smooth over the contestations between different people's perspectives, I have attempted to preserve them, even to amplify them. As a historian and as an author, I see my role to be fundamentally about composing a framework for understanding and making meaning out of historical moments. Within that framing, I contend that we need to hear and to engage with all the different voices, rather than seek to winnow away or silence the ones that are not 'true'.

Throughout the book, I have presented a series of discrete stories. For each story, the people I've interviewed have contributed their understanding of 'what happened'. However, no one that I spoke with told me *only* 'the truth' about any particular event. As is only natural, everyone I spoke with also told me *why* things happened the way they did. It matters how we interpret these events, because it is the interpretations that go along with the stories that give them meaning. While I have allowed myself to indicate at times whether a particular position is plausible – in light of other information gleaned from my research – in the main I don't believe it is my job to be the arbiter of these different interpretations of the past. My hope is that I have presented everyone's positions accurately and thoroughly, such that the reader can determine for themselves where the truth lies.

This approach to oral history feels particularly important, given the subjects that are at the heart of this book. Within the underground movement, there was a wide range of debates about strategy and ideology, constantly. Even among close comrades, these debates raged on. These different stances were further compounded by both the fact of having been infiltrated by the security police, and people's suspicions around the constant possibility of spies, arrests or other forms of state-sponsored attacks on the movement. In such a context, so much of what people 'know' about a given situation amounts, in fact, to what they *think* they know. Therefore, much of the book deals in the domain of speculation, educated guesses, rumour and hearsay. Added on top of all of this, there is also the not insignificant fact that the interviews I conducted took place forty to fifty years after the fact. So, there are inevitably gaps in people's memories, as well as knowledge obtained after the fact now being applied to history as if it was something known at the time.

I can appreciate that the reader may at times feel frustrated by the lack of solid ground and the depths of speculation involved in narrating these stories. I can assure you that all of us – not least, the participants themselves – would love to know 'for sure' what happened. However, in many instances, this is simply not possible. Therefore, I invite you to read these moments of speculation not as if they are somehow inadequate, but rather to see them as essential components of the world of underground radicals and spies.

This is a living history. That is to say, the research required for this book relies heavily on the memories and analysis of people who are still alive.

It should be remembered that this book draws on interviews with both members of the ANC (and other anti-apartheid activists) as well as Craig Williamson. On both sides, there is a heightened sensitivity to the way that this history is narrated. Therefore, throughout the process of writing and revising, these individuals have passionately provided feedback. This feedback spans the range from seemingly subtle or simple details to overarching interpretative disagreements, fiercely argued.

The stakes of this book exist as much in what is contained in the final draft as it does in the deletions that I was asked to make along the way, the things that people would not say on tape, and the people who refused to speak at all.

# Acknowledgements

While the bulk of the writing took place during the darkest days of lockdowns and mass death from Covid-19, this book is now eight years in the making. Before being a book, this was a dissertation, and before that simply a series of research trips and short conference papers. For conceiving the project, I am indebted to Professor Teresa Barnes, my bridge from the University of the Western Cape to the University of Illinois. Her idea of tracing a path from John Harris's 1964 bomb in the whites-only waiting room of Park Station, Johannesburg to the 1984 parcel bomb in Lubango, Angola got me started, although I was forced to admit that I could not accomplish such a grand mission.

Also at Illinois, Sundiata Cha-Jua remains the fiercest ally I've ever had in the academy, and also one of the few people who can critique me fiercely enough to grab my attention. Jim Brennan's steadiness, his patience and attention to detail got me over the finish line. As an external adviser, I could not have asked for better than Neil Roos. His scholarship on ordinary white people in South Africa is an inspiration for my own work and, for years now, I have come to rely on his thoughtful and warm encouragement.

During the final revisions of the manuscript of the book my colleagues in History and African Studies at St Lawrence University were enormously supportive in many ways. Many thanks also to the Academic Affairs office and the Departments of History and African Studies at St Lawrence University for providing the funds for the publishing subvention costs.

During an early phase of my research, I was invited by the Hoover Institute at Stanford University to participate in a two-week long research seminar on 'Authoritarianism and Democratic Breakdown'. Mine was only one of two projects that understood the word 'authoritarianism' to pertain to right-wing states – the rest equated communism with authoritarianism. The joke on the first day was that the archives were located in the basement, 'so that the communists can't find them'. In addition to my time at Hoover, I also received funding from the Association for the Study of the Middle East and Africa (ASMEA). After presenting my paper at their conference, I was horrified to learn that ASMEA exists as a Zionist break-away from the much larger Middle Eastern Studies Association. I acknowledge these two sobering experiences, because both of them helped me understand the potential pitfalls and culs-de-sac involved in studying the strategic thinking of the apartheid state.

My research path has followed the central characters in this book from South Africa to Botswana, Angola and multiple sites in Europe. At the simple logistical level, all of this was made possible thanks to a Fulbright DDRA Fellowship, which provided funding for nine intensive months of research. For my success in obtaining the Fulbright, I am deeply beholden to Ken Vickery, an absolute genius at editing and revising external funding applications and a genuinely warm-hearted man.

Beyond covering expenses, in all of the places that I conducted research and wrote, I received support – in the form of shared meals, excellent conversations, advice and encouragement – from so many people, without whom this book simply would not exist.

## South Africa

Cape Town was in many ways a home for me, for over a decade. Tony Morphet's home with Ingrid Fiske was – for many years – a special kind of refuge for me. Tony and Ingrid always pushed me to think more clearly about my project, asking all the best questions, and adding a healthy dose of laughter too. I found refuge among many other excellent people with whom I had the pleasure of crossing paths while there, including Maya Goldman, Simone Haysom, Jessica Wilson, Paul Khupethewa, Hedley Twidle, Heidi Grunebaum and the Mathibela family.

While Tony was unable to witness the full completion of this book, the fact of its fulfilment nonetheless owes a great deal to him. After patiently seeing me through my MA thesis and biography on Rick Turner, Tony was the first person to insist that I pursue a PhD. Throughout the years of research and writing, his incisive intellect and undying sense of humour steered the way forward. To the extent that the writing contained here succeeds in answering the ever-essential question, 'What is your thesis?' it is a reflection of Tony Morphet's relentless pursuit of fresh thinking. Any errors of approach and analysis are entirely my own.

On the research side, Horst Kleinschmidt and Terry Bell both patiently opened up their homes to me so that I could spend hours reading through their carefully catalogued private archives. Meeting with Jonathan Ancer on multiple occasions was crucial for understanding how to proceed in an interview with Craig Williamson, and how to write about it. At the Parliamentary Library, Sedack Cassoojee went above and beyond his job duties to track down a seemingly lost treasure trove of files from the Schlebusch Commission. I am also grateful to have spent many days researching in the Special Collections at the University of Cape Town, before a devastating fire destroyed much of the collection in 2021. Also at UCT, early drafts of writing for this project were workshopped by the excellent folks at the Archive and Public Culture Research Initiative. Quite a few of the interviews for this book were conducted in Cape Town, as well as a few that didn't make it into the final draft: Michael Savage, Clive Keegan and Geoff Budlender.

In Johannesburg, I had the honour of being hosted by the History Workshop at the University of the Witwatersrand. Among the many fine folks at the History Workshop, I am particularly beholden to Noor Nieftagodien, Arianna Lissoni, Antonette Gouws, Laura Phillips and Luke Sinwell. Also at Wits, Historical Papers is perhaps the warmest and most emphatically radical archive ('THE PEOPLE SHALL GOVERN!') in the world; a great space to spend weeks on end reading through files from the 1970s.

Living at Cranwell Hall, I befriended Fiona Lloyd, who shared memories and files from her beloved Hugh Lewin and hosted a vital meeting between myself and Sherry McLean. I carry with me – as a kind of moral compass – Sherry's deep disdain for Craig Williamson, her urgent longing for justice. Sherry read many early drafts of my writing and provided thoughtful feedback. In addition, she assisted me in connecting with the Curtis family and helped me try to locate Jenny and Katryn's graves in

Luanda. Early on in my research, Fritz Schoon graciously met with me for lunch. Fritz was friendly and encouraging. In addition, he connected me with his attorney, Karien Norval, and with his friend Terry Bell. These acts of kindness were absolutely vital to the success of this project.

Without Peter Swanepoel's patient assistance, I would not have been able to interview Craig Williamson. On a related note, Jacob Dlamini connected me with Hennie Heymans, who helped me understand the mentality of apartheid security police officers.

Among the many interviews I conducted in Johannesburg, my repeated meetings with Denis Kuny were particularly special. I will always remember our journey to Liliesleaf Farm together, with his little white dog sitting on my lap, and I will always remember Denis saying, 'to answer that, you've got to go back to 1960'.

My colleague Doug Jones spent many hours with me in the archives, humbling me with his diligence and rigour. And through it all, the discussions and meals with Jonathan Cane were vital to making peace with life in Joburg.

## Angola

Before going to Angola, I spent a week doing archival research in the Centro de Intervenção Para o Desenvolvimento Amílcar Cabral (CIDAC), which is an NGO in Lisbon with an extensive archive of books, newspapers, pamphlets and other material related to national liberation struggles in Africa. In addition, I reached out to a number of scholars with knowledge of Angola. This included Lara Pawson, a British journalist and author of *In the Name of the People: Angola's Forgotten Massacre*. Pawson spent an afternoon in London with me, talking through the project, and then followed up afterwards with an exhaustive list of names of people who might be able to help. One of Pawson's suggestions was Jenny Morgan, a South African living in London since the 1970s and a documentary filmmaker who worked for the BBC, including a film about Angolan women, shot in the 1980s, at the height of the civil war. Another suggestion was Joana Henriques, a Portuguese journalist and author of the book *Racismo no País dos Brancos Costumes*, which outlines the racist history of Portuguese rule in the five African colonies. In South Africa, I met with Claudia Gastrow, an anthropology professor, and Ruth Castel Bronco, a sociology graduate student. These individuals gave advice on everything from how to navigate the labyrinthine visa system, which neighbourhoods to stay in in Luanda, as well as suggestions of readings.

I timed my trip to Angola to coincide with Marissa Moorman's own research trip. Moorman is a historian of Angola, with more than twenty years' experience, and she has a genuine fluency for Angola; she not only speaks *Angolan* Portuguese, she moves through her days there with a genuine sense of calm and pleasure. Without being introduced to Marissa Moorman's version of Angola, my capacity to do research there would have been seriously limited.

There was one archive inside Angola that Moorman strongly encouraged me to consult. This was the Associação Tchiweka de Documentação, which is a family archive, comprised of the lifelong collection of Lúcio Lara, the second-in-command of the Movimento Popular de Libertação de Angola (Popular Movement for the Liberation of Angola – MPLA) during the war for independence. I was, in a sense, hosted by the Lara family while in Angola. Wanda's brother Bruno was a fantastic host in Lubango. The Laras set up a number of important meetings for me with students and colleagues of the Schoons, as well as helping me connect with translators. In addition, when the police began asking one of the teachers I was meeting with where I had come from, she simply answered, 'I don't know; as far as I know, he comes from Luanda, from Wanda Lara.' Without all these different layers of support, I simply wouldn't have been able to conduct any research in Angola.

## England

Over the years of research, London was a critical hub for my trips in and out of South Africa. On one such journey, having flown in overnight from the States, I met with Gillian Slovo for tea and an informal conversation. While I didn't take any notes during our discussion, I still remember the meeting vividly, and remain grateful that Gillian took the time to meet with me. I spent a couple of days in London at the Institute for Commonwealth Studies, reading through the wonderful letters between Gillian's mother, Ruth First, and her father, Joe Slovo. While the story of the Slovo family is largely beyond the scope of this book, it is of course very much in parallel, with many overlaps. Ruth First will always stand out to me as an exemplary scholar, passionately committed to revolutionary change.

My time with Nigel Watt was also vital. In addition to patiently sitting for an interview, Nigel also hosted a dinner at his home (where I was a guest for a night), which provided me an opportunity to chat with a number of British people who had been volunteers with the International Voluntary Service (IVS) during the 1970s and 80s. This dinner discussion deepened the understanding of IVS that I had gleaned from my time reading the archival collection up in Hull. Of course, the entire story of IVS contained in this book would not make much sense at all without the internal documents from the Foreign and Commonwealth Office, which I encountered at the very end of my nine months of research, in the British National Archives.

In addition to my time in London, a trip to Birmingham allowed me an opportunity to reconnect with Michael Hubbard, the beloved brother-in-law of Rick Turner. While visiting Hubbard, I was also introduced to Petra Röhr-Rouendaal, whose fabulous poster against the South African Special Branch still hangs on the wall above where I make my espresso.

## Denmark

My time in Copenhagen was brief but packed with intriguing meetings with Danish intellectuals and activists; their combined commitment to ending apartheid (and support for my research) was humbling. I am grateful for the warm hospitality and conversations with Gorm Gunnarsen, Steen Christensen, John Graversgaard and Henrik Berlau. Most of all, I am indebted to Henrik Thomsen for his diligent and persistent research into Craig Williamson's 'Operation Daisy'.

## Home

Through it all, none of these journeys could have amounted to anything without a solid home base. Whether in the prairies of Illinois, the mountains of Hawaii, the coast of the Beara peninsula, the endless sunshine of Nihomo, the bitter cold of Canton, or the cobblestone streets of Angra do Heroismo and Arraiolos, my beloved Lisa Fay has been right beside me, through every step of this process. On hundreds of long walks and over thousands of delicious dinners, Lisa and I have discussed this project, with a level of depth and care that is unparalleled. There is no one else who knows the subtle intricacies of these complex stories better than Lisa Fay.

Day by day, month by month, year by year, our time together grounds me and allows me to return to the writing studio, again and again. Lisa Fay never allows me to give in to my doubts, and she brings layers of light and playfulness into the marathon days of writing a book.

From years spent as Lisa Fay's biggest fan in the audience, I have learned a great deal about the craft of composing and the necessity of asking 'radically effective questions'. Furthermore, as a writer, I have drawn inspiration from Lisa's sustained commitment to rehearsing, and rehearsing again, and again … a fierce attention to detail, a deep striving for perfection.

For all that is excellent in this book – and in me – I am forever grateful to my Lisa.

# Acronyms and abbreviations

ANC     African National Congress
ARM     African Resistance Movement
BOSS     Bureau for State Security (in common usage among the opposition)
EDA     Environmental and Developmental Agency
FCO     Foreign and Commonwealth Office
IAS     Industrial Aid Society
IPRD     Internal Political Reconstruction and Development (ANC project)
IUEF     International University Exchange Fund
IVS     International Voluntary Services
MK     Umkhonto we Sizwe (the Spear of the Nation)
MPLA     Movimento Popular de Libertação de Angola (Popular Movement for the Liberation of Angola)
Nusas     National Union of South African Students
PAC     Pan-Africanist Congress
PST     Prisoners Support Trust
SACP     South African Communist Party (renamed after the CPSA was outlawed in 1950)
Sactu     South African Congress of Trade Unions (ANC aligned)
SADF     South African Defence Force
SAIRR     South African Institute of Race Relations
Sana     South African News Agency

| | |
|---|---|
| Sapet | South African Prisoner and Education Trust |
| Saso | South African Students' Organisation |
| SNS | Solidarity News Service |
| TRC | Truth and Reconciliation Commission |
| UCM | University Christian Movement |
| Zanu | Zimbabwe African National Union |

# Timeline

1948     The National Party wins the election. The beginning of apartheid.

1950     The Suppression of Communism Act bans the Communist Party and illegalises a wide range of activities that could purportedly be understood as 'communist' in nature.

1960     The Sharpeville Massacre kills 69, wounds 178 ... and becomes *the* turning point in the anti-apartheid struggle.

1961     Umkhonto we Sizwe (MK), the armed wing of the ANC, comes to life through a wave of bombings on 16 December (an Afrikaner holiday that glorifies violent conquest).

1963     On 11 July, the police raid Liliesleaf Farm in Rivonia, arresting 19 leaders of the ANC, most of whom would then be imprisoned on Robben Island after what came to be known as the Rivonia Trial. The General Law Amendment Act is passed, authorising detention without charges for up to 90 days.

1964     On 4 July, police arrest members of the African Resistance Movement (ARM). Along with the arrest of John Harris, an ARM member who bombed the Johannesburg train station on 24 July, the organisation is effectively smashed. Marius Schoon is sentenced to 12 years in prison for attempted sabotage.

1966     Rowley Arenstein, a white communist, ANC supporter and pacifist, is put on trial for furthering the aims of the ANC, despite his non-violent convictions.

1967     The annual National Union of South African Students (Nusas) conference requires segregated accommodation, forcing Black students to sleep off campus in the townships on the outskirts of Grahamstown. This outrages young Black leaders and is a pivotal moment in Black Consciousness.

1969   A group of Black students pulls out of Nusas and forms the all-Black South African Students' Organisation (Saso), the first Black Consciousness organisation. This creates a crisis of purpose for white liberals within Nusas, which gives way to a new radical politics.

1970   Neville Curtis is elected president of Nusas and takes the organisation in new, radical directions.

1971   Nusas initiates Wages Commissions on campuses throughout the country, a student initiative to support a living wage for the Black industrial working class. Jenny Curtis is one of the leaders of this project.

1972   The Schlebusch Commission begins. Craig Williamson arrives at the University of the Witwatersrand as a police infiltrator.

1973   Eight leaders of Nusas are placed under banning orders, following the recommendations of the Schlebusch Commission. Less than two weeks later, eight leaders of Saso are also banned. Neville Curtis flees the country as a result and Jenny moves to Johannesburg. The Industrial Aid Society (IAS) is formed, with Jenny Curtis among the founding members.

1974   A military coup in Portugal overthrows fascism, leading to the end of Portuguese colonial rule in Africa. Saso leaders at a Durban rally in support of Mozambique's Frente de Libertação de Moçambique (Frelimo – Front for the Liberation of Mozambique) are arrested, leading to a high-profile trial against Black Consciousness leaders. Nusas runs an extended campaign of education and protest calling for the release of all political prisoners in South Africa. Craig Williamson is elected to the executive leadership of Nusas.

1975   Breyten Breytenbach enters the country hoping to build a clandestine organisation of white radicals, called Okhela. Breytenbach and nearly 20 others, including Jenny Curtis, are detained as a result. Shortly after these white leftists are released from detention, a number (including Curtis) are banned and a handful of others are indicted in a high-profile trial against Nusas, accused of conspiring to support the ANC and SACP. They are acquitted. Angola becomes independent, and the South African military invades.

1976 The Soweto uprising begins on 16 June and continues for multiple months. Thousands of young Black radicals leave the country to join the exile movement. There is also an uptick in young white people leaving the country, in disgust and to avoid military service. Craig Williamson leaves in December, under the guise of being a South African 'refugee'. Marius Schoon is released from prison.

1977 Jenny Curtis marries Marius Schoon and on their wedding night the couple flee to Botswana to join the ANC in exile. Steve Biko is arrested and severely beaten in police custody, leading to his death on 12 September. A widespread crackdown on Black Consciousness organisations follows Biko's death.

1979 The Schoons' ANC cell in Botswana determines that Karl Edwards is definitely a police officer and Williamson is likely one as well.

1980 Craig Williamson is exposed as an undercover agent at the International University Exchange Fund (IUEF) and is forced to flee Geneva, returning to South Africa as an anti-communist hero. In July, arrests begin of activists connected to the Schoons, starting with Devan Pillay and Guy Berger.

1981 The round-up of white leftists linked to the Schoons continues, including Alan Fine, Barbara Hogan and Auret van Heerden. They are detained for months and often tortured in detention. In September, the Schoons are hired as co-directors of the International Voluntary Service (IVS) in Botswana. This sparks a campaign by the British Foreign and Commonwealth Office (FCO) to have them removed.

1982 On 5 February, Neil Aggett dies in detention. The authorities declare it a suicide, though activists continue to believe Aggett was murdered. Trials commence against the group of white radicals. Craig Williamson and Karl Edwards testify for the state. Alan Fine is acquitted; the rest are sentenced to at least two years and, in the case of Barbara Hogan, 10 years. On 14 March, the London headquarters of the ANC is bombed. No one is killed, but this is a clear act of terror carried out on European soil by the apartheid security services, including Craig Williamson. In July, Medu Art Ensemble hosts the 'Culture and Resistance' festival, bringing together hundreds of artists and members of the ANC in Gaborone. On 17 August, Ruth First is killed by a parcel bomb in Maputo, Mozambique, sent by Craig Williamson's unit of the security police.

1983   The FCO campaign against the Schoons escalates, leading to their decision to leave Botswana in July. Around Christmas the Schoons arrive in Angola.

1984   On 28 June, Jeanette and Katryn Schoon are killed by a parcel bomb, which explodes in their apartment in Lubango, Angola. The bomb was sent by Craig Williamson's unit of the security police.

# Introduction

> Racism, in its first and last instance ... is about controlling white people: reinforcing an amoral self-abnegation and attenuating moral accountability in order to exact compliance with the administrative, ideological, and material annihilation of black and non-black people.
>
> — Tiffany Willoughby-Herard, *Waste of a White Skin*

This book focuses on a small group of white radicals, centred on the experiences of Jeanette (Jenny) Curtis and Marius Schoon, between 1972 and 1984. In large part, the individuals who are at the core of this book are largely absent from the existing historiography of the anti-apartheid struggle. Jenny's story has been told, in part, via a memoir by her father, Jack Curtis,[1] and Jonathan Ancer's 2017 biography of Craig Williamson.[2] Interviews with Marius Schoon were included in *The Rift*, Hilda Bernstein's collection on the exile experience,[3] as well as Julie Frederikse's book on nonracialism, *The Unbreakable Thread*, published in 1990.[4] Beyond this, there is little to speak of. Unlike their better-known contemporaries, Joe Slovo and Ruth First, no full biographies have been published for either of the Schoons and neither are they generally spoken of in books that cover the armed struggle or the ANC. Part of the reason for this absence, I argue, is because the Schoons' story is – in important respects – 'unusable' in the sense that neither their participation in the anti-apartheid struggle nor the multiple moments of tragedy in their lives fits neatly within a triumphant narrative.[5] However, it is precisely the fact that this history is not easily contained within the standard narratives of the liberation struggle that it deserves to be researched and analysed.

This book is not a biography of either Jeanette or Marius Schoon. To the extent that what is contained here is of a biographical nature, I've taken inspiration from a growing trend among historians to write 'biographies of a generation'. Luisa Passerini's *Autobiography of a Generation*, for example, analyses the radical upheaval in Italy in 1968, while Robert Foster's *Vivid Faces* depicts the Irish generation that fought for independence around the turn of the twentieth century.[6] The term 'generation' is not a precise category. In the South African context, a 'generation' of political activists might be understood as lasting more than a decade, or as short a time as a couple of years. Given that Marius Schoon was more than a decade older than Jeanette, one might even argue that the two were not from the same generation. Nonetheless, there are some important biographies and memoirs that capture the generation that is the focus of this book. The texts that most closely relate to this book are Glenn Moss's *The New Radicals: A Generational Memoir of the 1970s*,[7] Barry Gilder's *Songs and Secrets*[8] and Judy Seidman's *Drawn Lines*.[9] Moss's memoir is the most thorough account so far of the white leftists who came through student activism in the early 1970s and became 'post-student people' – New Left Marxists. Gilder and Seidman's memoirs are markedly different from one another – due to their unique personalities and roles – but both capture different layers of the cover stories and undercover stories of the ANC in exile in southern Africa.

Given the extent to which histories of this generation of white radicals so far exist primarily via memoirs, this book will be the first scholarly work on these topics, based on extensive archival research and interviews with participants from this period.

In focusing on this group of white radicals, I by no means intend to imply that their contribution to the struggle was in any way more important than that of their Black counterparts. To the contrary, I am intensely aware that anti-apartheid white activists contributed to a Black-majority and Black-led movement. Within this context, white activists necessarily developed their understanding of both political and ethical priorities – and their own role in relation to the overall struggle – informed by both the political thinking and organisational infrastructure created by Black South Africans. In every aspect, white people's engagement with the struggle was shaped by Black people. For example, as this book details thoroughly, student leaders of the Black Consciousness Movement played a tremendous role in encouraging young white people to abandon liberalism. Later, Black leaders were influential in steering white people into the ANC, and once these people entered the ANC's exile structures, they were a small minority among thousands of members. Given these crucial facts, I have attempted to place the efforts of this small group of white activists within the context of the larger liberation struggle, throughout the book.

However, at the same time, white South African radicals remained unavoidably members of an apartheid society. That is, the dictates of a heavily racialised and divided society meant that a large portion of white South Africans' daily lives – even for those who were deeply invested in fighting against apartheid – took place within a whites-only context. Therefore, while white radicals were heavily influenced by developments in Black politics, much of this process took place internally, through extensive debates in living rooms of houses occupied by white leftists, in whites-only neighbourhoods. Even in exile, the realities of race and class limited the extent to which white radicals could engage with their Black comrades.

While it goes without saying for those who have spent time in South Africa, it is worth stressing that apartheid not only isolated white people from the Black majority, but also provided them with an almost unimaginable degree of privilege in relation to Black people. By certain measures, the wealth gap was as high as 50 to 1, protected by an aggressive set of legislation to enforce the 'Colour Bar' and to severely curtail Black trade unions. Strict legislation also reserved large swathes of urban areas for whites only. White people – even young leftists – regularly relied on Black domestic servants to take care of their homes and children.[10]

Furthermore, as this book analyses on numerous occasions, white people were also 'privileged' in terms of the ferocity of state repression. While white radicals were certainly subjected to various forms of abuse by the police and security services – including severe violence, such as torture and killings – such brutalities occurred far less often than they did to Black people. In addition, as this book also discusses in multiple instances, state repression against white activists was often carried out with an air of familiarity, or in a so-called 'gentlemanly' fashion. That is, white leftists were often regarded as errant family members, whose behaviour might be corrected via a stern talking to, rather than as sub-human or uncivilised rebels, who could only be contained through violence.

By necessity, white people's experiences within the anti-apartheid movement were distinct from the Black majority that they supported. Understanding their role, therefore, requires a distinct process of research and analysis. The Schoons and their comrades played several different roles within the anti-apartheid movement, including student protest, trade union organising, as members of an anti-apartheid arts ensemble, and clandestine political and armed struggle. As white South Africans, their engagement in these political modes were all necessarily a *different* form of treason from that carried out by their Black counterparts.

## The apartheid state

> ... our knowledge of how the regime functioned, how its leaders understood the challenges they faced, how they rationalized the hostile world around them, are little more advanced today than they were when the regime collapsed more than twenty years ago.
>
> — Jamie Miller, *An African Volk*

There is no such thing as 'the apartheid state'.

However coherent apartheid might have been, the state was not, in fact, a monolith. No matter how unified or cohesive the Afrikaner Nationalist project was, there were different ideologies at play, and multiple understandings of strategy and of the enemy. The state was therefore contradictory and confused, inefficient and imprecise, even, in some important respects, illiterate. Nonetheless, one of the central tasks of this books is an interrogation of the apartheid state. To be clear, I have not attempted a thorough ethnography of the state during apartheid. Rather, what follows is a narrower, nuanced study of a very particular section of the state apparatus.

The apartheid state was brutal in dozens of aspects, and yet also capable of strategic thinking, as well as determined to present a coherent ideology at its core. Therefore, this book follows two principal paths: one that investigates the 'violent arm' of the apartheid state and the other focused on what I'm calling the 'thinking arm' of the state. The violence of the apartheid state took many forms, personified through the military and police, but also through the security police, who were given extensive powers not only to surveil but also to abduct, torture and murder opponents of apartheid. While the malevolence of apartheid is undeniable, it is made illegible if it is understood simply as raw, unthinking power. The 'thinking arm' of the state includes commissions of inquiry, parliament and the courts; all of these were used to articulate apartheid ideology, but also to steer the violent arm of the state. The lines between these two categories were often blurry. For example, many security police officers studied Marxism, while prisoners awaiting a fair and impartial trial were often tortured for months in advance. These overlaps between thinking and violence are not simply of interest, but rather a fundamental component of what is analysed here.

## Overview

At its narrowest, this book centres around one question: how did the apartheid state's security forces decide to send the bomb that killed Jeanette and Katryn Schoon on 28 June 1984? It argues that the targeting of Jeanette Schoon was neither random nor thoughtless, but the result of years of intelligence work. Therefore, this book traces a trajectory from the first moment that Jeanette Schoon (née Curtis) became an object of state scrutiny, through an escalating thicket of entanglements, leading up to the assassination. Is it possible to establish a link between the 'rational' intellectual arm of the state in the early 1970s and the assassinating arm that struck out over a decade later?

Jeanette Schoon's story is used as a central narrative thread to provide insights into larger questions related to the state's capacity to understand the threats posed by white opposition to apartheid and the shifting set of repressive mechanisms that were deployed by the state in response. I argue that the assassination of Jeanette and her daughter must be understood as connected to other mechanisms of apartheid repression, from commissions of inquiry, to banning orders, political trials, detention without charge and torture. Throughout, this book grapples with the strategic thinking of the apartheid state by relating acts of state-sponsored violence to the apartheid state's overall strategic interests and understanding of the threats posed by the opposition. In my analysis of the apartheid state, I am concerned with the tensions between violence and rationality, which constantly contradicted and reinforced one another.

The book addresses the complex interplays between the apartheid state's security services and its radical opponents. In narrating this dual story of duelling undercover realities, the structure of this book encourages readers to hold onto the perspective of the apartheid state and their radical opponents – at once and in parallel. There is no way cleanly or entirely to separate out these two opposing viewpoints, as they were always operating in conversation and contestation with one another. Nonetheless, to the extent that it is possible, I have attempted to foreground one perspective at a time. The aim of this structure is to allow the disagreements, contradictions and overlaps between the resistance and the repressive apparatus of the state to be seen in stark relief.

Jeanette Schoon's life – and death – was irreparably woven together with Craig Williamson, a security police officer who infiltrated the white left in 1972 (simultaneous with the Schlebusch Commission of Inquiry into student organisations) and surveilled Jeanette and her comrades for over a decade. Williamson confessed to his role in killing the Schoons and received amnesty from the Truth and Reconciliation Commission (TRC). But despite Williamson's confession, there is still a great deal about Williamson's broader role within the apartheid state that has remained either unknown or contested.

Through original archival research and interviews with both Williamson and numerous individuals who were negatively impacted by him, this book offers perhaps the most in-depth scholarly account of Williamson's inglorious career to date. The research contained here shows that Williamson sabotaged the anti-apartheid struggle in a wide range of ways, beyond being a murderer. For example, Williamson spent years as an undercover agent inside a European philanthropic organisation, the International University Exchange Fund (IUEF), where he successfully commandeered funds intended for the anti-apartheid movement and channelled them towards the security police. Most importantly, this book analyses the ideological role that Williamson played in defence of the apartheid project. Williamson was a virulent anti-communist. He believed that the South African government could never win against a broad-based revolutionary insurrection and so he sought to obliterate the distinction between political and military opposition, to force the anti-apartheid struggle into an all-out war, fought along Cold War lines.

A key contribution of this book is that it insists on narrating the histories of what is known in South Africa as the 'aboveground' opposition – legal, non-violent political organising – alongside the histories of exile and armed struggle. The life stories of Jeanette and Marius Schoon show that the boundaries between these politics were fluid, as both of them were, at different points in their lives, members of the ANC, the South African Congress of Trade Unions (Sactu) and the Communist Party, as well as active in independent opposition structures, which were cut off from the more prominent liberation organisations. Analysing these different layers of political engagement provides a more nuanced and complete portrait of the anti-apartheid movement. In addition, the complexities of the Schoons' contribution to the struggle complicates our understanding of what the apartheid state deemed threatening. Contrary to Williamson's attempts to smear everyone who supported the ANC as 'violent', it is critical to acknowledge the subtle, creative and explicitly non-violent aspects of the radical politics that the Schoons and their comrades engaged in.

In the context of the ANC in exile, everyone was obligated to maintain a 'cover story' alongside their role within the underground. However, an unavoidable irony of this mode of living was that the cover work had to be genuinely engaged in. Even so, it often had a political content, in and of itself – for example, teaching at a socialist university, running an anti-apartheid news service or participating in an arts ensemble with a pro-liberation struggle stance. Narratives of the anti-apartheid struggle that stress the importance of the armed struggle tend to negate or obscure these subtle modes of radical resistance.

At the same time, the rituals of the underground – coded messages, dead letter boxes, noms de guerre and so on – were also the stuff of spies. As Williamson said, the modus operandi of the security police and that of the ANC underground was very similar. Sadly, while revolutionaries went underground in order to hide away from the state, in a certain sense they actually made themselves more visible in the process. This book interrogates an extended campaign of infiltration, surveillance and sabotage carried out by (Williamson's unit of) the security police, targeting one section (the Schoons and their comrades) of the anti-apartheid movement. Understanding this phenomenon provides critical insights not only into the apartheid state's security services, but also into the fragility of the anti-apartheid movement's efforts to build a revolutionary underground.

## Structure

In classic detective novel format, the story opens with an account of a double murder – that of Jeanette and Katryn Schoon, whose lives were brutally and tragically ended when a bomb exploded in their apartment in 1984.

The book is not a 'who done it', however, as the perpetrator, apartheid spy Craig Williamson, confessed to his role in the assassination of this mother and her six-year-old daughter. Rather, it provides a context for understanding the assassination, within a much larger campaign of state surveillance, sabotage and suppression.

It is impossible to simply present 'the' story of the murder. Given the complex mix of muddy memories and archival absence, the account of the assassination as described in the Prologue by necessity is not a single account. In fact it offers multiple accounts. Although they cannot all be true at once, each of them is in some way plausible and grounded in evidence.

We then move backwards in time, to 1972. This is an important year, because it was when the apartheid state explicitly named Jenny Curtis, as she was known at that time, as a subversive element. It was also the year that Craig Williamson first arrived on the campus of the University of the Witwatersrand as an undercover agent posing as a student radical.

The story then unfolds chronologically, in four distinct but interconnected parts – Part 1: From Student Radicals to Post-student People; Part 2: Cover Stories and Undercover Stories, Botswana and Geneva; Part 3: Furthering the Aims; and Part 4: Forced Asylum – which trace the intersecting lives of Williamson and the Schoons through an escalating series of entanglements.

Crucially, each part builds upon and references back to previous parts. This same pattern repeats with all of the parts, so that by the end of the book one finds that the earlier chapters have an entirely new meaning, in light of subsequent developments. For example, the dynamics of Williamson's career as a leader within the National Union of South African Students (Nusas) are critical to understanding his infiltration of the IUEF that followed. Williamson's credentials as a Nusas activist gained him credibility in Europe. Meanwhile, genuine Nusas activists (turned ANC underground members) based their mounting suspicions of Williamson on problems that they had first noticed years before, as student radicals.

A key component of the book's structure is an attention to the ways in which each of the stories contained here have been used as evidence, at a later stage. In some instances, I mean this quite literally. Chapter 8 (Part 3) deals with a series of political trials, while the Epilogue addresses Williamson's amnesty case at the TRC. It is important to understand that the political trials were a public platform for Williamson to weaponise his years of undercover surveillance to bolster the prosecution's case. In addition competing narratives regarding Williamson's exposure as a spy play a pivotal role in determining Williamson's motives for murder.

## Part 1: From Student Radicals to Post-student People, 1972–1976

This part contends that the decision to (re)turn towards an embrace of the ANC was a choice that was made gradually and that many young radicals were motivated in this direction in large part due to the repression of the apartheid state. In outlining this argument, I reject the pro-ANC framework that insists that a strong ANC underground was in operation throughout the period in question and that the ascendancy of the ANC was an inevitability. This position is best characterised by Raymond Suttner in his book *The ANC Underground in South Africa*:

> In the end it was the slow and patient reinsertion of the ANC into the country, taking advantage of the loyalty and sympathy of veteran members, that ensured that when the time came, the ANC would emerge as the pre-eminent anti-apartheid force in the process leading to establishing a democratic order.[11]

My research offers a very different depiction of this process.

There is one story that is central to this part, that of Marius Schoon. Schoon spent 12 years in Pretoria Central Prison for attempted sabotage. He was incarcerated in 1964, at the age of 27, and released in October 1976. Schoon described the nine months after his release from prison as the 'most important political work' of his lifetime. For Schoon, these nine months were especially fulfilling because they were spent actively pushing white leftists towards an embrace of the ANC. According to Schoon, the great majority of the white people whom he met were at least sceptical of – if not hostile to – the ANC. For every one who was inspired by Marius Schoon's vision of politics there were many others – from their first encounter, as well as in the years to come – who insisted that Schoon's politics were excessively dangerous and should be avoided at all costs.

Jenny Curtis was unique among her peers in terms of her willingness openly to advocate for the ANC within the social and political climate that began with the banning of the Nusas 'leadership clique' identified in the report of the Schlebush Commission in 1973, and continued through to the nine months she spent with Marius Schoon at the end of 1976 and into 1977.

Part of what made the politics of this period unique was the consistent refrain of feeling 'cut off' from prior generations of struggle and in particular the leaders of the mainline liberation organisations, the ANC and the SACP (with many of the leaders either incarcerated or in exile). This feeling of being unable to access the bearers of political prestige and memory was largely regarded as a detriment, a drag against the capacity to take effective action. At the same time, being adrift in this way inevitably led to a level of experimentation, which would not otherwise have been present. The sense of being without an older generation to connect to or take direction from, and the existential destabilisation caused by Black Consciousness, combined to forge what Glenn Moss refers to as a 'homespun' Marxism. Part 1 therefore addresses the monumental shift among a growing number of these young leftists, *away* from the politics that they had developed independently and *towards* the ANC.

Jenny Curtis came of age in the aftermath of the Liliesleaf raid and the Rivonia trials, and the smashing of the African Resistance Movement (ARM). She was among a generation of white student members of Nusas whose politics were fundamentally transformed by the emergence of Black

INTRODUCTION

Consciousness's powerful critique of white liberalism and multi-racial organising. Young white students radicalised, embracing a version of New Left Marxism.

In response to these new modes of radical politics, the apartheid state initiated the Commission of Inquiry into Certain Organisations in 1972, which became known as the Schlebusch Commission.[12] One of the key recommendations that the commission made was an order to place the so-called 'leadership clique' of Nusas under 'banning orders'. Included in that leadership was Jenny Curtis's brother Neville and others with whom she worked closely.

Chapter 1 of Part 1 provides an in-depth account of what banning orders meant for the leadership of Nusas. By tracing the impact of the banning orders that were placed on activists in the aftermath of the commission, I argue that the sheer relentlessness of restrictions contributed to a political climate where clandestine activity increasingly appeared unavoidable, rather than unimaginable. While a couple of these individuals were compelled back towards liberalism because of the restrictions, the majority either found illegal routes into exile, or radicalised, or both.

In chapter 2 I describe the transformation in Jenny Curtis's political ideology and projects, responding to this climate of repression. Initially, Curtis continued to engage in legal modes of activism, such as supporting trade unions through the Industrial Aid Society (IAS) or working as an archivist at the South African Institute for Race Relations. However, even these activities put Curtis into a position of increased surveillance and harassment. At the same time her archivist work allowed her time and space to engage deeply with Communist Party readings; it also put her in direct contact with recently released political prisoners. At the end of 1975, Curtis was among a group of 17 people detained in connection with writer Breyten Breytenbach's tour of the country in support of the clandestine organisation, Okhela, he planned to form. Following her release from detention, Curtis was placed under a banning order.

By the time Marius Schoon was released from Pretoria Central in 1976, Jenny Curtis had already seen numerous friends banned and was herself a banned person. She had suffered a period of detention without charges, and had been working as a conduit between the white left and the ANC for several years prior.

In conclusion, rather than offering a clean, linear narrative, where the ANC returns to its natural place of prominence, I insist that the process of moving towards the ANC needs to be understood as gradual and constantly contested. Given the predominance of Black Consciousness at the start of the 1970s – and the relative absence of the ANC – it was by no means inevitable that a group of white Marxists would choose to align themselves with the ANC within a few short years. Therefore, this dramatic political transformation ought to be engaged with as a critical question for historians to attempt to answer, rather than simply taken as fact.

Furthermore, the significance of the ANC's ascendancy needs to be analysed through the lens of the apartheid state's strategic interests, as well. While it is seemingly logical to understand a group of young people radicalising in response to repression as an *unintended* consequence of state policies, this seems to be a question that begs analysis. As will be discussed in later chapters, Craig Williamson was at least one (particularly vocal) member of the security forces who actively sought to force the struggle against apartheid into the shape of a straightforward war.

Not very long after Marius Schoon was released from prison at the end of 1976, he and Jenny Curtis developed both a political and romantic partnership. The couple got married in 1977 and went into exile immediately afterwards.

## Part 2: Cover Stories and Undercover Stories, Botswana and Geneva, 1977–1980

In a sense, Part 2 represents the 'heart' of the book. It was during these years that the Schoons and Craig Williamson most directly and explicitly lived intersecting lives. The stories of Williamson's undercover work in Geneva and the Schoons' underground work for the ANC in Botswana are intimately connected, on a number of important levels. To underscore this fact, the four chapters of this part flow continually back and forth between Botswana and Geneva, reminding the reader to stay attentive to the fact that the Schoons and Williamson were always parallel, crucially interconnected in a series of critical ways.

Both the Schoons and Williamson left South Africa via Botswana and much of the work Williamson did for the IUEF had a link to that country.

## INTRODUCTION

One of the more devious and ingenious mechanisms that Williamson used to establish legitimacy as a radical was to help ferry young activists out of the country. Many of the individuals who left South Africa via this security police 'railroad' were members of the Schoons' social and political networks in Gaborone. Furthermore, as the Schoons attempted to maintain communications with white radicals inside South Africa, they chose Karl Edwards, a friend and colleague of Williamson, as their 'courier'. All of this combined meant that Williamson had intimate and in-depth knowledge of Jenny and Marius Schoon's lives in Botswana; he was even a guest in their home on more than one occasion.

During the years that the Schoons lived in exile in Botswana, Williamson was in Geneva, having successfully infiltrated the IUEF. Despite the distance between them, the Schoons' world within the ANC exile structures and Williamson's world of espionage overlapped repeatedly and perniciously.

In the limited literature on the ANC in exile, Botswana is a rarely addressed small corner of the exile experience. There are numerous accounts of the Medu Art Ensemble – of which the Schoons were members – but much less on other layers of this period. The Botswana sections of Part 2 grapple, therefore, with the substantial barriers facing historians who hope to write an in-depth account of the political and armed underground of the ANC in Botswana. Based on interviews conducted with numerous comrades of the Schoons, I have attempted to provide as accurate a depiction of the role that the Schoons played within the ANC as possible. However, this account is necessarily complicated by multiple contradictory versions and void spaces within people's memories and narratives.

In taking stock of the barriers that I faced while writing the Botswana portions of this part, I believe my experience as a researcher was fairly typical. Padraigh O'Malley, for example, conducted over 200 hours of interviews with Mac Maharaj, who was one of the Schoons' superiors within the ANC hierarchy while they were in Botswana. In particular, Maharaj was tasked with running a section of the ANC called the Internal Political Reconstruction and Development (IPRD) programme. Based on O'Malley's exhaustive time spent talking with Maharaj, one would imagine that the resulting biography, *Shades of Difference*, ought to be essential reading for understanding the Schoons' work with the IPRD. However, according to O'Malley, 'Mac's account of this time conceals as much as it illuminates'.[13] That Mac Maharaj does not (or cannot) 'illuminate' much about the IPRD is not surprising when one hears that, soon after being put in charge, when he asked for the IPRD files he was 'handed an empty file. There were no records at all about previous activities.'[14] Given such an endemic culture of silences within MK and the ANC, it seems historians will have to rely largely on anecdotes, rumours and speculation.

On the other hand, Part 2 contains the most substantive account of Williamson's time at the IUEF to date, much of it as a result of extensive original research. It draws heavily from the archives of the IUEF, which includes numerous letters and internal memos, from Lars-Gunnar Eriksson (director of the IUEF) and Williamson, as well as financial documents and reports. Furthermore, this part relies heavily on the report of a commission of inquiry, which was convened by the IUEF board in the aftermath of Williamson's exposure as a spy. These sources allow for a detailed accounting of Williamson's tangible impact on the IUEF's operations. In addition to archival research, I also conducted an interview with Williamson himself. While remaining keenly aware of Williamson's skills in evasion and dishonesty, I was nonetheless very much interested in the justifications that Williamson might offer for his own actions. In taking stock of the damage Williamson caused while in Geneva, it is crucial to grapple with his strategic thinking and goals as a saboteur. What is striking is that, in a large number of cases, what Williamson understood about the role that he played and what the IUEF commission of inquiry concluded about him resonate strongly.

As the title of Part 2 suggests, cover stories for those who went into exile and engaged in underground work were a critical factor. In this setting, everyone was obligated to maintain a cover story alongside their role within the underground structures of the ANC. Their cover work was real work, however (teaching or lecturing, for example), although it often had a political content, in and of itself. Since this work occupied a significant portion of people's time in exile, in chapters 3 and 4 the need to understand the political content of people's cover stories is stressed repeatedly. The Schoons and their comrades in Botswana lived complex double lives, where they were obliged constantly to straddle the line between their cover stories and their roles within the ANC's underground structures.

## INTRODUCTION

Living and working in exile meant moving into a domain where secrecy was the dominant mode of interaction, even among friends who were close enough to regard one another as members of a shared family. In Botswana, while the Schoons were busy developing a network of ANC supporters inside South Africa, they were also teaching English at a secondary school, were members of the Medu Art Ensemble, and participated in the South African News Agency (Sana) and the Solidarity News Service (SNS). Both Medu Art and the SNS had many ANC members and produced pro-ANC art and news. Some of the projects these activists were engaged in – particularly Sana – were funded directly by the IUEF, and were therefore monitored closely by Craig Williamson.

Williamson's closest collaborator, Karl Edwards, ran another 'front' NGO, the Environmental and Development Agency (EDA). Building on his credentials and contacts at EDA, Edwards became a courier for clandestine messages sent back and forth across the border, between friends and comrades of the Schoons.

Meanwhile, Williamson's 'cover story' was his role as the deputy-director of the IUEF, which organisation he had successfully infiltrated in Geneva. There he used his position in charge of anti-apartheid funds to surveil the underground movement and serve the needs of the security police. The position granted Williamson a substantial amount of control over IUEF funds, which were intended for the anti-apartheid movement. At the height of his influence at the IUEF, Williamson was authorised to direct a secret Liechtenstein bank account, known as Southern Futures, while donors to the IUEF had no knowledge of its existence. Managing these funds allowed Williamson to engage in extensive surveillance of activist recipients of the funding, to channel funds into multiple 'front' organisations (under the direct control of the security police) and to outright steal money for security police uses.

In analysing this small sector of the ANC in exile, what comes through clearly is that there was a substantial amount of debate – even tension – around the relationship between political work and the armed struggle. A number of the individuals interviewed for this part-would concur with Mac Maharaj's assessment of the period that 'There was no political underground. The struggle was being pursued almost exclusively in armed terms ... The de facto position now was that *only* the armed struggle was the way forward.'[15] Within a context where many in the movement felt that the ANC was overly reliant on a narrow vision of guerrilla warfare, the role and substance of political modes of resistance were fiercely debated. Accordingly, these debates are extensively examined, in an attempt to treat all perspectives with respect.

While ANC comrades were busy building an (armed) underground infrastructure, Craig Williamson was busy pushing the IUEF *away* from supporting the Black Consciousness Movement and *towards* an open embrace of the ANC. Perhaps counterintuitively, Williamson viewed this ideological shift to be the greatest success of his time in Geneva. Within Williamson's political framework, the apartheid state would have more favourable odds fighting a war against an enemy that could be brandished as tied to 'the Moscow line' rather than fighting a diffuse, independent uprising such as began in Soweto in 1976. Williamson's intervention to push the IUEF to support the ANC had a direct impact on anti-apartheid initiatives inside South Africa, depriving the Black Consciousness Movement of one of their largest funders. In addition, Williamson's vocal support of the ANC earned him the tacit trust of the ANC's exile leadership, which allowed Williamson's network of undercover officers considerable latitude to sabotage the Schoons' exile structures in Botswana.

While the Schoons and their comrades were dedicated to keeping the substance of their underground activities shrouded from one another, the cruel fact was that underground activity was in an important sense *more* legible to the security police than legal activity. As is brilliantly depicted in Jacob Dlamini's book *Askari*, the shared terrain of the radical underground and the security police spawned a relentlessly complicated and contradictory web of allegiances and betrayals.[16]

In the Schoons' case in particular, their network was heavily infiltrated by Williamson's group of security police officers. While they were not able definitively to prove it, many of their comrades had deep suspicions about both Craig Williamson and his partner Karl Edwards. Several members of Nusas as well as of the ANC underground had deep suspicions throughout this time. Multiple people attempted to notify the IUEF's Lars-Gunnar Eriksson of their concerns about Williamson. Steps were taken to warn both the IUEF and the ANC, and even explicitly to expose the spies, but most of these warnings were ignored by the relevant leadership.

The ANC leadership did not take any firm action against Williamson during this period and concerns were largely shrugged aside as mere 'rumour-mongering'.

Meanwhile members of the Schoons' ANC cell set a trap for Karl Edwards, in an attempt to confirm their suspicions, and – it worked. Not long afterwards, in January 1980, Williamson's own cover was blown. He was formally exposed as a spy and forced to flee Geneva and return to South Africa. The story of Williamson's exposure and his final days in Geneva are recounted in detail in chapters 5 and 6. While the story may read like a spy novel, it is ultimately a tragedy. For a brief period of days – perhaps only hours – there was the possibility of turning Williamson over to the Swiss police, where he could have been indicted for espionage and appropriately incarcerated.

## Part 3: Furthering the Aims, 1980–1983

> I don't regret anything I did, and would have undertaken the same or a similar task no matter what.
>
> — Craig Williamson in Neil Hooper, 'Our Man in Moscow'

Within a few months of Williamson's return to South Africa, the apartheid state embarked on an extended crackdown on the Schoons' network of ANC-aligned leftists. This took the form of dozens of arrests, widespread torture and a series of political trials. Several of their closest comrades were arrested, tortured and tried for the crime of 'furthering the aims of the ANC'.

The political trials against this group of white radicals are of particular importance to the central questions of this book. Aided by the so-called 'expert' testimony of Craig Williamson – and his co-infiltrator, Karl Edwards – the state argued that the ANC was by its very nature a violent organisation. According to this logic, the ANC's decision to build its armed wing, Umkhonto we Sizwe (MK), forced all ANC members into the position of aiding the armed struggle, regardless of an individual's convictions on violence, and irrespective of each person's particular role within the organisation.

This ideological framing of the violent threat of the anti-apartheid movement did have precedents in earlier high-profile political trials, such as the 1966 case against Rowley Arenstein, and the 1976 trial of Breyten Breytenbach. Nonetheless, the indictments against Alan Fine, Guy Berger, Devan Pillay, Barbara Hogan and others represented an important intensification of the apartheid state's decision to criminalise non-violent resistance (such as trade unionism) within the framework of counter-insurgency. The majority of these young radicals were sent to prison.

When Craig Williamson returned home to South Africa he was fêted by the white community as a hero of the anti-communist cause, as a 'super spy'. The *Sunday Times*, for example, ran a full-page spread under the headline 'Our Man in Moscow', celebrating Williamson's achievements for the security services. Williamson told the *Sunday Times*: 'I don't know how many communist organizations and terrorist movements I infiltrated in all ... there were so many. We are still drawing up a list.'[17] In this triumphant frame of mind, Williamson remained employed by the South African security services, but no longer as an undercover agent. In the next few years after his return (1980–1984) Williamson engaged in an aggressive campaign to decimate the white left wing, whom he had spent eight years impersonating and surveilling.

This campaign was carried out first of all through a wave of arrests and indictments, which targeted a great number of people (of all races) who were suspected of being aligned to the ANC, including a handful of young white radicals, who were charged with treason *explicitly* on account of their connections to the Schoons. While the state initially imagined a large conspiracy trial, this proved to be an impossible goal, and the cases were eventually tried separately. The basic indictments were essentially identical, as the banning of the ANC allowed the state to indict people merely for 'furthering the aims' of the ANC, which was an intentionally vague legal standard.

Part 3 tells the story of the arrests, detentions and trials of a number of the Schoons' comrades. Chapter 7 focuses on the pre-trial events, while chapter 8 deals extensively with the actual arguments presented by both the prosecution and defence in the ensuing court cases. They draw extensively from interviews with, and affidavits written by, the activists themselves, including Guy Berger, Devan Pillay, Auret van Heerden, Alan Fine and Barbara Hogan. In foregrounding these voices, my interest is in understanding how this group of young people navigated their options in the face of a police and legal infrastructure that was monumentally brutal. The stories that these individuals tell of their time detained in apartheid prisons are horrific. The details of their treatment are horrible, as is the fact that such treatment was both widespread and relentless. While a number of these activists stressed the fact that police terror was racialised – that is, far worse for Black people – nonetheless the depictions of what was done to the young white people contained in this chapter are no less gruesome. The decision to provide an in-depth analysis of torture is not intended to diminish the horror that these individuals survived. Rather, I hope this chapter moves towards a deeper understanding of the interplay between violence and 'the rule of law' under apartheid.

I argue that one can see a clear pattern connecting the torturous, murderous modes of state power and the legal mechanisms of apartheid repression, such as political trials. A brief outline of a few moments of apartheid violence that are directly relevant to this book, all of which took place during just one year – 1982 – is intended to illustrate this pattern. Perhaps the most high-profile case of torture in detention was that of Neil Aggett, a young white activist in the trade union movement, who was found dead in his cell on 5 February 1982. Just a month after Aggett's death, Craig Williamson was involved in orchestrating a massive bombing of the ANC's offices in London, on 14 March 1982. Although no one died in this attack, it nonetheless registered as a serious act of warfare, targeting people thousands of kilometres away from South Africa. A few months later, Williamson once again was involved in an act of war, by sending a bomb to Maputo, Mozambique. This parcel bomb took the life of Ruth First, a prominent ANC member and communist intellectual. Not at all incidentally, this bomb also severely damaged the space where she worked, the Center for African Studies at Eduardo Mondlane University (an explicitly socialist academic environment, built by a newly independent African state). Also not coincidentally, this bombing took place on 17 August 1982, which was the day before Craig Williamson testified in the treason trial against Barbara Hogan.

In sum, one must understand apartheid as *per se* violent and therefore should not be confused about the purportedly non-violent or democratic arms of state repression.

During the months of detaining and torturing the group of radicals accused of furthering the aims of the ANC, there was no evidence that the state was engaged in anything like a thinking process. While the police interrogators asked questions and demanded written answers, this was by no means a nuanced or reflective process concerned with the actual intricacies of politics. Nonetheless, this period did give way to a series of court proceedings. In taking stock of the significance of these trials in terms of the apartheid state's capacity to have a public forum to present an ideological set of justifications for draconian measures, it is important to remember that court cases were never entirely one-way affairs. In spite of the intensely unjust laws and the extra-legal abuses of the police and prison system, the courts themselves remained governed by at least a modicum of adherence to the principle of 'the rule of law'.

In fact, Denis Kuny, who was an advocate for hundreds of anti-apartheid activists (his career spanned from 1960 through the 1990s), including dozens of people who were Communists, ANC members, and people engaged in the armed struggle, insists that during apartheid there were always 'proper' trials:

> I've always said that as difficult as it may have been in those years, the fact is that we had *proper* trials. We were able to prepare. We were able to have documentation. The state was often prepared to co-operate with us. We were able to go and consult with the accused, in jail or in the cells at the court. We were able to put them [the accused, political prisoners] in a witness box to talk. Whatever they may have said – which otherwise wouldn't have been reported – would be reported, as proceedings in court. In other words, they were able, through the back door, to be able to present their point of view. They wouldn't normally have been able to do that through a publication or a newspaper.[18]

Especially within a context of escalating censorship and repressive legislation, political trials represented a rare – if still limited, and skewed – forum for political discourse. That is, the state could attempt to slander and condemn their opponents, but those opponents had the right to slander and condemn the state as well.

Chapter 8 analyses three different political trials: (1) The State vs. Berger, (2) The State vs. A.M. Fine and (3) The State vs. Hogan. While one of these trials – that of Alan Fine – ended in acquittal, the defence lost both of the other two. Consequently, Guy Berger and Barbara Hogan were given prison sentences, as was Devan Pillay. I argue that beyond the threat of sentencing, what was at stake was also an ideological and political battlefield. While all of the defendants were sympathetic to the ANC – and connected to the Schoons' exile structures – the substance of *all* of their political work was essentially non-violent. That is, they participated in reading groups, organised trade unions, and supported workers' struggles through protests and writing. Given this, the defence case was grounded in the idea that it was possible to be a member of the ANC without engaging in the armed struggle in any form. However, as this chapter demonstrates, the capacity of the defence to articulate a viable vision for non-violent participation in the ANC was fraught with difficulty and aggressively countered by the state.

These trials were an important mechanism for the state to define the ANC as a treasonous, violent organisation. In each of these trials Craig Williamson (and at times Karl Edwards, as well) served as an 'expert' witness for the prosecution. In his testimony for the prosecution, Williamson's primary aim was to argue that there was no possible way to be sympathetic to the ANC and still advocate for non-violence, or to consider one's own role as being non-violent. In this chapter, Williamson's testimony is analysed in depth, both in terms of the specific form of his argument and also in terms of the larger strategic purpose of it.

I contend that the framework for understanding the ANC that Williamson articulated had a devastating impact, not only on the specific defendants in these trials but also for the ensuing decade of the struggle against apartheid.

## Part 4: Forced Asylum, 1981–1984

This part covers the final three years of Jeanette Schoon's life. During this period, the Schoons' room to manoeuvre – their capacity to determine their own destiny – became increasingly curtailed by several external factors. In addition to being targeted for surveillance, harassment and – eventually – extermination by the apartheid state, the Schoons were also hemmed in by interference from the British government (while they were in Botswana) and then by the extended civil war in Angola. In the midst of being boxed in and bounced about, the Schoons continued to seek out ways to remain engaged in the anti-apartheid struggle, while also struggling to keep their young family as safe as possible, given the circumstances.

In the Schoons' last few years in Botswana, they both worked for the International Voluntary Service (IVS), a British peace organisation. Crucially, chapter 9 addresses the reasons for the Schoons' hasty departure from Botswana in June of 1983. Throughout the nine months of my research for this book, I was under the impression that the Schoons needed to leave Botswana because their lives were at risk, presumably in the form of an attack carried out by the apartheid state. In light of the bomb that killed Jeanette and Katryn a year later – and the relentless campaign of harassment and attacks that ANC activists in Botswana regularly faced – this explanation seemed entirely plausible. In fact, this story is so widespread that it was repeated to me by everyone I interviewed and was further confirmed by interviews conducted by others with Marius Schoon. However, perhaps the most groundbreaking revelation of my archival research was an extensive body of evidence that shows that the commonly accepted story is absolutely false and was intentionally designed by the British government to be a false narrative.

One of the most important findings of my research was evidence that the Foreign and Commonwealth Office (FCO) played a profound role in actively forcing the Schoons out of their positions as co-directors of the Botswana branch of the IVS. In the eyes of the FCO, Marius Schoon was a 'terrorist', who would inevitably put British citizens in danger. As soon as the Schoons were hired by the IVS in 1981, the FCO began putting pressure on the organisation to get rid of them. It was as a result of this pressure that the Schoons left Botswana. Despite Jeanette having a sister in England and an Irish passport, the FCO opposed offering the Schoons any form of a visa or asylum in the UK.

The revelations contained in this chapter are the result of original research within the archives of the FCO, which have never been addressed by historians previously. Broadly speaking, historians know that 'throughout the 1970s and into the 1980s, Washington and London provided South Africa ... with significant covert support'[19] in terms of suppressing the anti-apartheid movement. Further, according to James Sanders, the 'British

Special Branch spied on members of the [Anti-Apartheid Movement] as late as 1983'.[20] However, many of the specific details of these collaborations between the British and South African intelligence services still need to be researched in greater depth. The archival documents discussed in this chapter detail an extensive and relentless pressure campaign designed to force the Schoons out of IVS and, consequently, out of Botswana. When the Schoons were hired by IVS in September 1981, the FCO immediately objected. Their concerns were voiced ever more vociferously over the following two years, until the IVS had no option but to assist the British government in forcing the Schoons to leave Botswana. Essentially the IVS was blackmailed by the UK government, which threatened to withdraw all funding for IVS overseas initiatives if they refused to fire the Schoons. In today's value, this funding would equal roughly one million British pounds, which was used by IVS to sustain development projects in multiple countries.

It seems clear that the FCO was opposed to the Schoons on purely political grounds. That is, the FCO understood the Schoons – and Marius, in particular – to be not only members of the ANC (a fact that troubled them) but also 'terrorists' engaged in clandestine military activities. The sources of the FCO's 'intelligence' on these matters has been redacted in the documents, with the clear implication that the British government was in direct communication with the South African security services. Far from expressing concern for the well-being of the Schoons, the FCO went to great lengths to ensure that these 'terrorists' would not endanger the well-being of any British citizens who might encounter the Schoons in IVS. Furthermore, the FCO was at pains to ensure that the Schoons would not seek asylum in the UK after leaving Botswana, as this would be tantamount to the UK 'harbouring terrorists'.

In chapter 10, the narrative returns to the site of the first and most central story of the entire project. Having addressed the assassination in detail in the Prologue, what remains is an investigation of the *life* of the Schoons during their short time in Angola. This account is necessarily hemmed in by two profound problems. First, there are substantial barriers to conducting archival research in Angola. Second, as Angola was a critical location for the ANC's military infrastructure, there is a deep-seated reticence to share any substantive details related to the inner workings of the organisation there. Nonetheless, based on a research trip to Angola, archival research in Lisbon, and interviews with ANC members who were willing to provide 'educated guesses', I have reconstructed at least some of the probable parameters of what the Schoons did in Angola.

The book begins in Angola, with the assassination of Jeanette and Katryn Schoon. Now, having analysed the fifteen years prior to the assassination, we have come full circle – back to Angola, back to 1984. In order to make any sense of the assassination, we have to try to understand why the Schoons were in Angola in the first place and what their lives were like while they were living there.

Given all of the secrets and silences contained in earlier chapters, what is truly staggering about this final period is how little can be said definitively about it. When the Schoons left Botswana, they entered into a domain of statelessness and security concerns that far outstripped their earlier modes of operating within the ANC underground. Before the Schoons were deployed by the ANC to Angola they spent nearly six months in some form of limbo, perhaps in Lusaka, but just as likely in a handful of other possible places. Then, once in Angola, the Schoons lived within the high intensity and intense deprivation of a society embroiled in a decades-long civil war. In light of these circumstances, this chapter necessarily relies heavily on a great deal of speculation and educated guesses.

In fact, since it would be virtually impossible to provide a 'definitive' account of this period, this chapter proceeds as if a series of different scenarios could all plausibly be true. Of course, these scenarios all run at cross purposes to one another, so they cannot possibly *all* be true. For example, I give an account of the role that the Schoons *might* have played, working in the service of MK while carrying out a cover story as English teachers at a teacher training college. In another section of the chapter, the school that the Schoons taught at is analysed in terms of the explicitly Marxist pedagogy offered to students. In this section, it appears plausible that the Schoons were *just* English teachers, without any military or underground role whatsoever. Both of these conflicting depictions are based on 'facts' to the extent that these exist, as well as on the reasonable assumptions of friends, family members and comrades, both in Angola and within the ANC.

Perhaps the Schoons loved their time in Angola because they wanted to be a part of a fledgling revolutionary socialist nation. Or perhaps they resented being deployed to Angola, especially in terms of the severity of war and the sustained hunger that their children were forced to endure. Perhaps the Schoons never wanted to be in Angola and instead longed to be safe and sound in Ireland. Perhaps the Schoons held the idea of exile in Europe in disdain and desperately wanted to be as close to the frontline as possible, to contribute to the ANC's just war against apartheid. Perhaps ...

My attempt here is not to settle the contradictions between different possible narratives of this time period, but rather to present them all as coherently and confidently as possible.

## Epilogue: Amnesty and Justice, 1995–2007

The assassination of Jeanette and Katryn Schoon has played a unique role in post-apartheid contestations around the need for amnesty and justice. Surviving members of the Schoon family – and Marius, in particular – tenaciously refused to reconcile with Craig Williamson and the other security police officers responsible for the deaths of Jeanette and Katryn. The Schoons' stubborn search for justice provides valuable insights into the contemporary stakes of this book.

The epilogue outlines the extended attempts to bring Craig Williamson to justice for the murders of Jeanette and Katryn Schoon, Ruth First and the bombing of the ANC's London headquarters. Williamson's remarkable capacity to evade justice is just one piece of the broader tragedy of post-apartheid South Africa. The simple fact is that a large portion of the crimes of the apartheid state remain unresolved – and the guilty continue to roam freely within the society.

However, even as I write these words, multiple efforts are under way to re-open cases previously considered closed, to force members of the apartheid security services to be held accountable for their crimes. For example, an extended inquiry into the suspicious death in detention of Neil Aggett was conducted simultaneous to my months of writing this book. Some of the individuals I interviewed also testified before this inquiry.[21] Further, in recent years there has been a concerted push to have more than 300 cases that the TRC passed on to the National Prosecuting Authority (NPA) in 2003 re-opened.[22] Given these ongoing initiatives to redress past crimes, it is clear that this book's depiction and analysis of the assassination of the

Schoons is not merely for posterity's sake. Rather, they may play a critical role in any future efforts to bring Williamson to justice.

Once again, this is a living history.

As the epilogue amply demonstrates, the key questions that this book grapples with are also alive today. Many of these debates are not yet 'settled'. The central characters of this book continue to contest both the significance of the events described here, as well as the contemporary processes to rectify the grievances of the past. These ongoing contestations have a profound impact on the stakes of this book.

Any book that attempts to grapple with the history of apartheid South Africa, must – as I have attempted to do, throughout – push against long-established habits of secrecy and long-coveted nostalgia. Historians of the apartheid state and the armed struggle alike must find creative methodologies to think through the thicket of obstacles that both armed combatants and the security services have constructed, if anything more than a superficial understanding of the underground and undercover history of apartheid South Africa is to be produced.

This book represents only a small piece of the important work that historians are currently engaged in, producing new histories of the armed struggle against apartheid. In doing so, this book addresses only a tiny corner of the ANC's underground, and the tiny corner of the massive apartheid state apparatus that was tasked with surveilling and sabotaging them. Nonetheless, researching and writing about this pocket of South African history brings to the fore all the challenges that any historian of this period must confront.

The stakes of this book exist as much in the specific stories that are told here, as in the *way* that these stories are told. It is vital that histories of the anti-apartheid struggle are written without relying on – and reinforcing – the triumphant narrative arc of the dominant nationalist party, the ANC, leading the people to their inevitable victory. What is needed now – at this particular historical moment – are stories that retain all of the contradictions, blind spots, and messiness of what was – without a doubt – one of the most courageous and admirable struggles for human liberation yet to surface.

# Prologue | The Assassination, 1984

Jeanette and Katryn Schoon were killed on 28 June 1984. The young mother and her six-year-old daughter died after a parcel bomb exploded inside their apartment in Lubango, Angola. Craig Williamson and Jerry Raven, South African security police officers, together confessed to manufacturing the bomb and sending it to Angola. These are the facts that can be stated without dispute or hesitation. Beyond these details, however, the story of Jeanette and Katryn Schoon's last moments alive drifts into speculation, contradictory and contested narratives, and supposed conclusions based on unverifiable evidence.

The questions related to how and why the assassination of the Schoons took place is a central concern for this book. To the extent possible, based on interviews Marius Schoon gave while he was alive, the memoirs of Jeanette's father, Jack Curtis, and my own research in Angola, I have attempted to reconstruct the likely chain of events on the day of the bombing, and the immediate events that followed. In narrating these details, I have drawn inspiration from Luise White's book *The Assassination of Herbert Chitepo*. For White, the purpose of studying an assassination is *not* to confirm, once and for all, the facts of the matter. Rather, the study is done 'in pursuit of history, of how narratives about the past are produced and reproduced and how power is produced and reproduced by these narratives'.[1] In the case of the Schoons, the different narratives of the assassination demarcate critical fault lines, which have been used to argue both for and against amnesty for the killers. In addition, the contestation around whether apartheid operatives deserve amnesty for this double murder hinges around determining where the line exists between being a 'combatant' within the ANC's military infrastructure and merely being a member of the political underground. At best, the line here is subtle, and difficult to draw clearly and cleanly. At worst, the line simply doesn't exist.

For Williamson and Raven to receive amnesty from the TRC, they were obliged to argue that the bomb was an act of war, targeting a soldier. The pair claimed that Marius Schoon was involved in supporting MK while in Angola and was therefore the intended target of the bomb. In other words, Jeanette's death was unintended. Further, the death of young Katryn was simply a mistake, based on false intelligence that the Schoon children were living with Jeanette's sister in the UK. Friends and family of the Schoons fought bitterly against Craig Williamson being granted amnesty. In fact, a crucial reason Williamson applied for amnesty was that Marius Schoon instigated legal charges against him for the murders of Jeanette and Katryn. In order for the Schoons and their comrades to argue against amnesty, they were obliged to argue that while living in Angola, the Schoons' role within the ANC was entirely political. In this framing, the Schoons could not have been legitimate targets of a targeted killing inside a foreign country. Instead, this group argues, based on over a decade of overlapping lives, Williamson was motivated by personal malice towards Jeanette Schoon. Perhaps even more damning, they argue that the death of Katryn is clear evidence that the parcel bomb cannot be described as a conscious political act. Simply and plainly, it is murder. Alternatively, if Katryn's death must be seen as an act of war, then it is a war crime. All these contested meanings of the assassination are contained within the narratives that continue to circulate, decades later.

Luise White insists that different narratives are not simply 'different perspectives on the same event, each narrated from a different position'.[2] That is to say, these narratives cannot simply be cobbled together to produce one clear mosaic of 'the truth'. Instead, it is crucial to acknowledge that

> All of them have loose ends and contradictions, and many seem unlikely, but I do not think they should be simply dismissed as coerced or contrived; they contain too many traces of the past to be discarded altogether ... each one a way of fixing the assassination

that is a frame, an either/or analysis, that both provides a structure for and limits our understanding of the events it describes.[3]

With this interpretive framework in mind, I have chosen to present the story of the assassination of Jeanette and Katryn Schoon through different 'takes', all of which contain both overlapping and contradictory details with the others. Throughout, I provide an analysis of why these differences matter.

Before we can engage with the larger significance of the assassination of the Schoons, we must first describe what happened on 28 June 1984 as well as possible.

## Take #1: The Vietnamese man

Jeanette Schoon always received her mail at work.

Like all of the other teachers at Lubango College, now called ISCED (Instituto Superior de Ciências da Educação – Higher Institute of Education Sciences) – the socialist teacher's training college in Lubango, Angola – Jeanette lived in an apartment building run by the school, just a few blocks away. So, on 28 June 1984, when a package arrived from her sister in England, Jeanette hurried home, with her two small children in tow (Katryn, aged six, and Fritz, two years old) to see what it was. Jeanette's partner, Marius, was away, in the capital, Luanda.

The apartment building, which was known as Simpor, housed all of the teachers who had come to Angola from other countries; the housing was considered part of the salary. The Schoons lived on the fourth floor. One of their neighbours and friends was a Vietnamese man. On that day, this man showed up at the door, hoping to speak with Jenny about borrowing a tape recorder. However, a moment after he arrived, a bomb went off. The force of the blast shook the whole building and sent shards of glass and debris out across the street, four stories down below. Jenny and Katryn were killed by the blast. The Vietnamese man was badly injured and lost his hearing as a result, but he survived. Little Fritz was forced to endure the horrific trauma of being one of the first witnesses to the deaths of his mother and sister. But ... he also survived.

This is, as they say in Portuguese, 'mais ou menos' (give or take) the whole story of the murder of Jeanette and Katryn Schoon. At least, this is one of the many tellings of how the day of the murder happened, without any analysis added in. In fact, any attempt to reconstruct the story in greater detail than this immediately runs into competing narratives, contradictory details, hearsay and rumours. I will not attempt to resolve these contradictions or provide a definitive answer as to 'what happened', because I don't believe that this is possible, at least not in this case. Instead, I will try to present as many details as I can, which means also retelling the story from a few different angles. Then I will offer some analysis as to what these different narratives 'mean' in terms of both our understanding of the specific assassination, as well as of the larger political and military dynamics at play in the death of this one young woman, and her much younger daughter.

To start with, most accounts of the assassination of Jeanette Schoon include the Vietnamese neighbour, in one form or another. There is a fair bit of agreement that this man was a witness to the killing, and that his hearing was badly damaged as a result; and multiple people speak of speaking to him, although they don't remember or don't mention his name. Marius Schoon was interviewed by writer and filmmaker Julie Frederikse in 1986, just a couple of years after the assassination, and in that interview, he recounts his version in a fair bit of detail:

> I spoke to a Vietnamese comrade who'd been in the flat when the explosion took place. He'd been badly injured in the explosion – he was very, very shocked when I saw him. His face was badly cut, his hands were badly cut, but he'd actually been in the room when the explosion took place. Now according to him what happened is that he came in to borrow the tape recorder, and Jenny ... was sitting at the table reading something, and Katryn was sitting on the floor playing with something more or less next to her chair, and when he came in Jenny offered him coffee ... and as she got up she pushed the table away from her, and she took two or three paces and then the explosion came.[4]

Given that this is the surviving husband speaking, one might presume that this is a more accurate telling than other recollections, given by people who were at a greater remove from the tragedy. Further, the description of the

Vietnamese man's wounds, just a day after the explosion, is gripping, and seems unlikely to have been misremembered. However, what is most striking in this account is the fact that it describes the bomb as if it is something that has been *placed* into the apartment, sitting on the floor, somehow unnoticed. The only problem with this idea is that members of the South African security forces – Craig Williamson and Jerry Raven – later testified that the bomb was a parcel bomb, which they had manufactured using a package that was intercepted, and then redirected to Angola, after having explosives installed. After this testimony at the TRC, the bomb is almost universally spoken of as a letter bomb, both by South Africans as well as by those who knew the Schoons in Lubango. Nonetheless, in 1986 Marius Schoon was inclined to believe that the bomb had not been sent through the post:

> Now I think our security in Angola is reasonably convinced that ... a very, very powerful explosive device had in fact been placed under the table and that pushing the table activated the tumblers. However, it is possible that it was also some form of a letterbomb. I don't think it matters.[5]

Why doesn't it matter whether the bomb was sent via the post, or somehow placed under the table by an assassin? What Marius intends to say is that in either case, he was entirely sure (from the first second) that it was the apartheid state who had blown his family to pieces. In this light, perhaps the specifics don't matter. Still, the simple fact that there is a dispute regarding this relatively basic-seeming point is in and of itself intriguing.

There is a very tangible and significant difference between the apartheid state using the postal service to murder someone, at a great distance, rather than the levels of organisation and capacity that would be required to infiltrate an intimate space of a family living in exile in order to place a bomb under the kitchen table of a fourth floor apartment in Lubango. In whose interest would it be to believe that the apartheid state had the wherewithal to kill Jeanette Schoon in such an intensely intimate way? When Marius speaks of 'our security in Angola', does he mean the intelligence services of the Angolan state, or of the ANC? Would either organisation have had the resources and skills required conclusively to determine the nature of this bomb? If they did solve this, why wasn't the answer widely publicised?

Most accounts of the assassination not only assert that the bomb was sent via the post; they also tend to add several details about who sent the parcel, who it was addressed to, or what the parcel looked like. For example, Jeanette's father, Jack Curtis, wrote in his memoir about the parcel as follows:

> Jenny had, after leaving Katryn and Fritzie at the play centre, gone as usual to the university. On leaving at the end of the morning session she had collected two large envelopes addressed to Marius, but with an unusual juxtaposition of names and initials, and apparently containing printed matter; she had not opened them there but collected the children and returned to the flat to give the children their lunch.[6]

It is striking that Jack Curtis describes the writing on the parcels so confidently, even though he was thousands of miles away when they arrived. Who would have told him that the letters had 'an unusual juxtaposition of names and initials'? Who said that the parcels apparently contained 'printed matter'? Furthermore, Jack Curtis declares boldly that the packages were addressed to Marius. He is not unusual for insisting that the letter bomb was addressed to Marius – and, by implication, *not* addressed to Jeanette. In fact, many of the people I met in Lubango insisted that this was the case, without offering any evidence to support it. I heard this even from people who were completely disconnected from the murder. In these cases, I took this certainty about the intended recipient of the bomb to reflect how particular people understood the differences between Jeanette and Marius, in terms of their demeanour, their teaching and their politics. In short, saying that the letter bomb was addressed to Marius seems to signal a belief that Marius was the more politically active person, and therefore the one most likely to be a target for assassination. There is a lot that could be said about this position, but to say the least, it is a belief presented without any solid evidence.

Not everyone insists that the parcel was addressed to Marius. A couple of people I spoke with were adamant that the parcel had arrived from England. Jeanette had a sister living in the UK, so the presumption was that the parcel was sent by the sister. This makes sense both because Jeanette often got mail from her sister, but also because Williamson and Raven testified that their standard practice in such bombings would be to intercept mail that had been sent by someone close to the intended target, and then they would 'repurpose' the package, before sending it onwards. From the assassin's perspective, it was critical that the parcel appeared to be a genuine communication from a loved one, rather than something suspicious, or foreign. A few people who knew the Schoons have said that both Marius and Jenny were always extra careful with their mail, because they were very much aware of other casualties of apartheid parcel bombs. Judy Seidman, a friend of Jenny and Marius, related a story about attempting to send some spices to Jenny while in Angola, and having used a spoonful of curry before sealing the package. Jenny sent a furious letter in reply, explaining that when they saw the curry had been opened, they had thrown out the whole box for fear that the spices had been poisoned.[7]

There are numerous examples of targeted parcel or letter bombs, just a step removed from the Schoons, most notably the assassination of Ruth First in Maputo in August 1982, and the killing of Black Consciousness leader Abraham Tiro in Gaborone in 1974. Even closer to home, Jack Curtis relates a couple of bombings against people whom Jenny knew personally:

> Among their immediate friends they had, in Gaborone, been in daily contact with John, a brother in an Anglican Church Order, who had lost a hand in a letter bomb explosion in Maseru in Lesotho, in which Phyllis, the person to whom the letter was addressed, had suffered severe bodily injuries.[8]

Since the Schoons were habitually careful when dealing with their mail, the question of who opened the package, and why, is a driving concern in all of the accounts of the assassination. As Jack Curtis puts it,

> Whether Jenny, believing that in Angola they were beyond the reaches of the murderous activities of the Security Branch of the ANG [Afrikaner Nationalist Government] had opened an envelope before ensuring its contents were harmless, or whether Katryn had accidentally gained possession of it in her playing, will never be known.[9]

While the truth of who opened the letter bomb will never be known, this doesn't mean that people did not make various speculations about this. One version that I was told – once again based on the Vietnamese man as the key witness – comes to the harrowing conclusion that it was Katryn who opened the letter bomb, and therefore suffered the most immediate impact of the blast. I spoke with a woman who had been a student at Lubango College during the time that the Schoons lived in Lubango. She began our discussion by insisting that she would 'only tell what I know'. Nonetheless, when it came to discussing the finer details of the explosion, her narrative drifted in places, and I got the impression that at times she was simply guessing, even though she said that the famous Vietnamese comrade had recently emailed her and shared his side of the story. In this version, the Vietnamese man knocked on the door, and Jenny answered. Jenny held the door open, and the two began speaking, while still in the doorway. Meanwhile, Katryn was playing by herself, and she noticed the package, and knew that it was sent by her aunt in England, Jenny's sister. Excited to see what her aunt had sent, Katryn opened the package, and detonated the explosives. The Vietnamese man lost his hearing because of the blast, but since he was standing on the other side of the door, his life was spared.

Now, Katryn was a small girl, only six years old. There is no getting around the fact that a high-powered explosive device would do brutal damage to such a small frame. But the impact one imagines when picturing a small girl opening a parcel bomb and feeling the full and immediate impact of the blast is simply grotesque to the point of being almost impossible to comprehend. Why does this woman, who was impacted by the blast, of course, on account of being a citizen of Lubango, and more so a member of the Lubango College community, but not a bystander, prefer to believe that the killing happened in this way? Could it be that, as a mother, and on account of her closer connection to Katryn (her own son was at the same elementary school as Katryn, just a few years older), she chooses to remember the assassination in such a way that Katryn was the principal victim?

In conclusion, while multiple people agree that the Vietnamese comrade was a witness to the assassination, they nonetheless do not all remember him *in the same way*. For example, Jack Curtis does not mention that the man is from Vietnam and doesn't claim that the man was a direct witness to the explosion. Instead, according to Curtis, 'he was climbing the stairs when, at a point where he was just able to see through into Jenny's and Marius's flat through the open doorway, an explosion occurred which blew him backwards down the stairs'.[10]

Despite this unnamed neighbour from Vietnam being a central thread in many accounts, the details about him are elusive, and contradictory. Furthermore, the details of the incident itself vary widely, and disagree on the most fundamental points, such as whether the bomb was sent in the mail or placed inside the room by the assassin.

## Take #2: The neighbour

Once it became known that I was researching the death of Jeanette Schoon, the people in Lubango who offered to help with my project (mostly younger people, not people who knew the Schoons at all) began to reach out in every direction that they could think of, to connect me with anyone who might know something. I got taken to a family lunch, in order to meet someone's father, who was in Lubango in the 1980s. Sure enough, the father remembered the story, and told his version of it, which is interesting in and of itself, but he wasn't able to add any specific information. Other people said yes, they'd be happy to meet, but then later cancelled, for reasons that were not explained. One man I was introduced to, who seemed friendly enough, and happy to chat about the Schoons, I was told afterwards was a police officer. Sure enough, in the days that followed, the Seguranza do Estado (State Security) started showing up, and calling my supportive contacts, trying to learn more about who I was and what I was studying. In case there are ever situations where 'normal channels' of research exist, Lubango in the aftermath of nearly forty years of civil war was not one of them.

During my time in Lubango, many of the details of my research happened, as they say in Angola, 'mais em cima' (higher up, over my head). Meetings were scheduled on my behalf by a sympathetic contact and then I would be driven to the meeting at the appropriate time. One of the most notable of these moments was when someone who had been helping with translation during interviews told me that their mother knew a woman who used to live in the Simpor building and was home when the bomb went off. Excited to meet this person, my translator gave her a call. 'Yes, she says that she will meet with us. She's in the middle of having her hair done, but we can come.' We went to the courtyard of an apartment building (not Simpor) where I was introduced to the neighbour of the Schoons, and we all sat down on plastic chairs in a circle, so we could talk.

> 'Do you remember Jeanette Schoon?'
> 'Yes, I remember her. There was also a daughter, but she didn't die.'
> An awkward pause.
> Finally, we muster the courage to attempt tactfully to say, 'No, the daughter died, as well.'
> 'Oh, yes, I remember her. Yes, yes, she died ... But I don't remember any other child.'
> An awkward pause.
> Again, we find a way to say, 'There was another child, a little boy.'
> Again, 'Oh, yes, I remember him.'[11]

After this quite stilted beginning to our conversation, the whole tone of the interaction changed. I suppose, having feigned ignorance at first, the neighbour had determined that we already knew some amount about this story, and so it was, relatively speaking, safer to speak to us. Having crossed this hurdle, the woman began to tell her story, which went like this:

She had a daughter about Katryn's age and the two girls played together regularly. They were close friends. On 28 June 1984, when Jenny and the kids came home to Simpor, Fritz and Katryn went upstairs, to the sixth floor, to be looked after by this friendly neighbour. After a while, Jeanette called her children to come back downstairs. The children all came running, including the young Angolan girl. Katryn arrived first, in time to see her mother open the package. Young Fritz and the other child were still in the staircase when the explosion went off. When she first heard the explosion, this woman sitting across from me in her plastic chair was absolutely horrified because, as far as she could know in the moment, her own daughter had just been killed. Furthermore, it was hard to believe that such a gigantic explosion could have been contained inside of a package, which is what she was later told it was. The blast shook the whole building, such that she could feel it up on the sixth floor and she could see glass and debris flying down onto the street below.

What happened to young Fritz, I wondered. Would this mother, who had just been looking after him a few moments before, then take care of him for the night, since his mother had just been brutally murdered and since his father was far away. No, she didn't take care of him, she says. Who did look after Fritz? She cannot say.

In fact, in answer to all of my questions about the aftermath of the explosion, her comments hint at a deep-seated, long-lasting fear.

'Do you remember what happened after the bomb went off?'
'Yes, the police came.'
'Do you remember what happened when Marius came home?'
'Yes, there were many police with him.'[12]

In other words, beyond the extremely precise imagery of the exact instant of the explosion, with three small children running down the stairs towards catastrophe, this person seems to have made a conscious decision to *try not to know*. Of course, the most glaring omission in this telling of the story is the Vietnamese man. Why would he be left out of the story? Having heard and felt the bomb go off, wouldn't she have run down the stairs to see what just happened, to try to find her own daughter? In the process of doing this, wouldn't she have seen the Vietnamese man, badly injured, alongside Jenny and Katryn's dead bodies? Or did she choose not to look that closely, afraid of getting too close to a clearly horrific crime scene? Was there never any comrade from Vietnam, or has this one witness simply blocked him out of the story entirely?

## Take #3: The cigarette

Shortly after the blast, Paula Dias and another colleague from Lubango College (a male nurse) came to the apartment. They were the ones who carefully, lovingly, cleaned the bodies and wrapped them in white sheets, to prepare them for burial. Reflecting back on that day now, Paula says, 'The job was terrible. I couldn't sleep for a month afterwards, because of the images of the corpses. Mainly Katryn.'[13] According to Paula, Katryn's body was totally broken into pieces. Jeanette's face was totally blown off, 'just the hair remaining'. At the same time, Jeanette 'still had a cigarette in her hand', gripped tightly in between her two fingers.[14]

Beyond the grim specificity of this account, what does Paula's version add or change? For one thing, her description of Jeanette's face strongly suggests that the bomb *was* contained inside of a package, and that Jeanette opened it. It would not have been Katryn who opened the package, and it wasn't an explosive device sitting underneath a large table. Jeanette must have been looking straight at the bomb when it exploded.

As a witness and a narrator, I'm inclined to trust Paula Dias over all of the rest, because she had the most unfortunate task of handling the bodies of the dead, very shortly after the bomb went off. If she was haunted enough by what she saw to have troubled sleep for a long time, then I believe that she still remembers the crime scene, as vividly as if it were yesterday.

Nonetheless, there are real limits to what Paula is truly able to speak to. She had no first-hand knowledge of the package itself, nor of the moments immediately *before* the bomb went off. Only the killers could tell us whether it was a package or a bomb and, if it was a package, who it was addressed to. Only the Vietnamese man could tell us what happened immediately beforehand, and we don't even know his name, or whether he was actually in the room.

Another striking absence in Paula's account, like all the rest of the accounts, is Fritz Schoon. What really happened to Fritz during and immediately after the bombing? According to Marius, in an interview he did with Hilda Bernstein in 1990:

> It's come up from subsequent discussions, remarks he's made, that he was clearly in the room when the explosion took place. So, I mean, he saw everything. It is miraculous that he wasn't hurt, at all. His ears were burned; he was deaf for a couple of days ... the first day, he didn't speak at all. Even the next day, he hardly said anything, and I actually thought the child was never going to speak again. I was frantic about it.[15]

This all sounds entirely plausible, and of course it seems unreasonable to question Marius's version of what happened to his own son. But, where in the room could the boy have been such that he escaped the explosion with less damage than the Vietnamese man? Was he on the staircase, like the neighbour said? To further complicate matters, in a front-page article printed a few days after the assassination, the *Rand Daily Mail* (the principal English language liberal newspaper, in Johannesburg) reported that Fritz Schoon was 'at a nearby creche' when the bomb went off. It is not clear who may have told the newspaper about Fritz's whereabouts. The only sources the article mentions are Jenny's parents and, intriguingly, the British intelligence services.[16] In sum, there are some who say that Fritz must have been in the same room, others that he was on the staircase down the hall, and others that he was somewhere else entirely.

Perhaps the only thing that really unifies these different accounts of the day that Jeanette and Katryn Schoon died are the absences. None of these narratives is complete enough, or coherent enough, to serve as a suitable explanation. Each of these tellings of the story begs more questions than they answer. There is something else that unifies all of these stories, however. Throughout, one can hear clearly, after all these years, and despite all that is still not known, the *feeling* of it all, the sense of absolute horror that pervades every second of it.

## 'This plane is yours, and I am yours'

Jeanette's husband, Marius Schoon, was away in the capital, Luanda, on the day of the bombing. This fact has many layers of significance, but the simplest of them is that he was not also a casualty, and that there was some delay between the bombing and Marius's arrival on the scene. Marius's description of the moment he heard the news is heartbreaking:

> I was in Luanda. I was staying with Jane Bergerol – a very dear friend, a very good comrade. We'd had supper. Jane was upstairs working. I was sitting downstairs, listening to music and reading. There's a knock on the door. There's the ANC chief representative, with two comrades with him. He comes in and says to me, 'I'm afraid I've got very bad news.' He then said to me, 'I have to inform you that we've just heard from Lubango that Jenny and Katryn are late.' I was completely numb. Then I asked for details. He said, 'We

have no details; all that we know is that there was an explosion.' I still didn't understand. I kept on saying to him, 'I understand that Jenny has been killed, but Katryn is in hospital; how badly is she hurt?' And the chief said to me, over and over again, 'Our intelligence is that both the comrades are late.'[17]

That Marius's host was Jane Bergerol was absolutely critical. Jane was a British socialist, who was firmly aligned with the ruling party in Angola, the MPLA. In fact, her support for the party was so strong that she was the co-author of an important English book about the Angolan revolution. In the book, Bergerol defended the MPLA position, in defence of what is now understood clearly to have been the slaughter of thousands of left-wing dissidents in 1977.[18] However shameful her association with the MPLA, her connections proved to be tremendously useful on the day of the assassination:

I went upstairs, and I told Jane. Jane knew everybody in Angola. She'd been in Angola since the day before independence. She knew all the senior people in the party. She knew people all over. So, Jane immediately came down and discussed with the chief [representative of the ANC]. It was decided that I would fly down the next day, with a comrade. Now, flying in Angola is not easy. You have to have passes, to move from one area to another. Getting onto an internal aircraft is an absolute shambles because they just sell as many tickets as people want them, and you just take your chances about getting on. So, Jane took the chief to go and see a very senior Air Force officer. The arrangements that were made were that I would go to the airport and if the commercial flight was flying – one never knew if it was flying or not – I would definitely get onto the commercial flight (we were given some sort of passes) and if it wasn't flying, there was a military aircraft going down later in the day, and we would go down on the military aircraft.[19]

As a member of the ANC in exile – supported by the chief representative of the party in Luanda as well as by Jane Bergerol – the Angolan socialists treated Marius as if he was an esteemed diplomat. Not only was he flown down to Lubango in a military airplane, but furthermore, upon landing Marius was told by the pilot, 'the aircraft is under your command – it will stand on the strip at Lubango until you order me to take off, whether it is today or whether it is in a fortnight's time.'[20] Following this dramatic declaration of support, 'The Angolan head of security – the man we'd had dealings with, because we used to have to get permits from him, every time we went to Luanda – was waiting on the tarmac when the plane landed. He just walked us through all the formalities. He took us into the arrivals hall.'[21]

No matter how much the logistics of getting back to Lubango were facilitated by the MPLA, there was still the inescapable fact that Marius's reason for taking the trip was horrific. The reality set in straight away. Marius's depiction is worth recounting in full.

> As we came up to the arrivals hall, through the window I could see one of the ANC comrades who was teaching in Lubango with us, with Fritzy in his arms. I rushed over, and I took him, and he was absolutely rigid; he was stiff. He just put his arms around me. He only said two things to me. In fact, I thought the child was never going to speak again. He said two things to me. He said to me, 'I thought I'd never see you, as well.' Then, the comrades from the students' union had come in a vehicle, to fetch us. We went into town, in the Land Rover. Fritz sat on my lap, with his arms around my head, and he whispered in my ear, and he said, 'Marius, you know the enemy didn't kill Jenny; they just broke her apart.' He had just turned two.
> They took us straight down to the flat. Now the street was cordoned off. There was no traffic in the street. We came through the security checkpoint. The whole street was covered in glass. It was a four-storey block of flats, and the explosion had blown out virtually every pane of glass. I mean, the street was covered in glass. We went upstairs to the flat. It was terrible. On the floor of the flat, there was a heap of blood, mixed with flesh. That had clearly been Katryn. Then, across the one wall – the whole wall – was just absolutely covered in blood. That is where the explosion had thrown Jenny. It was too ghastly.[22]

Marius and Fritz, with the help of students and colleagues from Lubango College, then set about the ghastly task of gathering the remains of Jeanette and Katryn and preparing for their burial.

## Burial, fire and rubbish

> I have heard about the memorial services held at home in Cape Town, in Johannesburg; about memorial services in Harare, in Gaborone, in London and in various Australian cities ... I have seen this too by the hundreds of letters I have had from all over the world. Many of them from comrades and friends. Many of the most moving of these letters from people who are complete strangers to me. It is as though the deaths of Jenny and Katryn have come to epitomize for many people the horror of apartheid, the senselessness of apartheid, the waste of apartheid.
>
> — Marius Schoon, interview by Colin Buckley, 29 August 1984

Together with virtually all of the students and staff of Lubango College and encouraged by the support and warm wishes from strangers in the streets, the coffins containing Jeanette and Katryn were transported to the airport, where something of a funeral took place, on the landing strip. After this airport funeral gathering, the Schoons – and a number of their supporters, both Angolan and ANC – boarded a military airplane that was entirely at their disposal, and flew up to Luanda for the actual burial and the funeral service. That the Angolan military provided an airplane to the Schoons was remarkable, and Marius underlined this point: 'In a war situation, the Angolan government had diverted an aircraft – which they could ill afford to do – purely to take Fritzy and myself, and comrades from Lubango up to Luanda.'[23]

According to the secretary general of the ANC, Jeanette Schoon needed to be buried in Angola, in accordance with the 'long standing practice by our movement to bury its deceased in the countries where they die'.[24] Jeanette and Katryn were buried on 6 July 1984 in Luanda. According to Marius, Jeanette and Katryn were buried alongside soldiers of the ANC and of the MPLA, the most prestigious burial possible in Angola at that time. 'The bodies were taken ... to a hall built into the wall of one of the major cemeteries in Luanda, a hall which is normally only used for the bodies of FAPLA [People's Armed Forces for Liberation of Angola] heroes who've died in action.'[25]

Clearly, the support from the MPLA for Marius in the aftermath of the bombing was total. Reflecting back on this some years later, Marius concluded that

> The government and the ANC couldn't have done more for us. This is something I've got to make myself remember. Because, as you know, there are times when I am so irritated with various things that the movement does. But I will be grateful, forever, for the support and comradeship that I received during that period.[26]

Not surprisingly, the immediate news coverage of the killing, in Angola, was based entirely on the analysis of the ANC, affirming the immediate realisation that the deaths of Jeanette and Katryn was a targeted assassination. On 3 July 1984, the *Jornal de Angola* reported that 'Agentes de Pretória Assassinam Militante do ANC no Lubango' (Agents of Pretoria assassinate an ANC militant in Lubango).[27] Intriguingly, the article further links the assassination to similar attacks by the apartheid state, against Joe Gqabi, who was killed in July 1981, in Harare, and Ruth First, who was murdered in August of 1982, in Maputo. While the links to Gqabi's death may be more metaphorical, it is of course now conclusively established that the assassination of Ruth First is not only reminiscent of the killing of the Schoons, but explicitly linked, and was carried out by the same members of the security apparatus.

A few days later, on 6 July, the paper printed a second article about the assassination, this time focused explicitly on the views of Marius Schoon. In making sense of the killing of his wife and daughter, Marius was adamant that this murder proved that 'terror – as much inside South Africa as well as outside the borders – is the nature of the heinous and retrograde system of apartheid'.[28]

These depictions in the *Jornal de Angola* are markedly different from the reporting done by South Africa's *Rand Daily Mail*. In the article on the assassination printed on 30 June 1984, the newspaper focused on the fact that the Schoons were 'self-exiled' from South Africa, and that they had already previously been warned by the British intelligence services of the danger to their lives.[29] In combination, this depiction implies that the Schoons were somehow responsible for their own assassination, in that they put themselves in danger, despite being warned in advance. Gone entirely from this account is any of the appropriate outrage that one might expect to find, in the aftermath of a young woman in her 30s and a six-year-old girl being blown up by their own government.

*

Jenny's parents, Jack and Joyce, flew up from South Africa for the funeral, along with Neville Curtis, Jenny's brother, who had been forced into exile in Australia as a result of his leadership of the student movement.[30] Jack Curtis, in his memoir, offers the following account of the burial of his daughter and granddaughter:

> Katryn and Jenny were buried in adjoining graves. Our attempt to have them buried in the same grave was frustrated by the rigidity of the regulations governing interment. Jane had miraculously managed to garner a small bunch of flowers, which save for the bare earth, was all that showed where their bodies had been laid. We had not asked to have the coffin lids raised when they lay, with a guard of honour, in the chapel at the cemetery. We knew that what lay inside bore no resemblance to the vital living beings who had gladdened so many hours of our lives. Tributes were paid to Jenny by those with whom she had worked and then in a slow march we followed the carriage conveying the coffins to the grave side. The burial service was conducted by a priest from the Cathedral and their bodies committed to the earth 'in sure and certain hope of the Resurrection'.[31]

Marius remembered the funeral simply as being 'very emotional, very harrowing'.[32]

Initially, there wasn't time to produce a gravestone for Jenny and Katryn. A year later the family returned to 'dedicate the gravestone and plaque, which joined their graves into one'[33] on 26 June 1985. By a cruel irony of apartheid brutality, this anniversary funeral was only days after members of the South African Defence Force (SADF) conducted a raid in the city of Gaborone, ransacking the homes and offices of friends and comrades with whom the Schoons had worked closely, and killing a dozen people.[34] Given this atrocity, it seems quite appropriate that the second funeral ceremony was not overseen by a priest, but rather by Marius and Jane Bergerol. Jack Curtis described the ceremony:

> This time we had brought some proteas with us, the floral emblem of South Africa. Jane Bergerol had produced, out of flowerless Luanda, a bunch of roses, and these were tenderly and reverently laid on the gravestone on either side of the plaque signifying that although their bodies rested in a foreign land they would always be remembered for the traditions in which they had been raised and the country which had been dear to them. Marius spoke of all that Jenny had been to him and the children, her devotion to the cause to which they were committed and the need to continue the fight until victory was won.[35]

\*

Based on the information about the burial in Marius's accounts, I made multiple attempts to visit the grave of Jenny and Katryn Schoon. There were only two cemeteries in Luanda in 1984, and I was assured that one of them, Alto Das Cruxes, would have been the site where any honoured citizen would be buried. This makes sense, as the cemetery is in the wealthy Miramar (View of the Sea) neighbourhood in Luanda. The cemetery is bordered by foreign embassies and wealthy homes set atop a cliff, overlooking the city and the bay. On my first visit to the cemetery, I spoke to an older gentleman, who seemed to have been working at the cemetery for many long years. I explained to him what I was looking for, in my imperfect Portuguese. In reply, I heard the words *fogo* and *lixo*, but with my limited language skills, I didn't immediately believe my ears. Did the man say 'fire' and 'rubbish'? Then, to underline his point, the man produced a pile of battered old books and slammed them down onto the counter in front of me. These were the registries of the dead, which catalogued every new burial in the cemetery and marked out exactly where the bodies were placed. He wanted me to see these few books so that I could understand that the vast majority of such records were destroyed by fire, or simply trashed, over the long years of warfare, with various waves of people coming into the cemetery and causing havoc of all sorts. As he and I walked together through the grounds, looking more or less blindly for some sign of the grave, I could see the signs of decline and disarray, in all directions. Even if Jenny and Katryn were granted pride of place in their initial burial, with roses flown in especially for the affair, it seems unlikely that the gravesite remains in anywhere near the same condition at this point.

Part 1

# From Student Radicals to Post-student People, 1972–1976

# 1 | Student Radicals

They are, according to the evidence which your Commission has before it, and this includes the oral evidence of some of the leaders themselves, opposed to the entire existing order in South Africa, including, to mention only a few aspects, the capitalist system, existing moral norms and any form of relationship of authority, inter alia that between parent and child, teacher and pupil, and university authorities and students. They reject liberalism as a political approach. The issue here therefore involves far more than opposition to the policy of a ruling party, even the artificial division of the whole population into black and white polarities and the fanning of a confrontation between these two polarities.

— Alwyn Schlebusch, Report of the Commission of Inquiry into Certain Organisations

## Leadership clique

Jenny Curtis first became a target of state scrutiny in 1972, when the Schlebusch Commission determined that Curtis was one of the 'leadership clique' of Nusas.

The three interim reports of the commission's findings (which all pertain to Nusas) were produced rapidly – nearly a year before the final product was published – and the commission explicitly stated that this was necessary because, even during their investigation, events were unfolding that required an immediate response from the state. The commission was under the impression that the political climate was escalating at a frightening pace, which might soon spill over into some form of violent action against the state. The perceived threat of violence here was both literal and vague, paranoid and deeply rational. Given the fact that anti-apartheid organisations (including some members of Nusas) had already turned towards armed struggle over a decade prior, this fear was far from groundless.[1] However, there seems to be no foundation to the idea that Nusas was at the time – neither in terms of individual leaders nor on a broad organisational level – participating in any form of clandestine or armed struggle. For example,

> This *Newsletter* report on the seminar [April 1970] put it explicitly in words that were underlined, that NUSAS could have nothing to do and should have nothing to do with violent change. Why this was necessary, the Commission does not know. Possibly the fact that it was a public document, reflecting the public image of NUSAS in contrast to its secret image, had something to do with it.[2]

It is deeply significant to read how the commission interpreted an explicit statement against violence 'in words that were underlined' as potentially evidence of some form of clandestine engagement with revolutionary violence.

One of the persistent lenses of the state was to assume that secrets were being withheld from them, that the real sphere of power within the opposition was somehow off stage. However, regardless of their delusional inability to take student activists at face value, the commission nonetheless correctly understood a shifting political *mood* within the organisation, wherein a radical rupture was increasingly both within the realm of imagination and even desired. 'This situation is fraught with dangers ... the possibility of dangerous outbursts must always be borne in mind, and this calls for constant vigilance and readiness for quick action.'[3]

Having established – to their own satisfaction – that Nusas was rapidly becoming more threatening, the question remained as to what actions against it would be most effective. The commission needed to decide whether the organisation *as an organisation* was to blame or whether it was a problem of leadership. As they had already done with the South African Communist Party (SACP), the ANC and the Pan-Africanist Congress (PAC), the state could well have decided to simply declare Nusas an illegal organisation. However, in the end, the state chose to focus their repression on a small group of people within the organisation.

> In conclusion your commission wishes to stress that in bringing out this report it has in mind action against individuals and not against NUSAS as an organisation ... it will not recommend the banning of this organisation. A national students' organisation functioning from, through and for students is certainly desirable.[4]

The Schlebusch Commission's view of Nusas was essentially of an organisation that had been hijacked by revolutionaries, who not only did not represent the viewpoint of most students, but were not even 'proper' students, but rather 'professional politicians'. While the commission did not assign the same importance to Jenny Curtis as to her brother Neville's role within Nusas, it is nonetheless clear that they were keenly aware of her extended role as a student leader:

> Jeanette Curtis was NUSWEL[5] secretary-general for 1972 (after she had already been national director of welfare, benefits and fundraising in 1968/1969 and Transvaal regional director in 1969/1970).[6]

According to the commission, the entirety of the leadership 'clique', minus one person, were all living together in Cape Town during 1972, in two houses which were described as communes in the evidence:

> Resident at 100 Belvedere Road, Claremont, were:
> Philippe Anthony David le Roux
> Jeanette Eva Curtis
> Margaret Paula Ensor
> John Gavin Frankis
> Neville Wilson Curtis
> Done James Christopher Wood
>
> Resident at 21 Milldene Avenue, Claremont, were:
> Ian Barry Cadman Streek

Paul Joseph Pretorius
Renfrew Leslie Christie
Nicolette Anne (Nikki) Westcott.[7]

This listing of names is significant. In fact, the Schlebusch Commission explicitly recommended banning most of these individuals, at the end of their hastily published Second Interim Report:

> These persons' continued participation in student politics is undesirable in the extreme. They all gave evidence on subpoena before your commission and also had the opportunity of submitting facts or arguments themselves. Every one of them, except Chris Wood, was assisted by a legal representative.[8]

The above declaration was printed on 23 February and three days later, the minister of justice served this group of eight (most living in the previously mentioned 'communes') with banning orders.[9] As it happened, these eight people were not simply removed from 'student politics', but largely removed from South Africa entirely, in one form or another. A number of these individuals later fled the country, Rick Turner was assassinated in 1978, and the assassination of Jenny Curtis (Jeanette Schoon) was only a few years after that.

## Bannings begin

Jenny Curtis was not one of the student radicals placed under a banning order on 27 February 1973. However, of the eight Nusas leaders banned on that date, four of them were Jenny's housemates – and one of those was her brother, Neville Curtis.[10] One of the other banned students, Paul Pretorius, lived just a few blocks away, in a house shared with a number of Jenny's friends.[11]

In contemporary South African society, both 100 Belvedere Road and 21 Milldene Avenue are well-kept, well-to-do homes. While located on the less affluent side of Claremont's main road, the community remains quite privileged, relative to other parts of the city. Although the South African suburbs are no longer racially segregated by law, Claremont remains a majority 'white' space, in the shadow of Table Mountain, with the UCT campus just a short drive away. It is hard to imagine such houses as communes, or as the headquarters of white student radicalism.

Among those who lived in these houses, and spent time in them, the idea that these were 'communes' isn't quite right; or, at least not in the way that the state intended that word.

Clive Keegan, one of the banned eight, didn't live in either house, but spent a lot of time socialising there. From his perspective, 'It's rubbish to call them communes. They weren't dens of iniquity. Obviously, they were intensely political places. But no insurrections were plotted there. If you were a police spy, you frankly would have been very, very bored.'[12] Charles Nupen, who was elected the president of Nusas after the 1973 bannings, was also a frequent guest at Milldene Avenue and described the house as 'an intellectually very stimulating environment, because people would constantly talk about affairs of the day, hoping to advance the cause of human freedom'.[13] Nicki Westcott, who lived in the same house, is even more emphatic about the intellectually stimulating environment at Milldene Avenue:

> When I think about how my children [now in their 20s] spent their student years, I'm always struck by how little they sit and discuss ideas. We would sit up until the dead of night, every night, discussing. We had people studying history, psychoanalysis, politics, communism etc. We used to read a lot too, and we would discuss each other's work. So, we had these really fascinating discussions.[14]

Despite their shared enthusiasm for the way of life at Milldene Ave, Westcott insists that calling it a commune 'was intended by the government as a slur',[15] and the furthest Nupen will go is to call it 'a rather middle-class type commune'.[16] By 'middle-class', Nupen meant that the housemates were busy with their studies (of law, medicine, botany and other disciplines) and enjoyed activities like hiking Table Mountain and rooting out non-indigenous plants. Paula Ensor, who lived with Jenny and Neville Curtis at 100 Belvedere Road, would not agree to call her home a commune, because:

> The idea of a commune suggests people in sandals and long hair who never bathe and who smoke lots of dope. Well, I think there

was a huge amount of wine drunk and a lot of bridge was played. We ate very good food and coffee ... but we were kind of a disciplined bunch. It was a very hard-working environment. Everyone was very committed and worked incredibly hard. I mean none of us smoked dope, actually. There was a strict rule that you never smoke dope in your house, because it would just be asking for trouble. If we're gonna get into trouble then it must be for political reasons, not for smoking dope. But we shared a lot as well. There was a lot of movement between the two houses in terms of sharing of meals and conversations and stuff like that.[17]

The distinction between Paula Ensor's conception of a commune as a slanderous designation and how she and her comrades lived together in those years is subtle. Ensor remains – as she was in her student days – proudly political, a dedicated Marxist. She remembers the atmosphere at her home on Belvedere Road as a 'disciplined' and a 'hard-working environment', where she and other radicals prioritised their political work above other considerations. At the same time, her recollections of daily life together are warm, with 'good food and coffee' and even 'a huge amount of wine' to go along with the hard work of political struggle. Nonetheless, Ensor insists that this way of sharing their lives was not communal living, because the choice to live together was more pragmatic than it was political. That is to say, they lived together because they shared a politics, but the politics they shared happened *elsewhere*, outside of the home.

Regardless of whether this group of young radicals believed that living together was in and of itself a political act, the banning orders forced the issue. The intention behind banning orders was to confine left-wing intellectuals to their homes, to separate them from all forms of public discourse. A critical irony of this policy, which united the experiences of all banned people, was that the years under a banning order provided ample opportunity for banned people to delve more deeply into their studies. Paula Ensor's decision to 'read all three volumes of *Capital* while I was banned' was a fairly typical response. In addition, it was quite common for banned people to decide, as Paul Pretorius did, that one 'could *not* comply with the banning order'.[18] This non-compliance had two meanings. First, banned people were naturally inclined to disobey the apartheid state, and their desire to resist unjust policies only accelerated due to the bannings. Among this group of eight, there were many versions of carrying on with political protest, while banned. Pretorius's first act of non-compliance was to mail the banning order *back* to the minister of justice, along with a scathing letter, written on his behalf by Roy Ainslee, which is worth quoting:

> Dear Sir,
> While Mr Pretorius will have no choice but to comply with the provisions of this iniquitous document, it should be made clear that such an order is morally repugnant to him as it is to all decent and thinking people. Therefore, although it requires his obedience, it will never command his respect.
> The banning order is returned to you as a mark of contempt both for the order and the injustice it represents ...
> You are hereby called upon to revoke this banning order forthwith and you are invited to bring Mr Pretorius to trial if he is believed to have committed any offence.[19]

In addition to this symbolic gesture of repudiating the banning order, Pretorius also attempted to pressure the minister of justice to explain the reasoning behind the banning. Pretorius claimed that 'it has come to my notice that I am entitled by law' to such an explanation.[20] However, recently declassified internal memos of the Department of Justice show clearly that the state felt absolutely no obligation to explain themselves to banned people. 'The information which induced the Minister to issue the abovementioned notices can, in his opinion, not be disclosed without detriment to public policy.'[21] Therefore, Pretorius was only given a bland, vacuous reply, which reiterated that Pretorius was determined to be 'furthering the aims' of communism.

Paula Ensor carried on with the organising work she had been doing with Jenny Curtis for the Western Cape Workers' Advice Bureau by having one-on-one meetings in her home. Paul Pretorius requested, and gained, an exception for his banning order, to be able to open a record store. As a playful provocation, Pretorius decided to name his shop Cold Storage, 'because that's what the Minister of Justice said in Parliament, that those of us who were banned were just "in cold storage for a while"'.[22] Meanwhile, another of the communards, Chris Wood, created a new political party called the Alliance for Radical Change (ARC) and ran as a representative of the party in municipal elections. The idea behind ARC was provocatively to exploit an intriguing loophole in apartheid law. On the one hand, Wood was expressly forbidden to engage in politics in any form, to publish any kind of political writing, and certainly to engage in political conversations. On the other hand, since the apartheid state sought to present themselves as a functioning democracy, any pamphlets or posters related to an election could not be censored or banned. Therefore, the ARC was able to distribute a pamphlet calling for 'BLACK MAJORITY RULE NOW' and stating that 'VORSTER IS UN-SOUTH AFRICAN'.[23] The ARC addressed the issue of running a banned person directly:

> The person who ARC has invited to stand is a person who is banned and restricted, and whose ideas this government is committed to killing. Although the candidate may not address meetings, campaign or be quoted – he will not be silenced. The ideas of ARC and the platform we represent cannot be banned or stopped.[24]

Of course, a political party running on a platform that 'Black people know better' in a whites-only election in Cape Town, 1974, had no chance of winning. Nonetheless, the ARC represented explicit defiance, and a clear refutation of the power of the state to silence dissent.

## A leadership vacuum

The significance of banning eight Nusas leaders was both immediate and profound. The apartheid state consciously created a leadership vacuum within Nusas to open up space for undercover security police officers to infiltrate the Nusas executive. While security police officers were a constant presence on university campuses during apartheid, I contend that the infiltration of Craig Williamson (and, to a lesser extent, Karl Edwards) into the student movement was intimately interwoven with the Schlebusch Commission.[25]

Craig Williamson entered the student movement at precisely the same time as the Schlebusch Commission began its inquiry into Nusas. Williamson first became a police officer in May of 1968. According to the stories he told, and his CV, his first years in the South African Police (SAP) were spent as an alternative to the mandatory military service required of white men at that time. It isn't clear when during this period Williamson became a security police officer, but it is certain that he was working for them by the time he entered the University of the Witwatersrand, in 1972. While Williamson now says that he 'was probably more suitable to have been on the conservative side' of university politics, he was assigned to infiltrate the left wing.[26] Within the political climate of Nusas in 1972, Williamson was an unlikely candidate for leadership within the student movement, as his appearance and mannerisms were more formal and conservative than his peers. In fact, Jonathan Ancer's biography of Williamson documents multiple incidents where Williamson was openly brutish and even explicitly racist, such as drunkenly calling Ian Kitai, a Nusas member, a 'k---boetie'.[27] Patrick Fitzgerald, who was active in student left-wing circles at the time, described Williamson as 'pig ignorant'. That is to say,

> He was devoid of any cultural background that lefties had. He was married, and he lived in a middle-class house in Houghton, a very posh suburb in Joburg. There was nothing about him that came across as progressive. He used politically incorrect language when it came to gender issues. Craig was a posh rich bastard.[28]

In spite of these obvious shortcomings, Williamson gradually established credibility for himself as a student radical.

One of the keys to Williamson's success as a police infiltrator was his willingness to do 'the non-glamorous tasks that student activists weren't interested in taking on: organizing events, balancing the books, handing out flyers and putting up posters'.[29] Williamson was elected onto the Wits Student Representative Council (SRC) in 1973 and then the following year he was elected to the national executive of Nusas, as finance officer (a full-time, paid position). Crucially, Williamson was *good* at handling financial affairs. In fact, Williamson 'was widely credited with having nursed the national student body, which was on the brink of bankruptcy, back to financial health'.[30]

According to Williamson, his initial instructions from his commanding officers were relatively vague. He was simply expected to engage with the student radicals, with the general goal of gathering intelligence related to the presence of the ANC and SACP on the campuses. This was an Afrikaner Nationalist government fiction; neither organisation was active at that point among white student radicals. Nonetheless, Williamson said: 'Once I got elected to Nusas, that's when the planning started more. Then obviously, the people who were controlling me were more interested in where the money was coming from, who was behind supporting these organisations, and what their actual objectives were.'[31] Something is clearly amiss in Williamson's depiction here. Once again, the apartheid state had clearly been 'interested in where the money was coming from' for years prior to 1974, as is well documented in dozens of pages of the Schlebusch Commission's report. It seems entirely plausible that the commission's catalogue of the chaotic state of Nusas's finances would have been essential reading for an undercover officer working as a finance officer inside the organisation. Furthermore, the commission had clearly articulated what they understood to be the 'actual objectives' of Nusas's funders, in no uncertain terms. In fact, given the intensity of the commission's animosity towards the IUEF, it seems entirely possible that Williamson would have been given explicit instructions to engage with the IUEF, in any way possible.

The same year that Williamson was elected finance officer was also the year that parliament passed the Affected Organizations Act. This law earmarked particular organisations as 'affected' and thereby blocked them from receiving overseas funding. The links between the Schlebusch Commission and this new legislation were explicit. In the concluding section of their report, the commission recommended 'that measures be considered to prevent political activities in South Africa from being supported and influenced by financial help from abroad'.[32] Once again, the Schlebusch Commission played a critical role in steering this repressive act. On the surface, the link here is unclear, due to the timing of the published report, which was not published until 12 August 1974. By that time, the Affected Organizations Act had already been law for nearly half a year, having passed through parliament on 1 March. In other words, it appears that the commission officially recommended what was already a matter of fact. It should not be forgotten that the commissioners were themselves MPs. Furthermore, according to Michael Lobban, in his book *White Man's Justice*, the final report on Nusas was 'written in September 1973'[33] and then held back from public view for nearly a year. Therefore, it is highly likely that the members of the Schlebusch Commission brought their proposals regarding blocking overseas funding directly to parliament long before the formal publication of their report. In this sense, it seems that Williamson is correct to state that the commission was used to 'justify decisions that have already been made'.[34] As Nusas had previously received such a large percentage of their funding from overseas, they were heavily curtailed by the new law. As finance officer, Williamson was expected to find ways around this dilemma.

Looking back on this process fifty years later, Williamson smugly claims credit for the leftward shift within Nusas:

> I must say, I was very involved in pushing Nusas left. The whole Release Mandela Campaign. That suited two purposes. One, the authorities were happy to see Nusas shifting more and more left, which made action against them easier and more justifiable. Also, as the individual officers, such as myself, were seen to be supporting that approach, that also increased my credibility.[35]

I am sceptical of the idea that Craig Williamson had as much influence over the radicalisation of young white people within Nusas as he now claims. Nonetheless, the idea that the security police actively *preferred* radicals to liberals, because that made 'action against them easier and more justifiable', sounds plausible and is an important insight into the strategic thinking of the state at that time. While Williamson referred to these independent socialists as the 'lunatic fringe', he was nonetheless employed to study their thinking, and now insists that he took that task quite seriously, far more seriously than many of his colleagues within the security police:

> I would write analyses of the different views and interpretations of Marxism, which meant nothing to most of the people who were reading the reports, because some of those people were only interested in, 'can we prove that these people are committing an offence?' From our perspective, it was very important to know the ideological positions of people on the left.[36]

As much as Williamson may have sincerely attempted to grapple with the fine distinctions between Trotskyism and Stalinism, workerism and political trade unionism, and so on, it is important to remember that Williamson saw such study as a component of warfare.

'Revolutionary war is not only people blowing things up, or shooting with bullets, it's to do with the mindset of the population.'[37]

## 2 | Post-student People

The state's concerted campaign against Nusas put Jenny Curtis's generation of student activists into a precarious position and forced them to re-evaluate their politics. Surrounded by banned people, Jenny found her room to manoeuvre seriously curtailed. The space for resisting apartheid – legally, openly – was narrowing, and fast. After her brother Neville's dramatic escape to Australia (sneaking aboard a boat, using a friend's passport) others soon followed in his path. Three more of the Claremont communards (Chris Wood, Paula Ensor and Philippe le Roux) were living in exile by 1976. For many young white leftists, there was a sense, as Barbara Hogan remembers it, that

> there wasn't a place for white South Africans, so the only moral thing you could do was to leave the country. For many of the young white men it was either that or conscription. What about those of us who chose to stay? Did we have a place or a legitimate place?[1]

Responding to this rapidly deteriorating political climate, Jenny Curtis and her comrades were largely on their own. They had become 'post-student people'.[2] That is to say, having developed their politics inside Nusas, they now found themselves older than and also intellectually and emotionally beyond the confines of campus politics. The interaction with the Black Consciousness Movement and the repressive tactics of the state had forced these young white people to reject liberalism, and to radicalise in various ways. At the same time, the even heavier repression of the 1960s meant that Curtis's generation was more or less entirely cut off from previous generations of struggle. As Glenn Moss described it, 'there was very little contact with the past because those who had been involved in the past were either in jail, or banned, or house arrested, or dead, or in exile'.[3] For Barbara Hogan, this separation from older activists meant that 'we weren't given the givens'.[4] In other words, the process of radicalisation that this group of young people experienced happened largely without the possibility of being mentored, or sculpted, into accepting the so-called 'correct line'. Cut adrift from the major African nationalist organisations and the Communist Party, this group, says Hogan, 'developed our own homespun brand of what it means to be a Marxist in South Africa. We didn't call ourselves communists. We called ourselves Marxist and I think that was very much a trend of our generation.'[5] According to Glenn Moss, this 'homespun' Marxism was 'absolutely and quite consciously' critical of 'what is seen as Soviet communism. There was an explicit attempt to critique and reject a mechanistic or Stalinist Marxism.'[6] As a result, the politics that developed among this group in the early 1970s was 'actually quite utopian'. What Moss describes as utopian is 'a sense that one would actually be helping to create links between students and people off campus, trying to raise the tone of political engagement'.[7] As post-student radicals, they knew that they needed to develop a politics that was relevant to the broader society, and they tried to make that aspiration tangible, however they could.

After Neville went into exile, Jenny Curtis moved up to Johannesburg. There, she once again developed a group of politically active friends in the suburb of Yeoville.[8] In addition, Jenny also worked as an archivist (she was a librarian by schooling) for the South African Institute of Race Relations. While this was a solidly liberal institution, her job put her in a position to make regular contact with communists and ANC members who were being released from jail after the major wave of repression in the early 1960s. In addition, it allowed her to read the periodicals produced by those (now illegal) organisations.

According to Barbara Hogan:

> Jenny played a very pivotal role because she was archiving Communist Party documents and through a lot of her research and archival work she linked up with remaining members of the Communist Party and the ANC. And they were threadbare. But

she created a very important linkage for particular people here in Johannesburg between that older generation of ANC and a younger generation. She kind of brokered a relationship, inviting us to come and have dinner and those kinds of things. And I think some of us learned at the feet of those people, more what Congress was about.[9]

There are a couple of important components to Jenny Curtis's role creating links between older leftists and her peers. In Barbara Hogan's memory, Jenny was uniquely well suited to begin to establish these connections. First of all, 'Jenny came to work on genuinely archival work, and she was a good archivist'.[10] So, she was respected for her expertise, and not seen as a troublemaker. Hogan also describes Jenny as a 'hospitable, sociable person', who was well liked. 'Wherever Jenny worked she set up luncheons, where people came with great vats of soup ... she just had that hospitality streak in her.'[11] Still, no matter how likeable she was, no matter how much soup was served, connecting with an older generation of radicals would have been impossible if they were all still in jail. Crucially, Jenny Curtis was only able to interact with ANC and SACP members because after 1974, a number of 'people started to come out of prison, who were sentenced in 1964 to 10 years for sabotage'.[12] Even though it was only a small number, the slow release of political prisoners allowed Curtis's generation an opening to pivot away from the earlier modes of independence and isolation that had characterised white opposition politics for many years. For example, after Indres Naidoo was released from Robben Island in 1973 (having served 10 years for his membership in MK) Jenny Curtis and her comrades became regular guests at the Naidoo home. Alan Fine remembers his time with the Naidoos (including Indres's sister Shanti and brother Prema) as his first significant exposure to in-depth discussions about 'the movement', that is, the ANC.[13]

One of the most direct connections that Jenny Curtis had with the ANC, Hogan says, came by working alongside a young man whose relatives remained in jail and in exile:

Pindile [Mfeti] worked with Jenny at Race Relations, in the archives. And he was the nephew of Govan Mbeki, cousin of Thabo Mbeki.[14] Pindile was sort of a generation that was older than us but young enough to have been influenced by Black Consciousness.[15]

In addition to their jobs at Race Relations, Curtis and Mfeti were founding members of the Industrial Aid Society (IAS), one of many initiatives in urban areas throughout the country designed to support and assist efforts to organise the Black working class. According to Glenn Moss, who later became one of the IAS directors, the other founding members were Steve Friedman, a white radical from the Nusas Wages Commissions, and Miriam Sithole, 'who had worked with Sactu in the early 1960s'.[16] Furthermore, 'in setting up the IAS, Jeanette and Pindile had solicited the support of a group historically associated with Sactu in the Transvaal, as well as individuals who had histories in the ANC and SACP'.[17] Therefore, IAS was from its inception a project that bridged the older tradition of Congress-aligned trade unionism with the homespun Marxism of Curtis's generation.

Soon after its inception at the end of 1973, Jenny Curtis was elected to a leadership role within the organisation and oversaw a flurry of activity:

> Jeanette agreed to fill the role of administrative organizer. Her early reports to the steering committee provided a window into IAS activities: a complaints and advice service; development of material for worker education courses and literacy; training of trainers for worker education and literacy; training of organizers; proposed legal aid, medical and dental clinics; a fund (15 cents a week contribution) providing death benefits; distribution of pamphlets and a worker newspaper at the gates of factories and at homes in the townships; development of a library and resource centre; and research into different industrial sectors.[18]

While IAS was not in and of itself a trade union, it was nonetheless explicitly intended to support union organising. Playing this supportive role allowed this group of post-student radicals to straddle the line between the highly intellectual politics of their student days and direct engagement with Black workers. The literacy and workers' education programmes allowed young radicals, such as Barbara Hogan, to put Paulo Freire's politics into practice in a South African context. Training workers to take over the teaching of these courses was in the leadership empowerment spirit of union organising. Further, while white intellectuals clearly participated in producing pamphlets and 'a worker newspaper', they did so in collaboration and/or under the direction of Black radicals such as Miriam Sithole, who 'was producing a fortnightly IAS newsletter for distribution at factories where organization was taking place'.[19] Black leaders within IAS had a profound impact on the organisation's capacity to connect with Black workers outside the factory gates and in their homes in the townships. This aspect of IAS work was the most tangible and explicit way in which Curtis's generation of white leftists began to step off the university campuses. While this group of Marxists remained committed to in-depth study of revolutionary theory and robust debate, establishing a concrete link to South Africa's Black proletariat had a profound impact on their political perspective. In addition, IAS leaders such as Curtis and Moss soon found themselves swept up in the non-stop intensity that is typical of the union movement. As Moss remembers it, 'the demands placed on those individuals were considerable, and many of us were working very long days and then meeting late into the evening, six or seven days a week'.[20]

Jenny Curtis's work with IAS represented a pivotal shift in her engagement in the anti-apartheid struggle, tilting towards the clandestine world of the ANC and SACP. There was a growing hunger among her generation to *connect*, to find a way to see their own efforts within the context of a Movement, with a capital 'M'. However, since both the ANC and the SACP were banned organisations, connecting with members of either organisation meant entering a terrain of illegality, of coded communication and subterfuge, a far cry from the robust debates on Milldene Avenue. Glenn Moss recounts in his memoir the way that the ANC underground directly supported the establishment of IAS:

> Shortly after starting work at the IAS, Jeanette Curtis had taken Steve Friedman and me to see Eli Weinberg. On a few occasions, he had handed over cash amounts for IAS set-up costs. We were aware that these were funds probably channeled from Sactu and the SACP.[21]

While this connection to Eli Weinberg was mutually beneficial, it was also, in Moss's memory, almost entirely devoid of intellectual/ideological engagement.

> If you're working with somebody like Eli Weinberg ... the one thing you never talked to Eli about was ideology. You certainly did not talk to him about Communism or Marxism or something else like that. And that would be true for most of them. I'm not sure they were ideologues ... Sydney Bunting once said that the South African Communist Party is the only communist party never to have had a Marxist as a member. That's very crude, but it has a point.[22]

The motivation for connecting to the political underground was more pragmatic than it was utopian. If they were now post-student people, and if the politics developed within Nusas was no longer viable, then perhaps the underground could provide a way out. Once again, the fact that Jenny Curtis helped to broker these nascent connections is not surprising, as she was far less oriented towards intellectualising about politics than many of her peers. As Barbara Hogan contextualises it,

> Our very intensive intellectual exploration of Marxism and its relevance to South Africa really emerged when we were at university and Jenny kind of missed that kind of engagement and she was always less intellectually and ideologically engaged and focused more on the practicalities of organisation. That was a great strength of hers. So, she was a bridge ... she had the linkages into the Congress networks and was respected, but she also understood the debates that were going on about race and class in the younger generation.[23]

Even if the clandestine connections to the ANC and SACP happened largely without ideological discussions, the *fact of it, the desire to connect* represented an important ideological shift that was under way. By 1974, the stubbornly independent impulse, the longing to be a 'new' left, was starting to crack and give way. Part of this shift in perspective had to do with a slow reassessment of Black Consciousness, and white people's role in relation to it. Five years after the dramatic rupture of the creation of the South African Students' Organisation (Saso) in 1969, Black Consciousness no longer carried the urgent potency that it once had. Also, as once-liberals came to accept the Black Consciousness critique of liberalism, and came to understand themselves as Marxists, their central concerns shifted towards the working class. Going back to the formation of the Wages Commissions in 1971, and straight through her work at the Western Cape Workers' Advice Bureau and the IAS, Jenny Curtis played a critical role in developing both a body of work and a corresponding politics that prioritised organising the working class. As it was happening, as people began to think through a 'class struggle' lens, it wasn't immediately obvious that they were drifting away from Black Consciousness. For example, in Paula Ensor's experience:

> Black Consciousness was hugely important in terms of framing my initial political ideas. I don't see it as a question so much as moving away from it, but rather deepening it by embracing much more profoundly a class analysis. I don't think that the two things are in contradiction with each other at all. But Black Consciousness as such made very little impact on the working-class movement in South Africa. When I came to Cape Town, I was stunned at how little resonance there was with Black Consciousness ideas. It was very much an ANC tradition.[24]

Black Consciousness urged white people to play a supportive role for Black people to determine how to liberate themselves. Given that the overwhelming majority of Black people in South Africa were workers, it was not surprising that many young white people responded to this provocation by seeking ways to assist the Black working class. However, this decision led them to focus heavily on the question of 'organisation', which meant a gradual embrace of the more mechanistic modes of Marxism that they had earlier shunned, including the idea (which is very much counter to Black Consciousness) that they might understand themselves to be members of a revolutionary vanguard. In addition, the shift towards trade unionism led many white leftists towards a gradual embrace of the idea that the ANC was the most prominent, popular, and therefore most important organisation of them all.

Crucially, some members of the ANC had their own reasons for connecting with IAS, seeing the nascent organisation of the Black working class as a vehicle for building an armed underground. According to Glenn Moss:

> Robert Manci was an ANC veteran who had served a sentence on Robben Island and had been banned ... One of the youngsters Robert Manci brought to IAS classes on Saturdays was Bafana Mohlayaneng. When 'Sammy', as he called himself in IAS classes, appeared as the fourth accused in a major ANC trial, charged with undergoing MK military training, it became apparent that at least one ANC group was using IAS facilities to recruit and educate potential members for MK.[25]

Given the extensive involvement of Sactu, SACP and ANC members in IAS, it is not surprising that the group caught the attention of the apartheid state. According to her father, Jenny Curtis was 'continually followed and harassed'[26] by the security police, because of her work with IAS. For example,

> One afternoon Jenny was handing out leaflets with a black colleague publicizing the activities of the Industrial Aid Society at the Hoek Street entrance, observed, as she was constantly by the Security Branch. She was accosted, her leaflets confiscated, and she was taken into custody for interrogation on the 9th floor, the Security Branch section of the notorious John Vorster Square Police Station.[27]

On this occasion, Jenny Curtis was released after a relatively brief detention, without charges. Nonetheless, moments such as these punctuated the new normality for Curtis, as so many of her friends and family were targeted by the state (even her parents were being spied on by neighbours, who gave information to the security police)[28] and as she increasingly came to be viewed as a 'person of interest' as well.

## Bannings again

Jenny Curtis was among the nearly 20 people detained in connection to Breyten Breytenbach's ill-conceived trip to South Africa, attempting to recruit members for his clandestine group, Okhela. As Jack Curtis remembers it,

Early one morning, at about 5.30 am, Janet, one of Jenny's flat mates, rang to tell us that at 4 am the Security Branch had arrived to search the flat, interrogate its occupants, and then had taken Jenny into custody in terms of the Detention Act ... Other calls coming in made it plain that a number of Jenny's colleagues and associates had also been detained. We went around to the flat to console Janet, who, having no sisters of her own had looked on Jenny as one. Inquiries finally elicited the information that the detainees had been taken to Compol House in Pretoria, the headquarters of the Security Branch, and were being held there. No communication with them was permitted neither to father, nor mother, nor other family members, nor to an attorney, nor a doctor, nor a priest.[29]

Jack Curtis doesn't explain the extent to which his daughter was genuinely interested in Okhela, nor does he speculate. Glenn Moss suspects that Jenny Curtis didn't even meet with Breytenbach, but may have connected to another Okhela member, from the Netherlands, who was in the country at the same time. Nonetheless, according to Breytenbach, conspiracy was the principal charge that the state intended to use:

The charges sheet was a very hefty document indeed. It accused me, amongst other heinous crimes, of having smuggled weapons across the border, of having plotted violent acts of sabotage, of being involved in spying activities in the ports. And conspiracy! Conspiracy is a heavily punished crime in No Man's Land. The court is not so much interested in what you've actually done, but in what you *intended* doing, and especially the *implications* of what you were conspiring to do.[30]

At first, the state proceeded with the detention of suspects as if they were building a major show trial, as they had attempted to do with the Treason Trial in the 1950s, and so on. For example, Glenn Moss remembers being treated as a dangerous guerrilla fighter:

When I was transferred from Johannesburg to Pretoria I was handcuffed in the back of the car and chained to the supports in the car and on the road from Joburg to Pretoria there were armed police watching. I don't know what they thought they had there. I didn't have a lot of friends who were going to rescue me – least of all with arms. But they were behaving as if they had something absolutely massive.[31]

Despite these theatrics of subduing a dangerous criminal, Moss remembers that he was 'often surprised about what they didn't ask about. That, to some extent could have been so as not to reveal Williamson and Edwards, both of whom would have been reporting on me.'[32]

Remarkably, while Moss and many others were detained and being interrogated, Williamson was dutifully playing the role of a concerned comrade on the outside, hustling to pretend to help get people released:

> With the leadership in jail, Williamson was left in charge of Nusas … Williamson went from campus to campus, shouting slogans and making rabble-rousing speeches with Helen Suzman … He also led a Nusas delegation to see the Minister of Justice and the Police, Jimmy Kruger. Williamson's Special Branch colleagues thought this was uproarious because while Williamson sat with the delegation demanding the release of their comrades, the paperwork for his promotion to lieutenant was on the minister's desk.[33]

On one level, it appears that the aim of detaining this group of 17 white leftists was quite simply to detain them, to remove them from daily life for an extended period, without having, in any way, to prove any form of guilt. It is hard to ascertain what the aims of interrogating them may have been, or the extent to which the strategic thinking about them changed over time. Jack Curtis believes that his daughter was interrogated 'for long periods', although the extent to which the police believed Jenny was an important suspect is not clear.

> Jenny's incarceration, since she was female, and white, did not involve any physical molestation. Just the deprivation of solitary confinement with nothing to read except the Bible, no communication with any person except for long periods of interrogation

by relays of interrogators and the knowledge that she was completely at the mercy of her jailers.[34]

Jack and Joyce Curtis were allowed to see their daughter while in prison only once, after six weeks, for half an hour. Jenny was on the other side of a plate-glass window, surrounded by a warder and two burly security policemen, and they were forbidden to discuss anything regarding politics, or her treatment inside Pretoria Central. 'That was the only contact we, or anybody else other than police and prison members had with her during the 65 days of her detention.'[35] As Jenny Curtis and her comrades had been gradually moving in the direction of clandestine politics, they had consciously attempted to study the conditions and treatment of white political prisoners at Pretoria Central. In fact, according to Glenn Moss, it was Curtis herself who initiated this study. 'Jeanette circulated Hugh Lewin's just-released but banned book, *Bandiet*, detailing his experiences as a detainee and political prisoner ... She had been advised that this was essential reading for anyone who might be detained or jailed in the future, and I devoured its contents.'[36] Despite this advanced preparation, the long stretch of solitude at Pretoria Central deprived of human contact – as well as any form of intellectual stimulation other than the Bible – had a profoundly damaging effect on Jenny Curtis. Her father remembers how, upon returning home, 'Jenny would wake up in the night shouting "they are coming to get me!" trembling violently. Joyce would assure her that all was well and that she was in her own home, and so she would sink back into sleep.'[37]

Shortly after being released from detention, Jenny Curtis was served a banning order on 3 November 1976, alongside several other activists in trade union struggles. Having spent years living in the intensely stimulating atmosphere of the Claremont communes, it is not surprising that Jenny Curtis maintained a politically and intellectually active lifestyle, despite the restrictions placed on her by the banning order. Barbara Hogan describes how she and other comrades were able to continue their engagement with Curtis during this period:

> Jenny was doing her BA Honours, in development. There were four of us: Alan Hirsch, me, Jenny and Mark Lavender who were doing honours together. Jenny wasn't allowed on campus. So, we used to

repeat all the tutorials and all the work with her off campus. Of course, it was illegal for all four of us to do it. Jenny would pick us up in a Volkswagen, and we'd all have to lie down on the bottom of the back seat, so that the security police wouldn't see that she was travelling with us. We had to set up places where we would be safe to meet, without getting busted by the security police, who kept tabs on all the comings and goings at our house. It was very difficult logistics, but that's how it was operating. The lecturers would also come. Those like Sheldon Leader and those who were less afraid would also come out and talk with us and lead discussion sessions. It was very rigorous. It was very important for us because we needed to make our way through a very complex time.[38]

The image of this group of young Marxists literally repeating in-depth classroom discussions for the benefit of their banned comrade demonstrates a remarkable commitment to education as a component of radical struggle. Clearly, by the time she was banned in 1976, Jenny Curtis had seen enough of apartheid repression, and had established enough connections to the underground, that she was increasingly prepared to contemplate going underground herself.

## Bandiet

Marius Schoon was released from Pretoria Central Prison on 17 September 1976, having served a full twelve-year sentence for sabotage. Upon release, Schoon was immediately served with a five-year banning order. The long years in prison were particularly brutal for Schoon. Schoon's close friend Heinz Klug said this was especially so because 'the South Africans hated Marius. For them, as an Afrikaner, he was a traitor. So there was a particular bitterness towards him.'[39] Klug offers a devastating example of the way that this bitterness played out at Pretoria Central:

Marius's first wife committed suicide while he was in prison. After this, they went into his cell, where he had been close to other people, they took him out and put him in an isolation cell and said to him, 'Your wife committed suicide. It's your fault.'

Then they left him there. Just shit like that. There was personalised, nasty stuff, in respect to Marius.[40]

In addition to the abuses Klug outlined, Marius Schoon also testified to the fact that 'the prison authorities, to rehabilitate me before going home, put me on my own for the last four months, in the condemned cells in Pretoria'.[41] While the time in jail was unspeakably difficult for Schoon, it also was an important period of political development. One of the ironies of racial segregation in the prison system is that it brought white radicals together, which allowed them – albeit in an entirely circumscribed setting – to discuss and learn from one another.

Hugh Lewin's prison memoir, *Bandiet*, remains, as it was for Jenny Curtis and her comrades in the 1970s, the authoritative source on this group of prisoners. Lewin provides a summary of the white political prisoners' backgrounds and political persuasions:

> The group included one Q.C., two attorneys, one artist, two engineers, three university lectures, two teachers, a doctor, a professional photographer, two business secretaries, one accounts clerk, one businessman, one surveyor, one salesman, three students and four journalists ... Twelve of us had been sentenced for sabotage, three under the Explosives Act, and the other twelve under the Suppression of Communism Act ... Sixteen of the twenty-seven admitted to being members of the Communist Party, with leanings to Moscow. Another one, a former expelled member of the Party, leant to Peking. He had one supporter and achieved one conversion. One other had been an avowed Trotskyite. Four of us had once been members of the Liberal Party, and had been expelled.[42]

In other words, the assembled group of white prisoners was very well educated, and the vast majority of them were socialists, in one form or another. Another layer of the political atmosphere at Pretoria Central was the arrival of Breyten Breytenbach, for the last year of Schoon's sentence. According to Jack Curtis, 'Marius and Breyten had a long-time friendship from their student days at Stellenbosch'[43] and communicated regularly while imprisoned together. All in all, Schoon's company at Pretoria

Central included quite a remarkable collection of dedicated revolutionaries. Heinz Klug describes the profound effect this environment had on Marius Schoon's worldview:

> Marius came in as this fairly young, naive bohemian. He was naturally a bohemian, all his life. He didn't change really. That's Marius. He was a young Afrikaner, and there was this radical group of Afrikaans poets in the 1960s; Marius was part of that group. At first, he was a liberal, counterculture Afrikaner. But he ended up in prison with Bram, and Marius completely worshipped Bram. That's where Marius no doubt became a communist.[44]

Whether or not Marius Schoon's commitment to communism can be linked solely to Bram Fischer, it is nonetheless clear that Schoon left Pretoria Central with a deeper, more determined and more focused commitment to revolutionary struggle than when he had entered prison in 1964. This much was patently obvious to the South African Police, who had been dealing with Schoon for over a decade:

> Schoon has not deviated 1 inch from his political stance, I would reckon he is now even more hardened in his political sense than 12 years ago. I will put him 2nd on the list of incitements. He is the type who does not accept no as an answer, he is backbiting, cunning and always suspicious. I am convinced that if he is released from prison he will immediately and surely again join his evil organizations and continue his devilish works, more determined than ever to achieve his goal.[45]

At the same time, in a very similar vein to the warders' attempts to 'save' Breytenbach from his treasonous ways (such as taking him to the Voortrekker Monument), the commissioner of prisons nonetheless retained some faith, and hope, that Marius might be persuaded to 'swing to the right' upon being released:

> It will appear from these reports that Schoon will continue as he did prior to his arrest. However, the possibility always exists that if he is brought under the influence of others whose ideology is

more acceptable to the democratic rather than the communistic outlook – more especially family, who will not be treated with contempt and suspicion, as was the case while in prison, then he may swing to the right. This however is a matter of pure conjecture with absolutely no guarantee of any success. However, where there is faith, there is hope.[46]

If there was any substance to the apartheid state's faith and hope that Marius Schoon might redeem himself upon his release, it had to do with an exchange between the minister of justice and Marius's sister Linde. According to classified documents of the Department of Justice, on 5 May 1976, while Marius was still imprisoned, 'His brother-in-law and sister, Mr. and Mrs. Barrett, wrote on his behalf to the minister to inquire, "what will be allowed for him after his dismissal."'[47]

Now, why were the Barretts concerned to advocate on Marius's behalf, and why was the state prepared to listen? First, it should be understood that when Marius's wife committed suicide, his daughter Jane was, in effect, adopted by his sister. So, the Barrett family had a greater than average stake in the affairs of Marius Schoon. From the police perspective, the Barrett family were people of good character and they had 'raised Schoon's daughter and they may also be able to exert a good influence on him'.[48]

Even given all of this context, the exact nature of the Barretts' request is striking on multiple levels. According to their letter to the minister of justice, Marius 'would like to settle in London by the end of September 1976 if the Minister does not object and he can obtain the necessary approval from the British authorities'.[49] As to how Marius Schoon arrived at the idea of 'settling' in London upon his release from prison, neither Mrs Barrett nor the minister of justice can say. However, apparently, 'Mrs. Barrett discussed Schoon's planned departure abroad with the Minister as early as October 1975'.[50] In other words, this was an idea that had been gestating for nearly a year before Schoon was released. The plan was so well worked out that the request to the minister of justice included a rough draft itinerary, from the moment of leaving Pretoria Central until his arrival in London:

> Should Schoon be allowed to leave the country, he would like to stay in Johannesburg until 22 September 1976 to make the necessary

financial and other arrangements and then visit the Barretts in Paddock, Natal until he leaves for abroad. Schoon's daughter lives with the Barretts and this will give him the opportunity to get to know his daughter, who is 15 years old.[51]

In other words – aside from essentially 'meeting' his 15-year-old daughter for the first time – Marius Schoon had essentially no desire or ambition to stay in South Africa. For all of his stubborn socialism, Schoon was not itching to rejoin the anti-apartheid struggle; he wanted to go and live in London. This is remarkable because it completely shatters the standard heroic narrative arc of participants in the anti-apartheid struggle. Another remarkable aspect of this story is the fact that the state was more or less content to allow Schoon to leave. According to a message from Compol, the headquarters of the Security Branch of the South African Police, to the minister of justice, on 15 June 1976:

> This department does not intend to apply for the above restriction after his release from prison. If the British authorities are willing to grant him permanent residence, his application for a departure permit will also not be opposed by these departments. In this case, for humanitarian reasons, there will also be no objection to him visiting his sister and daughter for a limited time.[52]

In other words, just three months before Marius Schoon was released from Pretoria Central, the police had decided that there was no reason to place him under a banning order, and that they would support his desire to go to the UK. The police did, however, include one (relatively huge) caveat, which would potentially nullify any goodwill that they were prepared to offer Marius Schoon:

> If his application for permanent residence in Britain is not successful and he is forced into the R.S.A. should remain, there will be no objection if he accepts work for which he is academically competent, provided that he refrains in all respects from any subversive activities and liaison with left-wing elements, which could possibly lead to restriction.[53]

There is no record in the declassified Department of Justice files regarding the final outcome of Schoon's application for a visa to the United Kingdom, if such a request was ever made. What is known for sure is that Marius Schoon did not undergo the 'good influence' of his sister, failed to 'swing to the right' and refused to 'refrain in all aspects from any subversive activities'. Therefore, he was swiftly subjected to a banning order. Nonetheless the reputation that Marius Schoon carried with him among some on the left was, still, as something of a wild card as a result of his engagement in the 1960s.

According to Glenn Moss:

> Marius battled like hell in the 60s. He was mistrusted by the ANC and the Communist Party. They thought (on a very spurious basis) that he was probably a security police agent because he was Afrikaans. There was a sense in that period that Marius was almost trying too hard to be radical or to be accepted. So, Marius was considered to be sort of wild, and ungovernable, way back in the 1960s. His attempted bombing of the Hillbrow police station was a totally un-sanctioned mission. That means that when he comes out of jail there's also a sense that this is somebody who you tread carefully with. He may actually be unnecessarily dangerous.[54]

While some people on the white left, such as Moss, had concerns about Marius's past, many others had a growing desire to find ways to connect to the mainline liberation organisations – the ANC and SACP – and Marius Schoon provided a unique opening into this clandestine political world.

## The most important political work

The political climate in South Africa changed dramatically during the 12 years that Marius Schoon was in jail. The year 1964 marks a critical transition in the struggle against apartheid, as a major portion of those who had turned towards armed struggle (both Black and white) were imprisoned, more or less simultaneously. This pushed the armed struggle to develop a clandestine and exile infrastructure and left the domestic opposition scrambling to adapt to the new limits on political activity. The development of the Black Consciousness Movement, which provoked white liberals towards a New Left radicalism, took place in the years that Schoon was imprisoned. If Marius Schoon had been released from prison five years earlier, or even a year earlier, he would have encountered a political climate that was largely foreign to him, and largely disinterested in his political perspective. As it was, there was a level of mutual wariness between the homespun Marxists on the white left, and Marius's adherence to an older generation's doctrinaire positions.

> Marius was having to deal with a generation of people who were not the kind that he was used to, who were outside of the formal fold of the Communist Party and the Congress movements. And I think that was difficult for him to understand initially. There were some very robust debates with Marius.[55]

The extent to which Marius Schoon was at all warmly received – even to agree to have robust debates – by the younger generation of white leftists was due in large part to the fact that he met Jenny Curtis, and the two fell in love.

When Marius Schoon got out of Pretoria Central, he began studying towards an MA. He met Jenny Curtis as a student. However, at that point, both Curtis and Schoon were banned. So, in their first months together, everything that Jenny and Marius did, both personally and politically, was illegal. Despite these limitations, Jenny and Marius grew close quite quickly. Jack Curtis remembers this burgeoning romance warmly:

> We had observed the deepening relationship and were not entirely surprised when Jenny, radiating with the glow which only a woman in love can display, informed Joyce and me that 'Marius had paid her the honour of asking her to be his wife' and he would, with our consent, ask for the opportunity of approaching us in person. Consent duly given they exchanged rings, but since every meeting, even as man and wife, would be illegal, they did not fix a wedding day.[56]

In addition to loving one another, Marius and Jenny loved the work that they were doing together politically. In an interview with Hilda Bernstein in the early 1990s, Marius remembered that time period tremendously fondly:

> Jenny and I spent the next nine months doing what I think possibly was the most important political work I've done in my life. We both ignored our banning orders, more or less completely. We saw literally hundreds of people. We spoke about the Movement. We argued against the Ultra-Left positions that they were taking. We did what I think is really solid political work. And during that nine months, in fact, we swung opinion foremost amongst the White Left to support of the ANC.[57]

While no one can take away from Marius Schoon his sense of pride and fulfilment, or his understanding of what was 'the most important political work' of his own lifetime, nonetheless it is clear that his description of what happened in those nine months is overly simplistic, and rosy. There are a couple of important distinctions that must be made in order properly to evaluate the impact that Marius Schoon had on shifting the white left towards embracing the ANC. First of all, it is important to understand that the shift towards the ANC was a gradual process, which had been under way for a number of years before Marius Schoon arrived on the scene. Second, it is important to be clear that some amount of this shift in thinking was also – and, perhaps, primarily – the result of tangible changes in the realities of struggle, rather than the changing of 'minds' pure and simple. Lastly, it is essential to grapple with the fact that a number of people remained sceptical of both Schoon and the ANC, and that these fears were grounded in tangible dangers, which *did* come to pass in later years.

By all accounts, Jenny Curtis played a pivotal role in the ongoing process of connecting young white leftists with the ANC. By 1976, Curtis had been moving steadily in this direction for at least three years, since the bannings at the start of 1973. As Barbara Hogan understood it,

> Jenny was ahead of the time in many ways in the way she operated. She had networks and I suppose for Marius it was rather lovely to come out of prison and find someone who had networks with old

> comrades who were still in the country but also had networks right into where things were happening on the white and Black left.⁵⁸

While Marius Schoon could not have been aware of all the subtleties of these shifts over time, he nonetheless recognised straight away that the 'one real exception' to the 'very hostile' attitude of the white left towards the ANC 'was Jenny, Jenny Curtis, as she then was'.⁵⁹ While Jenny Curtis's unique position is important to acknowledge, the differences were not as stark and binary as Schoon makes them out to be. Glenn Moss, who was among those whom Schoon would have considered hostile, nonetheless insists that there were multiple different views of the ANC being debated among the white left at that time.

> When Marius comes in and says the white left is opposed to the ANC, I'm not sure which white left he means. There is the position that said that national liberation movements seriously undermine working-class organisation and that historically and throughout the rest of Africa one actually sees something of a sell-out of working-class interests when national liberation movements reach power. There's the idea that by virtue of being a multi-class alliance, national liberation movements are dominated by non-working-class interests. Then, there's another position, which was trying to explore ways of strengthening working-class interests within those alliances. That's the position I was associated with, and the position that Jeanette was associated with at that stage.⁶⁰

In other words, these different political tendencies had been developing for years, and Marius found himself amidst these ongoing debates. In addition to the various interpretations of Marxism and how to organise the working class, there was also, throughout the first half of the 1970s, a great deal of sympathy for Black Consciousness among white radicals. Paula Ensor explains why she was initially far more captivated by Black Consciousness than by the ANC:

> I met a lot of ANC people, but I found the Black Consciousness people much more appealing. There was more energy, there

was more enthusiasm, there was more vigour, there was more determination. But the ANC did not inspire me with a great deal of enthusiasm. There seemed to be very little going on on the ground in South Africa. I didn't believe that the guerrilla struggle was ever going to achieve anything. Not in South African conditions.[61]

However, Schoon was correct in his assessment that many white leftists were largely ill-informed about the ANC. Barbara Hogan freely admits this.

> We did not know many ANC people. There was a bit of an old guard (Black and white) but they were not too integral to our thinking … and there was a lot of disinformation and also correct information about the ANC (some of it fiddling by Craig Williamson and those types). I think Marius was quite useful for many of us in terms of actually dispelling some of the myths about the ANC and explaining more carefully what it was about.[62]

Marius Schoon counts Hogan as one the people he converted during this period. According to Schoon, Barbara Hogan was 'taking a very intellectual, workerist position about everything. Well, during those nine months, we actually convinced Barbara.'[63]

While Hogan herself acknowledges Marius's influence, she doesn't explain her own transformation in quite the same terms. For Hogan, the decision to align herself with the ANC was largely the result of the political upheaval brought on by the Soweto uprising in June of 1976. Hogan explains how '1976 was for many of us evidence that if you did not take political sentiments and movements seriously that were happening in the townships, you lost the plot completely'.[64]

The insurrectionary protests of 1976 were entirely the product of the Black Consciousness Movement; the leadership, the language, and the methodologies of rebellion all came from Black Consciousness. By no stretch of the imagination could Soweto be described as a successful initiative of the ANC. Since at least 1969, 'the language of the time was Black Consciousness. People weren't talking about a "nonracial democracy".

They were talking about "Blacks are going to take over the country".[65] Nonetheless, for a variety of reasons, in the aftermath of a massive Black Consciousness-inspired uprising, the momentum and centre of gravity of the anti-apartheid struggle shifted quickly towards the ANC, in ways that hadn't been true since Marius first set foot in prison.

Devan Pillay, who grew up in East London and was racially classified as 'Indian', describes how in his youth 'everybody – if you were black – by black I mean generic black, (African, Indian, Coloured) you identified yourself somehow with Black Consciousness'. However, after 1976, this began to shift, so that, 'within the Black Consciousness framework you had people who were ANC. Black Consciousness was now being infiltrated by the ANC.'[66] In other words, within the Black movement, an internal debate was under way. As more and more young Black people left the country, seeking military training, the ANC – who ran the military camps, and who insisted on ideological 'unity' – became a more viable politics. In addition, as the Black Consciousness movement had grown in numbers and strength, a fringe that expressed explicit racial hostility developed, which hadn't been present in the original conception of Black Consciousness. Within this atmosphere, many young Black people grew more receptive to a politics of nonracial socialism. As Pillay puts it,

> For us, as young activists, who were not quite attracted to the hardcore Black Consciousness perspective – that is, the anti-white perspective – we were becoming more and more interested in the class analysis and a Marxist analysis of capitalism.[67]

As the momentum of Black politics started to shift towards the ANC, a number of white Marxists followed suit. Black Consciousness had been 'extremely important in reasserting that [the struggle against apartheid] was a black struggle'.[68] The generation of white people who were radicalised during this period had long ago accepted that their role was primarily to be supportive. Therefore, it was an entirely natural decision to support the ANC, if the ANC was going to be the organisation that would lead the Black struggle. As Ensor explains,

What I came to understand is that the ANC couldn't be judged by its manifestation in exile. The ANC needed to be judged by what people inside the country thought of it and I came to the view (not alone, with many others) that the ANC is the traditional organisation of the mass of black people in South Africa and that when mobilisation took place there would be a gravitation towards the ANC or organisations closely aligned to it. And that's exactly what happened. So that's why we decided to work within the ANC and to argue our position within the ANC.[69]

Amid these major shifts in the larger dynamics of struggle in South Africa, Marius Schoon's capacity to garner sympathy for the ANC among the white left makes a lot of sense. Even Glenn Moss admits that 'it is absolutely true that Marius had an influence on a young group in Johannesburg'. At the same time, Moss adamantly refused to get involved:

I wouldn't work with Marius. I thought he was dangerous. I was reasonably hostile (as were many people, it doesn't make me actually so unusual) to what Marius was doing. This was complex, because Jeanette and I had a very close historical friendship and involvement in working together. But I thought it was dangerous, doomed to failure, deeply infiltrated (which it was) and that there were good reasons to steer clear of it. I don't think that one avoids danger (obviously doing underground work is dangerous in and of itself). But I think you must actually make strategic decisions about what danger you expose yourself to. Marius's approach was unnecessarily dangerous.[70]

With the benefit of hindsight, Glenn Moss can point clearly to the exposure of Craig Williamson as a spy, the assassination of Jenny Curtis, and the arrest, torture and imprisonment of many of those young comrades who were recruited by Schoon as clear evidence of the fact that 'Marius's approach was unnecessarily dangerous'.

# Part 2

# Cover Stories and Undercover Stories, Botswana and Geneva, 1977–1980

# 3 | Cover Stories

**Botswana: Wedding day departure**

Despite Jenny Curtis and Marius Schoon's defiant enthusiasm, the banning orders did eventually take their toll. When 'Marius received a tip that he was going to be arrested',[1] due to his communication with Breytenbach while at Pretoria Central, he decided that his only viable option was to flee the country. Consequently, Jenny Curtis decided that they would need to get married straight away 'so that, should Marius be caught and imprisoned, she would be able to visit him'.[2] However, figuring out how to marry two people who were under banning orders was by no means straightforward. As Jack Curtis explains, 'This presented a knotty problem. A magistrates' court was out of the question for the wedding, and any minister of one of the established churches was likely to hedge at being party to an illegal gathering.'[3] In fact, as early as March of 1977, both Curtis and Schoon applied to the minister of justice for an exemption to marry. In a provocative attempt to give these applications additional weight, the couple had their letters hand-delivered by Helen Suzman, the Progressive Party MP, who could add a personal touch to the appeal. Suzman attached a note: 'You once said in the House that you are "a kindly man" – maybe you will react accordingly to the requests I was told were contained in the letters.'[4] In addition to requesting an exemption to marry, the couple also requested permission to visit Marius's sister in Natal, and 'Schoon also requested a variation of his restrictions to enable him to live with Curtis at her address'.[5] Unsurprisingly, none of these requests for exemptions was granted. Even though the applications were submitted during April, the minister of justice made no reply whatsoever, through all of April and May. Therefore, the couple decided that the wedding needed to proceed illegally. On 3 June 1977, Jenny Curtis and Marius Schoon were married.

> Fortunately, the Rev. Theo Kotzé had retained his license as a marriage officer ... Our good friend Mary Taylor had given Jenny a key to her flat in a nearby suburb; this would be the venue; Joyce and I would be the witnesses and would go first to the flat; each of the other parties would then arrive separately by diverse routes ... Marius arrived in a well pressed lounge suit, Jenny in a smart frock with her well-beloved poodle which, in the middle of the ceremony, managed to wrap his leash around her skirt. For the reception we had wine and biscuits. We then went our separate ways, Jenny clutching to herself her marriage license.[6]

While a part of the initial motivation for the marriage may have been to allow Jenny Curtis to visit her husband in prison, by the day of the ceremony she had decided to go into exile as well. Within hours of the wedding, the young couple embarked upon the perilous illegal crossing into Botswana. Since Jenny lived with a group of activist friends (similar to the house in Cape Town) both the wedding and the escape were kept a secret from her comrades. Alan Fine, who was one of Curtis's housemates, insists that

> This would have been the right thing to do in those kinds of circumstances. Jeanette didn't want to put us in any danger. None of us were invited to the wedding. Because in fact none of us knew that they were going to leave. Jenny had a very close friend, Sue de Villiers (who eventually became an ANC MP) who invited us over for dinner that night, so that Jeanette and Marius could make their departure from the house without having to explain to us why they were going. It's quite a nice story, actually.[7]

While the wedding went relatively smoothly – with as much celebration and camaraderie as possible, given the extremely restrictive circumstances – in leaving the country, disaster was only narrowly averted. The first hiccup happened right away, at Marius's Johannesburg apartment. When Jenny arrived there, she found that the security police were in the middle of raiding the place. She hid in the shrubbery outside the apartment and waited until 'the raiding party, having found nothing to which they could take exception, departed'.[8] The newlyweds were remarkably fortunate that the security police didn't see anything suspicious in Marius's home that night, and did not become aware of Jenny in her hiding place. Perhaps this narrow miss strengthened their resolve to leave the country. The plan was to be driven by a friend towards Botswana, and then, as Jenny's father describes it, 'at midnight, on a dirt road close to the border, Marius and Jenny got out of the car, bade farewell to their friend and set out due west over rugged country'.[9]

The illegal border crossing and journey into Botswana would be arduous, but the Schoons were well prepared for this, as Jenny's father describes:

> Since they would be confronted with a six-hour trek on foot through hilly scrub covered country when they reached the border, before encountering a road on the other side of the border, Marius and Jenny were equipped with a topographical map, compass, torch and water bottles. Jenny's love of 'little picnics' was well known. She prepared tasty snacks and liquid refreshments to consume on the road.[10]

Jack Curtis then continues to explain how, despite all these preparations, the pair got badly lost while walking through the bush in the middle of the night. Their compass turned out to be broken, and so they drifted for hours, along a path, and over a fence, which they believed was well inside of Botswana.[11] Around dawn they came upon a stranger, who assured them that they were still in South Africa. It seemed they had walked in a wide semi-circle back to their starting position. In the daylight, they walked on for six more hours before 'a passing truck gave them a lift into Gaborone and at 1 pm they sank down gratefully onto benches at a roadside hotel'. According to her father, 'Jenny's first thought was to reassure us and having got through to us by telephone, we were able to hear her voice before the call was cut off.'[12]

Only after word arrived in South Africa that the Schoons had fled did the minister of justice feel it necessary to close out the file requesting permission to marry. 'In the circumstances Compol[13] feel that it will serve no purpose to comment on the application.'[14] In addition, despite having had officers inside Marius Schoon's Johannesburg apartment on the night of their departure, the minister of justice only learned of the marriage by reading about it in the newspaper.[15]

Upon arrival in Botswana, the Schoons were first hosted by Michael Hubbard, a white South African liberal economist, and the brother-in-law of Rick Turner, the white radical professor whom Jenny had known well during her days as a student activist within the Wages Commissions.[16] In Hubbard's memory, there had been no communication regarding the plan to come to Botswana, prior to their dramatic arrival – 'I think they just arrived.'[17] Hubbard had previously shared his home with Chris Wood, another refugee from the South African white left, and a former resident of the Claremont house where Jenny Curtis had once lived. 'Obviously, Chris got hold of me and asked if it would be okay if Jenny and Marius stayed at the house.'[18] Michael Hubbard was a gracious host for the Schoons, and they lived there for a few months, without any difficulty. However, given Hubbard's strong commitment to liberalism and the Schoons' strong desire to connect to the ANC's exile infrastructure, the couple would not have felt entirely at home with him. 'I would have been seen as someone who was really not on their side. I was a pacifist. I was not about to take up weapons', Hubbard said.[19] Of course, there was a mutual wariness between Marius and Michael. In fact, Michael Hubbard was openly sceptical of Schoon's stubborn adherence to old-style communist views of the world:

> Marius was 40, and I was shocked seeing him. He looked much older. He hadn't looked after himself very well. He was a chain smoker, and a drinker as well. A nice guy, a gentle guy and well spoken. He was a helpful, careful man; he'd learned carpentry in jail. But he felt that he had the answers. I remember we discussed economics in Botswana, and he said, 'they should go for heavy industry,' which is the result of reading books about the Soviet Union. I said, 'Not in Botswana; no way you'll make steel here. That's the last thing you would want to do.'[20]

Understandably, the Schoons soon moved out into their own home, and began to establish a life for themselves in Botswana.

To live as a South African in Botswana required applying for political asylum. The South African security police were soon notified of the fact that the Schoons had 'applied for political asylum with the Botswana government under membership of the African National Congress. In all likelihood, his application will succeed.'[21] Being so close to South Africa, and also bordering Zimbabwe, Zambia and (at the time, occupied by South Africa) Namibia, Botswana played a critical strategic role in the 30 years of slow-fuse warfare against apartheid. As a landlocked country with a deep economic dependency on South Africa, Botswana insisted on a level of neutrality. They refused to allow the ANC to establish military bases in their country, but members of MK, the military wing of the ANC, moved through Botswana constantly nonetheless, both on their journey to military camps further north and (less often) as they headed south, back across the border to carry out military actions in South Africa.

Over the years, a kind of truce developed between the government of Botswana and the ANC. ANC members would be offered asylum in the country as long as they agreed to hide that fact, never exactly admitting to their true allegiance. They were granted political asylum, but their actual political work had to remain under the radar, as much as possible. Therefore, ANC members were required to sustain functional 'cover' in the form of decent, legal employment. According to Judy Seidman, an American radical artist who lived in Botswana for a number of years, 'if you were ANC and not registered as a refugee and didn't have a legal standing, they would definitely arrest you and deport you to someplace farther north, not south (whereas, for example, in Swaziland if they arrested you, 50/50 they put you to South Africa, which you might not survive)'.[22] This was the rather awkward peace within which the Schoons operated; it was essential that they furnish a reasonable cover story for themselves in order to live comfortably in Botswana.

## Geneva

> I would like to add that in the case of an obvious 'plant' by the South African government arriving in Botswana, a cable will be sent to the IUEF, Geneva, reading: 'Freeze Botswana Scholarship'.
>
> — Lars-Gunnar Eriksson, Strictly Confidential memo

In 1975, Nusas sent Craig Williamson on a trip to Europe, which was his first occasion to meet Lars-Gunnar Eriksson, the director of the IUEF, and others within the fund's leadership. This trip was highly significant. By all accounts, Eriksson was immediately fond of Williamson, and trusted his radical credentials easily. Importantly, the IUEF had set up security measures to ensure that communication related to 'politically sensitive' projects took place exclusively between the president of Nusas and Lars-Gunnar Eriksson. However, Karel Tip, the president of Nusas in 1975, 'identified for Eriksson a person within Nusas whom Eriksson could trust politically and who had administrative skills. This was Williamson.'[23] Therefore, when the two men met again, in July of 1976, and Williamson shared his secret plan to flee South Africa, Lars-Gunnar offered him a job in Geneva. 'It has in principle been agreed that [Williamson] will be employed by the IUEF ... His intention is to leave illegally at the end of the year via Botswana where arrangements have been made with Ranwedzi to get him cleared.'[24] That Eriksson went to such lengths to support Williamson's departure from South Africa, and to help him get established in Europe, is particularly striking in light of the fact that 'it had been the IUEF's practice not to employ refugees and Eriksson foresaw trouble if he employed a white and not a black South African'.[25]

This whole process took place during the massive nation-wide upheaval which began in June 1976 in Soweto. As a result of the uprising, thousands of South Africans were fleeing the country. Responding to this mass exile of young volunteers for the armed struggle, the IUEF sought to assist them, from afar. On 19 August 1976, Lars-Gunnar Eriksson announced to his staff that the IUEF would be initiating 'a special fund for freedom fighters who come across to Botswana wounded or otherwise in need of assistance. The fund will also cover assistance as needed to white deserters/defectors, etc. from South Africa.'[26] The security police hoped to slide Craig Williamson out of the country amidst this flood of 'freedom fighters' and 'deserters', and straight into the willing arms of the European social democratic movement. Sadly, even though Lars-Gunnar Eriksson had anticipated the possibility of such an 'obvious plant' arriving in Botswana, seeking assistance from the IUEF, these precautions did not apply to Williamson, whose dramatic escape from apartheid South Africa went off without a hitch.

Part of what made Williamson's escape story seem credible was that he took Eric Abraham along with him. Abraham was the founder of the South African News Agency (Sana) and had faced considerable harassment from the police while in Cape Town, so he was truly desperate to leave the country and to re-establish himself in exile. Williamson pretended to offer sympathetic concern towards Abraham, but in fact viewed him as merely, 'like a lot of people, a useful person'.[27] Bringing Eric Abraham to Botswana was useful for Williamson not only because it made his own escape look better, but also because it was the first journey of what Williamson later referred to as the 'railroad' of security police-operated escapes for South African radicals. Furthermore, Williamson encouraged Abraham to relocate Sana to Gaborone and this project was then funded and directed (by Williamson) by the IUEF.

Before carrying on to Geneva, Craig Williamson 'acquired ... a Botswana Travel Document No. 59 ... current until at least 19 January 1981, under which there is the right to return to Botswana'.[28] This was an important step for establishing his cover story, as it allowed Williamson to travel extensively without making use of his South African passport, and therefore to appear to be a genuine political refugee. In addition, having rights to return to Botswana was particularly helpful to Williamson, as much of his surveillance work in the coming years was focused on the ANC underground in Botswana.

Initially, Craig Williamson was hired by the IUEF as an 'information officer', to focus on publications and other matters related to southern Africa. He quickly built on his rapport with Eriksson, however, and 'supplanted at least one other who had formerly provided Eriksson with such information and advice'.[29] After about a year at IUEF, Williamson was promoted. On 27 June 1978, Lars-Gunnar Eriksson sent out a memo to all staff within IUEF, declaring that Craig Williamson had been chosen as the deputy director and that he was looking forward to 'what I hope will be many years of close cooperation with Craig'.[30] Eriksson later claimed that it was not his original intention to put Williamson in the role of deputy director. There was a months-long search process; a number of external applicants had been considered as well as the possibility of transferring another member of the IUEF staff. Furthermore, Williamson was vetted by 'making reasonably wide but informal checks, most on the level of should a *white* South African be appointed',[31] and not at all in terms of the possibility that he was an undercover agent. Again, Eriksson was quite fond of Williamson, and it seems that, at least at first, so were many of the other members of staff at IUEF. According to later testimony from his colleagues,

> Williamson's advancement from Information Officer to Deputy Director was accompanied by a marked change in his personality and popularity within the secretariat. From being well-liked, outgoing, and easy to get on with, he became authoritarian and abrasive.[32]

Despite being abrasive and unlikeable, as the deputy director of IUEF, Craig Williamson was granted an incredible amount of control, both in terms of the finances as well as the political direction of the organisation.

## Botswana

> For a front to be a front, you've got to do it. No question.
>
> — Heinz Klug, interview

In 1978, the Schoons found jobs at a secondary school in the small village of Molepolole – population roughly 40 000 – about an hour outside of Gaborone. At that time, the village had limited resources: scarce running water, no grocery store, and a butcher shop without any refrigeration. Despite these limitations, the people lived with a great deal of dignity.

Botswana during those years was relatively vibrant, as the newly independent nation sought to educate its children and build up a community of adults with the skills needed to be truly independent. The students were generally quite poor and often came a long distance to study (living locally as boarders) but they were dedicated students who were eager to learn.[33] Botswana in the 1960s and 70s actively welcomed skilled workers from abroad, without prejudice to nationality, including quite a large number of European teachers. You could be hired if you had a university degree, though you would be declared as having a lower level of qualification, and would teach at a lower rank.[34] For example, both Jeff Ramsay, from the United States, and Gary Wills, from the United Kingdom, were colleagues of the Schoons at the Molepolole Secondary School. Both have remained as teachers in Botswana, more than forty years later. According to them, the country has developed from a shortage of teachers to having a full cadre of young Black Batswana teachers, more than enough to sustain a highly literate, well-educated country.[35]

Jeanette and Marius Schoon were genuinely teachers, and they were warmly received as such. As much as teaching functioned as a cover story for the Schoons, it was nonetheless what they *actually did*, and they did it well. The couple taught English (both grammar and literature) to a group of students of all ages (advanced children were encouraged to start school straight away, as were eager young adults). These young Black people who had white political refugees from apartheid as teachers remembered them as very serious about their subject matter, as well as being deeply committed to nonracialism, and justice broadly. For example, Salome, one of the Schoons' students, now works in the Department of Economic Development for the Botswana government. The main lesson she learned at Molepolole Secondary School was that she could do and be anything that she wanted to be. According to Salome, the Schoons (and other white teachers) helped to reinforce this message. Another student, Wilheminah, who now owns a bed and breakfast on the outskirts of Molepolole, remembers being taught *To Kill a Mockingbird*. In her memory, Marius Schoon's teaching exuded passion and offered a real-life portrayal of Atticus Finch's determination to confront racism, as a white man.[36]

The Schoons were seen by their students and colleagues as rather bohemian, relaxed individuals; Marius was 'weathered' looking, with a full, bushy grey beard (often with bits of tobacco in it, from hand-rolled cigarettes) and Jenny with long, flowing hair and matching free-flowing long dresses.[37] The Schoons 'had the use of a comfortable furnished cottage'[38] on the grounds of the secondary school, and the community took note of the fact that they regularly hosted guests from South Africa. As their colleagues Gary Wills and Jeff Ramsay remember it, these parties were not lavish – as in 'bring your own metal plate and a tin cup'.[39] However, it is probable that people like Wills and Ramsay were not privy to the real nature of most of the gatherings at the Schoon household in Molepolole. Heinz Klug, a white South African comrade of the Schoons, who went to Botswana about a year after they arrived, remembers the gatherings in Molepolole with a great deal of warmth, but stresses that the true function of such events 'could never be open'.

> When comrades' parents would visit, families would come from South Africa to visit exiles, Marius and Jeanette, up in Molepolole, would throw a lunch. My parents came to visit. At the lunch, Makghoti would be sitting there, a coloured person sitting there, someone else from Robben Island down there, you know, comrades, sitting around the table. There was no talk of the ANC, and my parents had no idea. None. Partly just saying to the parents, 'Look, there's a community here, you don't have to worry about your kid.' But partly also a subtle education. It doesn't matter if he was on Robben Island, he's a human being, a perfect gentleman. They did that not just for the young whites like me, but for the young African comrades, as well, whose families would come up from Soweto, and so on, to visit. There was a different kind of space in Botswana. It was really extraordinary. But it could never be open.[40]

Many people concur with Klug's assessment, that Botswana was a 'different kind of space' at that time. In fact, Jack Curtis's description of visiting his daughter and Marius in Molepolole closely echoes Klug's description.

> We were now able to visit them frequently, staying over for weekends and meeting many other refugees from South Africa, both black and white. Among them all there was an openness and camaraderie not possible in the restrictive political and social milieu of South Africa.[41]

The biggest difference was simply the very basic fact that Botswana was an independent Black nation, without any hint of apartheid. Therefore, people were able to interact across racial lines without any suspicion or fear. Beyond this, it was also significant that the ANC was able to exist in the country, even if doing so required a level of silence and secrecy. Still, it was a significant improvement on South African daily life to be able to engage with other members of the ANC, including people who had been political prisoners, on a social level. Heinz Klug himself stressed the significance of maintaining a social connection with the Schoons.

> They used to come down to town [Gaborone] on the weekends. That's where I got close to Katryn, because I would take care of her while they dealt with other meetings. So, there's also kind of a social world going on. Even when I was no longer in a unit [of the ANC] with them, I still continued to socialise with them, right through.[42]

While the Schoon household was surely a space of inter-racial solidarity and connection on many occasions, the Schoons also hosted Foszia Fisher for a dinner, on 8 January 1978, the very night that her husband, Rick Turner, was assassinated in his Durban home. Even though the exact details of Turner's murder remain unresolved, there is some possibility that Fisher's visit to the Schoons – listed communists and fugitives from their banning orders – may have escalated the security police's concerns about Turner, who was also under a banning order, and may well have been seen as a flight risk. Fisher herself is sceptical of this theory, and insists that 'there wasn't enough time for this process to occur. I don't think it was me going across the border that made them think, "Now it's time to go kill Rick." I don't think so. I think, and I don't know why I think this, that the plan had been put in place. It wasn't spontaneous.'[43]

Rick Turner was someone who was resolutely opposed to clandestine activity. He had been attempting for some time to receive a legal exemption to leave the country. Foszia Fisher's reason for going to Botswana at that time was to connect with a German journalist, whom she hoped would help put pressure on the South African government to grant Turner an exit permit. Fisher insists that the couple were not planning to leave illegally, and that, in any case, if they were to do so, 'we didn't need help. There were already ways of leaving. It's a big border.'[44] Nonetheless, the fact that Fisher visited with the Schoons may have sent a signal to the state that Turner was losing patience and contemplating crossing the border illegally, as the Schoons had done just half a year earlier. In any event, on the night of 8 January 1978, Foszia Fisher left the Schoons' house in Molepolole and drove back to Michael Hubbard's house in Gaborone. Hubbard remembers the moment they heard the news:

> Suddenly we got this phone call. It must have come through at around 1 am. Ilona Kleinschmidt was on the phone with Foszia. All I heard was, 'What? What? Is he badly hurt? Is he badly hurt?' And she just slipped down to the floor and curled herself up in the fetal position ... and Foszia was saying, 'There's no point. There's no point ...' There was just crying and crying. There was no question of going back to sleep.[45]

In moments such as these, the devastating reality of apartheid repression haunted the Schoons in Botswana, regardless of the important ways in which Botswana functioned as a legitimate space of asylum for them.

Before too long, the Schoons were forced to deal with harassment from the apartheid security police, despite being safely across the border. On one occasion, Marius was hospitalised with malaria. Jenny's mother Joyce was in Molepolole, helping Jenny to look after baby Katryn, who was born at the hospital in Molepolole in 1978. Back in Johannesburg, Jack Curtis 'took a call from Molepolole to the effect that "Marius had died, and I must come immediately to Molepolole." The caller said he was phoning from the hospital at Mrs. Curtis's request.'[46] Jack Curtis drove quickly to the Schoon cottage, expecting to find his family grieving, but everyone was doing fine, going about their day normally. 'Somewhat nonplussed I asked Joyce when she had last seen Marius; she replied, "in the hospital at about nine o'clock that morning." "How was he then?" "Sitting up and having his breakfast."'[47] The family quickly figured out that the phone call earlier in the morning (before 9 am) had been fraudulent. When they investigated the matter at the hospital, the staff there confirmed that two South Africans had visited the hospital that morning, one of whom must have made the phone call. A few months later Jack Curtis received another prank call from the security police, this time claiming that Katryn was 'gravely ill with encephalitis'.[48] By themselves, such incidents don't amount to much – and certainly were far less troubling than the daily indignities of a banning order – but with hindsight, and in the larger context of repression, small nuisances such as these appear to be systematically nasty.

Furthermore, there were other, scarier moments of harassment. Heinz Klug remembers an occasion when 'Marius was driving in Gaborone and a man pulled up next to him and pointed a gun at him'.[49] Incidents such as these, Klug says, required the Schoons to be constantly vigilant. For example, 'We would be at parties and if Marius had to stay to talk to somebody, I would walk Jeanette and Katryn home, to make sure they were protected. There was that level of tension and concern because they were under direct pressure.'[50]

Despite the risks, Botswana was for many anti-apartheid activists – Black and white – an important political environment, which allowed people to engage in struggle far more openly than staying in South Africa. While the Schoons were in Botswana, the exile political community expanded dramatically, particularly because of the Soweto uprising, which significantly reshaped the political terrain, both internally and in exile. In addition, the South African invasion of Angola in 1975 greatly escalated the conscription of white soldiers, which therefore also provoked many white leftists to go into exile. Barry Gilder, who had been active in the cultural wing of Nusas as a young man, remembers this time:

> At the end of 1975, I got a call from my mother on Nusas's phone, which was obviously tapped, telling me that the military police had visited her in the middle of the night. The police told her that I was to report for duty, to go to Angola with the South African Defence Force. So, I skipped the country.[51]

While the Schoons overlapped and worked closely with many of these young radicals (especially the white ones) people's paths in and out of Botswana were varied, and often circuitous. While Gilder left South Africa in January of 1976 – more than a year before the Schoons – he did not arrive in Botswana until July of 1982. In between 1976 and 1982, Gilder changed his 'base' repeatedly, moving back and forth and all around Europe and Africa in search of a space to contribute to the struggle.

Mike Kahn, who joined an ANC cell in Botswana in the late 1970s, echoed a common sentiment among his generation when he declared that, 'I just felt that white student politics had reached a dead end. So, I wanted out.'[52] When Kahn first left South Africa in 1969, he first spent a number of years studying and raising his family in London. However, he missed Africa, and didn't like being at such a distance from the struggle against apartheid. Kahn was another South African exile who was first welcomed into Botswana by Michael Hubbard.

> Michael Hubbard sent me a newspaper clipping (tiny) tucked into one of those aerograms that you're not supposed to tuck anything into, and it said, "Wanted: lecturer to train physics teachers." I was a physicist of sorts, though I never worked in the field. To my amazement, I got the job; no interview, no CV, no certificate vetting, nothing. So, we went to Botswana. When we arrived in Gaborone, we stayed with Michael Hubbard and his family.[53]

Having been supplied with both housing and a reasonable 'cover' as a physics lecturer, Mike Kahn and his wife Carol established a home in Botswana, and stayed active in the exile ANC, until the formal unbanning of the organisation in 1990.

Both Kahn and the Schoons were active in the Medu Art Ensemble. Medu was a wide umbrella organisation comprised of separate 'units': Theatre, Graphic Arts and Design, Publications and Research, Film, Music, Poetry and Photography.[54] A wide range of artists participated in these units, including both white and Black South Africans, Batswana and expatriates.[55] Medu also ran art classes, and writers', theatre, music and photography workshops, from primary school age upwards. Defining themselves as 'cultural workers', Medu's work was explicitly intended to be political. It is easy to see the political content in the dozens of posters created by the Graphic Arts unit, for example. However, Medu insisted that all forms of art could – and must – be produced within the context of fighting for liberation.

According to Mike Kahn, 'MEDU was arguably created as a front organisation by the ANC to provide cover for senior cadres, who had some kind of arts media background, to remain in Gaborone.'[56] Judy Seidman, who was also an active member of Medu, disputes Kahn's characterisation and offers a different historical context for the organisation:

> Medu was actually not set up by the ANC, despite claims to the contrary by various people, mostly in the ANC. It was actually set

up by a bunch of artists who were in exile from South Africa, most of whom were Black Consciousness when they first set up the initial structure. And in fact it was initially for Blacks only. It was only just before I got there that there was quite a shift, from being pro-Black Consciousness to being ANC. Botswana was one of the places where that shift was thoroughly debated and not-quite violent. There had been white artists (one or two) who worked with them in the past, but they weren't part of the organisation.[57]

By the time Kahn and Seidman arrived, the 'not-quite violent' transition to ANC nonracialism was complete, and white artists were welcome within Medu and, hopefully, they came with a requisite awareness of their impact on the dynamics within the organisation. Having begun as an all-Black ensemble, Medu always remained a majority Black project, driven by the creativity and leadership of numerous radical Black artists. In Heinz Klug's experience of ANC-aligned politics in Botswana, understanding 'white people's role' in relation to a Black majority – and Black-*led* – struggle required taking a step back, and taking time to listen carefully,

> because we had university educations, and the conversations were in English, so shut up and listen. First of all, we were not the chair holders in the meetings, but maybe we should take notes, as the more educated people. That was the consciousness. That taught me a lot, too, by having to listen to people from very different cultures and communities. I learned. My experience in Botswana was an amazing experience.[58]

A number of white South Africans in exile got involved with Medu.[59] Mike Kahn's role within Medu was head of Photography. 'We did posters which were smuggled in. I did trainings for cadres in the photographic arts for reconnaissance and intelligence gathering. I maintained my own darkroom, which was equipped to do monochrome and colour if necessary.'[60] Kahn worked closely with a Black South African photographer, Tim Williams.[61] Marius Schoon was a poet and, according to Kahn, was 'very active [in Medu], from a literary perspective. He played quite a strong role in the organisation.'[62]

Judy Seidman arrived to Medu through a very different path from that of Kahn or Schoon. Seidman was raised by socialist parents from the United States. Early in her childhood, her family began travelling extensively. First, the entire family lived aboard a small ship, with the children being home-schooled at various ports. Next, the family moved to Ghana, where Judy completed her secondary education. When Judy was a young adult, her parents were living in Lusaka, Zambia. There, they worked as professors, in close contact with ANC stalwarts Ray Alexander and Jack Simons. In addition, Judy's younger sister had a job in the ANC headquarters. In 1972, Judy Seidman visited her parents in Lusaka and ended up staying for an extended period. 'In the process, I got married and also became quite involved, even at that stage, with people working with the ANC.'[63] In the Lusaka context, Seidman felt immediately welcome within the ANC. 'I just felt these were people that I could really talk to. I didn't actually feel I was permanently challenged by race issues. I certainly did not feel that I was being judged by my colour.'[64] In short, unlike some South Africans who crossed the border into Botswana in the *hopes* of connecting with the ANC, by the time Seidman arrived, she had already experienced a number of years of deep engagement with the ANC, in multiple different exile settings. This background gave Seidman a different entrance into Medu and the Botswana ANC network. As far as cover, Seidman lived in Botswana on a US passport, married to Neil Parsons, a historian employed at the University of Botswana. On the underground level, Seidman arrived in Gaborone having been previously 'vetted' by the movement, elsewhere.

For Judy Seidman, Medu was not a cover per se, in the sense that her artwork has been her life's work, and her art has always been explicitly political. At the same time, being openly identified with Medu did not *quite* equate to being openly in the ANC. Medu always remained 'definitely separate, as a structure. Politically it had to be and legally it had to be.'[65]

The only possible exception to this clear separation was the 'Culture and Resistance' festival, held in Gaborone in July of 1982. This festival brought together hundreds of artists and activists from both the exile community as well as those still living in South Africa. Organised under the leadership of Medu and the ANC's cultural wing, the festival thoroughly showcased the wide range of artistic and political activities undertaken by cultural workers affiliated with the Congress movement, including 'literature, visual arts, theatre, film, photography, music and dance'.⁶⁶ Among the participants at the festival were immensely talented and famous people, such as Hugh Masekela, Abdullah Ibrahim, Nadine Gordimer, Mongane Wally Serote, Jonas Gwangwa, Lindiwe Mabuza, Richard Rive, Chris van Wyk and many more. The Schoons were active participants in this festival. It was also the first occasion where their paths crossed with Barry Gilder, who arrived not only in his capacity as an ANC operative, but also with a guitar in hand, singing political folk songs.

Despite the strenuous efforts to keep Medu distinct from the ANC, Medu did serve as a functional cover story for many people. According to Wally Serote, the ensemble made a conscious decision to provide refuge for young South Africans, who poured into Botswana in large numbers in the aftermath of the Soweto uprising. Many of these youths had been heavily influenced by the Black Consciousness Movement and had a strong desire to fight against apartheid, but were not necessarily able easily to access the infrastructure of the exiled liberation movement.

> Tensions developed between the Batswana and the young South African refugees who were not integrating into any liberation movement or going to school or being employed. It became Medu policy to recruit and train these youth ... removing the South African youth from the streets and from mischief and keeping them organised, resulted in creating good relations between Batswana and South Africans.⁶⁷

## Geneva

> As long as money was being spent for the so-called struggle, within the budget, you could do what you wanted with it.
>
> — Craig Williamson, interview

At the most basic level, Craig Williamson's role as an undercover agent at the IUEF was about controlling the money.

In passing the Affected Organizations Act in 1974, the apartheid state had severely curtailed the capacity of anti-apartheid groups inside South Africa to access funds from sympathetic sources overseas. Of course, as Williamson understood all too clearly: 'It's like water and gravity. People overseas want to support the struggle. So, if you block that way, they'll find another way.'[68] For example, an internal memo of the IUEF, which was labelled 'Strictly Confidential', analysed the consequences of the Affected Organizations Act. The anonymous memo noted that the law 'would encompass all the organizations I can think of except pure small-scale political conscientization organisations ... this means that all these organizations become effectively under state scrutiny.'[69] Therefore, the memo concluded, 'this is merely another step forcing the internal projects closer to almost total clandestine methods of operation.'[70] As the IUEF grew to accept that the anti-apartheid struggle was becoming almost totally clandestine, the organisation – and Lars-Gunnar Eriksson especially – grew to accept that the need to find 'another way' in the midst of intensifying state repression meant being increasingly comfortable with breaking the law, or at least bending it. This widespread acceptance of 'irregular channels' provided a fertile atmosphere for Williamson to infiltrate and, over time, to manipulate funding towards his own ends, in profound and irreparable ways.

There were a number of layers to Williamson's manipulation of IUEF funds. The first layer was the creation of a series of false – or, at least, partially run by the security police – structures for operating projects that had been previously run by legitimate anti-apartheid organisations. The archives of the IUEF include hundreds of coded letters, budgets and memoranda all about these various means of laundering anti-apartheid money for the security police. For example, a file labelled 'Clandestine Funds' includes expenses for 'Charles' (both daily operating expenses, and also funds for Cape Town and Botswana trips), 'Paul', and also 'Horses' and 'Livestock'.[71] Some amount of this coding is straightforward enough, such as referring to smuggling activists across the border as the 'railroad'. While many of the other security police officers are still not known (and certainly not in as much depth as we know about Williamson) it's reasonable to presume that Charles, Paul and others were cops.[72] Other pieces of the puzzle remain elusive, such as the 'livestock,' or the 'ball bearing business'. Furthermore, much of the code refers to family members, and it is not entirely clear whether the family is the IUEF, the police, or some combination of both. Despite these difficulties, there is a fair amount about how IUEF money was misdirected that *is* possible to reconstruct.

Not surprisingly, Nusas was a principal target of these initiatives. According to Williamson, international funds

> had to be moved away from Nusas, per se, because we were no longer in control of Nusas. It had gone back to being a liberal organisation, broadly opposed to apartheid, but totally opposed to the armed struggle. What we did then was to create other organisations. EDA [Environmental and Developmental Agency] was one of them. That's how we maintained control of the money.[73]

The EDA, which is the only 'one of them' that Williamson explicitly named, was run by his partner in the operation, Karl Edwards. By all accounts, Edwards was sincerely an environmentalist, and the EDA legitimately took on projects related to the environment. Furthermore, the organisation drew in a number of young and idealistic leftists, such as Cedric de Beer. Therefore, EDA was not entirely a fabrication, but nonetheless it provided Williamson with a clear channel to move funds out of the IUEF and directly under the supervision of the security police. As the director of EDA, Edwards was not only able to direct where the funds were distributed, he was also able to use these grants as an intelligence-gathering mechanism for the South African government. As Williamson explains it,

> we now had all sorts of informers, people who were giving us information, because we were giving them someone else's money, and they had to justify what they were doing with that money. So, they had to tell us what they were doing with the money, who they were giving it to etc.[74]

This combination of directly funnelling money into the hands of the security police and intelligence gathering was broadly the model of the whole operation.

There were, however, some variations on the theme. For example, Williamson and his gang took a slightly different approach when it came to supporting political prisoners. The South African Prisoner Education Trust (Sapet) was a project created by Nusas. In its inception, Sapet was designed by student radicals who were attempting to find ways to connect with and offer solidarity to older generations of the movement, who had become political prisoners in the escalating repression following Sharpeville. In order to exert influence over Sapet, the security police created a separate organisation, the Prisoners Support Trust (PST) that was then responsible for dispersing all of the funding from IUEF on to activists inside South Africa. As Williamson explained in an internal memo to his colleagues at IUEF, the scheme went as follows:

> The original intention of the PST was to act as a channel for IUEF funds to SAPET and other prisoner/detainee and dependents support schemes ... However, this mechanism must be safe so that if someone receiving cash is ever arrested or interrogated, the names that they can give will not lead to our people or the closing down of the operation ... The overall impression I have of this plan is that it is foolproof.[75]

Here one can see the cunning, almost playful side of Craig Williamson. How can Williamson possibly claim that this system of illegally moving funds into South Africa is 'foolproof'? Well, of course he can confidently declare that the police will not close down the operation because the whole thing is, in fact, the product of the police. At the same time, by taking on the language and posture of someone taking risks for 'the struggle' Williamson made the whole endeavour more enticing to the IUEF and moved suspicion away from himself.

However, not everyone was easily persuaded by the charade of the PST. An intriguing example of this is a letter from George Sehl, the director of Amnesty International in West Germany, to the IUEF. While Sehl attempted to be courteous in his letter, his sense of unease is palpable throughout. The letter opens by declaring that 'we have some doubts to write to this Trust, because it is unknown to all people... which we have asked about it'. After outlining all of the different organisations in Europe that either had not heard of, or at least could not speak to the merits of the PST, Sehl then closes the letter by repeating, 'Can we trust this Prisoners Support Trust? ... We are rather suspicious about this Trust.'[76]

Craig Williamson's reply to this letter, dated 15 July 1977, was insistent:

> Your suspicions about the Prisoners Support Trust are unfounded and ... I am disturbed that you have been making public enquiries all over Europe about this group and I hope that it does not result in the police in South Africa acting against the Trust. Incidentally, you may be interested to know that the full-time worker on the Trust himself served 10 years on Robben Island. I have informed the Trust of your attitude and they would be glad if you would not contact them again.[77]

This is another example of Williamson attempting to take on the tone of a cocky radical, someone suitably appalled by the paternalism of an organisation like Amnesty International. Nonetheless, Williamson's bitter dismissal of George Sehl's suspicions belies the tremendous fragility of security police officers pretending to support prisoners. One of the ways that Williamson sought to minimise the risk of these police-run projects being exposed was to find ways to enlist actual radicals into the project, such as the ex-Robben Island prisoner working for PST. In this vein, Williamson explained in his memo to the IUEF that, 'the main activity I see for PST is the supplying of cash to individuals nominated by ANC, PAC, or BPC'.[78] Getting these groups to play an active role in choosing which prisoners to support not only gave Williamson's work additional credibility, it also provided the security police with further intelligence, as they could easily see which prisoners mattered the most to the movement.

One of the most important components of Williamson's manipulation of IUEF funds was a secret, separate entity, formally known as Southern Futures Vaduz (SFV), which was opened in Liechtenstein. On 19 May 1978, Lars-Gunnar Eriksson sent a memo to a select group of staff, which quite bluntly detailed the structure and function of Southern Futures:

1. Southern Futures exists in order to hide IUEF involvement in certain transactions made in relation to South African affairs ...

2. On <u>NO</u> account is anything to do with SFV <u>ever</u> to be dealt with under IUEF cover.
3. Nothing to do with SFV is ever to be sent out except on specific instruction of Lars-Gunnar.
4. Unless the person you are talking to is known by you to be involved in SFV affairs, you have never heard of SFV.[79]

Given that Southern Futures was so secretive, and apparently so tightly controlled by Lars-Gunnar Eriksson, it may seem logical that Craig Williamson was entirely unable to have any influence over this set of money. In fact, Williamson said as much when I asked him who controlled Southern Futures. Williamson insisted that he had 'no control' over Southern Futures. 'It was Lars-Gunnar, and Leslie Rubin.'[80] In saying this, he admitted, at least: 'I was given the money, yeah. I was told to do this with the money, yes. But they used to have their board meetings and issue checks, and sometimes I cashed them, but no, I had no control.'[81] Having been to the archives of the IUEF, this was one moment in my interaction with Williamson where I could be confident and clear about the fact that he was lying to me. Perhaps at the beginning, when the secret fund was first established, Eriksson did attempt strictly to control what was done with it. However, by November of 1978, Craig Williamson was explicitly and directly granted full control over Southern Futures. In a Strictly Confidential memo to the relevant staff, Eriksson declared:

> As from Monday November 20th all financial matters regarding Southern Futures will be handled directly by Craig. Therefore, in time for Monday, you should prepare a balance sheet and hand over the whole file, cash-book, etc. on SF to Craig. Before that, I would also like to check it myself to ensure that this has been properly done.[82]

What this memo from Eriksson proves is that, for at least a year and perhaps more, Williamson was given free rein over substantial sums of money; and that several people within the IUEF helped him do it.

A full cataloguing of the uses and misuses of these funds is impossible at this point, because the accounting was intentionally kept vague, as well as the fact that many of the files that did exist were likely stolen by Williamson himself. Nonetheless, the truth is clear enough in Williamson's cavalier depiction of Southern Futures as 'a secret account in Liechtenstein … that became like a slush fund. As long as you could give a report to the donors that the money has been received by whatever project, then you could keep the slush fund going.'[83]

To this day, Williamson is sensitive to the accusation that what he did amounted to stealing. 'A lot of people say we stole the money. We didn't steal the money. We gave it to people. We used it. We did with it what the donors had hoped we would do with it.'[84] It is difficult to fully comprehend how Williamson can make a claim like this, forty years later. In part, Williamson was merely expressing his own complicated sense of the guilt he carries. That is, to succeed in his role as an undercover agent at the IUEF, Williamson *did* to a substantial degree have to make sure that money that governments and organisations donated to the anti-apartheid struggle actually made it into the hands of the movement. To this extent, Williamson is haunted by the fact that he was forced to fund his enemies. Nonetheless, to simply shrug off the fact of his theft is deceitful at best and despicable at worst.

Williamson's cabal used IUEF funds to buy Daisy Farm, a secluded property outside of Pretoria. Williamson admitted this ('yeah, we did buy a farm') but still insisted that this was, more or less, what the donors had intended the funds would be used for. As evidence for this claim, Williamson explained that he brought Poul Brandrup, a representative from a Danish NGO,[85] down to Daisy Farm, 'and he knew the farm had been bought with Danish government and other government funds, and he was very happy that we had this base where these liberation activities could take place, within sight of Johannesburg and Pretoria'.[86] These liberation activities? What might that mean? Williamson's explanation that 'the money was given for leadership training' is less than vague. So, did this mean that anti-apartheid organisations used Daisy Farm to train their leadership? 'No,' Williamson admitted. 'It was our place.'[87] From this one might deduce that the only 'leadership' that was being trained at Daisy Farm were security police officers. According to Williamson, the only time anti-apartheid activists ever set foot on Daisy Farm was when they were being smuggled out of the country by Williamson's 'railroad', which they believed was run by the anti-apartheid movement:

> Some of the people who were taken out of the country would be taken there, but they wouldn't have known where they were. It was, in those days, right in the bush, near Lanseria airport. It was 20 minutes down a very difficult road. So, they'd be taken at night, and then kept there and then taken to the Botswana border.[88]

According to Williamson's testimony at the TRC in 1998, there was at least one other way in which Daisy Farm was intended to be used for leadership of the liberation movement. That is, the security police would often joke to one another about how the basement of Daisy Farm was 'Slovo's suite'.[89] The fact that such jokes were made just a couple of years before a parcel bomb ordered by Williamson murdered Joe Slovo's wife makes the crime of theft seem tiny, in comparison. Sadly, even Williamson's cruel jokes mask the true depths of cruelty that took place at Daisy Farm. Williamson's casual, offhand chatter about the farm is intended to conceal the fact that the farmhouse basement was regularly used by the security police as a torture chamber for anti-apartheid activists.[90]

# 4 | Undercover Stories

**Botswana**

While everyone needed a cover story, not all covers were as clean cut as being a teacher or an artist; in some cases, cover stories could have an *under*cover side to them as well. Heinz Klug and Patrick Fitzgerald's exile years in Botswana are perhaps the most complex – and also the most compelling – cases in point.

Klug had been a journalism student, and part of the radical leadership of Nusas, after the entire executive disbanded in 1976, and after Williamson's flight from the country. Klug had been living in Durban when Rick Turner was killed and had experienced a nasty increase in harassment from the police in the aftermath of the assassination. At the end of 1978, Klug moved down to Cape Town and began an MA in January of 1979. Meanwhile, Klug continued his radical organising, often focused on opposing the conscription of white men into the apartheid military. 'The pressures were building, and all of a sudden I got a letter that said that they had cancelled my deferment.'[1] In response to being called up by the military, Klug attempted to organise a group of students to all refuse to serve, together. However, the state strategically offered deferments, to whittle down this group of conscientious objectors. Furthermore, Nusas had decided that they were unwilling to encourage young white men to resist conscription.

> I told exactly two people, close friends, that I was planning to leave the country. One of these friends invited me to beer at the Pig and

> Whistle in Cape Town. My friend wasn't there when I arrived. Karl Edwards was sitting there, and he said, 'I hear you're leaving the country.' I said that I had no idea what he was talking about. He said, 'Well, look, if you decide you'd like to leave, there's this project in Botswana called SANA [the South African News Agency]. They need somebody to take it over. So, it's a job ...' I asked what SANA was, and he said, 'Oh, it's funded by the International University Exchange Fund.' I had no idea what that was. Karl explained further, 'It's Craig Williamson; he's in Geneva now.'[2]

At the time, Heinz Klug knew that he didn't personally like Edwards, and he knew that many people were suspicious of Edwards, knowing that he had once been a police officer. Klug had never interacted with Williamson before, so he started asking friends about him. 'About Williamson they were very confused. Some people said, "Don't trust him." Others said, "He's fine, he left the country, he must be okay." Some others said, "Maybe he's a spook for the British or somebody else."'[3]

Despite the various concerns about Edwards and Williamson, and the bizarre exchange in the pub, which amounted to a job offer, Klug took the offer seriously. Furthermore:

> When I spoke to ANC contacts, they said, 'Take the job.' I didn't know what the hell I was getting myself into though ... I crossed the border on June 26th, 1979. I went to a house in Gaborone, and who was there? Patrick Fitzgerald, who was just in the papers as a public deserter from the South African army. I had known Patrick from Nusas. I told him that I was supposed to take over SANA. He said, 'There it is.' It was this house, with electricity, but no water; you had to go outside to the stand-pipe.[4]

Patrick Fitzgerald had deserted his conscripted military service with the SADF and had arrived in Botswana hoping to connect with Jenny (whom he knew previously) and Marius (whom he was meeting for the first time).

> Marius saw me – I was clean-shaven and fit – and he was terrified; he thought for sure I was from the special branch. He flinched,

and reached as if he was looking for a whip. Jenny said, 'No, this is Patrick Fitzgerald, he's a friend ...' I thought I was on my way to MK, but as soon as they learned that I had political connections, they detained me to work in the political underground structures.[5]

Having been assigned to the political underground, Sana provided a credible cover for Fitzgerald to have a job at a legitimate news service, with a political content. The irony of this assignment was that Fitzgerald arrived in Botswana carrying deep suspicions towards Williamson and Edwards – which he was quite explicit about – and working for Sana meant engaging with them both.

When I arrived to Botswana, I was debriefed by Henry Makghoti and Marius Schoon. The first issue they raised with me was, 'What do you think of Williamson and Edwards?' My answer was that I thought they were security agents, and I thought everyone knew that. Marius smiled and said, 'That's what we think, but it seems we can't convince some of our ANC colleagues.'[6]

So, ANC leaders were quite aware of the suspicions that Williamson and Edwards were infiltrators, but encouraged both Klug and Fitzgerald to take positions at Sana all the same. Essentially, these two young members of the ANC underground were tasked with joining an organisation run by police infiltrators.

At the time that Klug and Fitzgerald arrived in Botswana, Klug says, 'the police were running Sana, there was no question about that'.[7] How did it come to be that Sana was based in Botswana and functioned as a surveillance mechanism for the security police? The first step in this process was a relentless campaign of harassment against Eric Abraham, the original editor of Sana while the project was still based in Cape Town. Jacob Dlamini's *Terrorist Album* documents extensively what was done to Abraham:

On December 9, 1976, Abraham opened a case of harassment against the police, saying that unidentified individuals were making his life a living hell. Anonymous harassers ordered a consignment of alcohol to be delivered to his flat without Abraham's knowledge; they had flowers and a card congratulating him on his banning order conveyed to his apartment; they sent a hearse allegedly to collect his corpse from the apartment; and they repeatedly made phone calls threatening to kill Abraham.[8]

As a result of having to endure this string of abuses, Abraham developed a habit of sleeping 'in the bath "since my studio had two large windows onto the street and I was very vulnerable"'.[9] In addition to attacking Abraham on a personal level, the police also attacked Sana. 'After two or three bulletins had been produced, the Sana offices were raided, and the Security Police took away every document in the office.'[10] The final nail in the coffin came in the form of an offer from Craig Williamson, who was keenly aware of the devastating circumstances for Abraham and Sana. Williamson shrewdly intervened by offering to help Abraham cross the border into Botswana (Abraham quickly continued on to a life in exile in the UK). Sadly, Abraham was prepared to trust Craig Williamson because he had the backing of people Abraham trusted:

> On [my] arrival at Jan Smuts Airport in Johannesburg, Jeanette Curtis picked me up and took me to her labor union office to collect something. It was here that I met Craig Williamson for the first time. To me he looked like an Afrikaner policeman and I was taken aback by his feigned familiarity, which jarred with me. It was Jeanette and Lars Gunnar Eriksson's bona fides about Williamson that persuaded me to talk to him, which I did only two or three times between 1973 and 1976. I was told he was Lars Gunnar's undercover representative in SA and had Lars Gunnar's full trust and confidence.[11]

Abraham's recollection is remarkable in that it indicates that Williamson and Curtis had a working relationship going as far back as 1973 – and that Curtis went so far as to openly encourage others to take Williamson seriously, at that time. Furthermore, the story of Abraham's meeting of Williamson indicates how simply and casually the security police were able to manipulate activists. Persuading Abraham to flee the country under the care of Williamson was a tremendous coup for the security police.

Once Abraham was out of the picture as the editor of Sana, the project was re-established in Gaborone, run by other South African exiles, and funded by the IUEF. According to Klug:

> A guy named Julian Sturgeon – another young white South African who was running away from the army – took over SANA. Sturgeon left in early 1979, which is why there was an opening. But it was IUEF who was putting people there, not the ANC, not anybody else.[12]

In other words, Heinz Klug was part of a succession of directors of Sana, all of whom were white leftists eager to get away from apartheid repression. For the security police, having nominal control over Sana provided an avenue to help shuttle people out of South Africa, under a cover that seemed reasonably legitimate. Being able to assist anti-apartheid activists 'escaping' South Africa also gave additional legitimacy to Williamson and Edwards, since their 'railroad' service had an air of revolutionary risk-taking to it.

While the ways in which the security police controlled Sana were all too real, there were other important dimensions to the project. Like all cover stories, Klug and other members of Sana *did* the work that they said they were doing; they actually ran a news agency. Sana produced a publication that was intended as a summary of news that would be relevant to the anti-apartheid movement throughout the world. 'There were reports about trials, reports about bombings or other MK attacks,' says Klug. 'We were also making our own stories out of the news, because we thought we were a news agency.'[13] Six months after taking over the news agency, in January of 1980, Klug and Fitzgerald divorced the project from the IUEF and stopped sending the paper to Geneva, due to their serious concerns about Williamson and Edwards.

The news agency project lay dormant for a period, until Klug and his comrades revived it at the start of 1983 and changed the name to the Solidarity News Service (SNS). In the project's new incarnation, the news agency became a very different kind of cover story. The SNS operated as a thinly veiled publication of the ANC. As Klug explains:

> When the [SADF] attacked the news agency in 1985, they claimed that it was an intelligence agency for the ANC. Well, to the extent that open intelligence is intelligence, sure. But we weren't ANC intelligence. This was an open, public entity. But if you read the pieces, you can see that they're very steeped in the ANC positions of the time. We were not objective. We didn't claim to be.[14]

In addition to generally printing news with a pro-ANC perspective, SNS also operated as a direct forwarding service, to gather South African news in Gaborone and to send it on to ANC headquarters.

> We sent a daily telex to Lusaka. First thing every morning, we would be outside the Botswana Book Centre to buy all the South African papers. Anything related to what we knew Lusaka was interested in, we would send an open telex ... and for Lusaka it was the most direct information they were getting about what was happening inside the country ... Otherwise, they would have to wait days.[15]

The South African News Agency – reborn as the Solidarity News Service – effectively played an undercover role in support of both the apartheid security police *and* the ANC, all through essentially the same organisation. The story of Sana/SNS is unique, but it nonetheless sheds light on the broader phenomenon of engaging in 'undercover' political work.

## Geneva: Black Consciousness and the ANC

Perhaps the most intriguing contribution that Craig Williamson made to the state's counter-insurgency campaign was his framing of the threat posed by the ANC. In his characteristically smug fashion, Williamson now claims that 'Umkhonto we Sizwe never worried us'.[16] Such a blanket declaration of confidence reeks of propaganda, on its face. However, if one digs deeper, and listens carefully, what Williamson is attempting to articulate is the crude calculus of the Cold War. Within the frame of an international battle against the red menace, fighting an extended guerrilla war campaign against an enemy that was funded by the Soviet Union, trained by the East Germans, and so on, was literally playing right into the hands of the apartheid state's greatest strengths. The more the enemy was communism, rather than nonracialism, democracy, human rights, and so forth, the easier it would be to marshal support (both domestically and internationally) for apartheid. Therefore, from Williamson's perspective, the *best-case* scenario for the state would be for as much of the anti-apartheid movement as possible to *align themselves with the ANC*, which he often spoke of as adopting 'the Moscow line'.

An intriguing insight into how Williamson understood his role in relation to pushing the anti-apartheid movement towards the ANC is his hand-written autobiography, penned during his detention in an Angolan prison, in 1996.

> The major change I made in the IUEF after my appointment as Deputy Director was that I got IUEF to recognize the ANC as the leading liberation movement in SA. This made the ANC very happy as they now had some say on IUEF funding to SA … my bosses in Pretoria were happy because they remained worried about the BCM and its potential and they also wanted to be able to 'brand' all anti-apartheid organizations as Moscow/Communist and so the more the ANC controlled all anti-apartheid forces the happier they were.[17]

It is absolutely striking that Williamson would claim the IUEF's declaration in support of the ANC as the 'major change' that he was responsible for, and one that made his bosses in Pretoria especially happy. To understand the substance of this claim, and why it makes sense, it's necessary to take a step back, to understand the political context that Williamson was grappling with while working for IUEF.

Before Williamson arrived in Geneva, the IUEF had made a conscious decision actively to support the Black Consciousness Movement and explicitly to keep a distance from the ANC. Crucially, the IUEF was funded (and quite heavily) from the social democratic movement in Europe, and particularly by Scandinavian governments. According to

Williamson, the IUEF hoped 'that the Black Consciousness Movement would be a social democratic bulwark against the Communist dominated or controlled ANC'.[18] It is perhaps fair enough to say that social democrats are anti-communist, in the sense that they oppose Stalinism, or authoritarianism. However, it is important to clarify that Lars-Gunnar Eriksson (and many others, such as Olaf Palme) were solidly on the left of the social democratic movement, meaning that they were interested in an independent and democratic form of socialism. Considering this, it seems clear that IUEF support for the Black Consciousness Movement was not merely *anti*-ANC or even the Soviet Union, but also, crucially, *an investment in* a new and experimental political movement. Therefore, when Williamson boasts of pushing the IUEF to support the ANC, he immediately clarifies that 'Eriksson accepted the situation after long arguments with me, but he was not 100% happy and his BCM/PAC/Zanu friends were furious that the IUEF had been "hijacked" by a white communist'.[19]

Craig Williamson's campaign to shift the IUEF's position on the ANC was subtle, stubborn and slow; but he started in on it early on. In his first few months in Geneva, Williamson reached out to the ANC office in London, attempting to undo the ANC's natural reticence towards interacting with the IUEF. In a letter sent on 24 May 1977, Williamson shrewdly misrepresented the IUEF's actual stance towards the ANC, and instead claimed that it was merely a problem of ignorance:

> I feel that any lack of ANC information in IUEF publications is probably due to lack of contact between us and I hope to rectify this as soon as possible. I will be in London from Tuesday to Friday next week ... I hope we will be able to sort out any problems which exist.[20]

While certain ANC members now deny or downplay the fact, it seems certain that Williamson did engage with the London ANC office on several different occasions during his time in Europe. Furthermore, while the levels to which Williamson was regarded as a bona fide 'member' of the organisation is still hotly contested, it seems that at least some members of the ANC regarded Williamson as a bona fide supporter, and openly supported him in return. One of the most striking examples of this is the fact that the ANC agreed to provide Craig Williamson's wife with an official letter of recommendation so that she could get into medical school. On 21 October 1978, Williamson appealed to the ANC, seeking a letter of recommendation for his wife, Ingrid: 'She is determined to complete her medical studies so that she will be better able to serve the South African people and the movement.'[21] Williamson signed the letter 'Power to the People'. Nonetheless, the ANC took his request seriously, without any irony, and produced the following recommendation:

> This letter serves to confirm that Ingrid Williamson is a supporter of the African National Congress and is a de-facto refugee from [South Africa] ... The ANC ... is striving to develop a sufficient degree of medical resources and expertise to allow the movement to become self-sufficient in aspects of medical health care of the thousands of refugees under ANC care in various African states. In addition, this committee seeks to follow the necessary strategy needed for healthcare in a future liberated South Africa ... For these reasons the ANC commends Ms. Ingrid Williamson's application.[22]

According to James Sanders, writing in *Apartheid's Friends*, Williamson's wife, after arriving in Geneva with the ANC's blessing, directly engaged in espionage activities while there. 'Working closely with his wife, Ingrid Bacher, they would spy through the night at IUEF, as they "photocopied memoranda, receipts, orders and private correspondence, rifling through files and drawers".'[23]

Beyond whatever personal charm Williamson may have mustered to endear himself to the ANC, he was also working simultaneously on developing a pro-ANC stance within the IUEF. For example, in the beginning of 1978, Williamson made a trip down to Botswana, and used his report-back to Lars-Gunnar in Geneva to smear the independent left wing that the IUEF had traditionally funded (Black Consciousness and white activists in the New Left). 'There is a danger that these people may be banded together into a destructive group which will oppose the "national liberation movement".'[24]

That is, Williamson hoped to portray individuals and organisations as not only 'non-aligned' with the ANC, but actively opposed to them:

> Ranwedzi[25] says that he estimates that 99% of the kids leaving South Africa are anti-ANC. He says that even if they are non-aligned when they first leave, within a matter of days of being in Gaborone, they become anti-established liberation movements.[26]

Williamson's portrayal of South African leftists in Botswana being 'anti' the ANC put Eriksson, and the IUEF more broadly, in an uncomfortable position. While Eriksson and his donors may have been willing actively to invest in an *alternative* political trajectory to the ANC, they would not have been willing to see themselves as working *against* the 'liberation movements'.

It should be remembered that Williamson's pressure campaign was happening at a moment when the Black Consciousness Movement was in serious decline and the ANC was ascending. There are a couple of important layers to this. First, even though the Soweto uprising was without a doubt the result of Black Consciousness, the aftermath of the uprising primarily bolstered the ANC. In its aftermath, young Black Consciousness activists poured into ANC camps, seeking military training. At the same time as these dynamics were playing out within the exile movement, the apartheid state took increasingly aggressive measures to smash Black Consciousness inside South Africa. In September and October of 1977, a wave of repression shuttered multiple Black Consciousness organisations, banned their leaders, and murdered Steve Biko. Given this overall context, it is possible that the IUEF would have moved towards openly supporting the ANC without interference from Williamson. Within the formal declaration of support that the board of the IUEF drafted, on 21 July 1978, there is a clear recognition of the fact that the landscape of the anti-apartheid movement had shifted dramatically in the past two years:

> The groups which are supported inside South Africa by the IUEF have stated that they do not accord themselves liberation movement status ... They also regard the external political representation of the South African people and the implementation of the armed struggle as the duty of all liberation movements. The ANC

is the leader of the National Liberation Movement which is comprised of all South Africans who subscribe to the democratic principles and ideals contained in the Freedom Charter.[27]

This is a clear and sober assessment of the political situation in 1978 and it is not surprising that the IUEF took this stance, if they were genuine about their desire to end apartheid. Nonetheless, it is still significant that Williamson understood a major European funding organisation's decision to support the ANC as a strategic victory for the apartheid state.

There are two different reasons why Williamson saw IUEF support for the ANC as a victory, one ideological and the other practical. At the level of political ideology, Williamson understood the ANC's vision of the armed struggle to be fundamentally *less dangerous* to the survival of the apartheid state than mass mobilisation.

> The ANC, as far as I'm concerned, made an error by pushing the armed struggle as the be all and end all. The ANC wanted most people to the camps, in Angola. They still thought that they'd take all these kids and make them soldiers and then they'd go to South Africa and liberate it. For a long time, the ANC didn't see the power of mass mobilisation. It was only later, with the UDF [United Democratic Front].[28]

Williamson contrasts the ineffectiveness of the ANC's armed struggle with his nightmare vision of a successful mass mobilisation overthrowing the state:

> I remember getting lectures on what happened to the Shah of Iran. Exactly what happened to the Shah – one day a million people suddenly said, 'that's it!' What is the army going to do? So, mass mobilisation was the one fear.[29]

From Williamson's perspective, the Black Consciousness Movement had the latent potential of the Iranian revolution embedded within it. There was something unknown and uncontrollable about Black Consciousness, which might explode in an outpouring of refusal, such as the Soweto uprising. In contrast, the ANC's vision of an extended military confrontation against the most powerful army on the continent didn't seem so scary.

In addition to these strategic concerns, supporting the ANC 'reduced an administrative burden'[30] on Williamson and his fellow officers within the security services. Since Williamson was in the business of pretending to be a funder for the anti-apartheid movement, his work was a whole lot easier if everything he did was under the direction of the ANC.

> So, it was a matter of encouraging the ANC to follow their natural arrogance and their idea that they were the leaders of the struggle, and people should do what they said … That would be advantageous to us, from a state security perspective, because it allowed it to have more credibility, and built our intelligence gathering.[31]

What Williamson meant by allowing the ANC to 'follow their natural arrogance' is that he calculated (correctly) that the ANC would only agree to be the recipients of funding from the IUEF if they could have a direct say over who would receive the funds and also who would be excluded from funding. In July of 1979, Mac Maharaj, Thomas Nkobi and other representatives of the ANC met with the IUEF secretariat. Most directly, it was decided at this meeting that 'The IUEF is to provide 6,000 GBP to the ANC for their internal activities.'[32] More broadly, however, the ANC sought to have a full accounting of all the *other* organisations that were receiving funds from IUEF. In particular, Mac Maharaj wanted the IUEF to explain what support they had given to a series of BCM groups. As a strong indication of the new direction that the organisation had turned in the year prior, Lars-Gunnar Eriksson insisted that 'for the IUEF to carry out future funding for BCM activities will be very difficult unless the BCM can straighten out their relationship with the ANC'.[33]

Once again, it is more than probable that Eriksson and others within the leadership of the IUEF made a genuine decision to throw their money and their hearts behind the ANC. Still, it is worth pausing to reflect on the possibility that this was – in a tragic irony – the best-case scenario for the apartheid state at the same time.

## Botswana: the ANC underground

As one can hear firmly in Marius's recollections years later, he was a staunch supporter of the ANC, determined to do everything he could to support the organisation. At least according to Marius, Jenny's commitment to the ANC was just as fierce. Without a doubt, it was their underground work for the ANC that most occupied the attention of the Schoons while they were in Botswana. So, what exactly was the role of the Schoons in the ANC underground in Botswana? There are several barriers to answering this question.

Part of the difficulty in uncovering the realities of undercover politics is the fact that the organisation was, for obvious security reasons, divided into distinct cells, which had little to no contact with other cells. As Klug explains it, 'there were people in the ANC underground in Botswana that I wouldn't have known. There were people who I recruited and worked with, that other people wouldn't know. You kept within certain circles.'[34] The idea of using cell structures was not new, and had been practised for decades throughout the world, particularly among communist parties. What is perhaps not so obvious about this system is that the division into separate cells cut across close friends, even families. For example, Mike and Carol Kahn 'were placed in separate cells. Somebody gave us our noms de guerre. I was Farid, and she was Layla. In some way or other we were referred to as Farid and Layla, which suggests a relationship. But I have no idea who was in Layla's cell.'[35] The risks involved in undercover work – particularly at the military level – required an intense commitment to secrecy; so much so that Mike Kahn can still claim in all seriousness (and despite apartheid having ended 30 years ago) that essentially he had no idea what his wife was doing, or with whom. Similarly, Klug and Kahn lived together for a period in Gaborone, but operated in separate cells, so again, neither have anything to say regarding the other's activities. Having taken an oath of secrecy decades ago, it is now virtually impossible for those who were members of the ANC's underground to speak in any depth of detail about what, precisely, that meant. To be certain, if these men have nothing to say about the activities of those with whom they shared a home – even a bed – they certainly cannot say with any confidence what Jeanette and Marius were doing. As Kahn says, 'what he was doing, he was doing; what we were doing, we were doing. In theory, nobody knew what the others were doing. In terms of real underground work, between my household and theirs, was nil.'³⁶

Even Barry Gilder, whose role as an intelligence officer in Botswana would presumably have given him a higher vantage point within the ANC hierarchy, claims to have virtually no direct or concrete knowledge regarding the Schoons' role in Botswana. Gilder repeatedly stressed that a 'generation' within the struggle against apartheid was only a year or two long. Thinking of generations in this way, the Schoons 'were a short generation before me in Botswana, so I was not aware of what the particular work was that they were doing in Botswana'. Then again, Gilder was in Angola, as were the Schoons, but 'I had been in Angola three or four years before they got there'.³⁷ In sum, the combination of a strict cell structure and an organisational community that was transient for a myriad reasons (arrests, deportations, assassinations, shifting politics, shifting romantic relationships) makes it extremely difficult for participants in the underground to speak authoritatively about the experiences of their comrades. In fact, at times, there are important reasons why underground militants find it hard to speak even about their *own* experiences.

Judy Seidman is very aware of the ways in which the culture of secrecy that developed by necessity within the ANC underground limits and skews the capacity of historians to tell the story of the ANC in exile. At a very basic level, members of the underground grew accustomed to downplaying or evading any direct depiction of their involvement with the ANC. As Seidman explains:

> You often say that 'I'm not political' because that was also part of cover. You did not in Botswana announce at that stage – even if you were legal and with an American passport – you simply did not announce 'I am a functional member of the ANC,' in any way, shape or fashion ... My experience is, many people still do that.³⁸

According to Seidman, even thirty years after the unbanning of the ANC, people remain allegiant to the security ethos of the struggle days. In this context, uncovering the history of the ANC underground is akin to navigating a subtle minefield. This can be accomplished by drawing on what information comrades *are* willing to speak about at this point, as well as by reading between the lines what is implied, and what is *not said*.

One of the consequences of a commitment to underground political activity was that daily life, above ground, retained many of the qualities of a quiet, middle-class existence. Families such as the Schoons carried on all the routines of a young family, and their social lives functioned much the same as other families anywhere might do; that is, with the rather large caveat that the Schoons were white and foreign in an African country, and therefore their social world was largely separated from the Black majority around them. As Heinz Klug describes it,

> It's divided in the same race and class lines that happen in colonial spaces anywhere ... At the school where Jenny and Marius taught, all their colleagues were Batswana ... But essentially, our community was expatriate.[39]

Within these basic divides along race and class lines, the Schoons and their white comrades in the ANC – the Kahns, the Seidmans, Klug and Fitzpatrick, and others – spent a great deal of time together more as members of an extended family than as clandestine combatants. Mike Kahn says this explicitly:

> We were family. We were extended family. To the extent that we agreed, as things began to hot up ... we made a pact. The pact was simply this: 'Jenny and Marius, if they kill us, will you adopt our children?' And vice versa. So we were that close. It was at that very intimate level.[40]

Judy Seidman describes her relationship with the Schoons in very similar terms. In her memory, the primary connection between herself and Jenny Schoon was familial, and the political connection developed *after* that:

> Katryn and my daughter Annie are the same age and in fact became best friends. The kids were in the same crèche and we arranged to take them to school. Jenny and I became friends around that and it

was clear that she had political interests that matched my political interests. But I don't remember meeting her specifically and consciously in a political circle.[41]

To be clear, the decision to describe these connections as familial, rather than grounded in political principles, intends to express a *deeper* connection than mere convictions or organisational fealty. In fact, Judy Seidman echoed the Kahns' willingness to take on the Schoons' children as her own, as needed.

> I actually offered to adopt Fritz after Jenny was killed, and Marius's response was 'I'll be damned if I'm going to allow another child to live in Botswana, after we just lost one child'. But we had talked about that: if anything happened to one of or the other of us, we would take care of the kids.[42]

This familial bond among comrades even allowed political disagreements to be superseded, to some extent. Paula Ensor had been quite close with Jenny Curtis, from their time living together in Cape Town and working within the Western Cape Workers' Advice Bureau. After 1976, Ensor established herself in London, where she became active in the Marxist Workers' Tendency of the ANC. This group of socialists developed a strident critique of the ANC's approach to the armed struggle. According to the Marxist Workers' Tendency, the ANC was excessively focused on guerrilla warfare, which was doomed to failure, rather than focusing on building an armed revolutionary working-class movement. This critique put Ensor and the others in her 'tendency' into a sustained and bitter conflict with the ANC. By the time Ensor arrived in Botswana, in 1979, she had been suspended from the ANC. Within a couple of years, Ensor and the rest were expelled entirely from the organisation. In this context, it is not surprising that 'Marius Schoon made it absolutely clear that the ANC would act against me if they found me involved in any kind of politics at all'.[43] Despite the open bitterness, politically, between Paula and Marius, Paula and Jeanette 'kind of managed' to maintain a warm social relationship:

> Both he and Jeanette were homemakers. They loved having people around. So, there was a side of Marius that I really loved. But I

didn't agree with him politically. It created a tension, because Jeanette and I had to manage a very difficult situation. Obviously, she was very loyal to him, and she and I wanted to spend time together. We kind of managed it. If it was just the two of us it was fine. But when it was me and her and Marius it could be tense at times. Because he would want to know what I'm doing in Botswana.[44]

While the political divide between Paula Ensor and the Schoons was particularly glaring, it is important to reiterate that even among comrades who shared a deep political commitment, nonetheless the necessities of clandestine activity required that certain important aspects of their lives were simply impossible to discuss. Therefore, neither Judy Seidman nor Mike Kahn – both of whom had vowed to raise Katryn and Fritz, if needed – would have been privy to any discussions between Jenny and Marius regarding huge decisions, such as whether to engage in military activities, whether to leave Botswana, or where to go next. All these conversations would have existed solely among other cell members, or with commanding officers of the ANC. Such were the limits of the familial intimacy of the political underground.

In sum, being underground white ANC members in Botswana meant that a large portion of the substantive space for engaging with comrades happened at the level of family, of shared social space within the home, rather than centred around 'politics' in the traditional sense of that word. In addition, the houses themselves were one of the main ways that white members could contribute to clandestine activities. For Mike Kahn, this happened almost immediately after he had established himself in Gaborone. 'The next thing that happened after I got my university house, I got approached [by the ANC]. "Can you put up some draft resisters?" In effect, we then ran a safe house for the next thirteen years. By '78 I was working with MK people.'[45] The ANC needed safe spaces in Botswana, either to house young people leaving South Africa to gain military training, or to house trained MK soldiers as they attempted to infiltrate back into South Africa. White members were especially useful in this regard, as they often had stable jobs – such as Kahn's position as a lecturer – and comfortable homes (in Kahn's case, provided by the university). Heinz Klug also found a way to utilise the fact that he was often surrounded by expatriates to set up ANC safe houses.

> What I learned very quickly is that none of these communities spoke to each other: the Danes, the Swedes etc., they all spoke just to each other. In any summer period, or winter period, they would all go off on holidays, and we would look after their houses, and so I'd have five or six houses that I was looking after at once, with cats and dogs that I was supposed to feed. Those houses could then get used as safe spaces for ANC people moving north or south through the country.[46]

## Between politics and violence

At the most formal layer, the Schoons were part of the Internal Political Reconstruction and Development Programme (IPRD) of the ANC. Like all such titles, making meaning out of it may prove entirely elusive. It seems to mean that the Schoons were helping to build (or reconstruct, after the repression of the apartheid state) a group of individuals inside South Africa (internal, rather than in exile) that would be sympathetic to the ANC and may help to 'develop' a domestic underground ANC infrastructure. It seems certain that the Schoons' role within IPRD was focused on the white left. Specifically, according to Patrick Fitzgerald, their task was

> to pull the white left much more substantially into the liberation movement (ANC) camp. By that time, there was a white left orthodoxy that the ANC were either (take your choice) (a) terrible Stalinists who were completely out of touch with global realities of history, or (b) were basically chauvinist African nationalists. Also, that the armed struggle was pathetic and useless.[47]

Quite simply, this meant that the Schoons were tasked with carrying on the work that they had already begun while living in Johannesburg, by keeping in touch with that network of the white left and passing on information about their activities to the ANC headquarters in Lusaka.

The network of individuals inside South Africa that the Schoons were in contact with were primarily focused on trade union organising, study groups and publications: acts of political and cultural dissent. The ANC during this period was starved for information about what was going on inside South Africa, and desperate to build an infrastructure to pass on information. Telexes from SNS, as well as messages passed via clandestine channels from radicals still in South Africa to the ANC in Gaborone, served as vital conduits of information for the ANC in exile.

From Glenn Moss's perspective, having stayed inside of South Africa throughout this period, the tremendous effort involved in sending information about internal projects to the ANC in exile was both dangerous for the activists still inside the country, and largely superfluous. For example,

> Alan [Fine] was risking a hell of a lot to send legal publications like the *South African Labour Bulletin* and *Work in Progress* and things like that up to Jeanette and Marius in Botswana. I knew about this and I kept saying to him, 'Alan, they can subscribe. They can pay R12.50 to subscribe for a year. You don't have to bloody well service dead letter boxes and have couriers to do this.'[48]

Barbara Hogan, who worked directly with the Schoons in an ANC cell, and was actively organising support for trade unions inside South Africa, was intensely aware of the fact that her connection to the Schoons put both herself and her organisations at risk:

> That bedevilled all our politics during that period, because just a simple linkage to the ANC could put you in jail and put your organisation that you were working with in huge jeopardy. So there had to be real reasons why you were linked and there was a lot of emphasis within the ANC at that stage on MK networks. I said specifically that I don't want to be in MK because I knew that that was a shortcut to demolish any organisational base that was political because they just had to prove an MK connection and then just wipe out the organisation. And I wasn't convinced that armed struggle was the route that was going to rescue us. I wasn't hostile to it, but I still believed that organisation was more important.[49]

Barbara Hogan, Alan Fine and other comrades of the Schoons who remained in South Africa when others went into exile found themselves in a difficult predicament. On the one hand, the political initiatives they were engaged in had been developed largely independently of the ANC and had value in and of themselves. On the other hand, because they were eager to connect their efforts to the larger movement (led by the ANC), they found it worthwhile to sustain a connection to the Schoons. However, this connection caused them to be increasingly at risk of being implicated – either directly or by association – in the armed struggle.

According to Heinz Klug, there is a hard and fast line between political work and engaging in violence. 'We support the armed struggle, yes. But we support it *politically, unless we're actually combatants.*'[50] However, in practice, the line between the two is far from being so clear. In Barbara Hogan's case, she found it virtually impossible to maintain a clean separation from the armed struggle. Marius Schoon was one person who was entirely unwilling to accept her position.

> I think Marius was [involved in MK] but I declined to engage in that manner ... and yet he sent me a letter via dead letter boxes and asked me to set up a network of safe houses for MK people. I was *very* angry because he'd understood that that was a no-go for me.[51]

Why would Marius Schoon so flagrantly disregard Barbara Hogan's wishes in the way that she describes? Furthermore, what was his role within MK, such that he felt the need to pressure a comrade to assist in this way? Just because Schoon asked Hogan to set up 'a network of safe houses for MK people', doesn't mean that such a network ever existed, linked to Marius Schoon. It is not even clear that anyone else, other than Hogan, was ever asked the same question by Marius Schoon.

Cedric de Beer made several trips to Botswana while the Schoons were living there and regularly visited their home. On one of these trips, in 1978, De Beer had lunch at the Schoons' house. 'It was on this occasion that Schoon tried to recruit me to do work for him,' he says. They went on a drive together to a store, and Marius made his pitch. While De Beer does not elaborate on the specifics of the 'work' that Marius Schoon wanted him to do, the reply was, 'I was myself not prepared to engage in acts of violence.'[52]

There are a few factors that at least hint at the possibility that Marius Schoon was engaged in MK while living in Botswana. For example, Mike Kahn claimed that 'I didn't store stuff for them; I wasn't asked to.'[53] Now, one possible meaning of the phrase 'store stuff' could refer to weapons. Of course, on the other hand, 'stuff' could also be pamphlets or other printed material. Another grey area has to do with military training. The direct superior to the Schoons, Mac Maharaj, testified to the TRC that Marius *was* sent for military training. However, Maharaj clarified that this was only a brief course and solely focused on self-defence; it was of no more significance than the ordinary white South African learning to shoot a gun. Based on his experience in the camps in Angola, Barry Gilder affirms that some ANC members were sent to Angola for 'crash courses'. 'So, people – usually from the frontline or people who were going to be sent back into the country soon – would come to Angola for very short crash courses, maybe for a few weeks or so.'[54] Gilder further explained that these 'crash courses' were focused on self-defence. Still, the question remains as to why Marius Schoon was chosen – in particular – to go to Angola for one of these courses.

To complicate matters further, even if it appears likely that Marius Schoon was, in one form or another, involved in military activities, this does not necessarily mean that Jeanette was also in MK. Judy Seidman confidently declared, 'I'm pretty sure Marius had direct contacts with MK when he was in Botswana.' However, even though Jenny Schoon was active both within the ANC and SACP, nonetheless Seidman's 'impression was that Jenny did not have military training and was probably not involved in military structures. I could be wrong about that.'[55]

This clear demarcation between the role of Marius Schoon and the role of his wife Jeanette is a continual theme, both among friends and comrades, as well as from the perspective of the security police and the courts. This repeated emphasis on the difference between the two political positions and activities could simply be a substantive reflection of the reality on the ground, or could be a subtle form of sexism, or could be merely subterfuge. As Judy Seidman explains, many women who were active in the ANC – and MK – used their status as wives as a type of cover story. 'Many of us have commented over the years that the standard cover for women was "it's my husband". And it helped. I mean, you can claim all sorts of things for your husband.'[56] Seen from this angle, it is possible to imagine that Jeanette Schoon consciously cultivated an image of herself as being somehow less 'active' or less 'radical' than her husband, since being seen as the less militant participant of the couple would allow her significantly more room to manoeuvre than Marius, who was always in the spotlight and always targeted.

Then again, spiralling back to the beginning, even though Judy Seidman *was* certain that Marius was, in some sense, involved with MK, she nonetheless expressed some doubt as to whether he 'was working with MK *directly* when he was in Botswana'. What does it mean to work *indirectly* with MK? Seidman knew that Marius Schoon owned a gun, as she was the person whom he chose to give it to, right before heading to the airport to leave Botswana for the last time. However, this, for Seidman, was not evidence of being involved with MK. 'I'm sure he had the gun because he was under threat. There's no question about that.'[57] Fair enough. Still, what if Marius Schoon was involved in MK, but not in a way that required him to directly handle or use weapons?

As a final complication, while several comrades speculate on the degree of Marius's participation in MK, there are other comrades of the Schoons who entirely dispute this claim. Patrick Fitzgerald categorically insists that 'Marius had absolutely nothing – *nothing* – to do with anything even *approaching* MK'.[58] Fitzgerald is not simply guessing; he's basing his declaration on an extensive and intimate engagement with the Schoons during this period. 'I lived in their pocket. I ate dinner with them three, four, five days of the week. There was hardly a day I wasn't with them. I was privy to Marius's deepest confessions.'[59]

Part of what makes analysing the Schoons' (or anyone else's) involvement with the armed struggle so clunky and messy is that there were many ways in which a person might assist in the military work of the ANC, without themselves committing a single act of violence. This is a point that pacifists and police can easily agree on. While Heinz Klug acknowledges that there were lots of different ways that people could participate in the armed struggle – even 'indirectly' – Klug stridently insists on drawing clear distinctions between combatants and supporters:

> Say the guy that scribbles ANC on his mug at work, is he an armed combatant?[60] You could say he's a supporter. The moment you are in an ANC structure, does that make you a combatant? What if

you've never had military training? What if you are never asked to do military activity? It gets greyer because obviously a guerrilla movement operates in ways that are not explicitly political, in that people travel without bearing their arms publicly, they live in civilian houses, they aren't wearing uniforms. Are they still combatants? The Geneva Convention says yes, as long as they are carrying weapons; even if they are just travelling through the bush on their way somewhere, they are combatants. They don't have to be in battle. But there's still a big difference between that and an ANC member who says, 'I support the armed struggle.'[61]

In Klug's framework, had Barbara Hogan agreed to house MK combatants, then she could reasonably be considered a combatant herself, even if she never received military training or operated any form of weaponry. Mike Kahn, who *did* agree to offer his home as a 'safe house' for MK, does not quite regard himself as a soldier. 'We would probably not be regarded as fully fledged MK people. I did not take that oath. Not that it was ever asked. But I did not.' Nonetheless, Kahn accepted without reservation that opening his home to MK meant 'if a grenade had been tossed into the house, we would've gone alongside them. I think there were quite a large number of people in that position.'[62] Kahn seems to have embraced the fact that he put his – and his family's – life at risk. Hogan refused. But, does it matter simply that she was *asked* to do something of a military nature? What is at stake in drawing these distinctions between various levels of engagement in the armed struggle was quite simply life and death. As Mike Kahn says, with a soldier's resignation, 'Are you a combatant or not? If you're a combatant, then combatants kill one another in wartime. And that's that.'[63]

Heinz Klug was also active in the SNS and also received military training in Angola, so, based on his own definition, he accepts that he could be considered a combatant. Nonetheless, at the end of the day, Klug would rather be understood as having been a member of the political underground, and not a soldier. In fact, even though Klug is considered an MK veteran by the ANC government, he consciously refuses to draw a pension as a veteran. There are many motivations for this decision, not the least being that Klug has been living for many years in the United States, with a stable career as a law professor, and therefore has no need for the pension. However, on the philosophical level, Klug is opposed to being seen as an MK member, because he is opposed to the entire struggle against apartheid being collapsed under the banner of war.

> The value that the ANC in exile actually provided *was political*. It wasn't military. The military stuff was, as we saw it, armed propaganda. When they blew up SASOL,[64] that was great, everybody in Soweto could see the smoke rising. But ... to just collapse it all into a military structure, or a clear command that gave instructions all the way down, actually doesn't understand what was going on.[65]

Heinz Klug's emphatic defence of political struggle as the most important aspect of the ANC in exile affirms – in an upside-down kind of way – some of the critique waged by the Marxist Workers' Tendency. For example, Paula Ensor believed that one of the problems with the strong focus on armed struggle was that this created a militaristic climate within the ANC, in terms of the ways in which political debate and disagreements were handled. 'I mean arguing your position in the ANC in exile was never going to work because it was a very ossified, very centralised and bureaucratic operation. I mean the corruption was already evident in 1969. So, working in the ANC in exile was very difficult.'[66] To some extent, Heinz Klug echoes this sentiment, raising concerns about how military terminology permeated non-military political work, such that the distinction between the two was no longer visible:

> They used to train people in what was called MCW, Military Combat Work. That was underground work. How to set up dead letter boxes, how to communicate with code, and so forth. I thought it was a mistake to call it 'Military Combat Work'. That was an old Soviet term that was being used. We were using that for political purposes; not to move guns. You use those skills when you use guns, too – granted. But there is a line there somewhere, and I think it's quite important to hold that line. Otherwise, you can say, 'You oppose the government? And there are people out there with arms? So, you are all armed.' That's what it becomes, very quickly.[67]

In Judy Seidman's memory, the structures of command within the ANC were more nuanced than a simple military hierarchy. 'The issues around safety and security were pretty absolute. I mean, you followed orders.'[68] However, in defiance of Ensor's characterisations, Seidman stoutly defends the culture of discussion and debate within the ANC:

> One of the things that I admired about the ANC at that time was that despite [the necessary hierarchy around safety] we were very proud of the fact that people would discuss things. You challenged things if you didn't agree with them. If it was an intellectual question or a theoretical question or principle question, you could challenge it, you could fight over it, you could scream with each other. That was expected actually. When they had those conferences, they circulated the papers for months in advance and expected people to talk about them.[69]

Whether one agrees with Ensor (that the ANC stifled debate) or with Seidman (that the debate was vibrant) the important thing is that one way or another, debate definitely happened. Questions related to the armed struggle, including who and who was not involved, and where the lines exist between revolutionary politics and violence, were always contested, and these contestations were not easily resolved. As much as both the apartheid state and certain members of the ANC attempted to establish hard and fast categories, such as 'combatant' or 'legitimate target', the practical reality of these categories, on a daily basis, was far from clear cut.

# 5 | Exposing Craig Williamson

Above and beyond the general difficulties and complications of doing underground work for the ANC, in the Schoons' specific case, as Glenn Moss scathingly – and correctly – says,

> The damn problem with their network was that it was heavily infiltrated. It was not just Williamson and Edwards; everybody who went to Botswana to meet with them [the Schoons], something happened to them afterwards. People went there just to visit them as friends and were asked to bring back a document or something like that and they always got stopped at the border and searched ... people who touched that network would get into serious trouble.[1]

Barbara Hogan echoes Moss's sentiments regarding the Schoons' network, of which she herself was a member. Hogan's description of how she ended up working with the Schoons in this way is gripping, in that it reveals her deep misgivings and regrets:

> Mac recommended that I be shifted to the Botswana operation because Jenny and Marius were there. It was understood that I would work with the white left on shifting them to a Congress position. The white left punched above its weight at that stage because of its privileged position ... I was unhappy about going to Botswana, although I loved Jenny and Marius. I thought it was

a very leaky operation. Jenny and Marius weren't very good at managing security. The people who were messengers for them were security police. In actual fact, the work I did with Jenny and Marius I regard as the least important. My main interest was to look at how you organise the unemployed, and I was working with the unions down in East London.[2]

It is interesting that Hogan, a lifelong supporter of the ANC, describes her work with the Schoons as the 'least important' that she did during that period. If Hogan's priorities were to organise the unemployed and help build trade unions, was it worth the risk involved to send coded messages via dead letter boxes and couriers across the border, letting the Schoons (and the ANC, by extension) know about these activities?

Since both Craig Williamson and Karl Edwards have now definitively confessed to their roles as infiltrators, it is now possible to make these assertions without any hesitation.[3] But, what did people understand — or suspect — of this infiltration at the time? It is important to acknowledge that there were widespread suspicions regarding both Williamson and Edwards throughout the 1970s by those who knew them closely. To understand the nature and the significance of the security police's successful infiltration of a small group of the ANC's underground, it is necessary to understand the ways in which suspicions were raised over the years, and why more wasn't done to neutralise effectively the undercover police operatives within the underground.

As both Williamson and Edwards began their careers as undercover policemen within Nusas, the first people to grow suspicious of them were within the leadership of Nusas. While many people expressed doubts about Williamson, according to Moss, this was tempered by the fact that 'there were concerns and suspicions about lots of people, many of whom probably weren't spies'. However, the discomfort around Williamson always ran deeper than simple rumour. 'There were sufficient concerns to say that he shouldn't be allowed access to anything sensitive, clandestine or unlawful. That was a very consistent position, right from the early 1970s.'[4]

In an affidavit written in support of a lawsuit filed by Barbara Hogan against the Commissioner of Prisons Cedric de Beer describes his initial misgivings about Edwards while in Nusas, and offers an explanation as to why he did nothing about his misgivings, at first:

> It was only quite late in 1975 that I became aware of the fact that [Edwards] too had been in the police force. This began to look like too much of a coincidence, that two police officers should find their way onto the Nusas head office staff. However, they were both friends and colleagues of mine, and the suspicion did not really develop at this stage.[5]

De Beer's affidavit continues for nearly 50 pages and offers multiple glimpses into moments where something might have been done to expose Williamson and Edwards, and again and again either nothing at all or very minimal hesitant steps were taken to address the mounting evidence of infiltration. De Beer is at the centre of many of these critical moments, trapped between being a close colleague of Edwards (even a friend) and his own increasingly coherent description of Edwards' suspicious activities. De Beer's affidavit offers a concise and compelling description of why Edwards was a successful infiltrator of the white left in South Africa:

> Edwards has a peculiar charisma, and exercised an almost hypnotic charm over many people, particularly naïve young girls, of whom he seduced a great number. He also had an ability to portray himself as a fool and buffoon (the drunken life and soul of the party) which made people take him less seriously than they ought. Using both these characteristics, he recruited himself a loyal army of operators and friends.[6]

What is striking about De Beer's depiction here is that it presents the drunken foolishness of a police officer as a 'peculiar charisma', a strategic advantage for gaining the confidence of young radical white people. Another important piece of De Beer's analysis was his attention to the way that Edwards successfully exploited 'the sense of irrelevance' of the white left. 'All of this would be done with an excess of clandestine aura and was achieved by playing on the sense of irrelevance suffered by many young white radicals, their adventurism.'[7] In other words, as young white radicals felt that their previous political work was irrelevant, and actively sought out a politics with 'an excess of clandestine aura', they inadvertently placed themselves within a domain that the security police were quite comfortable with. If the homespun Marxists of the early 1970s had carried on along roughly the same political trajectory, would it have been possible for men like Karl Edwards to infiltrate successfully?

A critical component of Williamson and Edwards' success was their combined capacity to control a significant amount of anti-apartheid funds. The infiltration of IUEF would have been far less devastating if Karl Edwards and other undercover police had not stayed behind, playing the role of directly distributing the funds. Edwards used money to gain trust and loyalty from people who might otherwise have been expected to raise legitimate concerns about him. There were multiple organisational avenues for the security police to channel money in this way.

Karl Edwards' primary project was the EDA, which grew out of a wing of Nusas called Envirac, and became an independent entity in May of 1976.[8] As has been mentioned already, Edwards' knowledge of ecology and commitment to environmentalism were genuine. According to Patrick Fitzgerald, 'Edwards' cover as a progressive ecologist was much more credible than Craig's, who seemed to have no cover at all.'[9] Cedric de Beer also played an active role within Envirac, throughout the life of the organisation. In 1978:

> Tensions grew within EDA as Edwards did less and less work. Robert Berold, Dick Cloete and myself [De Beer] decided that we would try to get him to leave the organisation. At the end of 1978 Edwards disappeared without notice for about six weeks. When he returned, there began a series of meetings which took place over a couple of months. Finally, in March or April 1979 he resigned.[10]

In addition to simply doing 'less and less work', another key reason that Edwards was forced out of EDA was that he was found to have embezzled R50 000 from the organisation, which had been donated by the World University Service. Even as Edwards was viewed with increasing disdain and doubt by his colleagues in EDA, they nonetheless remained hesitant to confront or expose him directly.

Then in May 1978, Robert Berold, who worked with me in EDA, and whose judgement I trust, said to me that he felt that Edwards was working either for the ANC or for the police. He had no facts to go on, only intuition. This was another confirmation of my suspicions. My concern became something of an obsession.[11]

Given that Edwards was, in effect, working for *both* the ANC and the police, Berold's intuition was remarkably clear. As the evidence mounted, pointing more and more clearly to Edwards being an agent, De Beer continued to avoid directly confronting him, despite his suspicions having become 'something of an obsession'.

Continuing into 1979, still no one directly confronted Edwards inside South Africa. Even after Edwards was essentially forced out of EDA, he retained his position as an undercover agent. In fact, as late as September 1979, Cedric de Beer and Auret van Heerden were not yet prepared to confront Edwards or Williamson directly. In light of all of the moments along the way where people who knew Edwards well had good reasons not to trust him – and as it was always known that Edwards worked closely with Williamson – it is remarkable that nothing substantial was ever done to get in their way, at least not from those still inside South Africa.

## Geneva: rumour-mongering

> Eriksson's actions suggest to us that he was at this point more eager to quell rumours about Williamson than to see instituted any thorough investigation or inquiry.
>
> — International University Exchange Fund,
> Report of the Commission of Inquiry

Given the extent to which Karl Edwards and Craig Williamson were treated with suspicion and mistrust by anti-apartheid activists, the IUEF's commission of inquiry understandably dedicated a substantial amount of attention towards understanding how Williamson had gained – and maintained – the trust of Lars-Gunnar Eriksson for so long. Particularly now, in the contemporary political climate in South Africa, testimonials of suspicions about Williamson ought to be interrogated carefully, as the benefit of hindsight encourages everyone to distance themselves from Craig Williamson. To properly assess the damage that Williamson caused, it is important to face soberly the fact that a great many people *did* trust him, and to a considerable degree, for a number of years. Nonetheless, it is also important to stress that Lars-Gunnar Eriksson was warned about Craig Williamson, and repeatedly, over the years. In addition, the commission found that the ANC considered Williamson to be important enough to their *own* intelligence-gathering efforts that they were hesitant about taking a strong stance against him, despite whatever misgivings they may have felt about him.

As soon as Craig Williamson was hired, the South African Council of Churches 'sent warnings to the IUEF through a South African expatriate, Duncan Innes'. Innes had been a president of Nusas in 1969 and therefore would have been aware of suspicions circulating about Williamson within Nusas. Eriksson did not take this warning seriously. Duncan Innes again tried to warn Eriksson, in 1978, and was told that Eriksson would check in with Karel Tip about these concerns. Remember that Karel Tip (another ex-president of Nusas) had initially encouraged Williamson and Eriksson to meet. For reasons that are not entirely clear, 'Innes accepted that a clearance from Tip would be satisfactory'.[12] After Karel Tip sent word that he considered Williamson to be trustworthy, Eriksson decided that Innes's concerns were simply 'rumour-mongering'.[13] In addition to these warnings from Innes and the churches, a representative of the Zimbabwe African National Union (Zanu) told the commission that the organisation had been hinting to Eriksson that Williamson was an agent for some time. 'The Zimbabwe African National Union (Zanu) began investigating Williamson in 1978. Its concern had been aroused when it learnt that some information discussed only with the IUEF had reached Salisbury.'[14] The following year, Dr Mutumbuka, from Zanu

> warned Eriksson about Williamson on two levels: (a) that ZANU were unhappy that the IUEF was getting too involved in ANC work and was employing an ostensible ANC supporter, Williamson, in a high post; (b) that Williamson was a BOSS [Bureau of State Security] agent ... Dr. Mutumbuka gave Eriksson an ultimatum – that unless something was done about Williamson, ZANU would

find it difficult to work with the IUEF because security was more important to it than money. Dr. Mutumbuka felt that in this discussion, Eriksson was not prepared to look at Williamson objectively.[15]

Since Eriksson had been persuaded – by Williamson – to throw his support behind the African National Congress, logically the ANC would have been the most influential source to warn Eriksson of the dangers of working with Craig Williamson. Indeed, the strongest warning came to Eriksson because of Williamson's interactions with the ANC. Based on interactions between Williamson and the ANC in Lusaka, the Swedes had become concerned. Due to information given to the Swedes by the ANC, Thord Palmlund, Sweden's secretary of state for foreign affairs, was worried enough to reach out to Eriksson directly.[16] Palmlund sent a letter to Eriksson outlining his concerns. However, when Eriksson followed up on the warning, by scheduling a meeting with Thomas Nkobi, who was at the time the treasurer-general of the ANC, Nkobi downplayed any concerns as 'an unfortunate misunderstanding'. According to Eriksson, Nkobi 'cleared' Williamson 'in a quite unambiguous way'.[17] The ANC had reasons for treading carefully regarding Williamson and shielding him from accusations, even if they were simultaneously keeping him at arm's length. On the one hand, the commission found that

> the ANC headquarters itself remained suspicious about, and cautious in its dealing with, Williamson. His requests, from 1977 on, to join the ANC, were all rebuffed. The ANC's suspicions of Williamson persisted through 1978 and 1979. In his attempt to penetrate the ANC he began 'punching at different spots' and was, the ANC felt, 'pushing too hard' to establish his credibility. The ANC remained, therefore, hesitant either to confirm or dispel the rumours about Williamson.[18]

This all sounds quite plausible, except for the last sentence, which feels jarring and out of place. If the ANC had been rebuffing Craig Williamson's advances for years, why would that make them hesitant to convey their suspicions to Lars-Gunnar Eriksson? Intriguingly, the commission of inquiry believed that 'the ANC "went along" with Williamson in part because the information which Williamson supplied them with, especially about alleged IUEF support for the Pan-African[ist] Congress (PAC) and the ANC dissidents, was useful to them'.[19] In fact, from a certain perspective, rather than understanding the ANC as 'rebuffing' Williamson's advances, it may make more sense to understand these moments in terms of the ANC's desire shrewdly to steer Williamson in directions that would be most useful for them. For example,

> In November 1979, Williamson proposed to the ANC that he work out of the Lusaka office of the IUEF so that he could become more involved in the internal work of the ANC. The ANC replied that from its point of view, it would be better if he remained in Geneva and sent occasional reports as he had been doing.[20]

In other words, to the extent that the ANC understood that Craig Williamson was an undercover agent, they nonetheless strategically calculated that the benefits of gleaning intelligence from him (for their own 'counter-insurgency' measures, of sorts) outweighed whatever risks were associated with allowing him to continue to operate as a spy. According to the commission:

> The ANC did not want to tell Williamson there were doubts about his real identity and roles because it would spoil this important operation of establishing exactly how information networks of which Williamson was a part were working.[21]

Perhaps it goes without saying, but the commission of inquiry was deeply disappointed by Lars-Gunnar Eriksson's failure to take any further precautionary steps in response to the multiple warnings that he received regarding Williamson over the years. In particular, the commission was opposed to Eriksson's pleas for more concrete evidence against Williamson, which would have been difficult for any of the actors in question to provide. The refusal to act on 'rumours'

> seems inappropriate in the circumstances. When a second warning came from a different source, Eriksson could have been expected

to take decisive action to ascertain the truth of the warnings, or if he was not convinced by them, to ease Williamson out to the edge of the organisation, to a position in which he could have no access to further information likely to be of interest to the South African Government; even this was not done.[22]

## Botswana: exposing Edwards and Williamson

From the moment that he set foot in Botswana, Heinz Klug was immediately suspicious of Edwards and Williamson. Even though Klug took the Sana position on the explicit advice of the ANC, he nonetheless notified Lusaka of his concerns right away. 'In this report I said honestly that before coming I had consulted with some people, and some people said that Zack (the nickname for Karl Edwards) was definitely a policeman. Williamson, who knows, but there's suspicions.'[23] However, the ANC declined to take any action against Williamson, or to pass on Klug's concerns to the IUEF. Some people remain furious about the ANC's unwillingness to directly expose Williamson. From Glenn Moss's perspective,

> the ANC absolutely refused to hear that Williamson was a security risk and he was supported and protected by Ronnie Kasrils, Mac Maharaj, Reg September, the Pahads, etc. The ANC has a hell of a lot to answer for in regard to Williamson and those of us who were trying to at least say there are questions got hammered for it. We got turned into demons, had support cut and things like that.[24]

While the exile leadership in London quietly acquiesced to Craig Williamson's purported role (as a member of an ANC cell), on the ground in Gaborone, ANC comrades such as Heinz Klug had to figure out how to respond to a situation that they knew was fishy, at best.

Right from the start, Heinz Klug had an uncomfortable feeling about sending Sana material to Williamson in Geneva.

> Craig said to us, 'You write things up, and send us the information.' We thought, So that's what is going on. If he's working for

the other side, he's going to take the information we give him, and share it with them. We were supposed to use our illegal contacts, to get information on what's going on inside South Africa.[25]

In addition, Karl Edwards acted as a courier for communications between this group of white radicals in Botswana (Klug, the Schoons, Fitzgerald) and white leftists still inside South Africa. Given the nature of underground work of this kind, it is impossible to know precisely how often Edwards was used as a courier or the nature of the messages. While Edwards likely exaggerated the importance of his role as a courier, none of the members of the Schoons' cell deny that he actively played this role, for a period. However, in 1979, the group began to be suspicious of Edwards. As Klug remembers it,

> Karl at one point came to Botswana, and we noticed that he was very nervous. He wouldn't get out of the car and come into the house. He drove up and asked us to come out to talk to us. He said, 'Where's the stuff? You guys are supposed to be supplying information.' He wanted us to help him recruit people inside South Africa. We said, 'No, don't worry. No, thank you.' Then, at another point, he sent an African guy, who came up in a car from South Africa, with some bullshit information, claiming it was from 'the network we're building'. We realised what was going on ... So, part of my task, when I went into the country in late 1979, was to contact people and say, 'If Edwards comes around, just say "no, thank you." It's not from me. Cut that line.'[26]

As it began to feel increasingly clear that Edwards was dangerous, 'the four of us came up with a strategy (which the ANC approved) to try to work out whether Karl Edwards is a policeman.'[27] The Sana plan to expose Karl Edwards was ingenious, but also quite complicated. Therefore, it is worth allowing Klug to recount the full story, in detail:

> The next thing we did is we said to Edwards, 'You were nervous when you came here, and we're very worried about things as well.' Edwards said, 'Oh, yes, let's set up a dead letter box, at the border.' We looked at that and thought, Fuck, when they get tired of us,

they're just going to grab us there one day. Not so sure about that, but we're going to play the game, and this is an opportunity for us. What we did – myself and Patrick – in the middle of the day, we went out to the dam, near the border with South Africa. We took a camera, and very ostentatiously – because we knew we were being watched – we took photos as if I'm photographing down to where the dead letter box would be. Then I sent a long description to Edwards, attached to what supposedly were the photos, except there were none, because the camera was empty. I mailed that to the box number in South Africa, which we were using to communicate with Edwards. This black guy came to us and said, 'We received the letter, but where's the photos?' We had said in the letter that the photos were under separate cover. So, we said to him, 'Oh fuck, the photos must have been gotten by the security police. Just don't touch this; this is dangerous.' Then we got a message back that said it couldn't possibly be the police. Couldn't possibly be? How could you be so fucking confident that it couldn't be in the hands of the security police? When that happened, I phoned Williamson in Geneva. I said, 'This is a big problem. We don't know what's going on with Karl. We sent the stuff in, and some of it didn't arrive, so we're convinced that the security police must be in to it.' Williamson responded, 'You guys are confused. Karl is absolutely fine. There's no question that Karl's okay.' Again, that's not the response that someone has in these networks. If somebody says there's a problem, you worry. Two and two is making five here. So, we reported all of this to Lusaka. We said that Edwards is definitely a spy, and that we're not sure about Williamson, but he isn't acting right. The IUEF immediately cut our money. Williamson immediately offered Patrick and I full scholarships from the IUEF, anywhere in the world. We just said, 'No, thank you, we're fine here in Botswana.' So, he was trying to close us down. But that just made us more suspicious.[28]

Having trapped Edwards and Williamson in this elaborate ruse, Klug and his comrades were certain that they had effectively proven that the two men were undercover police officers. The ruse with the dead letter box and the photos was in October or November 1979, and Williamson was exposed in January 1980.

> Now, whether it's because we supplied information, or because of his story that it was a guy in London, whatever the reason, he ran. Now, does he believe that we were part of his exposure? I think so. In fact, as soon as he ran, we phoned the newspapers in Johannesburg, and we said, 'And Karl Edwards.' So, we did blow Karl Edwards from Botswana.[29]

In Judy Seidman's memory, there is no doubt that 'Jenny and Marius were instrumental in exposing him. They talked about that.' Furthermore, in the days after having exposed Williamson, Seidman heard 'stories about people being tailed, Marius and Jenny and one or two other people who were involved in exposing Williamson, and that they were actually scared for their lives'.[30] According to Heinz Klug, things could easily have been the other way around. That is, it could very well have been the case that Williamson was the one who was scared for his life, rather than the Schoons and their comrades:

> In 1979, we asked Williamson to come to Botswana. We wanted to grab him; the ANC wanted to grab him and figure out what the fuck was going on. He promised he was going to come in the future, and he never came. At the same time, Lusaka tried to get him to come there, and he never came. Williamson must have had indications that there were suspicions.[31]

In the immediate aftermath, at least, there was no evidence of Williamson facing any great (or small) difficulty from having been exposed as a spy. His co-conspirator, Karl Edwards, 'duck[ed] and dive[d] for a week or two',[32] immediately after word came out that Williamson was a spy, but also seemed to fare relatively well, all things considered.

## Geneva: the end of the game

> Then, suddenly he confessed:
> 'I've been a member of the SA Police since 1968 – and I still am.'

He explained he was not a member of BOSS.

'We're not as bad as you think. The BOSS – they're lunatics and prejudiced people. We're different. We police do a lot for blacks and people like you should understand.'

Williamson said that there was 'one common enemy: the Communist Party'. He also confessed he was a secret member of the SA Communist Party, as a spy.

— Hugh Lewin and Walter Schwarz, 'How Spy was "Blown"'

The story of Craig Williamson's exposure as an undercover agent is the stuff of spy novels, full of confusing twists and inexplicable missteps by all involved. The whole drama unfolded over a period of weeks, from just before the new year until 23 January 1980. Of course there are many different versions of this story, depending on who is telling it and why. Perhaps the most thorough account of Williamson's last days at the IUEF is the one produced by the Commission of Inquiry into the Espionage Activities of the South African Government in the International University Exchange Fund, which was convened by the board of the IUEF in the aftermath of Williamson's exposure. While this report still leaves many gaps in details and unanswered questions, it is still quite useful, because the commission not only attempted to reconstruct the story, but also aimed to analyse it. Therefore, the account that follows here will draw heavily on the Report of the Commission of Inquiry.

Williamson and his wife went away for the holidays to London. While they were away, on 30 December 1979, the British left-leaning newspaper *The Observer* published an extended exposé from Arthur McGiven, an ex-member of BOSS. When McGiven defected from BOSS, he smuggled out a large pile of documents, which he handed over to *The Observer* to substantiate his story. The article didn't mention Williamson or the IUEF explicitly. However, McGiven did explain that he had entered the security services at virtually the same time as Craig Williamson when both were officially students at the University of the Witwatersrand. Furthermore, according to *The Observer*, 'From 1976 he worked in the section [of BOSS] dealing with South African and overseas student groups',[33] with a particular focus on white groups. Obviously, Craig Williamson and Arthur McGiven knew one another, and Williamson would have immediately understood that McGiven had quite in-depth and specific information relating to his own role as an undercover agent.³⁴ So, aware that his cover could soon be blown, Williamson began taking steps to protect himself.

On 2 January 1980, Piers Campbell, 'Projects Officer' for the IUEF, met Craig Williamson at Heathrow airport and the two flew back together to Geneva. Over the next couple of days Williamson and Eriksson met to discuss Williamson's upcoming work for the organisation. This included an extended trip to Africa, planned to begin on 16 January. On 5 January, a Saturday, Campbell saw Craig Williamson in the IUEF office and noted that he had a suitcase with him. Williamson explained that the suitcase was full of documents that he was 'returning' to the office, although in hindsight it seems obvious that exactly the opposite was true, as the IUEF later learned that a large number of documents had been stolen by Williamson. The following day, Sunday, 6 January, a second article was published in *The Observer*. Under the headline 'The British Targets of Boss', McGiven explicitly mentioned the IUEF, but again didn't explicitly state that the organisation had been infiltrated by a South African agent. Rather, McGiven outlined the reasons why the IUEF was a cause for concern for the bureau.

> The involvement of foreigners in the affairs of South Africa's blacks is a constant source of suspicion and irritation, not least because the motives behind it are totally incomprehensible to the elite ... IUEF funds played a major role in the projects set up by the Black Consciousness Movement, which in turn helped develop a new mood of independence and self-pride amongst blacks ... Attempts have also been made to find out who is 'behind' the IUEF, starting with the CIA, and moving on to the Socialist International.³⁵

Even though Williamson had not yet been directly exposed as a spy, the publication of McGiven's article clearly escalated Williamson's concerns, as he began to take increasingly drastic steps. On Monday, 7 January,

> Campbell found in the office a note from Williamson saying that his wife Ingrid was sick and that he had gone to London. That evening, Williamson called Campbell to say that his wife had had

a nervous breakdown and had returned to South Africa and that he was shaken and being pursued by BOSS agents in connection with a recent escape from Pretoria Central, which he claimed to have assisted.[36]

After this quite bizarre communication, the IUEF received no further news from Williamson for the rest of the week. On Saturday, 12 January, Eriksson met with Campbell in Geneva. 'Both were worried by Williamson's silence.'[37] Eriksson called both the IUEF office in London and also Hugh Lewin, but neither had heard from Williamson. The following day, Sunday, 13 January, *The Observer* printed a rebuttal letter to the editor, from Lars-Gunnar Eriksson. In what is now a painfully stark moment of irony, Eriksson defended the IUEF against what he saw as the 'rumour and innuendo' that was being spread by the South African government, 'to which your article may have inadvertently given credence'. Most specifically, Eriksson was insulted by the insinuation that the IUEF was somehow a front for some other organisation, such as the CIA or the Socialist International. Eriksson insisted that the sources of the IUEF's funds were made publicly available. Further, Eriksson claimed that a copy of the IUEF's audited accounts had been 'stolen' by the South African government in 1978. This theft was not presented as evidence that the South Africans had infiltrated the IUEF, but rather that the government's fears regarding who might be 'behind' the IUEF were clearly baseless. Eriksson concluded his letter by confidently declaring that the IUEF was 'a fully autonomous and responsible organization and its activities are in no way directed or manipulated by any other governmental or political body'.[38] Beyond being embarrassing in hindsight, it is illuminating that Eriksson saw fit to go out of his way to draft this letter to the editor, even in the midst of the collapse of his relationship with Craig Williamson. Eriksson's insistence that his organisation was 'in no way directed or manipulated' serves as a startling indicator of just how deeply he had placed his trust in Craig Williamson.

On Monday, 14 January, Williamson called Campbell and said he was 'too frightened to come to Geneva',[39] but wanted to meet with Eriksson and Campbell somewhere outside Switzerland. The following day, Williamson called Eriksson and said that he 'did not want to come to Geneva then or ever again. He sounded confused', and again asked to meet somewhere else, such as Frankfurt. Eriksson offered to meet in Zurich, and Williamson 'agreed unhappily'.[40]

> [Later that Tuesday] Eriksson and Campbell discovered that Williamson's desk had been cleared out ... It could have been on Saturday January 5, when Campbell saw Williamson in the office with a suitcase ... both Campbell and Eriksson were worried that something was seriously wrong ... Eriksson at that time made joking reference in conversation with Campbell to the possibility that Williamson was a spy.[41]

While they may have joked about it in the moment, according to the commission, 'Both Eriksson and Campbell have said that they did not consider the most likely explanation for Williamson's erratic behavior in the first two weeks of January that he was a South African agent.'[42] On 17 January, Williamson called Eriksson to confirm the meeting. 'He was no longer confused and assured Eriksson he was now "clear".'[43]

On Friday, 18 January, Campbell and Eriksson flew to Zurich. Eriksson went to meet Williamson at the Hotel Central, telling Campbell to call the Swiss police if he hadn't heard anything by 2 pm. The meeting was full of 'random conversation' until Eriksson forced the issue, around 1 pm. Williamson confessed to being a member of the security police and explained how this was different from BOSS. Williamson then tried to persuade Eriksson that the security police were 'trying to do the same as Eriksson himself and that their common enemies were the communists'.[44] Williamson attempted to make a deal, asking Eriksson to allow him six more months within the IUEF, to complete his goal of infiltrating the ANC. Then, Williamson's boss, Brigadier Coetzee, arrived, to further discuss the details of this deal. Coetzee then 'made certain threats, against Eriksson and his family, against the organization'.[45] Eriksson said that he needed more time to think it through. When Eriksson met with Campbell that afternoon, he didn't divulge any of the details of the meeting. They flew back to Geneva separately, but met up again around midnight, after Eriksson had talked through the whole situation with his wife.

Late that night, and into the next morning, Campbell and Eriksson discussed three options: 'playing for time, doing the deal sought, and blowing the story. They chose to blow the story which seemed to require, given how Eriksson had interpreted certain things said in Zurich, that Eriksson's family be taken to a safe place of hiding'.[46] Accordingly, Lars-Gunnar Eriksson spent Saturday, 19 January trying to figure out how to get his family out of the country to safety. Eriksson sought assistance from the Swiss police. However, he did this, first of all, by calling the Swedish Foreign Office and urging them to put pressure on the Swiss authorities. This led to an argument between Eriksson and the Swiss police, which would later sour any attempt to get Williamson arrested in Switzerland. Eriksson and Campbell decided together that the Swiss papers would be unlikely to carry the story and decided instead to get the story published in English. Around 5 pm, Eriksson called Hugh Lewin and asked for advice. Lewin suggested getting the story published in *The Guardian*, aiming for Monday morning, and 'agreed himself, reluctantly, to attend an interview in Paris with *The Guardian*'s correspondent, Walter Schwarz'.[47]

Eriksson and Campbell left Geneva late on the night of 19 January and drove overnight to Paris. They met with the journalists at Charles de Gaulle airport, where they had a three-hour interview. Lewin and Schwarz had the article sent into *The Guardian* by 7 pm. However, '*The Guardian* feared an adverse reaction if the story were a fabrication',[48] and so attempted to verify certain details by reaching out to South African contacts. This slowed down publication of the article; it also meant that Williamson was not directly named in the article, only that an 'alleged spy' had infiltrated a 'relief agency'.[49] The story was published in a paper that did not reach Geneva until Wednesday, 23 January.

The commission concluded that Eriksson and Campbell had made a number of errors over the weekend of 19 January, 'the cumulative effects of which were to allow Williamson to leave Switzerland without being arrested and to render more difficult the handling of the affair by the rest of the IUEF staff and others associated with the organization'.[50] Especially in light of the devastating impact that Williamson had on the anti-apartheid movement in the years after his departure from Geneva, it is especially heartbreaking to realise that there was a possibility of having him indicted for his crimes, rather than allowing him to return home to South Africa.

As it happened, the IUEF seems to have been particularly incompetent in their handling of Williamson's final days in Geneva. The failure to apprehend Williamson in Geneva was not only terrible news for South Africa, but also had a substantial impact on the IUEF and led to its collapse, within a few months of Williamson's departure. According to the commission of inquiry, 'It is possible, even probable, that when [Williamson] realised his return was inevitable, or even imminent, leaving the IUEF in ruins behind him became a goal in itself and this may have been a major guide to his actions in January 1980, but probably not much before then.'[51]

At the meeting in Zurich, Williamson had agreed to return to Geneva on Sunday, 20 January, which he did, and come in to the IUEF office the following day, Monday, in order to return a number of documents. The commission found that Williamson arrived in Geneva confidently, without any apparent concern about being arrested or otherwise sensing he might have been in danger. Throughout his time in Geneva, no one at the IUEF took the necessary steps to have Williamson arrested. Piers Campbell agreed to meet with him on the Monday afternoon:

> alone, against the advice of the criminal lawyer and of other members of the IUEF's staff, on grounds (which he has given variously) of bravado, of a wish to stall to give the police time to act, and of a wish to confirm that Eriksson's account of what happened in Zurich was not fantasy.[52]

Campbell did ask a lawyer to get the police to come to the meeting, but the police refused to come 'until a formal charge had been laid in writing',[53] perhaps simply out of bureaucratic incompetence, or perhaps as a result of their argument with Eriksson a few days before. In any case, the meeting proceeded more or less without substance, and Williamson was able to board a flight to South Africa the following morning (22 January) without any difficulty. By the time the newspaper article reached Geneva, and by the time formal charges were submitted to the Swiss police, on Wednesday, 23 January, Williamson was already back in South Africa.

The IUEF's commission of inquiry reconstructed the events of Williamson's last days in order to make sense both of Williamson's goals in the midst of his exposure, and also in terms of the level of culpability on the part of Eriksson and Campbell, for their failures to stop Craig Williamson from fleeing Switzerland. The commission concluded that it was in the best interests of the IUEF for both Eriksson and Campbell to resign, as they both did. While there were a number of other, longer-term reasons for saying so, the handling of the 'Williamson affair' certainly added to the commission's sense that neither individual was capable of trustworthy leadership. It is striking that Lars-Gunnar Eriksson's letter of resignation, which he submitted on 6 February, long before the commission of inquiry had even begun, completely denied any sense of guilt or remorse.

> I am not resigning out of a feeling of guilt in regard to the Williamson affair nor in regard to some of the more unorthodox financial and administrative procedures and transactions for which I have been responsible. I would like to state unequivocally that all actions I have undertaken or endorsed have been deemed, on the basis of available facts, to be in the best interests of the objectives of the IUEF. My main concern and commitment has been to the liberation of all Africa.[54]

In spite of his confident posture, the fact that Eriksson was susceptible to being blackmailed by the security police remains troubling. While the commission of inquiry was unable to prove, in any concrete sense, precisely what 'dirt' Brigadier Coetzee and Williamson may have had on Eriksson, beyond simply the 'unorthodox financial and administrative procedures' at the IUEF, they were concerned that something else must have existed, in order for Eriksson to be as fearful and hesitant as he was in the moment. Furthermore, the commission was troubled by the fact that Coetzee had taken the quite unusual step of flying to Zurich, and exposing himself to Eriksson, especially in order to attempt to make a deal that was, in the commission's view, 'incomprehensible'.[55] In the analysis of the commission, the presence of Coetzee 'suggests the stakes could have been very high – higher than simply the continuation of Williamson's work in Europe, or the incrimination of Eriksson'.[56] In other words, the decision to send Coetzee to Zurich could indicate that the South African government strongly believed that Craig Williamson was on the verge of a major breakthrough in his undercover work. 'The stakes were high if Williamson genuinely felt he was on the point of breaking through to gaining the full confidence of the ANC, and if Williamson thought Eriksson's support could protect him against exposure.'[57] However, as the commission correctly ascertained, it was also possible that Williamson simply lied to his commanding officer, in order to inflate his own importance, and the importance of his work:

> This is to suppose Williamson was making grave misjudgments, which is not consistent with other evidence that he had a shrewd mind, at least on this level. Desperate that his mission be crowned with the spectacular success of infiltrating the ANC's inner councils Williamson may have deluded himself and his superiors into thinking those few more months were all he needed to 'crack' the ANC.[58]

Along the same lines of analysis, the commission also concluded that it may well have been important for the South Africans to turn the exposure of one of their agents – a failure, by any measure – into a glowing success story, the facts be damned.

> The possibility that the events at Zurich can only be explained in terms of the Special Branch itself requiring a spectacular espionage coup is enhanced by the fact that the South African police do appear to have gone out of their way to present Williamson as a more effective agent than he in fact was.[59]

Indeed, as soon as Williamson landed back home in South Africa, the police and the right-wing media began to tout the incredible successes of Craig Williamson's exploits. Minister of Police Louis le Grange[60] was emphatic:

> The position [Williamson] held not only allowed him to uncover the anti-South African activities of [the IUEF] but also those of the South African Communist Party, the African National Congress and the Pan-Africanist Congress. The information which he collected and channelled is invaluable to the security of South Africa.[61]

Meanwhile, the Afrikaans press reported glowingly that 'his enemies fear and admire him', and that Williamson had negotiated 'on behalf of leftist and communist organisations in Moscow itself'.[62] Throughout the 1980s (and indeed still to this day) Craig Williamson inflated his own importance, and arrogantly proclaimed his own status as a 'super spy,' again and again. This posturing seemed to suit the apartheid state, who played their part in propping Williamson up, offering him a promotion upon his return to South Africa, and giving him considerable latitude to take drastic action against the people he had worked closely with as an undercover agent. As Judy Seidman rightly insists, 'the security police have a long history of exaggerating how effective they were'.[63]

The purpose of analysing the limited success of white radicals to take any concrete action to stop Williamson and Edwards' operation is not to reinforce an exaggerated depiction of the effectiveness of the security police. Rather, it is vital to make sense of the fact that a police infiltration campaign survived as long as it did, in order to understand the weaknesses and blind spots *within the opposition* to apartheid. In particular, it must be acknowledged that – even at the time, and even among close comrades – there were grave misgivings about the effectiveness of the political network that was linked to, or 'run', by Jeanette and Marius Schoon.

Ultimately, whether or not Williamson and his colleagues inflated his importance, there is the undeniable fact that Williamson *did* have a damaging role – both within the IUEF and also within the ANC underground networks connected to the Schoons.

## 6 | The Damage is Done

The commission of inquiry that was convened by the IUEF in order to investigate Williamson's espionage was comprised of an international group of representatives from different governments. In addition to John Wilson, who had been the information officer at the IUEF office in London, the commissioners were:

> Mr. Sundie Kazunga, Special Assistant to the President, Zambia; Mr. Bertil Zachrisson, former Minister of Education and at present M.P., Sweden; and Mr. David MacDonald, former secretary of State and Minister of Communications and M.P., Canada.[1]

The commission met on three separate occasions, between April and June of 1980, in Geneva, London, Lusaka and Gaborone.[2] In addition to reading through whatever files were still held by the IUEF (as Williamson had absconded with a large pile of key documents) the commission also heard testimony from more than 20 different people, including staff of the IUEF, recipients of IUEF funding and representatives from the ANC (Mac Maharaj, Thabo Mbeki and Thomas Nkobi),[3] as well as representatives from Zanu. Arthur McGiven, the BOSS officer who initially exposed Williamson, also gave testimony.

The principal function of the commission of inquiry was to assess 'the extent of damage done to the organization, to the recipients of IUEF assistance, and to IUEF relations with other organizations'[4] as a result of Williamson's infiltration. The commission was concerned not only with the specifics of what Williamson had done (or intended to do), it also sought to probe more deeply into the structural problems within the IUEF, which (a) allowed the organisation to be infiltrated in the first place and (b) allowed a significant portion of well-meaning funds to be diverted and misused by the South African security services. The commission was influenced strongly by the stated concerns of the donors who provided funding for the IUEF. Crucially, since a great deal of the funding for the IUEF came from European governments,[5] there was a concern that widespread distrust of the IUEF as a result of Williamson's infiltration would have a negative impact on all attempts to fund the anti-apartheid movement. 'This was a clear and present danger judging by the various reports appearing in the donor countries.'[6] Therefore, the commission was not concerned simply or solely with the continued survival of the IUEF. In fact, they stated quite bluntly that they were 'of an open mind about the future of the IUEF'. This meant, on the one hand, that the commissioners were 'anxious to help save the organization, if we could, but not at any cost'. Furthermore, the commission 'did not dismiss the possibility that our findings would completely and irretrievably destroy the credibility and reputation of the organization'.[7]

While the commission of inquiry was necessarily focused on what went wrong, they also stressed that the organisation had been doing important work for nearly two decades and that these accomplishments should be acknowledged. One of the sad facts of this story is that Williamson infiltrated the IUEF in large part *because they were so effective*:

> In 1962, when the programme began, the IUEF supported about 20 students. By 1972 the IUEF was supporting more than 1,000 refugee students on scholarships. By the end of the decade the total numbers of IUEF scholarship holders had increased to more than 2,000 African refugees and almost 600 Latin American refugees.[8]

In the years since Williamson's espionage was exposed, most accounts of the IUEF (this one included) focus almost entirely on the last few years, when Williamson was steadily driving the organisation into ruin. It is important to acknowledge that the IUEF had a long history of successfully supporting students and organisations working towards the end of colonial rule in Africa, all of which cannot be properly analysed here. That said, it is also important to acknowledge that the IUEF was long saddled by structural weaknesses, which made it particularly susceptible to infiltration.[9]

The commission determined that Lars-Gunnar Eriksson's tendencies towards a top-down decision-making structure, combined with his willingness to be relatively loose in terms of managing finances, made for a particularly toxic situation, which Williamson effectively exploited.

> There is little doubt in our minds that Eriksson personally and the IUEF as an organization were to some extent vulnerable to pressures because of the way the organization had been run, because of the financial irregularities which had been committed and because the organization was in a very shaky financial position because of administrative overspending ... and a lack of effective financial control.[10]

As had been the case previously at Nusas, Williamson was able to move up within the ranks of IUEF in large part because of his accounting 'skills'. Having entered into an organisation that was struggling financially, Williamson ordered an audit in 1978, which showed that the organisation was in 'serious financial straits'.[11] However, it seems clear that Williamson's aim in having the audit done was not to resolve the difficulties, but rather to exacerbate them. One of the ways that Williamson destabilised the organisation was to play on 'Eriksson's worst instincts'.[12] That is, 'throughout 1978, and particularly at the time of the crisis in late 1978-early 1979, Williamson urged on Eriksson a centralised, authoritarian structure and way of running the organization rather than a more open, collective, democratic approach, with staff committees or unions'.[13] Centralised control of the organisation suited Williamson's needs because it meant that 'secrecy was endemic',[14] and since he had so thoroughly ingratiated himself with Lars-Gunnar Eriksson, his own position was strengthened. For everyone else within the IUEF, this authoritarian climate made for very low morale within the staff, and a high rate of staff turnover. 'About a score of people have left the Geneva office since January 1979.'[15]

Meanwhile, the financial situation continued to deteriorate, which was of course accelerated through Williamson's control of Southern Futures and his use of IUEF funds for security police projects. By 1979, 'the IUEF required an overdraft of more than 1 million francs'.[16] While all of this paints quite a damning picture of Williamson's capacity to sabotage the IUEF, the commission of inquiry speculated that the organisation may well have collapsed even without his intervention.

> The damage Williamson has done to the IUEF itself has been very considerable although, not to give him more credit than he is due, the organization would have been overtaken by a serious financial crisis in 1980 whether he had ever been on its staff or not. To some extent, indeed, Williamson did the IUEF a favor by bringing to a head the accumulated problems of financial mismanagement and administrative incompetence which have hampered the organization from doing effective work in recent years.[17]

It should be remembered that this commission was convened by the IUEF board, and its brief was to analyse the failures *within* the organisation in order to make recommendations for moving forward. Therefore, it is only logical that the report's harshest criticisms were, in some sense, reserved for Eriksson and others at IUEF, rather than Craig Williamson. In addition, Williamson's theft of critical documents during his last days in Geneva seriously curtailed the commission's capacity to analyse concretely the extent to which Williamson abused and stole from the organisation.

> Our work in investigating Southern Futures has been hampered by the fact that the basic documents of Southern Futures, except for a ledger book, have gone missing under circumstances unknown to us. Both Eriksson and Campbell suggested to us that Williamson took the Southern Futures files with him when he left the IUEF office for the last time.[18]

In addition to the limited details that the commission had access to, it seems that they were unaware of the full extent of control Williamson had over this secret fund. The commission's assessment of the problems with Southern Futures was based on testimony from Lars-Gunnar Eriksson.

Eriksson insisted that structures such as Southern Futures were the way that 'this work *had* to be done'.[19] The commission disagreed entirely. In addition, the commission concluded that 'Campbell was not just a functionary keeping the Southern Futures books but participated in the financial irregularities associated with the company'.[20]

In the main, the commission of inquiry did not attempt to assess the misuse of funds related to the fraudulent organisations, such as EDA and PST, which the security police created in order to redirect anti-apartheid funds. Either they were unaware of these facts or had no concrete evidence related to them. In the analysis of the commission, EDA was largely a failed initiative, on account of the fact that Karl Edwards was a sloppy undercover agent, and not trusted by the legitimate members of the organisation.

> His activities and lifestyle were such that the police could have been expected to pick him up – but they did not. Sometime in 1977/78 white activists were sufficiently uncertain about Edwards to, in effect, force him out of the Environmental Development Agency which he had founded.[21]

The commission had a similar analysis of the impact that Williamson and Edwards had on the South African News Agency. In sum, Sana 'never functioned effectively as a news agency, largely, some people associated with it came to believe, because [of] Edwards, who was "running" the internal network, and Williamson who … never had a great interest in its success'.[22] Beyond simply lacking interest in Sana, Williamson and Edwards were also unable effectively to use Sana as an intelligence-gathering mechanism because 'the two present Sana representatives in Gaborone were suspicious'[23] of Karl Edwards, in particular and, by extension, of Craig Williamson. Overall, the commission held a very dim view of Karl Edwards. In their attempt to take stock of other abuses of funds during Williamson's tenure, representatives from the ANC testified that

> one possible major misappropriation of IUEF funds occurred when, in anticipation of a restrictive act being passed, Williamson and Eriksson passed a very large sum to Edwards for which there

was no specific programme backing. Edwards' readiness with money and his extravagant style of living and working were only possible if he had large resources behind him.[24]

While Craig Williamson's boasts about his successes as an undercover agent were in many ways inflated, or outright lies, it is striking that the commission of inquiry largely confirms and even at times echoes Williamson in terms of his key impact on the IUEF's political and funding trajectory. It is worth quoting the commission's summary in some length:

> Williamson's first objective, in point of time, may have been to weaken and even get rid of the BCM [Black Consciousness Movement] which seemed to pose a more immediate threat when Williamson left South Africa than it did later. Once this threat appeared to have diminished, his attention may have turned more strongly towards penetrating the ANC. If the goal of Williamson and his superiors in the years 1976–77 was to destroy and discredit the BCM, then the IUEF, as a major external supporter of the BCM, was an obvious organization to penetrate. Some effort does seem to have been made to cool the IUEF off the BCM through Edwards feeding strongly anti-BCM reports from inside South Africa. This may also have been behind Williamson's working within the IUEF to promote a shift to a pro-ANC stand, for such a step would deprive the BCM of one of its most important sources of support. This is not inconsistent with Williamson's primary goal later being to penetrate the ANC, for once the 'threat' the South Africans perceived in the BCM had faded, the ANC was clearly the source of the major remaining threats to the South African Government.[25]

What is particularly instructive about this analysis is that it doesn't seek to quantify the Black Consciousness Movement as objectively more 'revolutionary' or more 'threatening' than the ANC, but rather sees the apartheid state making strategic decisions in response to changing circumstances. Obviously, Craig Williamson's role in Geneva – as a saboteur of the BCM – took place in a dynamic interplay with repressive measures carried out by the state in South Africa, and vice versa. On a related note, this attention to shifts in strategic thinking over time is also useful in terms of analysing Eriksson's role in terms of the IUEF's decision openly to support the ANC. The commission acknowledged that Eriksson's thinking regarding the anti-apartheid movement was shifting naturally. However, they still insisted that 'the fact that the shift coincided with Eriksson's own understanding of what was necessary does not mean Williamson did not have a hand in making the shift for his own purposes'.[26] Once again, in assessing Williamson's impact, it is crucial not to inflate his capacity to influence large-scale events, while still taking seriously the strategic thinking behind what he did accomplish. In terms of understanding Williamson's 'own purposes' in urging the IUEF to support the ANC, the commission of inquiry's assessment is eerily similar to Williamson's own depiction, as conveyed in our interview.

> His reports of meetings and conversations with these people in the IUEF files, read, now, as exactly what they are – intelligence reports ... Williamson's aim may have been not only to penetrate the organizations as far as he could but also to encourage the organizations to form links with the ANC, which could easily result in all opposition to the regime being depicted in South African propaganda as 'communistic'. This would also concentrate opposition in a disciplined, centralized organization which the South Africans may have felt they could cope with more easily than a more diffuse opposition made up of many groups with varying activities.[27]

## Further damage

> The unfortunate fact is that little can probably be done to protect or otherwise assist those on whom Williamson has incriminating (in South African eyes) documents or information.
> 
> — International University Exchange Fund,
> Report of the Commission of Inquiry

There is no denying that Craig Williamson's infiltration of the International University Exchange Fund had a devastating effect not only on the IUEF itself but also on the anti-apartheid movement more broadly. While Williamson's later efforts for the security police were quite literally lethal, his sabotage of the IUEF may well be the high point of Williamson's undercover career. As much as men like Williamson glorified the apartheid state's capacity to engage in counter-insurgency warfare, the decision to undermine the anti-apartheid movement through the manipulation of newsletters and ledger books once again demonstrates that the apartheid state was also and always concerned about the threats posed by legal, non-violent opposition.

In the conclusion of their report, the commission of inquiry admitted that they had been unable to assess the damage caused by Williamson as systematically as they would have liked. Nonetheless, the commission did make a sincere attempt to make constructive speculations regarding 'the incidents, some minor and others grave, in which the South African security police may have used information fed to them by Williamson while he was still based in Europe'.[28] The report details a few different moments where people were arrested inside South Africa, such as the arrest of Renfrew Christie, an ex-Nusas white leftist aligned to the ANC, and Winston Nkondo, an ANC member who was apprehended while attempting to fly to Lesotho. The commission believed these arrests may have been the result of intelligence sent to South Africa by Williamson. While this is troubling in and of itself,

> much more disconcerting is the possibility of a connection between Steve Biko's receiving funds from the IUEF and his detention. The IUEF does not appear to have made any effort after Biko's death to ascertain if there was any connection between his funding by and association with the IUEF and his detention and murder by the South Africans.[29]

Since 1980, speculation regarding Williamson's role in the detention and death of Steve Biko has only grown over time. However, the capacity to substantiate these concerns with evidence is as limited now as it was when the commission of inquiry first raised it.

In addition to grappling with the indirect casualties of Williamson's tenure at the IUEF, the commission also tried to anticipate any potential further damage. In the main, the commission was confident that the anti-apartheid organisations that Williamson had engaged with had taken concrete steps to insulate themselves against potential fallouts in the future. Sadly, the reality of Williamson's continued assault on the ANC in particular in the years to come shows that this was an overly optimistic assessment. The commission was more accurate in declaring that Williamson's espionage was unlikely to damage European anti-apartheid organisations, or recipients of IUEF scholarships.

The most concrete fear raised by the commission also proved to be the most prescient:

> Nevertheless, now that 'Operation Daisy' is, presumably, over, there is no reason for the South African government not to start picking off those who have been so compromised by Williamson's, and Edwards', activities. A 'round-up' may follow of people who have had contact with the IUEF ... It was suggested to us that Williamson's intimate knowledge of the white activist networks could allow the South African state to mount a conspiracy trial like the South African Students Organization (SASO) trial and Nusas trial of the mid-1970s.[30]

Within months of the publication of the commission of inquiry's report, the round-up of radicals who had been affiliated with Williamson and Edwards was under way. Furthermore, when these young people arrived at trial – after months of detention and torture – both Williamson and Edwards were in the witness box, testifying as expert witnesses for the prosecution.

Part 3

# Furthering the Aims, 1980–1983

# 7 | Arrests and Detention

## Conspiracy minded

Barbara Hogan estimated that 'a hundred or more' people were detained during her time.

> This was significant: it was African, it was Indian, it was coloured and it was whites; quite a lot of whites. It was firstly an indication that there was a big nonracial something happening, but secondly that whites were beginning to identify with the ANC ... certainly they also thought that they really had captured the entire leadership of this post-1976 mass movement that was Congress aligned. They were very cocksure of themselves. They were stupid. In the early phase of my interrogation, they were bragging to me that there would be van loads of us standing trial, the biggest treason trial, much bigger than the '56 treason trial. And they were cock-a-hoop. They really thought they'd cracked it. When they weren't able to establish the evidence that would stand up (even in a prejudiced apartheid court) of the linkages between the ANC and these activists, the organisational linkages, suddenly their case looked a whole lot weaker.[1]

Contrary to what the security police might have imagined at the time, the political climate among young opponents of apartheid in the late 1970s was fluid, contested and experimental. Devan Pillay, a young man raised in East London, classified racially as Indian, and studying at Rhodes University, found himself right in the middle of all of these different political trajectories. Along with his friend Lindy Harris and a white lecturer at Rhodes named Guy Berger, Pillay was part of a reading group, which had been organised with the explicit goal of understanding the ANC and Marxism more deeply. At the same time, Pillay had some contact with people who were active in the ANC underground, including Mandla Gxanyana, and a distant relative of his, whom the ANC sent to recruit Pillay. In other words, according to Pillay, 'I was sort of ready to be recruited into a political project … But I wasn't *yet* recruited.'[2]

Devan Pillay was arrested in July of 1980. Pillay's arrest represents a rather confused understanding – on the part of the police – of the political work that Pillay had been involved in. Counterintuitively, Pillay was arrested for attempting to convince Black people to be less bitter towards white people, and to adopt a nonracial politics:

> Mandla gave me these underground, photocopied pamphlets from *Mayibuye*, the ANC journal [including an article about Tim Jenkin, a white activist in the ANC[3]]. So, what I did was … I went into university, and I made copies of this. I thought I'm going to show this to my Black Consciousness friends to show them that not all white people are conservative, right? That's when I got arrested. Obviously, somebody must have seen me copying it at the library at Rhodes.[4]

While the incident with *Mayibuye* may have sparked the arrest, Pillay was immediately accused of participating in a much larger conspiracy, alongside Mandla Gxanyana and Guy Berger:

> Looking from the outside, you connect the dots, and you see one huge conspiracy. So, they arrested us all together. I was connected with Mandla, that would be one thing. And I was connected to Guy. So, actually, come to think of it – I was the common thread. But we were operating independently. That's the interesting thing. I was doing things on my own volition but inspired by these things I was reading and so on.[5]

Alan Fine, who was also engaged with the Schoons (and was himself arrested for it, roughly a year later), cautions against reading 'too much coherence' into people's political choices during this period of time. 'Actually, there were a hell of a lot of people who were in a grey area. Because I think there was enough sophisticated thinking that actually what was important was what work was being done, not whether someone was, as they called it, "under discipline".'[6] However, the security police were unable to conceptualise any kind of grey area in politics. They were conspiracy minded, and they assumed the worst of any kind of clandestine activity. Because Devan Pillay had interacted with Mandla, from the ANC underground, they assumed that Pillay was also an underground operative. In addition, because Guy Berger was in contact with the Schoons in Botswana, and because those communication channels were heavily infiltrated by the security police, the state also assumed that Berger was a member of the ANC's underground.

In fact, not only were the police certain that Berger and Pillay were conspiring together, but they also assumed – in typical racist fashion – that Berger, as the white man, must have been in charge of the whole thing. Berger himself rejects being cast as the mastermind, and particularly the police view that 'without white agitators, black people would be docile', and the need to have a 'genetic explanation for people's behaviour'.[7] Berger was 'surprised to be arrested, in fact, because I didn't think I was really doing anything very serious or effective. It would have been nice to be a hero, but it was actually small-scale stuff – helping a bit here or there.'[8] Through coded messages, dead letter boxes and couriers, Berger interacted with the Schoons about the trade union movement in the Eastern Cape. But, according to Berger, most of the messages were cryptic, such as 'how's the work going?' and this lent itself to being greatly inflated in significance by Karl Edwards and Williamson, who were able to intercept these messages.[9] Williamson was sent to interrogate Berger in detention, in the lead-up to the trial:

> They took me into this office in the security police headquarters, and there was this guy standing with his back to me, looking out of the window. His hands were behind his back. He turned around very majestically. I said something like, 'Good morning, Captain

Williamson.' He gave the impression he hadn't even heard me. He said, 'Do you *know* who I am?' He was really living it up. He had such a high opinion of himself![10]

In addition to flattering himself, Williamson also insulted Berger, calling him a 'useful idiot', and insisting that the ANC was just using him.

While the security police may have exaggerated the severity of Berger and Pillay's subversive activities, and misunderstood the complexities of their political thinking, this doesn't mean that they were simply making up the charges. As Denis Kuny stresses, 'I know of no case, certainly none of the cases that I was involved with, where it was a complete fabrication, from end to end.'[11] Both Pillay and Berger were legitimately interested in the ANC and doing what they could to learn more about the organisation, and what it might mean for them to move in that direction. They had no illusions about the fact that their study group was illegal, in that they were engaged in an extensive reading of banned literature. The study group met in secret, and the reading material was hidden away in a trunk. In fact, both Pillay and Berger each had a trunk full of illegal literature, and they both decided, separately, that the safest place to leave them would be at the home of Lindy Harris. Once detained, they admitted to the existence of these trunks, and the police found the following:

> *Time Longer Than Rope* by Eddie Roux ... *Mayibuye* ... *No Easy Walk to Freedom* by Nelson Mandela, *Guerrilla Warfare and Marxism*, edited by William Pomeroy, *The Park and Other Stories* by James Matthews, *Forced Landing*, edited by Mothobi Mutloatse, *African Patriots: The Story of the African National Congress* by Mary Benson, *The Barrel of a Gun: Political Power in Africa and the Coup d'Etat* by Ruth First, *Pedagogy of the Oppressed* by Paolo Freire, *Staffrider* ... *The South African Labour Bulletin* and the journal *Works in Progress*.[12]

In addition to reading banned literature, Berger and Pillay's dabbling into the ANC's underground may have been minimal, but it wasn't insignificant. However, the state never learned of a more serious act by Berger. When Berger was serving his mandatory period of military service, he obtained a copy of an SADF counter-insurgency training manual, which he photocopied and smuggled into Botswana, where he handed it over to Pete Richer, a comrade of Marius Schoon. Similarly, Devan Pillay was lucky to have not yet taken the step of agreeing to work within the ANC underground. Mandla was facing quite serious charges for his role within MK. At first the state hoped to try him alongside Berger and Pillay, but they soon realised that the connections between the three were too thin to hold up in court, and Mandla was tried separately.

*

Barbara Hogan was arrested very early in the morning on 22 September 1981. The police searched her home for a couple of hours, and seized the following:

> ... one *African Communist*; my whole filing cabinet with all the papers, posters on the wall relating to the Wilson-Rowntree boycott, the anti-Republic day, the Women's day; they took photographs of the wall and the posters; they took a poster relating to the Collindale Pineapple Factory. Cronwright was shouting all the time that the others must find union stuff ... they took personal photographs and letters.[13]

Immediately upon arrival at John Vorster Square (the central police station in Johannesburg) Major Cronwright asked Barbara if she was a member of the ANC, and she said yes.[14] Then the major asked, "'You want to know who is being detained?" and read out the list.'[15] Clearly, the police wanted Barbara Hogan to know that she was just one of many people who were being detained, presumably for being part of a larger conspiracy.

By the time that Barbara Hogan was arrested, she had actively considered herself to be a member of the ANC for about three years. Having begun her relationship with the ANC in exile via Swaziland, most of Hogan's work was in connection to Jeanette and Marius Schoon, whom she had already worked with prior to their time in Botswana. Hogan found the process of attempting to do political organising inside South Africa – legally, openly – while maintaining contact with the ANC in exile to be fraught with difficulties. In the days before her arrest, these problems accelerated dramatically:

> One day, Jenny's parents came for me and told me that there was a message from Botswana to say that I need to get out of the country immediately because an envelope which I had put a particular message in had been torn open, meaning my networks had been infiltrated.[16]

Even though Hogan wasn't sure whether the message she had sent to Botswana had actually been intercepted, she nonetheless started thinking about leaving the country. However, she found that she was being constantly tailed by the security police, which made her feel like it would be impossible to leave safely. At the same time, staying in Johannesburg under this intense level of surveillance felt increasingly dangerous.

> I just decided I couldn't go to meetings – I couldn't do anything – because I was now endangering anyone that I was meeting with. So, then I said, I've got to get out of the country because I'm now a danger to everyone. I don't know why I'm being followed but this is a precursor to being arrested and I don't know what I'm being arrested for.[17]

In this state of panic, Barbara decided to reach out to someone whom she knew to be connected to MK, to ask for assistance getting smuggled out of the country. Given her earlier reticence about being associated with MK in any form, this was clearly a drastic decision, but she felt it was necessary because she couldn't imagine leaving the country through any legal channels, under such intense scrutiny from the police. The MK member 'came back to me and said he had spoken to his handlers to see how to get me to a safe house. His handler then said they needed a list of people who I'd worked with politically, because they were worried about their security or whatever.'[18] In hindsight, being asked to write down a list of names sounds incredibly suspicious, but in the moment Hogan complied, believing that she was following orders from the ANC. She did ask whether the names ought to be written in code but was told that since it was such an urgent issue, there was no need. Sadly, the so-called handler was actually what was known as an 'askari', that is, someone who had been turned by the security police and had agreed to work for the state.[19]

> They were recording my meetings with him [the man Hogan understood to be in MK]. I'd meet with him on a bench in Yeoville and the security police were sitting around the corner, because this chap's handler was a security policeman. They were recording everything. They also had a report on the frustration I had with being linked into the ANC in exile, but operative here politically. They had this report from the moment I was arrested. That was supposed to be going to the ANC.[20]

In essence, Barbara Hogan had unwittingly handed over to the security police a great deal of evidence, which would prove damning not only to her but to a great many other people who were included in the unencrypted list of 'comrades' that she had written up. Within a few days of Hogan's arrest, wave after wave of arrests began:

> It became the first big nonracial arrest in a long time, and they were boasting that they were going to have the biggest trial since Rivonia ... But I was in detention for six months. And as they went on and on and on, they did reckless stuff of just picking up people all over the place; anyone who was politically active at the time, thinking that they would get a massive smashing of what they thought was an ANC underground. But they were still working based on an early 60s model that everyone who was politically active were members of the ANC ... and we weren't ... The problem was that they couldn't prove ANC linkages. I was the only person because of that interception.[21]

Among the dozens of people who were swept up in these raids were two people with whom Hogan had worked closely: Alan Fine and Auret van Heerden. Both Van Heerden and Fine were part of the white left wing that had grown out of Nusas and become increasingly active in trade union work, and New Left Marxism. Both of them were also to some extent interacting with the Schoons. While both later denied to the police and the courts that they were members of the ANC, they had clearly been connected enough to raise the suspicions of both other comrades and the security police. Since Alan Fine had been close to Jenny Curtis while she was in Johannesburg, and looked up to her as a radical mentor, he made a few visits to the Schoons once they left for Botswana, and even offered to join them in exile at one point. In the end, Fine had decided to stay in Johannesburg to work for the unions and sent information about the trade union movement to the Schoons in Botswana, using covert means. As soon as he was placed under arrest, Alan Fine understood that the police were already aware of his communications back and forth to Botswana:

> The security police arrived at my house at 4 o'clock in the morning on the 24th of September 1981. Warrant Officer Syffert looked at my bookshelves and, in addition to looking at the political stuff, he looked at all of the novels and said, 'Spies, spies, spies! No wonder you're a spy.' When he said that I knew he knew what I had been doing. In a way, it was quite a relief, for that to come out. Because, when you go into detention you have to work out very carefully what you're going to say and what you're not.[22]

It is too simple to say that the police 'knew' what Alan Fine, or Barbara Hogan, or any of the rest of them, had been doing. There was an amount that had been intercepted through infiltration and other means, but there was still a great deal of information that the state fundamentally didn't understand or refused to understand. To turn this mass wave of arrests into convictions in a court of law, the police needed to find concrete links to the ANC and/or the Communist Party and/or MK. This was a task that was simultaneously clear and entirely vague. Furthermore, the methods used to 'learn' such facts were primarily brutal, and much more often served as a means of terrorising detainees rather than anything resembling intelligence gathering.

## Systematic torture

> In that period, when you were politically active, the consequences were huge. So, you could not be reckless. Because you could be reckless and

implicate other people but also reckless for yourself, for everything. And it was a very hard time for people. Our political lives were beset with people being detained and horrifically tortured. A couple were destroyed by that.

— Barbara Hogan, interview

Already in the first few days of being detained, the police began to interrogate Barbara Hogan, using a combination of outright torture as well as the threat of even worse. Barbara's account of these long days of interrogation is harrowing, heartbreaking, and it gets exponentially worse as the process accelerates over time. Within the first encounter, the signs of the coming madness were already painfully clear.

> Cronwright came in and was shouting that I was a terrorist.
> Then, I was told that if I did not give the names ... 'the wolves would get me'.
> Later, Captain Visser said that they were going to break my arms. He said that he was very upset that they were going to do this to a woman.[23]

On one occasion, the interrogation continued until 'I semi-fainted and I had to be half-carried into Struwig's office by Knight and a black policeman. Struwig shouted at me and said that I was playing the fool.'[24]

In addition to the psychological stresses of interrogation, and being physically beaten on many occasions, Hogan also suffered a series of other ailments while in detention, such as internal bleeding and a severe toothache. Her interactions with the prison's doctors seem to have compounded the torturous experience, despite the attempts by the medical professionals to distance themselves from the brutality of Hogan's jailers. Unfortunately, even when the doctors were able to secure an amount of privacy for her, they could not realistically offer any genuine confidentiality, as medical reports were immediately transmitted on to the security police. Therefore, in essence, the doctors lacked the power needed to provide any real respite for Hogan. Nonetheless, it's clear from Hogan's account that she attempted, on multiple occasions, even desperately, to get the doctors to help take her pain away. For example, on her first visit to Dr Clinton, 'I was crying hysterically. I begged him to allow me to stay the night at the hospital. The supervisor came and said I had to stay the night. I was given sleeping tablets and Valium.'[25] The second time Hogan requested medical assistance, Officer Struwig informed her that this 'would be the last time that I would be allowed to see a doctor or a dentist'.[26] As it happened, Hogan was allowed to get dental care and returned to the doctor on a number of occasions. Nonetheless, the doctor visits remained cynically unproductive. Hogan's visit with Dr Jacobson was the starkest representation of her predicament in detention:

> 'Are you all right?'
> I pointed to my face.
> He said, 'What's been happening to you?'
> I started crying hysterically.
> He made me strip completely and he examined me, and he said that I had bruises.[27]

In spite of the obvious and ubiquitous evidence, Barbara Hogan urged Dr Jacobson not to report to the police that she had been assaulted, as she had been explicitly warned by Officer Deetlefs to 'just to say that I bruised easily'.[28] In other words, Hogan arrived at the doctor's office terrified that if she told the truth about what had happened to her, she would be beaten further, in retribution. As a result, when Hogan decided, months later, that she really ought to file a complaint against her torturers, she was informed that there was no evidence of assault in her medical files. 'I asked him to look in the file of the 23rd October and I saw that Jacobson had written down, "patient says not assaulted by the police", then he had detailed the position of bruises all over my body.'[29] Trapped within a structure that constantly brutalised her and also made it impossible to receive proper treatment for her wounds, Barbara Hogan 'tried to commit suicide. I tried several ways.'[30] Thankfully, she survived.

Meanwhile, the interrogations continued non-stop. The police were obsessed with learning 'odd things, for example the address of the Schoons'.[31] In Hogan's analysis:

> They were asking questions but not the kind of questions to get answers. They were shouting. It was intended to be disorienting.

> I was not allowed to go to the toilet. They were saying, 'do you want to get hit?'... Suddenly Prins hit me on my face on both sides. He did this several times. Approximately 20 to 25 times. He hit both my ears at the same time saying 'I'll break your ear-drums ...' They said they were going to make me into a vegetable – did I want to be a cabbage or a carrot?[32]

This pattern continued for weeks on end, sometimes continuing all through the night, with multiple interrogators, who were switched out every three hours. Moments of violence were interspersed constantly with moments of being asked questions, and these oscillated between sheer random topics ('For example, they asked me to do an analysis of the crisis in Afrikanerdom.'[33]) and pointed questions about the ANC and her relationship to the organisation, and to her comrades. For example: '... then he asked me to write out what the structure of the ANC was. I did this. They said that I was lying and that I must give them the internal structure as well.'[34] Barbara Hogan attempted strategically to answer these questions in such a way that she didn't give away too much about her comrades, and in particular those who were still inside South Africa. She co-operated to the extent of writing out statements about both the ANC and about her work in the trade unions. 'I spent the rest of Tuesday, the whole of Wednesday and Thursday night typing out the statement.' However, her interrogators were constantly dissatisfied with her statements, and accused her of lying or leaving out important details. 'On Friday I was told to tear everything up ...'[35] This cycle repeated itself many times. In the end, the police essentially drafted the document themselves:

> I would write out a couple of paragraphs and then Olivier would read them, and I would have to alter whatever he felt necessary. I cut out pieces from old statements and stuck them onto the new statement. This took approximately 3 weeks.[36]

In this fashion, the police succeeded in obtaining a 90-page document, complete with an index of relevant names, which was then used against Hogan in the ensuing court case.

In addition to the direct brutality inflicted upon her, Hogan was also regularly made aware of the fact that her comrades were suffering similar – or worse – fates in other rooms within the same building. At one point, 'a policeman came in with purplish knuckles. Struwig got up and said that he must go and stop them before they kill someone. I think this was Cedric.'[37] Despite the horrifying things that were done to Hogan, over an extended period of time, when I asked her about these experiences during our interview (nearly forty years later) she remembers her own experience as having been mild, relatively speaking:

> What is torture? Is it being kept awake? Is it being assaulted? All of those things which happened to me. But when you talk about systematic torture, like when people had their hands chained to the ankles and made to stand for days on end in that position, I was not tortured in that kind of systematic way. Others were, who were with me. I think the fact that they knew I was ANC actually protected me, because they didn't have to extract an ANC admission from me, whereas the others they would try to extract that. You know what I mean? But you know detention is always *unbelievably* brutal. Unbelievably brutal.[38]

Given the relentlessly gruelling details of Hogan's account of her time in detention, it feels like a not very helpful distinction to define Hogan's treatment as somehow not 'systematic' enough to be described as torture. Clearly, Barbara Hogan was tortured, and over an extended period of time. The fact that this process included random aspects, including things that were seemingly pointless, stupid or at least not explicitly vicious doesn't negate the fact that the process was 'systematic'. The people who oversaw Hogan's detention and interrogation – including the doctors, the magistrates and the lower-ranked Black policemen who carried her bruised body from the interrogation room when she was passing out – were all carrying out orders. In other words, the campaign of abuse and intimidation that Hogan was subjected to was in every way intentional, and part of a much larger campaign of systematically assaulting opponents of apartheid.

Nonetheless, there are certainly differences that are worth noting. Auret van Heerden was one of the 'others' Hogan mentioned, one of the ones who *was* systematically tortured. Van Heerden was a white radical, who had been the president of Nusas, and whom the state presumed was a member of the

ANC. He was arrested not long after Barbara Hogan, and Hogan herself was repeatedly interrogated about her connections to him. Meanwhile, Van Heerden was detained for 281 days, during which time he was brutalised and humiliated, through a wide variety of torturous tactics. A full rendition of what was done to Van Heerden would be truly unbearable to read – let alone to imagine what it must have been like to live through such treatment. Still, in order to understand the depths of apartheid savagery, it is important to face what happened to Auret Van Heerden in some depth. First, there is the image that Hogan remembers so vividly, decades later, of having your hands chained to your ankles. Van Heerden describes how this was done to him, starting at 8.30 am, on the morning of 18 November 1981. Once Van Heerden was bound in this extremely uncomfortable position, he was instructed that

> if I did not stand, if I sat or lay down or even if I just fell over, I would be assaulted ... I therefore did my utmost to remain standing.[39] ... Captain Olivier asked me after about half an hour of standing in that position, whether or not I thought I would be able to stand like that for an hour and I said that I would not. He also asked if I felt that I might be able to stand like that for a day and I said definitely not. As it turned out, I stood like that until 7 pm.[40]

Such abuse would have been traumatising enough on its own. In Van Heerden's case, the day spent hog-tied was just the beginning. After he was unchained at 7 pm, 'the electric shock and suffocation began'.[41] Van Heerden describes in excruciating detail the process of being waterboarded, with a canvas bag forced over his head, 'with the name of an Afrikaans banking concern which I cannot remember',[42] and then having electricity coursing through his body to the point of 'screaming and being unable to breathe'[43] at the same time. Following this, Van Heerden was then made to sit between the legs of Captain Visser, who wrapped a towel around Auret's neck and strangled him, 'I would say between 10 and possibly as many as 15 times ... Each time he applied the strangulation, he would look into my eyes ... and he would say that he was now going to kill me.'[44] Following this, Van Heerden was beaten and whipped.

> I could see that they were nervous about the possible effect on my neck because on the occasions that my head buckled, they warned

me to keep my neck and back in a single plane lest my neck get broken by one of the blows.[45]

The following day, 'I was then chained up that way again at some stage in the early hours of the morning and stood like that until 6 pm.'[46]

In light of this unfathomable series of events, it is clear why Barbara Hogan insists that the torture that she endured was of a markedly different calibre than what others experienced. Furthermore, the fact that Van Heerden claimed that 'since I have never been a member of the ANC, I could not answer the questions' seems to affirm Hogan's point that admitting to membership of the ANC in some sense 'protected' her. However, this feels virtually impossible to prove, one way or the other.

Devan Pillay was also tortured in detention, and much more extensively than his co-accused Guy Berger. Berger is aware that he was spared many of the worst abuses, but he nonetheless insists that 'the inhumane treatment was still effective'.[47] Berger was subjected to three days in a row of sleep deprivation, and was slapped around, and then spent many days in 'solitary confinement in a tiny grey cell for twenty-three hours a day. The window is painted black, and a naked bulb is on twenty-four hours. You don't know when this ordeal is going to end.'[48] While this experience was clearly dreadful, Berger stresses that he 'wasn't given electric shocks or made to stand on drawing pins',[49] like Devan Pillay was made to endure. Reflecting on the differences between his own experience in detention and Berger's treatment, Pillay came to believe that, as a general rule, 'They physically tortured the Black prisoners and they psychologically tortured the white prisoners.'[50] Given the tenacious desire of the apartheid state to racialise every single aspect of society, it is certainly true that the state reserved its most vicious and severe forms of brutality for Black people. Hundreds of Black freedom fighters were savaged by apartheid police and soldiers, in the most sadistic and inhumane of ways, up to and including burning people alive. There are certainly differences that are worth noting. However, the treatment of Auret van Heerden proves that the apartheid state was at least willing to physically torture *some* white people. Furthermore, even to describe what happened to Barbara Hogan as merely 'psychological' grossly understates the case. Hogan was the victim of violence on dozens of occasions and had any of her attempts to kill herself succeeded, it would seem inappropriate to call this 'suicide', since her jailers were clearly the cause of her desire to die.

During the time that Barbara Hogan was in detention, another white radical comrade, Neil Aggett, *was* found dead – hung – inside his prison cell.[51] Neil Aggett was trained as a doctor, but his sympathies for the anti-apartheid movement led him into the trade union movement. Aggett was detained, like all the others, on suspicion of being a member of the ANC, or at least someone who was furthering the aims of the organisation. Aggett insisted that he was a nonracialist and a pacifist, and not a clandestine operative for the ANC's armed struggle. But the state refused to believe him.

Given that it was undertaken immediately after Aggett's death, it is not surprising that the state-initiated inquest 'proved' that it was a suicide and exonerated the police officers involved. Nonetheless, the report of the inquest detailed the extensive interrogation that Aggett was subjected to, which was far more pervasive and pernicious than the state was willing to admit to.[52] As Barbara Hogan explains, Neil Aggett's death became an international embarrassment for the apartheid state:

> And of course, it just blew internationally. Because Neil was secretary of the Food and Allied Workers' Union, international trade unions started refusing to unload South African cargo, in places like Australia and all over the place and it became a huge international thing. Then of course just in Joburg alone seven people were admitted into psychiatric wards who were detainees because of the extent of the torture. Maurice Smithers, who was detained along with me, was able to smuggle out in a matchbox details of the torture that he'd seen of Neil Aggett and Helen Suzman read that out in parliament. The Nats[53] were denying that they tortured anybody. It totally exposed the security police for what they were. To the extent that even when I was in jail the wardresses would say to me that the security police mustn't tell us that they don't torture people.[54]

Despite all manner of violence and psychological abuse, and endless rounds of ripping up and rewriting confessional statements, the state's efforts to produce a grand treason trial ultimately failed. Therefore, with the few indictments that were remaining, the state found themselves determined to win an important ideological battle: to redefine the nature of non-violent protest, treason and revolution.

## Soul enriching

In preparation for their trial, Berger and Pillay were faced with the predicament of having several people close to them that might reasonably agree to testify against them. In trials such as these, where the 'crimes' were rooted in political beliefs, affiliations and actions, the apartheid state relied heavily on being able to coerce or 'turn' fellow comrades, to persuade them to testify against their friends. Devan Pillay understood this whole process – like so many other aspects of apartheid society – as playing out along racial lines.

> If you were a black African activist, the pressure in the townships on you not to testify were enormous. If you were an Indian activist, you'd have faced some pressure. If you're a white activist, the pressure would have been the opposite. Whites were really more tempted to testify.[55]

An extremely pertinent example of the difference that Pillay describes was the trial of Mandla Gxanyana, who was originally indicted alongside Berger and Pillay. Once Mandla's trial was separated out, the state was forced to try to find new witnesses to provide evidence against him. However,

> Mandla's chief witness in his trial was a trade unionist and he refused to testify against him. The irony of that saga was that Mandla got six months, because there was no evidence against him. And [the other guy] got one year for refusing to testify.[56]

In other words, this kind of solidarity among comrades, on the one hand, made it virtually impossible for the state to impose stiff sentences against activists facing political indictments. On the other hand, the punishments for staying silent and standing by your comrades were severe enough that many people, especially those with privilege, were too afraid to do the courageous thing. Regardless of the risks involved, Devan Pillay felt strongly that his white comrades ought to have been willing to refuse to testify, to at least reduce the sentences given to himself and Berger. However, Pillay was out-voted by Guy Berger and Denis Kuny. According to Pillay, 'There was a whole big thing about not wanting to put them through the trauma of testifying. Or not testifying and getting a sentence. That was also a big discussion.'[57] The two accused also were concerned that even if they succeeded in convincing some of their comrades not to testify, one might have still testified, and Berger and Pillay would have been convicted.

> In addition, in my case at least, there was Sydney Zotwana – a lecturer at Rhodes – whom they could have called to testify (I had shared ANC publications with him), and I did not want him to become a martyr (he had fairly recently just spent a year in prison for calling a stayaway, and some white left students had given evidence against him in that case). So, the issue was more nuanced, I think.[58]

Based on all these considerations, and to spare their comrades 'the trauma of testifying' or the risk of a prison sentence for refusing to testify, Berger and Pillay decided to plead guilty to the charge of furthering the aims of the ANC. As a result, Guy Berger was sentenced to four years, which was reduced to two, on appeal, and Devan Pillay was sentenced for half as long (two years, reduced to one, on appeal).

Even though Devan Pillay went along with pleading guilty, for the sake of those who might have testified against him, this was clearly a difficult choice to make. Reflecting back on his state of mind at the time, Pillay remembers feeling confident that white comrades refusing to testify would have sent an important political message:

> My view was that getting the sentence of six months for not testifying – that's good for them, for their political soul. Maybe I was being cruel, but I just thought that spending time in prison ... could be a huge political statement. Six months in prison as a white person was going to be soul enriching.[59]

Whether or not it is cruel to say so, Pillay's description of prison as being 'soul enriching' is based on his own experience inside.

> I found the prison experience to be so enriching even though it came with physical deprivations and torture. I was much more committed to the struggle after having been in prison, having spent time there. All my other political prisoners were black African, and we had political discussions every day and other activities together. It was a bit like a university.[60]

There is certainly something quite clear, and even compelling, about the image of a young radical like Pillay going to jail and ending up with a much deeper connection to other Black radicals, and therefore coming out of jail even more committed to the struggle than when he entered. In part, this sentiment underscores the common experience of many activists, for whom the escalating mechanisms of repression frequently escalated their determination and drive to resist. However, there is another layer of irony at play here, which seemed to slip out of view for Pillay, when he imagined his white comrades in prison. That is, apartheid necessarily separated all prisoners based on race. Therefore, despite Pillay receiving some small privileges (slightly better pants, bread instead of corn meal porridge) for being understood as 'Indian' racially, nonetheless he was imprisoned alongside Black prisoners, which meant having the easiest access to members of the ANC, and other Black radicals, than would have ever been possible as a 'free' man. However, for white prisoners, the situation was reversed. White anti-apartheid activists – people who had made conscious decisions to cross the colour bar, to build nonracial organisations, and to think seriously about Marxism – were only a tiny fraction of South African political prisoners. Hugh Lewin, who spent seven years (1964–1971) in jail for sabotage, said,

> I met altogether twenty-six other white politicals: as a group we never, at any one time, reached more than twenty-one and, by the time I left at the end of 1971, there were only nine whites left (but still some 400 blacks on Robben Island).[61]

As such, these white prisoners found themselves cut off entirely from Black people, and imprisoned alongside white criminals,[62] who not only generally accepted white supremacy as a given, but also had been raised in an intensely anti-communist society. Furthermore, white prison warders reserved a special space of hatred for white radical prisoners, and often subjected them to special abuses as a result. Therefore, rather than having an enriching experience of deep engagement with the Black majority and sustained political education, white political prisoners were comparatively isolated, relying only on their fellow political prisoners for support.

Confronted with the charge of furthering the aims of the ANC, young radicals had extremely limited options to defend themselves. One could attempt to deny any association with the ANC, but in many cases this merely escalated the ferocity of the police. By the same measure, admitting to being an ANC member would *not* spare people from being tortured and would undermine the legal defence in the trial still to come. Furthermore, the state could and often did pressure close friends to betray one another. Confronted with this threat, some chose to plead guilty (even if they didn't believe they were) in hopes of reducing their prison sentence.

In short, all available options appeared awful.

# 8 | The Trials

## Not a place of amusement

The trial against Guy Berger and Devan Pillay began in February 1981. Despite the severity of the charges levelled against them, Berger and Pillay took the proceedings as 'lightly and irreverently' as they were able.[1] After months in solitary confinement, the two took pleasure in one another's company. This irreverence from the accused was so noticeable that at one point the judge admonished Denis Kuny, their advocate:

> I would suggest that you also tell your clients not to find the proceedings amusing. I have noticed that Accused No. 1 has on a number of occasions found considerable amusement, Mr. Kuny. I suggest you just tell him that it is not a place of amusement.[2]

To make their case, the prosecution for the state made the rare decision to call Karl Edwards in to testify. However, at the request of the National Intelligence Services, Edwards' testimony was held behind closed doors, and the court was instructed that Edwards' identity could not be disclosed to the public, in any form. Denis Kuny, the advocate for the defence, asked Edwards to explain why the proceedings should be secret.

Edwards first replied, 'I have no idea, your worship.'

Then, when pushed a second time, Edwards asked, 'May I decline to answer that question, your worship?'

Finally, when the judge insisted, Edwards explained that 'Intelligence agents should have as little exposure to ... any members of the public for the reason that the more the enemy gets to know of one's modus operandi the weaker the organization, namely the N.I.S., is.'[3] In other words, the state was taking a calculated risk in allowing Edwards to testify.

According to his testimony, Edwards had been employed by the police as early as 1969, and had worked for the security services for a decade, since he entered Rhodes University in 1971, and immediately set about his work as an undercover agent, 'a vigorous member of the leftist community, but not necessarily outspoken'.[4] Alongside Williamson, Edwards joined Nusas and quickly moved up within the leadership structures of the organisation. Edwards first met Guy Berger in 1975, when Berger was a student at Rhodes.

One aspect of Edwards' role as an infiltrator was the pretence of being part of an ANC cell inside South Africa, which was in fact comprised of other security police officers. In this vein, Edwards testified before the court that 'formally I was recruited by Aziz Pahad, of the ANC in London'[5] in 1977. It seems highly improbable that the ANC genuinely understood Edwards to be a formal member of the organisation. However, this group of security policemen did carry out certain tasks for the ANC, such as distributing pamphlets, acting as couriers for coded communications and helping people escape the country. Karl Edwards played a critical role in these projects.

Edwards' role as a courier was most pertinent to his testimony against Guy Berger. Edwards testified that he had 'carried literally hundreds of letters to people inside South Africa from the ANC in exile to people within South Africa'.[6] When Denis Kuny declared that he was 'entitled to know, with respect, the other persons to whom [Edwards] is supposed to have delivered letters in connection with the ANC', Edwards demurred, saying that this information was 'highly confidential' and that 'indeed it would' be damaging to the security of the state to answer this question.[7] While the claim of 'literally hundreds of letters'[8] is likely an exaggeration, it seems certain that Karl Edwards did act as a courier for some portion of the messages sent between the Schoons in Botswana and ANC-aligned activists in South Africa, including Guy Berger and Alan Fine. According to Edwards, 'I was in and out of Botswana many, many times ... Virtually every six weeks ... Over a period of three years.'[9] Furthermore, Edwards testified that it was Jeanette Schoon herself who initiated using Karl

Edwards as a courier, not the other way around. Edwards returned to this point again and again, always stressing that 'Jeanette Curtis would not have approached me to deal with what must be considered sensitive material if I was not trusted by the ANC and in fact a member of the ANC.'[10] This is quite a striking claim, especially given the extent to which many activists did *not* trust Karl Edwards – and *he knew it*. Alan Fine decided to stop visiting the Schoons in Botswana as soon as he knew that Karl Edwards was their courier:

> When Jeanette and Marius told me that Karl Edwards had been part of the courier network, I took my stuff and left. For the ANC to have worked with Williamson and Edwards, when so many people had suspicions about them, is still reasonably controversial.'[11]

On the witness stand, Karl Edwards admitted that he likely failed to gain Berger's trust during five years of interacting. 'For a long time, he [Guy Berger] suspected me of being a possible spy.' Despite this, Edwards said, 'I think we had a fairly good relationship.'[12]

Karl Edwards' testimony against Berger included only two specific instances of communications that he had delivered to Berger, sent from Botswana by Jeanette Schoon. One of these items was just a social science newsletter, not even banned literature, of essentially no significance. The more important document was a letter that was allegedly sent from Jeanette, and delivered, by hand, to Guy Berger. Edwards claimed that this letter had been signed simply with a letter 'J' and that the decision to use only this letter, rather than a full name, represented a type of code. Edwards' testimony was meant to exhibit a certain expertise for coded communications. The exchange regarding this letter, however, developed a rather tragi-comic feeling: the letter Edwards brought to court was a photocopy of the original, with the all-important 'J' deleted. As this document served as one of the key pieces of evidence for the state that Guy Berger was connected to Jeanette Schoon, it was befuddling that the signature had been deleted prior to being submitted as evidence.

Adding to the tragi-comic feeling of this section of the trial, Karl Edwards began to feel light-headed, and became unable to speak properly, while still in the witness box and under oath.

Judge: Aren't you feeling well?
Edwards: It is alright, your honour.
Judge: If you're not feeling well, just say so Mr. Edwards.[13]

The court was forced to adjourn at a certain point. The next day, the prosecutor insisted on making a statement regarding the fainting, before the trial could resume:

> May I draw your attention, sir, to the report that appeared in this morning's Eastern Province Herald under the heading 'Government N.I.S. agent faints during evidence at security trial.' Your worship while the report is fairly accurate, I must make public my objection to the headline and state that the individual concerned did not faint, that he was indisposed and that he sweated profusely but that he did not go to the extent of fainting.[14]

Both before and after the fainting incident, Denis Kuny circled around the problem of the missing 'J' in his questioning of Edwards, probing at the absurdity of deleting the 'code' on a piece of evidence that was intended to prove that the defendant used coded communication. Karl Edwards claimed that his colleagues didn't need to know the names (even code names) of the actual ANC members. This was clearly ludicrous, and Kuny told Edwards that 'there would have been no reason at all to conceal their identities'.[15] More importantly, Kuny fundamentally disputed the idea that this letter was in any way evidence from the ANC:

> And you will agree, Mr. Edwards, that there is not one word in this letter which indicates that it emanates from ANC or has to do with the ANC?
> --- That is quite correct.[16]

Part of the reason why the letter from Jeanette Schoon couldn't be considered proof of a connection to the ANC was because, by Edwards' own admission, Jeanette was not herself a member of the ANC. Having testified that Marius Schoon was linked to the ANC, Karl Edwards was then asked by both the prosecutor and by Denis Kuny whether Jeanette was *also* linked to the ANC. On both occasions, Edwards replied, 'Not to my knowledge, no ... She is primarily concerned with Trade Union organization within South Africa and is linked to SACTU.'[17] This distinction, although seemingly subtle, and perhaps even immaterial in hindsight, proved to be a thorn in the side for the state.

## Reasonable doubt

> I am probably one of the luckiest people on earth because I did all this stuff, I got caught, I was detained for six months, I went on trial under the Terrorism Act and the bloody cover story that I'd worked out with Jeanette and Marius (I wasn't working for the ANC, I was working for SACTU) worked and I got acquitted.
>
> — Alan Fine, interview

The entirety of Alan Fine's legal defence rested on the difference between the ANC and Sactu, and Marius and Jeanette Schoon. During his trial, Fine admitted that he had travelled to Botswana, to the Schoons' house, but that he had only interacted with Jeanette, his friend from Johannesburg. Further, Fine admitted to sending information about trade unions to Jeanette, because he did consider himself to be a member of Sactu, but he insisted that he had no idea that Sactu was an organisation that had ties (ideologically and literally) to the ANC. Understandably, this claim was challenged by the prosecution, but Alan Fine was quick on his feet, and found creative ways to dodge the obvious fallacies in his story.

> One of the scariest things I had to do is the prosecutor said, 'Oh, you say you've got nothing to do with the ANC.' He then dumped every single edition of SACTU News on the desk and said, 'So, which one of these have you read?' I said, 'I can't quite remember. Please give me an hour to look through and see.' I had to very quickly page through every single one and I had to find a couple which had less emphasis on the ANC.[18]

Despite the extensive and explicit links between the ANC and Sactu, Fine's quick-witted scan of Sactu newspapers successfully avoided him having to admit in court that he had any knowledge of these links.

For Denis Kuny, formulating a defence strategy was not about either being truthful or lying, but simply about using the law to carve out whatever openings might exist, no matter how narrow. From Kuny's vantage point:

> If Alan said, 'I met with Jeanette, but I didn't meet with Marius,' then the state needs to prove the case beyond a reasonable doubt. If there wasn't a witness that would say, 'I was present when Alan met with Marius,' then there was nothing to contradict Alan's testimony.[19]

Furthermore, in Kuny's estimation, even if the state had been able to prove that Alan Fine and Marius Schoon *had* been in the same room at some point, 'merely to have a conversation with Marius Schoon wouldn't prove a common purpose'.[20] Understandably, Alan Fine was not entirely sure that this legal strategy would be effective, especially since he was facing up to 10 years in jail, if convicted.

> I suggested a couple of times, why don't we do a deal with the prosecution where I plead guilty to the lesser charge? If Denis had recommended that to me, I would have gone for it. But there's a principle of law, which says that you can only be convicted if you had an intention to break the law. Denis insisted that I had no intention to break the law, since I was unaware of the relationship between the ANC and SACTU.[21]

One of the difficulties that Alan Fine faced in his trial was the testimony of Craig Williamson, who testified at length regarding the nature of underground work, the role of trade unions within a Leninist political perspective, and the fact that 'I know Jeanette Schoon or Jenny Curtis very well and I had discussions with her on various occasions'.[22] Williamson's testimony was intended to prove that Jenny Curtis was, in fact, an ANC member and that her interest in trade unions was fundamentally a desire for revolutionary change. Furthermore, Williamson clarified that while it is theoretically possible to be a non-violent advocate for revolution, 'one of SACTU's beliefs is in the armed seizure of power'.[23] Williamson insisted, repeatedly, that anyone making any kind of contact with Jeanette Schoon would be the subject of a police investigation.

> Kuny: But as far as someone like Jeanette Schoon is concerned, she is, if one may use a colloquialism, poison for people to be associated with, in your mind?
> Williamson: Well, Poison Ivy.[24]

Denis Kuny used several tactics to undermine Craig Williamson's testimony. First, Kuny pointed out the glaring fact that Williamson's testimony was not in any way based on actual evidence regarding Alan Fine. 'You will realize that a great deal of evidence has been given covering a vast area and not one word of the witness' evidence touches on the accused himself.'[25] Second, regarding the revolutionary aspirations of the trade unions, 'the only other defence witness was Eddie Webster, who became quite good at putting before a judge the reformist view of trade unions'.[26] While both Alan Fine and Jeanette Schoon did, in fact, view their work within the unions as revolutionary, nonetheless the best defence for Fine was to introduce reasonable doubt about this. Lastly, the cleverest tactic that Denis Kuny employed was to use Williamson's purported expertise about clandestine activities as a way to introduce a further layer of reasonable doubt regarding Alan Fine's work with the Schoons.

> Kuny also got Williamson to agree that the reason that I did things in a covert way – like dead letter boxes for sending messages – was not because I knew what I was doing was unlawful but because people who had done *nothing* unlawful tended to get detained and arrested and banned. That was key to it all.[27]

This was a real stroke of genius on Kuny's part. Not only did this line of reasoning help get Alan Fine acquitted, it also forced a security police officer to admit that the general climate of surveillance and political repression pushed innocent people to try to be secretive, or inadvertently to break the law.

## Modus operandi

> Yes, your worship, as a security policeman and as a member of a covert ANC operation the modus operandi is very similar.
>
> — Craig Williamson, testimony, The State vs. G.J.E. Berger and D. Pillay

To establish his expertise, Craig Williamson spoke at some length – and repeatedly – about his life as an undercover police agent, and especially the time spent within (or at least among) the ANC. Williamson testified, much like Karl Edwards, that his affiliation with the ANC began as early as 1975, when he was on the national executive of Nusas. This seems like bravado, and is highly improbable. It seems much more likely that Williamson's contacts with the ANC became serious after his arrival in Europe, and with his role at the IUEF. According to Williamson, 'I was based in Geneva, but I used to travel to London, sometimes every week.'[28] Apparently, the ANC gave him some reading assignments, which later showed up as evidence for the state, against Hogan, Berger and Pillay.

> These documents are all copies of documents which were given to me as lectures, or as material which I was to learn, to enlighten myself about the strategy and tactics of the organizations involved.[29]

From the examples Williamson used in his testimony, and the general view of the lens he used to analyse them, it seems clear that the readings included materials related to the ANC, to MK and to the Communist Party – and that Williamson made essentially no distinctions between the three. For Williamson, the attempt to infiltrate the ANC was, by definition, also an attempt to infiltrate a communist project, and an armed organisation intent on overthrowing the South African government.

While Williamson was the public face, showing up regularly in London, he purportedly created an ANC cell that was comprised entirely of other undercover police:

> Kuny: The whole of your network, in fact, comprised people who were really members of the Security authorities.
> Williamson: That is correct, your worship.[30]

Williamson claimed that he, and other members of his 'unit', were given noms de guerre and training in underground operations, including military techniques. It is worth noting that in Williamson's testimony before the court, he often explains that he was uniquely adept at adopting the

ANC's structures for clandestine organisation precisely because these structures were so *similar* to techniques used by the security police. 'Some of the people who were working in my unit,' he testified, 'were in fact given sabotage training in London. I was given training in the manufacture of explosive devices ...'[31] This sounds fanciful at best, and more likely entirely a fabrication. What sounds much more likely is Williamson's description of an assignment given by the ANC to get a stack of fliers distributed in South Africa on the first anniversary of the Soweto uprising:

> Stephanie Kemp[32] visited me in Geneva and asked me to arrange for the urgent distribution of some propaganda material inside South Africa, which should take place shortly before June the 16th. I subsequently traveled to London where in a meeting with Ronnie Kasrils,[33] I was given several thousand of these pamphlets [announcing] a nationwide general strike from June 16th to June 18th 1977... packed into the false bottoms of – well, it was two suitcases, but only one was useable because the other one wasn't finished.[34]

An intriguing insight into the nature of Williamson's faux ANC cell is his admission that they *failed* to distribute this stack of pamphlets. Then, he clarifies, 'Well, we arranged for the attempt to fail, your worship.'[35]

At the centre of Williamson's claims to legitimacy and, indeed, relevance to the cases at hand, was his connections to the Schoons, and their work for the ANC while in Botswana. Intriguingly, none of Williamson's testimony on these matters provided any *direct* information regarding the accused themselves. Rather, Williamson attempted to present a general portrayal of the Schoons' aspirations, which would then indict people like Hogan, Berger and Fine through simply associating with the Schoons. Williamson testified to a series of visits to Botswana. The first of these meetings was on 20 January 1978. Williamson met up with Marius Schoon at the President Hotel, in the centre of Gaborone, along with Lauren Vlotman and Pete Richer, who were friends/comrades of the Schoons. The alleged purpose of the meeting was to discuss white people who were refusing to do their military service for the SADF.

According to Williamson, Marius Schoon also took the opportunity to explain, in depth, the structure and function of his work for the ANC:

> Schoon then told me that he was in fact in Botswana to work on behalf of the ANC and that his job was to coordinate a new and top-secret ANC project ... this IPRD, that is an abbreviation for the Internal Reconstruction and Development, was headed by Oliver Tambo and that various other ANC members were concerned, including Thomas Nkobi, the Treasurer-General of the ANC, Alfred Nzo, the Secretary General of the ANC and Henry Squires, or Makghoti ... He said that the four main objectives of the IPRD at that stage were to spot potential recruits for the ANC, to recruit such persons for the ANC, to gather intelligence for the ANC and to infiltrate and influence legal organizations operating inside South Africa.[36]

It feels hard to imagine Marius Schoon explaining all of the above to Craig Williamson, while sitting on the veranda of the President Hotel. Perhaps Marius would have admitted to attempting to recruit people into the ANC, as he had been actively committed to this task before his arrival in Botswana. What else would Marius have said so casually to Williamson? If even part of Williamson's account is accurate, it means that Marius either trusted Williamson a lot, or that he was quite sloppy, in terms of divulging so many details regarding this work, and in particular the names and ranks of his superiors within the organisation. Nonetheless, Williamson continually gave testimony in this vein, including at the trial of Barbara Hogan, adding in the accusation that 'one of the purposes of the Internal Reconstruction programme was also to identify young whites and to recruit them ... for Umkhonto we Sizwe'.[37] Would Marius have admitted something like this, directly to Williamson's face?

In Williamson's testimony, there is a clear attempt to portray his meetings with Marius Schoon, and other members of the ANC, as if he had always met with these individuals on equal terms, as if he was always treated as a comrade, as a fellow member of the same organisation. For example, Williamson testified that Marius Schoon had asked him to hand-deliver three letters to Lusaka, for Mac Maharaj, Henry Makghoti and Ray Alexander. 'I later carried them to Lusaka, where I could not find anybody except Ray

Simons to whom I surrendered all three letters as instructed. I did, however, gain sight of the contents of the letters before handing them over.'[38] If Marius did indeed give Williamson this assignment, it was a rather unusual choice, given the general concerns around security within the ANC's exile structures. Both Mac Maharaj and Aziz Pahad were upset that letters with such sensitive information had been carried by hand, by Williamson, to Lusaka.[39] They viewed it as a security risk. Pahad and Maharaj were right to be concerned. Using Williamson to carry these letters not only meant that he was able to pass on copies to his superiors in the security police, but also that copies of these letters were submitted into evidence at the trial against Guy Berger and Devan Pillay.

In late November of 1978, Williamson again returned to Botswana. This time he went to Molepolole, to the home of Marius and Jeanette. In hindsight, it is gruelling, horrifying, even perverse, to imagine one's killer being a guest in your home just a few years earlier. Friends and comrades of the Schoons acknowledge that Williamson was indeed a guest of the Schoons at some point. This fact, among many others, contributes to the general impression that Williamson's decision to send the parcel bomb that killed Jenny and Katryn was an act of personal malice, rather than simply following orders. There was only a hint of malice (or, at least, the absence of warmth) in Williamson's testimony regarding his visit to the Schoon residence. Williamson's attention was focused on the rather banal fact that the Schoons were openly communists, and ANC members:

> Swanepoel: Do you know whether the Schoons keep ANC or SACP literature in their house in Botswana?
> Williamson: Yes, large quantities, my lord. They keep not only ANC but also SACTU publications, the African Communist and a lot of other publications.
> Swanepoel: Is it locked away or is it ...?
> Williamson: Not while I was there my lord, it was quite clearly visible and available.[40]

In addition to taking note of what was on the Schoons' bookshelves, Williamson and Marius also discussed, once again, the courier system, the method by which Edwards testified to having carried 'literally hundreds' of messages between Botswana and South Africa. Williamson bragged about the effectiveness of the security police courier system, claiming that 'Marius Schoon told me ... we were running the only effective and efficient courier system'.[41] At the same time,

> [Marius] complained to me and asked me to improve the courier system between Botswana and South Africa. He was angry that one message which he had sent to Grahamstown in Easter of 1978 had taken 5.5 months to be delivered.[42]

This admission of Marius's frustrations regarding the courier system raises questions about the aims of a security police involvement in such tasks. Wouldn't the goal have been to carry out their work as well as possible, such that the police were able to glean a maximum amount of information from these communiques?

According to Williamson, he only visited Botswana on one other occasion while the Schoons were living there. In April of 1979, Williamson went to Lusaka, and from there, by plane, to Gaborone. This visit was notable because it was the only occasion where Craig Williamson claims to have interacted with Jeanette in any way.[43] 'I met Jeanette Curtis ... That is right, your worship, at the airport. We were both flying on the same flight ... She was in the company of two ANC protocol officials whom I know as comrades Shuta and Oshkosh.'[44] Apparently, Jeanette and Craig did have a discussion of some sort, but the prosecutor at the trial against Berger and Pillay did 'not wish to go into details of that discussion, your worship'.[45] What kind of conversation would not serve the needs of the prosecution? Was it just a chatty, irrelevant exchange? Did the two argue? Perhaps the details of this chance encounter in Lusaka would have revealed that Craig Williamson was not nearly so close to Jeanette and Marius as he liked to pretend.

Craig Williamson's testimony regarding his role as an infiltrator is intriguing, at times simply because it is a story of intrigues and betrayals, at times for the seeming clarity of what he depicts, and at other times for his pompous exaggerations. It is impossible to say that Williamson was merely a liar or a fool – that he somehow failed as an undercover agent. While he was surely never as much a member of the ANC as he boasted in court, he nonetheless did, at the very least, interact with several people within the organisation, on a few different occasions. Williamson learned at least something about the political work of the ANC, even if he inflated his own importance, as well as the dangers posed by the revolutionary left.

To say that the security police and the ANC had a very similar 'modus operandi' is a damning observation. If one strains to see things from the perspective of a security police officer, it looks like leftists were merely play-acting at tasks that men like Williamson had received paid training to do. It seems painfully obvious that infiltrating these clandestine networks must have been far easier than anyone involved in them would have liked to imagine.

At the same time, Williamson's testimony almost always lacks the kinds of intimate details that one expects from confessions related to eight years of undercover work. In Williamson's most compelling moments, the analysis of his subjects does ring true, but only at the level of basic intellect and superficial observations. Clearly, Williamson's 'expertise' about the ANC was only at the level of abstractions, of ideology. Williamson saw the organisation for what it said about itself and its goals, but somehow missed all the *heart*, all the passion, that undergirded the daily life of a revolutionary.

## The ANC per se

Initially hoping to smash an entire section of the opposition through one grand treason trial, the state gradually realised that this was an impossible dream. During the year that Barbara Hogan spent in detention, the state arrested dozens of people, and tortured them repeatedly, hoping to terrorise them into compliance. However, the friends and family of the tortured began to push back against the state. According to Hogan:

> Because so much of us came from privileged positions, this set of arrests hit the headlines bigtime. Then, friends and activists who were not arrested did the brilliant thing of setting up detainees' parents' support committees. There was a support committee around every detainee and family members used to meet with each other and with the lawyers.[46]

These support committees not only provided a mechanism for parents to support their children and one another, they also generated an embarrassing amount of highly visible protests:

> There were good solid white mamas standing outside John Vorster Square saying, 'Release my detainee.' It became a big issue. And that was the result of our privilege, which was leveraged very successfully by our friends out there ... With that the security police and the National Party were under huge pressure to prove that this was a serious case because the scope of the arrests was massive.[47]

Amid this escalating pressure, 'they were starting to look stupid. The prosecutors were saying "We've got to have a case."'[48] Meanwhile, Alan Fine was acquitted, Cedric Mayson (a member of Beyers Naudé's Christian Institute) was able to flee the country after being released on bail, and charges were withdrawn against a group of trade unionists from East London. 'This all meant that my trial had to be bloody significant', Barbara Hogan said, 'because that's all they had'.[49] In one sense, the case against Barbara Hogan was straightforward, since she had admitted from the first moment that she was a member of the ANC. At the same time, Hogan adamantly insisted that she had no part in the military wing of the party, or violence in any form. Therefore, the state used Barbara Hogan's case to redefine 'treason' to equal merely participating in the ANC and believing in the values that the organisation represented. The goal of Hogan's prosecutors was to prove that these acts – in and of themselves – constituted violence against the state.

Once again, Craig Williamson was called in to testify, in what would prove to be his most heroic role as an expert witness for the state. As he had done already in the previous trials, Williamson's testimony was devoid of any specifics regarding Hogan herself, but rather aimed to indict the ANC, *at the level of ideology*. At the heart of Williamson's testimony was his answer to the question: could a person join the ANC to pursue non-violent aims? Williamson replied:

> The ANC *per se* is inherently violent. So, I'm not denying that it is conceivable that somebody could join with those objectives. What

I'm saying, as I said a bit earlier, is such a person would be confused about the ANC.[50]

Williamson's articulation of this position at Hogan's trial was zealous and repetitive to the point of sheer fanaticism. In Williamson's mind, anyone and everyone participating in the ANC was complicit in the armed struggle. 'Even, I would go so far as to say, giving them [an ANC member] a telephone book. If done as an instruction as a disciplined member of that organization, then it is a revolutionary act.'[51]

For Williamson, the fact that most things that people actually *did* as members of the ANC were not, in fact, violent, made no difference whatsoever.

> The point is that the ANC is involved in what they call a process of armed revolutionary struggle and there is only one armed, revolutionary struggle. Most of the elements of the armed revolutionary struggle are not physically violent, but they are part of one single armed revolutionary struggle.[52]

While Williamson was nothing if not zealous on this point, he was not merely prejudiced. He had clearly read a fair amount of ANC and Marxist writings, prior to his testimony. He was very much aware of the fact that the ANC's theories of revolution were not solely focused on violence. However, in Williamson's view, all the other aspects of the struggle against apartheid ultimately existed only to lay the groundwork for violent revolution.

> So, there are aspects to the African National Congress, to Umkhonto we Sizwe, and to the South African Communist Party, which are not directly involved in military struggle. However, the activities of those units or aspects or divisions are part of an overall whose aim is violent revolution, the armed seizure of state power.[53]

Seeing everything that the ANC did as inevitably leading to one grand conflagration, Williamson slandered all members of the organisation as having blood on their hands, no matter what their actual roles were. In fact, Williamson understood the ANC's rhetorical emphasis on the need for political organising to mean that politics was a necessary ingredient for the armed struggle. 'In the theory of the ANC it is impossible to have successful armed struggle or military actions or terrorist atrocities without fundamental political groundwork being laid first.'[54] In other words, ANC members who claimed to be doing political work 'don't pull the triggers. They just select the targets.'[55] To the extent that Williamson accepted the idea that an ANC member might genuinely abhor violence, he nonetheless insisted that this person would be compelled by the organisation to support the armed struggle, at least at the level of policy.

> Nobody in the ANC is going to force a conscientious objector to pull a trigger, but they will ask him first of all not to object to the policy of the armed overthrow of the state and second of all, if he's an active member, he will be expected to carry out political work for the organization.[56]

Craig Williamson was an operative of a bitterly anti-communist government, working for the security services, which was arguably the wing of the state that was most heavily imbued with the missionary zeal to annihilate communism at all costs. Within this lens, Williamson understood the Communist Party to be the absolute driving force behind the ANC.

> In theory, the Revolutionary Alliance is made up of the main three organizations, ANC, SACTU and SACP, is an alliance of equal organizations under the leadership of the ANC. But that is the theoretical position; the de facto position is that the South African Communist Party, in my experience, is the dominant organization.[57]

Using an anti-communist lens (aided by some amount of genuine study of Marxist texts) Williamson wholeheartedly rejected any attempt to portray trade union organising, particularly for Sactu, as anything other than an attempt to bring about revolutionary change:

> Members of the ANC who are working in a trade union are people who by the very nature of things are involved in attempting to subvert the existing trade union or labour dispensation as part of

their ongoing process of subverting not only the current political system, but also the economic, social and cultural system.[58]

Williamson's point was that just because someone participates in a legal entity doesn't mean that they are not still working towards revolutionary aims.

## From our side

> From our side, the trial had its politics, in terms of showing white people, again, who were not Communist Party, but affiliating themselves with the revolutionary overthrow of the state.
>
> — Barbara Hogan, interview

What is striking about Craig Williamson's testimony, aside from the tenacious repetition, is the fact that so much of what he said was *rational*. That is, at least for a significant portion of the ANC, Williamson's depictions of their ideological priorities – if hateful and caricatured – were more or less accurate. It is true that by 1981 the ANC had spent two decades growing increasingly committed to the armed struggle, and not just in terms of building up the infrastructure of warfare, but also by developing a political consensus within the organisation regarding the necessity of violence. While they may not have been the dominant force within the ANC, there were certainly communists of many stripes who believed in building working-class organisations as a piece of a much larger revolutionary strategy.

However, the fact that Williamson's testimony was grounded in at least some amount of intelligent intellectual analysis did not reduce the menacing danger of his role. It is worth repeating that Craig Williamson gave his testimony against Barbara Hogan on 18 August 1982, which was only *a day* after a parcel bomb, sent at his direction, killed Ruth First. Williamson needs to be understood as a murderer, loyally carrying out the objectives of a deadly regime. Williamson's ideological analysis – that the ANC was a fundamentally violent organisation – was in itself a weapon, targeting not only Barbara Hogan and others facing similar charges, but absolutely anyone who might dare associate themselves with the ANC. As Denis Kuny explained, adopting Williamson's view of the ANC 'would mean that if a person in 1978, 1979, or whenever it might be, associates himself with the ANC and is subsequently charged with that association, then he may be confronted with anything said by any member of the ANC at any time in the past, to any person.'[59] In fact, the implications are even worse than being held accountable for anything that any member of the ANC ever said. In Williamson's view, ANC members were also implicated by the actions and intended actions of the armed wing, even if an individual was themselves unwilling to engage in violence. 'Well, your worship, as I have mentioned before, there are witting and unwitting collaborators ...'[60]

With the help of Denis Kuny, Alan Fine was able to pull off some skilful ideological acrobatics to claim that his interest in trade unionism – even Sactu – was rooted in a desire for small reforms of the capitalist system, rather than a revolutionary allegiance to the ANC. Given that this line of argumentation spared Alan Fine years of time in jail, one can hardly blame him for taking it on, even if it was (strictly speaking) dishonest. Barbara Hogan found herself in a very similar predicament but decided that she was unwilling to disavow her convictions, even though this ultimately led to a sentence of 10 years in jail.

> I had said that I didn't believe in violence, but I *understood* it.
> That was where I had no defence. As I said, we were all defenceless against it because it was true. We could argue that I was non-military and non-violent, but we could not argue that I was not revolutionary. Because it was so important in terms of nonracial struggle that whites align themselves with the revolutionary stance ... So yeah, my trial was a huge embarrassment for me because my prosecutor could tie me up in knots ... You know, there were people in my defence team who were just hoping that I would disavow all this stuff.[61]

Clearly Barbara Hogan had a great deal of courage confidently to declare before an apartheid court her desire to overthrow the state. It is worth underlining the fact that Hogan felt that such a stance was particularly important given the fact that she was white, and privileged. Hogan's sense of the importance of white people visibly taking a radical stand against apartheid has been repeatedly vindicated in the decades since her trial.

'I can tell you it's been a recurring refrain in my life where black people have said to me, "You know your trial made me realise that whites could be part of the struggle."'[62]

As much as Barbara Hogan's stance at her trial had an important political significance, she is also correct to recollect that the prosecution was able to tie her up in knots as a result. Reading the exchanges between Prosecutor Swanepoel and Barbara Hogan, one can easily see how narrow the knife's edge of reasoning was in this trial, as Hogan attempted to present a carefully nuanced position, in response to a brutal binary.

> Swanepoel: Mandela says here ... 'we felt that without violence there would be no way open to the African people to succeed in their struggle against the principle of white supremacy.' What is your comment, do you agree with that or not?
> Hogan: I can see why he said that, and I can understand why he does say that, but for me that is not the only way that I see open.[63]

Given that Mandela, the most esteemed representative of the ANC, says that there is 'no way open' without violence, how can Barbara Hogan possibly contradict this?

> Swanepoel: I think you have said that you believe the ANC can bring about change without using violence.
> Hogan: I believe that is still possible, yes.
> Swanepoel: ... What is your attitude about the use of violence by the ANC?
> Hogan: I regret any act of violence ... I believe that the ANC's purpose in those acts of violence is to try and break down the structures of oppression. They are waging, in a sense, a minor civil war. They are not trying to terrorize a population for the sake of terrorization.[64]

Despite Hogan's attempts to insist that other methods of struggle were still possible, and that violence was regrettable, she nonetheless conceded that the ANC was engaged in 'a minor civil war', which essentially affirmed and bolstered the state's case. Therefore, through sheer persistence, Swanepoel was able to force Hogan to concede, against her better judgement, that she actually condoned violence:

> Swanepoel: So you think it can be condoned?
> Hogan: I think that in the circumstances it can be condoned, but that is not the path that I have chosen ...
> Swanepoel: Not if you can condone it. Do you condone it or not?
> Hogan: Yes, I can condone it.
> Swanepoel: Do you or not?
> Hogan: Yes, I do.
> Swanepoel: Not can. You do?
> Hogan: Yes.[65]

While subtle, the line between testifying that you 'can' condone violence and that yes, you 'do' condone it was deeply significant. Despite Hogan's attempts to present herself as both believing in and working towards a non-violent struggle against apartheid, she could not, in the end, sufficiently distance herself from the violence – both real and imagined – of MK.

Despite Barbara Hogan's desire to be unabashedly revolutionary within the court, she was nonetheless facing charges of treason in a country with the death penalty. Hogan's legal team was determined to provide a vigorous defence, and their attempt to do so provides valuable insights into the possibilities and pitfalls of arguing against Williamson's dangerous interpretation of the inherent violence of the ANC. Barbara Hogan's advocates were Denis Kuny and George Bizos, both very capable lawyers, with distinguished careers spent defending a number of prominent anti-apartheid activists, including Walter Sisulu, Nelson Mandela, Bram Fischer and Steve Biko. Kuny and Bizos were, therefore, very familiar with the long trajectory of resistance to apartheid, including the ANC's earlier tradition of non-violent resistance, and the subsequent turn to armed struggle, after Sharpeville.

In addition to this general knowledge, Hogan's legal defence also called on the expertise of Tom Lodge, a left-wing historian who has studied the liberation struggle in South Africa extensively, throughout his lifetime. Lodge was tasked with reading through a wide range of ANC literature, including documents submitted by Williamson into evidence, Hogan's own writing, and other publications, both recent and historical. Lodge's role, as an academic, was to find a line of argumentation within this literature that could reasonably refute, or at least undermine, Williamson's ideological framework. The resulting memorandum is striking, both in terms of what it offers as a defence, and in terms of how hesitantly this defence was presented. Lodge opened the memorandum by saying, 'I have some reservations about this argument, and I think it needs to be advanced in a very qualified and careful fashion.'[66] The reason that Lodge had reservations about the argument he was offering is fundamental, striking to the heart of the predicament of Hogan's trial:

> I have found <u>no unequivocal evidence</u> that the ANC's leadership is prepared to accept as members people who openly admit having moral and political reluctance to accept the necessity of a violent strategy.[67]

In other words, Barbara Hogan's testimony that she condoned violence represented not merely a moment of weakness within a stressful interaction, but rather it was an inevitable concession, given the nature of the ANC at the time. Over 20 years of developing both the infrastructure and rhetoric of war, an organisational culture had developed within the ANC where advocating non-violence had become virtually impossible. This is all the more striking given the fact that the ANC had spent nearly fifty years as an explicitly pacifist organisation. In fact, the inception of MK was merely a few days after the president of the ANC, Albert Luthuli, had received the Nobel Peace Prize for his staunch commitment to non-violent resistance.[68] Nonetheless, by 1982, Tom Lodge not only could not find any unequivocal evidence that the ANC would welcome members who espoused non-violence, he also found quite a bit of evidence that suggested the contrary:

> A quantity of documentary evidence can be cited to suggest that the position of such people within the organization would not be easy, for example: 'the ANC in teaching its cadres it is not enough to die for freedom, we must also learn to kill for freedom' (*Sechaba*, August 1979, p. 22).[69]

As it was impossible to argue that the ANC embraced members who did not believe in violence, Tom Lodge recommended arguing that there were, at least, sections of the ANC's work that was not itself violent, and that this work was 'separate and isolated from Umkhonto we Sizwe'.[70] In full, Lodge recommended three basic lines of reasoning for Hogan's defence:

1. That since the formation of MK the ANC has continued to attempt to maintain a separate non-military organization within South Africa. That this organization works in isolation from the Umkhonto insurgent groups.
2. That the ANC advocates a multi-dimensional strategy and is sensitive to the dangers of 'militarism,' that is, the subordination of mass (non-violent) political work to requirements of military action.
3. That many of the tasks of the political organization do not have a violent military objective or function.[71]

In fact, Craig Williamson – and by extension the prosecution – did not deny either the first or the third points, although they interpreted them in the most sinister way possible. Therefore, Lodge recommended stressing the fact that the internal political work of ANC members and the armed wing were in important respects largely ignorant of one another:

> Lines of communication are vertical rather than horizontal: Individual units are linked with each other only indirectly through an external official ... and are therefore ignorant of each other's identity and activity ... This compartmentalization contributes to the organizational isolation of military from non-military spheres of activity.[72]

It was an intriguing choice to argue that the cell structure and chains of command created for MK actually provided a degree of autonomy to those members of the organisation whose work was non-military. However, at least in Barbara Hogan's case, this does not appear to have been an altogether accurate depiction. To be sure, as Lodge stressed in his second point above, Hogan *was* deeply concerned about the possible damaging impact of MK on her aboveground political work. The fact that Marius Schoon attempted to push Hogan to host MK cadres (against her wishes) demonstrates the inherently messy process of attempting to create clear and hard lines between military and non-military activity within the ANC's underground.

Throughout his interrogation of Hogan, Swanepoel repeatedly returned to questions such as 'The way you see it, the ANC concerns itself with workers just for the benefit of the workers? Not to bring about change in South Africa?'[73] In other words, despite Alan Fine's acquittal just a year before, the state was deeply sceptical of trade union organisers, whom they saw as manipulatively hiding their Leninist longing for revolution behind a concern for 'the workers'.

To respond to these accusations, Hogan's legal team – like Fine's before them – called on Professor Eddie Webster as an expert on trade unions. Webster's testimony was intended, first and foremost, to persuade the court that 'in themselves [trade unions] are not revolutionary institutions. Trade unions are not the institutions that conservatives fear, nor revolutionaries hope.'[74] Webster's testimony stressed the importance of the 1979 Wiehahn Commission's decision to move towards the legalisation of Black trade unions[75] in terms of understanding the increasing unionisation efforts at the beginning of the 1980s, which Fine, Aggett, Hogan and thousands of others were involved in. Nonetheless, Webster was at pains in his testimony to present workers' attempts to organise, and even major boycotts and strikes as being consistently grounded within legitimate grievances, rather than inspired by union organisers or – least of all – the ANC. '[T]he strikes that take place in South Africa are overwhelmingly spontaneous strikes ... it is sociologically inaccurate, M'Lord, to suggest that it is trade union leaders or trade union officials that are provoking strikes.'[76] Swanepoel challenged Webster on this point, and used writings by the ANC that spoke to the importance of organising the working class, in order to insinuate that underground ANC operatives were responsible for worker unrest. Webster responded:

> I have done detailed analyses which have been widely published of strike actions over the last three years, and M'Lord, I can only say that if these activities are taking place, they have been concealed from me, a zealous social researcher.[77]

Later, Denis Kuny returned to this same question, forcing Webster to answer it a second time:

> Mr. Webster, in your research into the question of strikes over the last two years have you found any evidence at all that any of those strikes have been initiated by, stoked up by the ANC or any political agitators?
> No, M'Lord.[78]

One particular exchange between Swanepoel and Webster encapsulates the tension between these two seemingly contradictory truths:

> Swanepoel: Would you say that a trade union can be used as a tool to bring about revolution?
> Webster: No.
> Swanepoel: Can workers be used as a tool to bring about revolution?
> Webster: Of course.[79]

This is perhaps one of the most cogent and honest exchanges of the whole trial. However, it seems unlikely that either Swanepoel or Judge Van Dyk comprehended the subtle distinction that Webster was attempting to make. Indeed, throughout Webster's testimony, Judge Van Dyk intervened on multiple occasions, expressing open distrust and disdain for Webster, and for the trade union movement more broadly. In the judge's mind, the goal of all working-class organising was always about 'crippling industry'. Consequently, Webster was forced into the unenviable position of claiming, repeatedly, that trade unions primarily existed in order to lessen disruptions to industry, and to blunt the rage of the working class by providing proper channels for negotiating with management.

The other academic who was called as an expert witness for the defence was Tom Lodge, who had already helped to prepare the defence strategy in advance of the trial. Lodge testified before the court on 30 August 1982. Swanepoel began by immediately attempting to insult Tom Lodge by calling him a communist, to which Lodge responded calmly and clearly:

> Swanepoel: Do you favor the socialist system of government?
> Lodge: Yes, I think I do.

> Swanepoel: ... But would you say that socialism could be the answer to the problems in this country?
> Lodge: If by socialism you mean a great deal of State intervention to ensure social justice, redistribution of wealth and so forth, yes.[80]

Furthermore, as to whether Lodge had studied the SACP, Lodge responded: 'It had to be stupid of me not to know anything about the South African Communist Party. An understanding of it is indispensable to an understanding of the other groups in this country.'[81]

In short, Tom Lodge was at pains to present himself not as a partisan witness, but rather as a serious scholar, with an interest in social movements. In outlining his expertise regarding the ANC, Lodge testified to reading through '60 reels of microfilm collected by American scholars of documentation on the ANC'.[82] His expertise also included a reading of *Sechaba, Mayibuye, The African Communist, Pakhati* and the *Voice of Women* journals, all produced by the organisation. Swanepoel questioned Lodge regarding these publications:

> Swanepoel: Would you agree with me that to get a proper understanding of what the ANC is, one will get the best information in publications published by the ANC itself?
> Lodge: No, not at all... It would be exceptionally naïve – for an academic that is – to take everything that is published at face value.[83]

Lodge's response here is intended to imply that the court would have to be 'exceptionally naïve' to accept Williamson's analysis of ANC materials as the indisputable truth of the organisation. However, Swanepoel was clearly sympathetic to Williamson, who sat next to the prosecutor throughout the two hours of questioning Tom Lodge, passing Swanepoel hand-written notes.[84] Therefore, Swanepoel attempted through his questions to present 'Major Williamson' as someone with equivalent expertise regarding the ANC as Tom Lodge. Further, Swanepoel implied that Lodge's decision not to consult Major Williamson in his research on the ANC was prejudicial. However, Lodge was willing to concede that it was important to hear 'both sides' on this subject. 'That is one of the reasons, for example, why I pay so much attention to Court records and to police testimony in Court.'[85]

Tom Lodge's role for the defence was like Webster's role, in that Lodge sought to downplay and dispute a depiction of the ANC as a violent, revolutionary organisation. 'I don't think [the ANC] is altogether revolutionary. Of the liberation organizations that I know about, it is one of the more conservative ones.'[86] This line of argumentation seems to go against the conclusion that Lodge had reached in his pre-trial memoranda that 'ultimately the SACP and ANC have convergent goals'. However, Lodge also admitted that 'I don't see where this gets us in furthering Barbara's case.'[87] Therefore, the strategic tack that Lodge followed was to attempt to place some distance between the ANC and communist revolution. This was linked to the strategic goal of undermining Williamson's expertise, by suggesting 'that CW's information and training came from a tendentious and unrepresentative source (most of ANC not communist, etc. etc.)'.[88] Along these lines, while on the witness stand, Tom Lodge portrayed the ANC as being unclear about their ultimate aims (in terms of a negotiated transition, an armed overthrow of the state, and so forth) and determined to inflate their own importance as an organisation.

The question that dominated Swanepoel's interrogation of Lodge – like the rest of the trial – was the violent nature of the African National Congress. While remaining polite, Tom Lodge did make some attempt to push against the state's portrayal of the ANC as an inherently violent organisation. 'I am sorry, I don't want to quibble, but violence and revolution are not synonymous.'[89] Tom Lodge sincerely believed that the ANC's turn to armed struggle was not nearly as inevitable as it was often portrayed at the time and is still often portrayed now. At the time of his testimony, Lodge had written an academic article that attempted to demonstrate that 'There were opportunities then for furthering its cause without turning to violence, which [the ANC] didn't take advantage of.'[90] In other words, Lodge held out some hope for non-violent solutions to ending apartheid:

> Swanepoel: A non-violent political revolution is a contradiction in terms. Do you accept this?
> Lodge: No.
> Swanepoel: Why not?
> Lodge: Because it is incorrect.[91]

THE TRIALS

However, Lodge's relatively innocent quibbling was quickly undermined by Swanepoel's line of questioning. For example, when Swanepoel sought to equate overthrowing the government with violence, Tom Lodge first was able deftly to evade this association:

> Swanepoel: Would you agree with me, the ultimate aim is to overthrow the government by means of violence?
> Lodge: Overthrow the present government, if violence will help to do so, the ANC will use it.

However, Swanepoel would not allow Lodge to make this distinction.

> Swanepoel: No, that is not the question. Is the aim to overthrow the government by means of violence?
> Lodge: I think the aim is to overthrow the government and the ANC has no scruples about using violence in doing so. So, yes.[92]

In fact, Tom Lodge was attempting to say something markedly different from Swanepoel in this moment. Therefore, the 'so, yes' at the end of the exchange marks a notable victory for the state's case, as Swanepoel had skilfully backed Lodge into affirming that the aim of the ANC was to use violence to overthrow the apartheid state. Swanepoel then won a further concession from Lodge:

> Swanepoel: So, if one calls the ANC a revolutionary organization, it is because the ANC employs violence?
> Lodge: Very well.
> Swanepoel: Do you accept that?
> Lodge: Yes.[93]

It is not at all clear – given the remainder of Tom Lodge's testimony – why he would have said, 'Very well,' and accepted the formulation that the ANC ought to be considered a revolutionary organisation merely because it utilised violence. Within the domain of ideological jousting that was The State vs. Hogan trial it seems that this moment marks (depending on one's vantage point) either a damaging blow on the part of the state or a serious strategic error on the part of Hogan's defence.

In addition to bringing in Webster and Lodge as academic witnesses, Hogan's defence team also had to grapple directly with Craig Williamson. George Bizos's cross-examination of Williamson was grounded in a series of questions that the defence team had drafted in advance of the trial. For example:

11. From most of the academic and popular studies of the ANC easily available to a student in this country what is the dominant impression one would receive of the ANC's ideological position?
12. How wide a circulation do you think documents like *Sechaba* have in this country even among ANC supporters?[94]

Based on these questions, George Bizos asked Williamson about a series of documents from the ANC to which young students might have access, which presented the organisation differently than the documents that Williamson submitted into evidence. Since all materials related to the ANC were banned within South Africa, and as Williamson had done his reading in exile, it was at least theoretically possible that Hogan had limited knowledge of the debates regarding the armed struggle, which would have been readily available outside of South Africa. If this were the case, then Hogan could have reasonably joined the ANC based on the organisation's history, and the documents available to her, without considering herself to be aspiring towards armed revolution, treason or terrorism. For example, Bizos used writing by Nelson Mandela to try to insist on the fact that the ANC was not led by the Communist Party, and also to insist on a certain set of reasonings behind the turn to armed struggle. Given his intensely anti-communist prejudice, Williamson refused to agree that Mandela should be taken as 'the' leader of the ANC, and also saw many of Mandela's statements – the ones that stressed a desire for nonracialism and democracy – as mere propaganda.

> One has to try always in analyzing documents of not only the ANC, any political movement, to make a distinction between propaganda and policy and a lot of the statements that the defence

has been alluding to, must by the very nature of those statements, fall into the category of propaganda.[95]

In addition, Bizos attempted to present the 1955 Freedom Charter, which outlines the broad ideals that someone sympathetic to the ANC might aspire to, as a foundational text of the ANC. Crucially, this document was drafted *before* the turn to armed struggle in 1961. Therefore, Bizos implied that it would be possible for someone to be an active supporter of the ANC, grounded in the organisation's earlier commitment to non-violent resistance. However, Williamson rejected this line of reasoning by highlighting the multiple possible interpretations of the Freedom Charter. 'Your worship, the Freedom Charter is an extremely sophisticated document allowing a veritable jungle of interpretations.'[96]

Another line of defence that Bizos attempted was to make a distinction between how Williamson interpreted ANC positions and how young idealistic students would have interpreted the same thing. While it is certainly reasonable to believe that a security police officer and a student activist would read ANC literature through an immensely different lens, Williamson rejected this idea entirely:

> I certainly never in my experience came across anybody in all my years ... who distinguished between the ANC and its violent methods of achieving its aims and goals. They were seen as being virtually one unity.[97]

Again and again, the fact that the ANC was, in fact, committed to a sustained armed struggle against the apartheid state beguiled all of Bizos's attempts to present Hogan's politics in a more nuanced light. Hogan's defence was to say that she was not personally engaged in any act of violence, and so the terms of conspiracy or treason should not extend to her simply because she was a member of a group that espoused violence. However, at the same time, Hogan herself admitted that the aim of the ANC was to overthrow the government by force.

Ultimately, the court accepted Craig Williamson's ideological line and charged Barbara Hogan with treason, even though the defence had demonstrated that she was not involved with the armed struggle in any form.

> That was the dilemma: I was not involved in MK. They didn't know how to charge me, and the judge said that nothing per se that I'd done was illegal except for being a member of the ANC. So, the only recourse they had was to charge me with treason.[98]

Judge Van Dyk did *not*, in fact, rule that 'nothing per se' that Hogan had done was illegal. Rather, in his ruling, Van Dyk profoundly redefined the terms of illegal activity in South Africa. As George Bizos noted during the trial, an important legal precedent was set by the case against Barbara Hogan. 'The State has for the first time to our knowledge, m'lord, in any case attempted to equate membership of the African National Congress with treason or terrorism.'[99] The state was willing to concede that Hogan's activities were in and of themselves not of a violent nature, but insisted that this fact, in and of itself, did not lessen the treasonous nature of the activity. Judge Van Dyk, in explaining his sentencing, summarised Barbara Hogan's political participation as follows:

> Through her actions she assisted the ANC in planning its strategy in the labour field to organize the mainly black working class in order to create a trade union consciousness amongst them which could by clever manipulation be converted into a political and class consciousness and ultimately into a revolutionary consciousness.[100]

According to Van Dyk, Hogan's work for the ANC had only one possible endpoint:

> The switch from a non-violent political struggle to a violent militant confrontation would follow almost as a matter of course.[101]

The idea that a person could be convicted and sentenced not for what they have *actually done*, but rather for the actions that 'would follow almost as a matter of course' was the most devastating and damning feature of the trial against Barbara Hogan.

This ruling was not only personally devastating to Hogan, who remained in jail until the unbanning of the ANC in 1990, but also set a vicious precedent for all future cases involving participants of the domestic rebellions of the 1980s. According to Hogan:

> All these people who later became [the United Democratic Front][102] would be charged with treason because they realised that the onslaught had shifted significantly from not only military onslaught but to mass struggle in a *very* powerful way, because it was organised struggle. They had to try and clip all of that in the bud and sort of make treason now to be extended to anyone who opposed the state. So, my trial was *very* important from that point of view.[103]

Hogan is correct to link her trial to a series of later trials. Judge Van Dyk was open about the fact that he intended his harsh treatment of Hogan to have a deterrent effect on other radicals:

> I do not agree with Mr. Bizos' further contention that a heavy sentence would, because we are dealing with people's political convictions, have no deterrent effect on similar would-be perpetrators.[104]

The new definition of treason that Hogan's trial unleashed not only empowered the apartheid state to use legal mechanisms to detain and imprison people for their treasonous belief in nonracialism and democracy. At a more sinister level, Judge Van Dyk's ruling against Barbara Hogan was quite explicitly framed within the logics of emergency wartime measures, and therefore Van Dyk was also quite explicit about the fact that the state was justified, under such conditions, to execute anyone they deemed to be guilty of treason.

> It stands to reason that in times of actual war the penalty for treason in an appropriate case may very well be the death sentence. The question may well be asked if South Africa today does not find herself already in a state of war, albeit of a somewhat unconventional nature. The ANC on the evidence before me, regards itself as being at war with the Republic of South Africa on all fronts. This the accused knew and admitted in evidence before me.[105]

The apartheid state's use of the court system to articulate Craig Williamson's view of the ANC meant the obliteration of the distinction between non-violent political work and clandestine armed activities. Beyond the courtroom, this ruling gave the apartheid state extreme latitude in taking military action against individuals engaged in radical politics, even if such military actions had 'a somewhat unconventional nature'. In other words, the ruling against Barbara Hogan implicitly sanctioned the killing of people like Jeanette and Katryn Schoon, regardless of their roles within the ANC.

# Part 4

# Forced Asylum, 1981–1984

# 9 | No Asylum from Her Majesty

**Another cover story**

In September 1981, Jeanette and Marius Schoon were hired as co-directors of the Botswana branch of the (UK-based) International Voluntary Service. The IVS developed as a pacifist response to world war, enabling people from different nations and backgrounds to work together as an antidote to militarism and patriotism. For example, in the aftermath of World War 2, British volunteers went to Germany and worked alongside volunteers from all over the continent helping to rebuild war-torn cities. The organisation also responded to natural disasters and initiatives that would now fall under the broad umbrella of 'development' work. IVS in Britain had joined with other UK agencies as part of the British Volunteer Programme, funded mainly by the government, and it had 'overseas programmes' in several other, mainly African, countries. In fact, according to Nigel Watt, who was the general secretary of IVS at the time,[1] 'budget wise, the overseas programme was the biggest because we got 75 per cent, sometimes more, from the government for this programme. It was kind of like the British Peace Corps in a way.'[2] Much of the overseas work had a strong emphasis on development, such as digging wells, building schools, and teaching and working at orphanages. There was, since the organisation's founding, a strong focus on the value of hard work on improving society. However, IVS staff would have resented being lumped together with

NGOs and charities that are paternalistic, who simply provide 'service' without a sense of mutual humanity:

> We tried to make it one operation, so that in those days when we sent volunteers to Botswana, say, as part of their preparation we would ask them to attend an international work camp here [in the UK] before they went, so that they would understand the whole ethos of volunteering.[3]

In fact, the situation in Botswana for IVS was substantially different from how one might imagine the Peace Corps operating in Africa. First, the organisation did not pretend to be politically neutral, but rather, 'we thought we were supporting anti-apartheid in a way by demonstrating that racial harmony can exist in the neighbouring countries [to South Africa]. I suppose that was the kind of motivation, you could say, for IVS as an organisation to be there.'[4] Beyond symbolic support, IVS also sought to provide direct assistance to Botswana, 'in order to help build capacity in the country. In those days there were genuine manpower shortages because under the colonial regime very few people had gotten an education.'[5] According to Watt, the way that the organisation determined precisely what jobs needed to be filled, or what skills would be of value was by sending someone down from the UK who would

> talk to people in the government, talk to local organisations, NGOs and so on to find out what the needs were, then come back with a shopping list of, you know, we need X number of teachers and whatever else. And then from general recruitment we would try to match them to a request we had for a volunteer. For example, out of a list of 82 requests we probably filled 20 of them ... a librarian, one in the newspaper, a couple were in the agricultural research station, there were a couple of midwives in the hospital in the north of Botswana.[6]

The phrase 'volunteer' is perhaps slightly misleading in this context. British citizens who were sent to work in Botswana (or elsewhere) received what was referred to as a 'volunteer salary', which was actually the same as what any local citizen would get for the same job, 'or even in some cases more'.[7] In Botswana, IVS volunteers worked directly shadowed by a local person, who was learning how to do their job. For example, a white journalist from England would have a Black African person at their side while out at meetings, doing interviews, typing up drafts, doing layout and editing and so on, constantly. In other words, the volunteer posting was not simply intended as a means to fill in gaps in the local skillset, but actively to build up those skills within the population. Furthermore, IVS in Botswana placed numerous volunteers in positions of support for the 'Brigades' movement, which was a co-operative rural development programme, started by a left-wing South African named Patrick van Rensburg.

After having attempted to run the Botswana programmes entirely from the UK in the past, by 1981 the organisation had decided that it was important to hire people locally to run the projects in the country. Therefore, Jeanette and Marius Schoon were, for IVS purposes, local. The Schoons were hired as co-directors. This was not uncommon at IVS, as many married couples shared their posts. Notably, however, Nigel Watt has entirely forgotten this fact, with the passing of time. In his memories, only Marius exists. Watt declared confidently that 'Jenny was not employed by us; it was just Marius. We have employed a couple of married couples as job shares, but I don't think Jenny was part of the job here.' What is striking about this omission is that Watt actually remembers Jenny being present, on a regular basis. Immediately after saying that she was not the co-director, Watt added, 'though she did come always with Marius when we had meetings and stuff. And I think she was involved, whether she did it as a volunteer or what'.[8] In another moment, Watt spoke about how 'Marius and Jenny would host volunteer meetings (apart from obviously having volunteers in for a meal, when they came to town or something) maybe three or four times a year, a meeting of all of the volunteers.'[9] Nigel Watt's erasure of Jenny's role is normal, in so far as she was ignored from essentially all sides, from the security police to the leaders of a peace organisation. Jenny Schoon exists at mealtimes, even at the meetings (for some forgotten reason), but not when it comes to having actual decision-making power or being a real political threat. For example, was IVS aware that the Schoons were members of the ANC? Marius, yes, of course. 'We knew that Marius was still involved with the

ANC and he was doing ANC work in Botswana. And we were happy with that as long as he behaved himself, sort of thing, didn't get us into trouble. He was, I think, reasonably efficient. As an older man he was kind of an uncle figure for the volunteers, who were mostly quite young 20s.'[10]

## Intolerable pressure

In the midst of an escalating campaign in South Africa against the underground political networks that the Schoons played a critical role in building, the Schoons found themselves, in Botswana, to be the targets of a related, but different campaign against them orchestrated by the British government. In fact, as soon as the Schoons took the job as co-directors of IVS, in September of 1981, they came under a new level of surveillance and scrutiny, not only from the South Africans but also by the Botswana government, and by 'Her Majesty's' government in London. According to the British FCO, the Botswana government was immediately uncomfortable with the Schoons working for IVS and sought to have the British block the hiring. At that time, the British FCO chose not to intervene. However, less than a year later, the British began receiving intelligence, presumably from the apartheid security services,[11] which persuaded them to take action against the Schoons:[12]

> In July 1982, a [redacted] report was received in London indicating that the previous month Mr. Schoon had taken part in a meeting in Botswana to discuss an operation designed to destabilize the South African 'homeland' of Bophuthatswana, and to assassinate its president.[13]

Without knowing the source of this information, and without any other corroborating evidence, it is impossible to either confirm or deny this accusation. No other source of either written or oral testimony refers to Marius Schoon as even tangentially engaged in anything along the lines of assassinating a president. Certainly, neither Marius himself, nor any of his closest friends and comrades – some of whom *were* MK soldiers – refer to him in this way. Nonetheless, this image of Marius Schoon as an ANC 'terrorist' (a term they explicitly used in later documents) took root in the imagination of the British government and began to impact their policy decisions. This process began gradually, almost at a subterranean level, but by the end of a year it had reached fever pitch.

Starting in August of 1982, the British government began a campaign of 'intolerable pressure', in hopes of forcing the IVF to fire the Schoons, or at the very least to get them out of Botswana. When speaking to the IVS, the representatives of the British government felt that it was impossible to speak candidly about their actual motivations for taking action against the Schoons. The information they had received that presented Marius Schoon as a terrorist was deemed classified. While British state operatives declined to pass on their 'intelligence' to the IVS, they formulated their message in a way that is striking, and quite significant. The IVS was informed 'that the linking of Mr. Schoon by the South African authorities with the ANC (through the Barbara Hogan trial) places IVS volunteers in physical danger'.[14] Three things are of particular note here. First, it is quite clear that the apartheid state's targeted campaign against Hogan, and other comrades of the Schoons, had the desired effect of sullying the Schoons and spreading the message internationally that there was a large (and violent) conspiracy against apartheid. Second, it is significant that the FCO phrased their warning in terms of a threat of physical danger. Third, it is worth noting that when the British government spoke of 'physical danger', they were speaking only of the risk to British citizens, who were working in Botswana, in proximity to the Schoons. What they did not say, what is maddeningly absent, is any mention of any physical danger to the Schoons themselves. It is clear from reading these documents – and this sentiment only becomes more pronounced with its repetition over time – that the British government did not intervene in this matter based on *humanitarian* concerns.

Nonetheless, the FCO began to 'suggest' that the Schoons must be fired. Even in the first of many meetings with IVS, the government underlined their suggestion by declaring that 'if IVS resisted this suggestion, our only sanction would be the withdrawal of financial support'.[15] This threat was quite severe. In the early 1980s, IVS ran volunteer programmes in several different countries, and these programmes were heavily funded by the British government. At the time when this threat was made, the total funding at stake was £314 000. At today's currency values, this would equal nearly one million British pounds. In this light, one can understand why

Nigel Watt, the general secretary of the IVS (and the man responsible for hiring the Schoons)[16] described the pressure that was put on him and his organisation as 'intolerable'.[17]

Initially, Nigel Watt made what efforts he could to resist the pressure being put on him by the FCO. For example, in an early meeting, Watt explained that IVS had a contractual obligation to retain the Schoons until August of 1984. To this, CW Squire, representing the FCO, insisted that 'certainly August 1983 was an outside date by which we felt the Schoons should be clear of any involvement with IVS volunteer program in Botswana'.[18] Exchanges such as these continued for many months between Nigel Watt and representatives of the British state. From the state's perspective, it was critical to induce Mr Watt's co-operation, to make IVS responsible for any action taken against the Schoons, rather than the state.

Quite unwittingly, it seems, Nigel Watt took one step, relatively early on, which significantly aided the state's campaign against the Schoons. In January of 1983, Watt sent out a letter to a dozen leaders of IVS, expressing alarm at apartheid raids into neighbouring countries and asking them 'to use what influence you have to help increase the pressure from this country to prevent South Africa violating international law again in the future'.[19] Unlike the motives of the FCO, it seems clear that Nigel Watt's motives for this letter stem from a genuine humanitarian concern. Watt was appalled by the brazen violence of the apartheid state and hoped to find ways to protect the hundreds of volunteers his organisation had stationed throughout southern Africa. However, Watt's letter was then forwarded to Stanley Cohen, an MP, and then onwards to the FCO. At that point, Nigel Watt's sentiment that 'in these circumstances, it is hard to maintain the kind of political neutrality which charity law demands'[20] was turned on its head by the FCO, who believed the letter 'hopefully strengthens our case and shows that IVS themselves are alert to the security threat to their volunteers in Southern Africa'.[21] They then used the letter as leverage to try and increase the pressure against Watt and IVS more broadly, to get them to get rid of the Schoons and to cut all ties to the liberation movements in southern Africa. While Watt (and IVS broadly) believed that the violence of apartheid required their members actively to oppose it, the government insisted (and even more bluntly, over time) that being a British 'volunteer' meant staying 'neutral' and that, in this case, 'neutrality' equalled distancing oneself from the struggle against apartheid as much as possible. Remember also that Nigel Watt's concern for the safety of his volunteers (and innocent civilians throughout southern Africa) may have been a convenient leverage point for the FCO, but it was by no means the initial impetus for their concerns regarding Marius Schoon. For the British state, the problem with Marius Schoon (and, to a lesser degree, by extension Jenny) was that he was an ANC member. This concern only translates into anything related to 'physical danger' in the context of a rogue minority regime that is willing to kill indiscriminately in the name of fighting 'terrorism'.

Looking back on it now, Nigel Watt insists that he and the organisation as a whole resisted the pressure being put on them by the government. 'We thought we're an independent organisation and we're not going to be told what to do. Least of all by the South African authorities.'[22] As late as March of 1983 – roughly half a year after the first 'suggestion' to get rid of the Schoons – Nigel Watt was still not persuaded to do so. Watt appealed to Lord Elwyn Jones, the British high commissioner in Botswana, at a meeting on 17 March, during which he insisted that the Schoons were capable directors of the organisation. They were people he would like to keep on the staff to expand the work of IVS in Botswana, he said. Further, Watt 'felt that the Schoons might derive some protection from being IVS representatives here and so be more at risk if they left that job'.[23] In hindsight, Watt's suspicion that the Schoons would be at risk after leaving the IVS was proven justified, a thousand-fold. Nonetheless, Lord Jones 'demurred, but it is irrelevant anyway.'[24] During this meeting, the two men discussed the possibility of allowing the Schoons to fulfil the remainder of their contract by taking on some other role within IVS, in the UK. For reasons that weren't explicitly stated, Nigel Watt wasn't sure whether the Schoons would even be interested in this offer. Still, it was a proposal he was prepared to make and, at this point in time at least, one that the British government was willing to entertain.

It is unclear how much of these machinations between the British government and the IVS (led by Nigel Watt) Marius or Jenny were aware of. When Marius was interviewed, roughly a decade later, by Hilda Bernstein,[25] Marius recalled only one meeting with Nigel, and he claimed that the meeting took place in May of 1983. In Marius's telling:

The General Secretary of IVS flew out from England, to tell us that he'd just been informed by the British Government – by the foreign office – that they felt that the lives of British volunteers were being put at risk, having us in the program and that we were to be terminated immediately (or else they were going to withdraw funding from the program). So, this happened in about May of 1983. Then, we were staying on in the program until a successor had been appointed. Jenny was due to fly to England in July of 1983, to be part of the interview process for the successor.[26]

Now, of course Marius's memory may have failed him to some extent, but it also seems clear from this account that Nigel Watt was not being entirely truthful with Marius. The idea that Watt had 'just been informed' severely underestimates the months-long campaign to have the Schoons removed from Botswana. Furthermore, it appears that Nigel Watt stressed to Marius the potential danger (not to the Schoons, but to volunteers, it's worth repeating), rather than anything about Marius's politics. Also, in Marius's version of the story, it sounds as if the Schoons accepted the idea that they were in danger and that they were willing to continue working for the IVS as amicably as possible, including Jenny's planned trip to England, to help to interview a successor for the job of co-director. The story contained in the archives of the British FCO unfolds quite differently from Marius's recollection.

On 8 April 1983, the British Foreign and Commonwealth Office noticed a job posting in the *New Statesman* periodical for a field officer for the IVF in Botswana; the job was due to begin in either June or July. So, clearly the decision to terminate and replace the Schoons was taken before May. Further, RFR Deare (of the FCO) documented a phone call between himself and Nigel Watt, on 20 April 1983. At this time, Watt explained that he had been down to Botswana in March, to talk to the Schoons. During this meeting, Nigel Watt offered the Schoons a job in the UK, after leaving Botswana and, 'much to his surprise they had shown considerable interest in this possibility, and IVS National Committee would this evening be considering what terms should be offered'.[27] It is intriguing that this offer to finish out their contracts in the UK is not something that Marius saw fit to mention when recounting the incident. Similarly, when asked to speak about this incident in a recent interview, Nigel Watt had no recollection of the 'considerable interest' that the Schoons indicated regarding working in the UK. In fact, Watt downplayed the significance of his offer by saying that, 'I mean, it wasn't that big of an office. We had probably in what we called the overseas department about four of us ... so we'd have given him some temporary posts ...'[28] Watt offered no concrete explanation of the job that the Schoons may have been offered, or why this path never materialised. He speculated that 'maybe the sort of work we were giving them might not have been very stimulating'.[29] Such a sentiment rings somehow false, given the 'considerable interest' that the Schoons indicated at the time. Further, this explanation seems to ignore entirely the fact that for the Schoons, moving to the UK would have been not only a job offer, but also an offer of genuine asylum, in terms of viable passports and the right to raise their children in a stable, developed country, rather than at the frontier of an extended armed conflict with a despised minority regime.

At the time, there was, however, a growing debate within the British government as to whether the UK should even be willing to allow such a thing to happen. On 20 April 1983, for the first time, hand-written in the margins, the FCO started to show discomfort with the idea of welcoming the Schoons into the UK by asking, '... but did he [Nigel Watt] not advise against this?'[30] It seems that the matter of allowing the Schoons asylum in the UK was far from settled, at least for the next month or so. Just a week later, on 28 April 1983, Lord Elwyn Jones met with Marius, and again the possibility of moving to the UK was discussed. According to Jones, Marius 'was not quite as responsive as Mr. Watt reported. He seemed quite ready to go quietly but was perhaps not quite so ready to accept that it was really necessary'.[31] In addition, Marius informed the high commissioner that Jeanette had Irish citizenship. 'Incidentally Mrs. Schoon's acquisition of an Irish passport is quite recent ... It should remove any problem of her settling in the UK *and so ease the way* [emphasis added] for her husband to be given permission to do so.'[32] For Jones at least (and he stayed fairly consistent in this stance throughout) the only reasonable course of action seemed to be for the Schoons to leave Botswana, and then to resettle in the UK. But once again, the reply in the margins was not nearly so friendly, as someone in London wrote, 'Not necessarily!'[33] A few days later, for the first time a representative of the British government sent a memo in order explicitly to declare that he was 'not convinced that we would be well advised to help them enter this country to take up work at IVS headquarters in Leicester'.[34]

Another important matter that Marius either forgot, or saw no reason to mention, was the discussion with Nigel Watt regarding the ANC. Nigel Watt told the FCO that 'while Mr. Schoon acknowledged membership of the ANC, Mrs. Schoon claimed that she was not a member.'[35] I [Deare] said that in practical terms the point was largely academic, given what had been alleged about Mrs. Schoon's activities during last year's treason trials in the Republic.'[36] What is striking about Deare's firm sense that Jeanette was a committed radical in her own right, regardless of her claim that she was not an ANC member, is the fact that his confidence is rooted in the testimony at the treason trials of comrades of the Schoons. In essence, then, Deare accepts without question the view of 'the Republic' in their accusations that the Schoons were members of a criminal conspiracy to overthrow the state through violent revolution. This is a particularly bold stance to take, given that Alan Fine was actually acquitted – by the South African 'Republic' (for terrorism) and his legal defence was, simply and plainly, that his associations were with Jeanette Schoon (a Sactu trade unionist) rather than with Marius Schoon (an ANC member).

As late as May of 1983 – despite all the pressure, and even though IVS was in the process of hiring their replacement – it seems that it was not entirely certain that the Schoons would actually be compelled to leave Botswana. A Mr Thorpe, from the Southern Africa Department of the UK, was travelling in Lesotho, and encountered Francis Johnston, an IVS representative who was stationed there. According to Johnston, Nigel Watt had convened a meeting of the southern African regional leadership of the organisation, where he had explained 'that as a result of pressure from the FCO the Schoons had resigned their role from IVS in Botswana. This news had apparently caused some concern amongst the volunteers who had at their initiative written to the Schoons to express sympathy and to say they should not resign simply because of possible danger to other volunteers.'[37] This gesture of sympathy and solidarity from volunteers within IVS (particularly others working in the southern African region, who were similarly in danger of apartheid attacks) is very significant. In moments such as these, it seems clear that the IVS, as an organisation with a set of principles, and as a collection of individuals, was not necessarily persuaded by the reasoning the British government used to try to persuade them to remove the Schoons. However, over time, the government tried less and less to persuade IVS, and more and more relied simply on coercion, insistence and, in essence, blackmail (the threat of withdrawing £314 000 annually).

On 24 May 1983, Lord Jones met with Marius Schoon. Marius acknowledged that his family and other volunteers were at risk from apartheid aggression, but Marius felt that the volunteers generally accepted these risks. In addition, Marius 'said that IVS was if anything even more opposed to violence than was HMG'.[38] On the face of it, this assertion is simply and plainly accurate, a bald-faced true statement. The IVS is a pacifist organisation, founded in the aftermath of World War 1, and Her Majesty's government were the perpetrators of the world's largest, and arguably most violent, empire in history. Nonetheless, Lord Jones retained his suspicions. Jones insisted that 'the Pretoria bombing increases my concern that there should be no delay in appointing a replacement'.[39] The Pretoria bombing was an MK attack, on 20 May 1983, which targeted the South African Air Force, and killed 19 people, injuring over 200 more. Many of these were members of the Air Force, but many others were civilians. It is therefore often referred to as a terrorist attack. An unintended irony of the British High Commission marking this bombing as a critical reason to expedite the removal of the Schoons from Botswana is that MK later explained that the bombing in Pretoria was meant (at least in part) as a retaliatory attack for the bomb that had assassinated Ruth First just half a year earlier. Of course, the men responsible for the bomb that killed Ruth First would later also take responsibility for the bomb that killed the Schoons in Angola.

By the beginning of June, the British government's determination to remove the Schoons from Botswana accelerated considerably, often on a daily basis. In addition to the Pretoria bombing by MK (which the British did *not* imply that the Schoons had any involvement in) the British government also received additional intelligence in May of 1983, once again from a redacted source (presumably the South Africans), which implicated Marius Schoon in another military attack inside South Africa. As a result of this accusation the 'Botswana Special Branch called in Schoon but found nothing on which to hold him'.[40] Adolf Hirschfeld, the head of the special branch in Botswana, 'took the line that they had warned us about Schoon soon after his appointment and that we had taken no action and were not likely to do so now'.[41] In spite of this, the high commissioner apparently felt unable to share his 'intelligence' with the Botswana special branch, nor to admit that in fact the British government had been steadily taking steps to have the Schoons removed, at that point for the better part of a year. Therefore, Jones felt that he was 'handicapped in making any move here'[42] and yet felt increasingly worried about the 'considerable embarrassment'[43] that would come to HMG if the Schoons were kidnapped or killed by the apartheid state.

Jones wanted to increase the pressure on IVS, to force them to remove the Schoons more quickly. However, as always, he felt that 'obviously IVS could not be given the full report'.[44] Therefore, he recommended telling IVS a summary version, which explained that the South Africans believed that Marius was involved in an MK attack in South Africa. It is not clear from the files whether this information, in any form, was ever passed on to Nigel Watt, or anyone else in IVS. Regardless of the specifics of what was said to IVS, it's clear that at this point in the process the British government was done with 'suggesting' and were at the point of absolutely insisting.

When Lord Jones sent a telegram to London on 3 June, communication began flowing between various individuals and departments of the government, analysing how best to proceed. In Thorpe's assessment, 'this poses serious personal danger for Mr. Schoon himself'.[45] What is striking here is that it was, in fact, the first time that anyone in the British administration admitted to any direct risk to the Schoons, at all. Of course, Thorpe did finish the sentence by repeating the refrain: 'and significantly increases the risk for British volunteers ...'[46] Just one paragraph later, Thorpe returned to this refrain, with more emphasis, declaring that, 'Our immediate responsibility is to the British volunteers in Botswana, and to the reputation of the British Volunteer Programme.' By now, 'the concern for the safety of Mr Schoon is limited to the fact' that the FCO is 'obliged to take reasonable action' in order to avoid being (once again) embarrassed by an 'incident involving Mr Schoon'.[47]

As a further indication of Thorpe's assessment of the risks facing the Schoons, a later proclamation by him is as troubling as it is bizarre. Citing no evidence, and no source (not even a redacted one) Thorpe wrote that, 'Mr. Schoon could also be a target of the ANC since he may be suspected (probably wrongly) of being a South African informer.' While the tone of

Thorpe's message was urgent, he nonetheless insisted that 'we cannot make Mr. Schoon leave'.[48] IVS had to be seen to be taking the responsibility for moving the Schoons out, as quickly as possible. Upon leaving Botswana, Thorpe claims that 'there are, as it happens, no reasons why Schoon should not come to the UK, if he wishes'.[49] That is, according to a redacted source, there is nothing on Marius's record that would bar him from the UK, and so, 'in the circumstances, we could tell IVS that Schoon would probably be admitted'.[50] This is, to put it mildly, the mildest possible offer of asylum one could make, especially if, 'in the circumstances' the person being offered asylum is at risk of assassination or kidnapping, and especially if he is married with two small children. In short, the UK government did not really intend to extend any genuine offer of asylum to the Schoons. In fact, their deeper allegiance seems to have been to the apartheid state. Thorpe warned that 'we must minimise the risk of leaving ourselves open to possible South African charges that we have supported the harbouring of an ANC terrorist in the UK'.[51] In addition, Thorpe underlined the fact that 'any proposal by IVS to employ Schoon here on work connected with the BVP program in Southern Africa, which is supported by government funds (314,000 GBP pa) would pose serious difficulties'.[52] Taken altogether, the claim that there was no reason why the Schoons should not come to the UK is actually hollow, a false invitation. In fact, the UK government was deeply reticent to allow them in, and absolutely uncomfortable with allowing them to work the one job that they were most likely to obtain.

On 8 June, representatives of the FCO (Thorpe, Squire and Hudson) met with Nigel Watt in order to accelerate the removal of the Schoons from Botswana, and to make it clear that they would not be welcome in the UK. According to Hudson, 'we made our position quite clear and offered no room for negotiation over our primary aim of ensuring Schoon left Botswana within the next week'.[53] Nigel Watt gave his consent to a telegram being sent out to Lord Jones at the High Commission in Gaborone, with talking points to pass on to Marius Schoon. This included the message that 'no more than about 24 hours grace would be allowed' as 'there was no time to waste'.[54] Nigel Watt attempted to have until August to send down a replacement field officer for the Schoons, and to allow the new employee to shadow the Schoons for the first few days. 'We said that this would not be acceptable, and Watt did not demur'.[55]

Despite the urgent desire to get the Schoons out of Botswana within the week, Hudson was still imagining that their next stop would be the UK (perhaps via Lusaka). 'The question of what Schoon might do on his return remains open. He might be paid off or he might be found work not connected with Southern Africa, although this would not be easy to identify.'[56] For sure, the option of the Schoons continuing to be engaged with the issues of the anti-apartheid struggle, or of building independent African states in the region, would not be permitted at all. From the perspective of HMG, it would be better to simply have the Schoons 'paid off', so that they stopped engaging in the anti-apartheid struggle. Of course, as the hand-written note in the margin reiterates, even to imagine that the Schoons would go to the UK, in any capacity, 'implies he [Marius Schoon] belongs to the UK!'[57] Ultimately, it seems, the decision was taken that, in fact, the Schoons did not 'belong to' the UK and need not be welcomed there.

Two days later, on 10 June, the FCO once again increased the pressure on Nigel Watt, who was told that 'a message must be urgently conveyed to Schoon to say he (Schoon) no longer has any discretion in this matter and, if he wishes to remain in Botswana for non-IVS reasons, he must either resign at once or face immediate dismissal'.[58] However, if the Schoons did agree to leave quickly, 'in the short term at any rate', they would 'enjoy continued remuneration by IVS'. According to the FCO, 'Watt accepts this' and agreed to pass it on via telephone later that day.[59] At the same time, an urgent telegram was sent to the high commissioner to Botswana, Lord Elwyn Jones, outlining the final decision regarding the offer of asylum for the Schoons. 'Home office have agreed that you may issue without reference to them a visa endorsed "short visit".' This sentiment is followed immediately by, 'home office stress they would much prefer Schoons to go elsewhere'.[60] Despite their contradictory nature, these two concise sentences soon became the official policy on this matter, which would henceforth be referred to as 'paragraph 4'. Finally, in a rare acknowledgement of Marius's family, the telegram ends: 'all the above applies to Schoon's wife and family as well.'[61]

The climax of nearly a year of gradually escalating pressure on IVS and the Schoons came on 10 June. Ultimately, it was Lord Jones, as the representative for the British High Commission, who was in the position of finding a way to enforce the removal of the Schoons from Botswana, and to ensure that this happened within the timeline set by the FCO, and with all their limitations on the Schoons' mobility intact. Nigel Watt passed on the FCO 'line' in the morning, and Lord Jones met with Marius that same afternoon. In his interview with Hilda Bernstein, Marius described this critical meeting with Lord Elwyn Jones. It is important to understand precisely how Marius understood this interaction, before grappling with Lord Jones' account of the same story:

> In the middle of June of 1983, we got a phone call, and we were called in to see the British High Commissioner. He said to us, 'I've been instructed by the foreign office to inform you that the foreign office has what they regard as "excellent intelligence information" that you – that is, me – are to be shot by the South Africans in Botswana. I have been informed by the foreign office, to advise you to leave immediately.' We were very skeptical. So, he picked up the phone, and he phoned Brigadier Hirschfeld who was at the time the head of the Special Branch in Botswana. We rode in an ambassador's car to police headquarters in Gaborone. We went in straight away to see Brigadier Hirschfeld and basically word for word, he said the same to us as the British High Commissioner had said, adding however that the information that he had came from a source different from the British. So, we went straight down and saw the chief representative [of the ANC]. He was actually flying to Lusaka that day. Within two or three days, the office got a telex from Lusaka saying that we should move ourselves from Botswana, immediately.[62]

Beyond the simple fact that this is an utterly gut-wrenching story, there are a few details that are important to highlight. First, in Marius's telling, Lord Jones told the Schoons, point blank, that the South Africans were planning to kill Marius. This doesn't seem like the kind of detail that someone would misremember or embellish after the fact; especially since he was told the same information *twice in a row*. Second, it is significant that Marius trusted Adolf Hirschfeld, the head of the Botswana Special Branch, more than he trusted the British. Lastly, it's clear that once the Schoons accepted that they were in danger, they handed over the decision of what to do next to the ANC leadership structures.

Having taken stock of Marius's recollections of his moment of being unequivocally forced out of Botswana, we can now analyse these same critical moments in light of Lord Jones' report. According to Lord Jones, Marius 'did not so much dispute' that his life was at risk 'as seek further information before he would move as rapidly as was being suggested'.[63] Marius expressed confusion as to what could have happened in the previous two weeks to have escalated the urgency from HMG so much. Of course, he was not told that the FCO understood Marius to be a terrorist. According to Lord Jones, Marius was also not told that the FCO had 'excellent intelligence information' that Marius Schoon was going to be shot. Rather, Marius was told that the threats to his family, and to British volunteers, 'was real'.

Then, 'when he remained querulous, I invited him to seek a second opinion from the Botswana government'.[64] Here there is a crucial discrepancy between Marius's understanding of what happened, and what was actually happening. In Marius's telling of the story years later, going to speak to Hirschfeld had a major impact on his willingness to take the threat seriously. In Marius's mind, Hirschfeld's opinion could be taken more seriously, as it represented a somewhat more independent, and perhaps even sympathetic, position than the British High Commission. Unfortunately, this impression was the result of an elaborate theatre, which he was subjected to by the British. Jones admitted that even before recommending that Marius speak to the Botswana authorities, 'I had already been in touch with [the] head of Special Branch'.[65] Presumably, the conversation between Jones and Hirschfeld set out the talking points that Hirschfeld was expected to use, and the intelligence officer merely complied. By no means can this interaction then be understood as a genuine second opinion that was offered to Marius. It was simply a second iteration of the same message, through a new messenger. Hirschfeld 'strongly implied to Schoon that the Botswana were on the point of asking the ANC to move him ... [and] at one point HB told Schoon that if he did not move soon the South Africans would either kill him or take him back to South Africa alive "and you know what will happen to you then"'.[66]

Given the other documents in the FCO files, which outline the intelligence offered (presumably) by the South African security police, there was, in fact, no mention whatsoever of *any* imminent threat to the Schoons, either of assassination, arrest or any other kind of attack. There were only accusations, or implications, that Marius Schoon was in some form involved in armed sabotage attacks. Based on this, there was the (perhaps quite reasonable) assumption that his role as a saboteur would motivate the South Africans to make a cross-border raid of some form, as they had done in other instances, and as they would continue to do in the years to come. In fact, roughly simultaneous to this dramatic warning from the British high commissioner (a couple of weeks to a month earlier) the Schoons had been the victims of a serious scare at their house. Judy Seidman remembers this incident as follows:

> Sometime in the morning, Marius and Jenny were both at work. Katryn was at a crèche. There was a child minder with Fritz. A person carrying a gun came to the house and knocked on the door. The child minder was holding Fritz when she answered the door. He pointed the gun at her and demanded to see Marius. She said, 'He's not here,' so the man came in and searched the house. Marius and Jenny figured that this was an assassination attempt. Nobody stayed in the house for the week after that and Fritz and Katryn stayed with me. Fritz was one and a half years old and was absolutely terrified. Fritz was having panic attacks. When anybody came to the door, he screamed and ran.[67]

Seidman has carried these harrowing memories with her for nearly forty years now. Since 1983, she has been thoroughly convinced that this 'assassination attempt' was *the* reason that the Schoons decided to leave Botswana. For Seidman, there has been no doubt whatsoever – the Schoons were in danger, as she herself was and as so many of her comrades also were. Given the relentless assaults by the apartheid state on anti-apartheid activists throughout southern Africa – all the losses and near-misses – it is not at all surprising that people like Seidman or the Schoons genuinely believed that their lives were at risk. Nonetheless, the fact that the story that Marius Schoon was told was *plausible* does not in any way lessen the sting of the fact that it was not *factual*. Despite the overall climate of danger that the Schoons lived with on a daily basis in Botswana, the warning given by the British government was not founded on any actual intelligence information. Sadly, Marius Schoon could not have been aware of all the forces that were conspiring against him, and lying directly to his face, pretending to care about his well-being. Marius was told that his life, and the lives of his wife and children, was in danger. He was ready to believe that and could not reasonably refuse to take action based on such a threat.

From the tone of Lord Jones' writing, it seems clear that he understood Marius Schoon to be a guilty man. Jones stressed that 'at no time ... did Schoon say anything to suggest that he had not been doing anything to warrant the threats'.[68] However, even if Marius Schoon were proven to be a member of MK, and engaged in armed sabotage efforts, by what kind of moral arithmetic does this mean that a state-orchestrated assassination, in a foreign, sovereign country, would be 'warranted'? Of course, the cruel irony of this whole exchange is the fact that in hindsight we can see clearly that the apartheid state *was* prepared to undertake a cross-border attack on the Schoon family, and Jeanette and Katryn would pay with their lives for this. This horrific outcome would have been far less likely if the Schoons had been allowed asylum in the UK and hadn't moved to a country that was actively at war with the apartheid state (and had been for nearly a decade). It seems that the notion that the Schoons might end up somewhere even less safe than Botswana did not enter into the equation for men like Lord Jones. Their only real concern was to get the Schoons away from the precious citizens of the United Kingdom.

Lord Jones also seemed troubled by the fact that Marius insisted on communicating with the ANC leadership before leaving Botswana. Rather than seeing this as a practical consideration of obvious importance, Jones understood it as a further expression of Marius's guilt. 'He seemed to me to put his loyalty and duty first to the ANC rather than IVS.'[69] The irony of this frustration with Marius's supposed lack of loyalty to IVS is that, thanks to the efforts of Lord Jones and others in the government, the Schoons were being entirely forced out of IVS, and entirely blocked from fulfilling even their initial contract with the organisation. In other words, Marius had no choice but to have a greater loyalty to the ANC than IVS.

Intriguingly, Lord Jones seems to have been unaware of the fact that the Schoons were not actually going to be welcomed into the UK. Jones wrote to the head office:

> I hope that I can have authority now to issue a visa, if he decides to travel with his wife in the next few days. If, however, the position is that Schoon must make an application first and we must await an answer on whether he can be admitted at all, neither he nor I will be able to reconcile it with the line IVS and we are taking.[70]

By saying that neither he nor Marius would be 'able to reconcile' the fact that the Schoons would not be automatically offered asylum, Lord Jones signalled the essentially criminal nature of the entire FCO campaign against the Schoons. In essence, the representatives of the UK government were well aware that their campaign to force the Schoons out of Botswana would put already stateless people into an even more precarious position, and nonetheless they went ahead with the process, without making any reasonable effort to offer them any asylum.

## Conclusion

The archival findings contained in this chapter are groundbreaking for a number of reasons. In terms of understanding the story of the Schoons' life, it is critical to understand that their lives were not actually in danger in Botswana and that they could have continued on there had it not been for the interference of the British government. Even if the Schoons were eventually convinced that their lives were in danger – by representatives of Her Majesty's government that lied to them – it is crucial to understand that a possible option for the Schoons could have been to carry on working for IVS by receiving asylum in the UK. With hindsight it is clear that moving to England could have saved the lives of both Jeanette and Katryn Schoon, as an assassination attempt on British soil would have been highly unlikely. In light of Marius Schoon's earlier application to move to London and the fact that Jeanette held Irish citizenship and had a sister living in the UK, it is reasonable to assume that this option was at least something that they considered and may well have chosen, had they been offered it. In any case, understanding the British government's role in the Schoons decision to leave Botswana puts their time in Angola in a considerably different light.

Beyond the specifics of the Schoons' lives, this story is critical because it sheds light on the complicity of the UK in supporting the apartheid state's attempts to suppress the African National Congress. Far from playing a neutral diplomatic role, the 'war on terror' framework that the British FCO utilised entirely echoed the perspective of the apartheid state. In fact, while the FCO claimed that they had evidence of Marius Schoon's involvement in MK, their position towards the ANC presumed that membership in the organisation was per se tantamount to being a terrorist, as Craig Williamson had argued. In fact, it is striking to note that the political trials against the Schoons' comrades were used explicitly by the FCO to show that the Schoons were inherently dangerous individuals.

In sum, the British government's sustained complicity with the South African security services complicates the simple narrative of the Schoons being targeted by the apartheid state. Without gaining access to the redacted sections of the FCO files, it is impossible to know precisely what the South Africa's precise stake was, in terms of urging for the removal of the Schoons from Botswana.[71] Given their earlier success in infiltrating the Schoons' networks, it seems plausible that the security police may have preferred to keep the Schoons closer, in terms of ease of surveillance. Or, perhaps after Williamson's exposure, and the ensuing incarceration of several of the Schoons' comrades, the Schoons were no longer considered a genuine threat. Did the South Africans push the British to pressure the Schoons, or did they merely serve as a useful bogeyman, to sell the story to the Schoons?

What is clear is that the Schoons were just one of thousands of families who were swept up in the multi-faceted Cold War, waged in various forms on dozens of battlefields, throughout Africa. Sadly, it seems impossible for the Schoons to have had anywhere near a full sense of the array of forces that were operating against them. Far from the relative safety of London, the decision to move to Lubango, Angola, would only cast them deeper into the depths of the Cold War.

# 10 | A Kind of Asylum

**Lusaka limbo**

If it were possible to reconstruct the Schoons' mindset at the moment of understanding that they needed to leave Botswana, it might be possible to understand the thought processes that went into the decision to go to Angola. However, there is about a six-month gap between their departure from Botswana in June of 1983 and their arrival in Luanda in December of that same year. These months are almost entirely unaccounted for, either by Marius or by anyone who might have known them and worked closely with them during that period.

There are a number of problems with reconstructing these events. First of all, it is important to understand that whether or not either Jenny or Marius were actively participating in armed activities, they were nonetheless, as disciplined members of the ANC in exile, 'under instruction', which meant being subject to a military hierarchy. This was especially true in terms of major life decisions, such as where to live or what work to do (even whether or whom to marry).[1] That is, in the language of the ANC at that time, the Schoons would have been 'deployed' to Lubango, and this would have been thought of in much the same way as any other soldier, for any army, being deployed into a given war situation. Other members of the ANC underground during that same period explained to me that it was possible – to an extent – to refuse a command from someone higher in the hierarchy, or at least to negotiate for another option. But this kind of negotiating had to be done within reason, and while understanding that the organisation had limited resources, spread out across multiple countries in Africa, as well as further afield. Also, at the end of the day, there was always the basic feeling that having committed oneself to the ANC meant surrendering to the larger needs of 'the movement', even in matters of life and death.

When Hilda Bernstein interviewed Marius Schoon in 1990, after the organisation's unbanning, and as he was preparing to return home, there are a number of moments in the interview where he expresses criticisms or regrets about the ANC. But if you read Marius's statements just a few years before, even in the immediate aftermath of the loss of his wife and child, he comes across as an intensely loyal person, determined to carry out the will of the ANC. A British friend and comrade, Colin Buckley, interviewed Marius on 29 August 1984. Colin asked Marius, 'What are you going to do now?' Marius's reply was typical of the general sentiment within the ANC at that time: 'I am of course an activist of the ANC. My future plans depend to a large extent on what the ANC wants me to do. I am of course prepared to serve the ANC in whatever capacity I am asked to.'[2]

So, given the structures that governed decision-making at the time, combined with people's continued allegiance to the organisation decades later, it is not trivial to gain a straightforward answer to a question such as: why were the Schoons deployed to Lubango, Angola? To gain a definitive answer, one would have to speak either directly to the Schoons, or to their direct superior within the ANC, Henry Makghoti, who could (if they chose to divulge such information) explain exactly what the decision-making process was, and so on. As all the most relevant individuals have now passed away, the only available path is to reconstruct this decision-making process via close friends and family of the Schoons. However, as none of the people I interviewed were present for the critical conversations – and as others indicated that they would not have been told any specifics, for fear of compromising one another's security – most of what there is to go on amounts to speculation.

All of this to say that there is, by necessity, very little to be said about the second half of 1983, when the Schoons were somewhere (or perhaps many places) in between Gaborone and Lubango. Marius says that this time was spent in Lusaka:

> The chief rep's advice was that I was not to go by car to Lusaka, so I flew up to Lusaka. Jenny, and the kids and the dogs came up by

Land Rover. We spent six months in Lusaka working in the offices of our Department of Education, and Department of Culture.³

Since the ANC headquarters was in Lusaka, it seems certain that at least some portion of the time was spent there. In fact, Patrick Fitzgerald recalled an interaction with the Schoons, while they were all still in Gaborone – where Marius explicitly said, 'We're good comrades, we'll report to Lusaka.'⁴ However, during this same discussion, Marius was adamant that he was *not* willing to be deployed for a long term to Lusaka. 'Lusaka is a hellhole,' he told Fitzgerald.⁵ In light of this admission, it is notable that Hugh Macmillan (the author of *The Lusaka Years*, now the definitive book on the ANC's infrastructure in Lusaka, and who was himself living in Lusaka in 1983) has no recollection of the Schoons living in Lusaka during this period. Therefore, Macmillan speculated that the Schoons may have travelled to any number of other locations within the exile world – Harare, London, even Moscow, or Cuba – during this period, using Lusaka as a plausible cover for their activities.⁶

Whether they were stationed there for six months, or merely in and out, what might the Schoons' lives in Lusaka have been like? According to Patrick Fitzgerald (who spent multiple years within the ANC in Lusaka and grew to enjoy it), being embedded within the 'ANC colony' in Lusaka was like a 'boarding school':

> Everybody knows everybody's business. You live in these ANC houses. You don't have a salary. They used to give us 30 kwacha a month; they used to call it cigarette money. That was all the cash you had. The ANC would buy you what you needed. Food would be brought once a week. Bales of Swedish clothes would arrive, and they'd open them at a party branch and there would be 50 or 60 people running in to get what they can. I quickly learned not to look for clothes that fit, just to take what you can. Then you can sell them on to Zambians for a few kwacha, so you can go out and buy a beer or whatever.⁷

Fitzgerald is certain that the institutional culture of daily life in Lusaka would not have suited the Schoons. Fitzgerald insists that the Schoons needed a level of autonomy, away from what he referred to as 'the ANC gossip machine'.[8] Having worked closely with both Makghoti and Barbara Masekela, Fitzgerald is certain that the Schoons could have served the ANC departments of education and of culture in Lusaka, for an extended period. Their roles would have been administrative, procedural work: handling bursaries for South African exiles, and so on. In sum, there was a possible future for the Schoons in Lusaka, but not one that they were likely to have chosen for themselves.

As for the decision to go to Lubango, there are only a few things that can be said definitively.

First, England was not an option. Based on the evidence uncovered for this book, it is now known that asylum in England was not possible, due to interference from the British FCO. However, even if the Schoons had no knowledge of this fact, they may nonetheless have decided against going to England. I met with one member of MK who told me that he was present at a meeting in Lusaka where the Schoons were directed to go to London, and they refused.[9] Now, there is absolutely no way to verify whether such a meeting ever took place. But, if this is a true story, then why would the Schoons have refused to go to London? They had two small children and had recently been told, by multiple sources, that their lives were in danger. Wouldn't they appreciate the offer of a relatively stable life in a developed country, far from the frontlines of apartheid aggression? Throughout my research period (and the years of writing that followed) I have asked myself versions of these questions, repeatedly and constantly. In the end, I'm grateful for Patrick Fitzgerald's insistence that the Schoons and others within the ANC underground

> made choices in a different paradigm. You think normal, sane people make decisions on a certain basis. That's not the basis we made decisions on. Nobody was trying to have a nice life or have a lovely safe place to bring up our kids ... No, it's not about having a nice time. I don't think we expected to have a nice time *anywhere*.[10]

Operating within this particular paradigm, Jenny and Marius may well have had an aversion to their vision of an exile existence in England, full of newspaper articles, placard holding, boycotts and being card-carrying members of the Islington branch of the Communist Party. As Fitzgerald put it,

> Going to London for people like Marius and Jenny is the epitome of defeat. That's like you gave up. You actually left Africa and went to join those absolute Stalinist narrow fuckwits in London who pontificate on some champagne circuit of the anti-apartheid movement, know nothing about and have no influence on what's going on inside the country.[11]

Fitzgerald's sentiments were echoed to me by many people who had been active in the anti-apartheid movement. There was a strong desire among many people to do whatever was in their power to stay on the African continent, and preferably to be as close to the South African border as possible. Perhaps Jenny and Marius felt similarly.

Without a legitimate option of asylum, and having fled South Africa illegally, the Schoons were effectively stateless people, and therefore were reliant entirely on the structures of the ANC and the solidarity networks that the movement could draw on. Jack Curtis succinctly summarised the two options that the ANC was realistically able to offer in this situation:

> The first option was to take up teaching or administrative posts at the African National Congress's self-contained development and educational institution for refugees and their children outside of Dar es Salaam in Tanzania. The second option was to teach English as a second language at the Lubango College of Luanda University in Southern Angola.[12]

As it turned out, Marius Schoon did end up teaching at the ANC school in Mazimbu, Tanzania, for about three years, after the assassination. Marius summarised his time at Mazimbu as follows:

> I can talk about Mazimbu in one sentence. If the new South Africa is going to be like Mazimbu, I don't want it. I would rather live in Ireland ... I feel the three years I spent in Mazimbu were a complete waste of my time. The things I tried to do at Mazimbu, I shouldn't think lasted for two days after I had gone.[13]

Maybe Marius knew in advance that the option of moving to Tanzania would be a complete waste of time.[14] In any case, in his own narrative of what happened in Lusaka, Marius made no mention of Tanzania; he said, simply, 'And then comrade Makghoti, who was then the secretary of Education, spoke to us and suggested that we should go and teach at the University in southern Angola. The ANC had gotten requests for English teachers, and he would like us to go there.'[15]

So, is that it? Was the process that simple? The ANC headquarters received requests from the Angolans to send English teachers, then the Schoons were asked if they would like to go there, and they agreed? Heinz Klug believes that this is precisely what must have happened:

> So, yeah, it was an extraordinary decision for them to go to Lubango. But it wouldn't have been an ANC decision … You were deployed by the ANC, but deployment was a negotiation. So, it was *their decision* [Marius and Jenny's] to go to Lubango. I have no doubt about that.[16]

Patrick Fitzgerald concurs with Klug's assessment, absolutely. From Fitzgerald's perspective, the option to teach in Lubango would have been immediately attractive to the Schoons, for a few reasons:

> (a) They were going to be university lecturers; (b) it was actually not one salary, but two; (c) they would have their own house (not an ANC house) and their own car (not an ANC car); and, again, (d) it was *not* London and *was* close to the frontline of the anti-apartheid struggle.[17]

These are all plausible reasons, which may have influenced the Schoons to make an active decision to go to Angola. Even so, it is worthwhile to think more carefully about the reasons that Angola may have seemed like the best available option at that time, as well as to compare whatever hopefulness the Schoons may have had against the actual conditions of daily life that they experienced upon moving. There are several layers to this, which both overlap and work in opposition to one another.

## Asylum in a war zone

> Lubango was quite scary. One would hear the shooting every night. The helicopters would be going over, day and night.
>
> — Marius Schoon, audio interview by Hilda Bernstein

If you fear for your life, then why go to a war zone?

If the ordeal with the British while in Botswana genuinely scared the Schoons, then the decision to move to Angola seems genuinely confusing. That is, unless one remembers Fitzgerald's dictum that the Schoons were operating within an entirely different paradigm. Within the paradigm of the ANC underground in 1983, 'you don't *not* go somewhere because there's a civil war'.[18]

It may be impossible to ascertain, at this point, how much Jenny and Marius understood themselves to be 'running for their lives', or seeking asylum in Angola. However, it is possible to evaluate the extent to which Lubango could have reasonably offered asylum to them, if that was what they were seeking.

Moving to Lubango at the end of 1983 meant moving into a war zone. Compared to other parts of the country, things in the city of Lubango were often quiet, relatively speaking. In fact, I was told by many people now living in Lubango that the city had absorbed thousands upon thousands of internally displaced people, seeking refuge, over the previous decades. While Lubango may have offered a margin of refuge to many (including the Schoons) it was nonetheless still a society at war, and Marius's description captures this fact in gripping detail:

> At the time, it was very much a military zone. It was very close to the frontline. The South Africans bombed the airport a couple of times. There was constant troop movement through the streets. And, the South Africans were making a major assault on Angola, starting more or less virtually when we got there, in December.[19]

Marius didn't specify precisely when in December they arrived, though he did say that their first week or so was spent in Luanda. In any case, if the Schoons got to Lubango in December of 1983, they would have been in town for a major aerial bombing of the surrounding area, which took place on 29 December.[20] South African troops remained in Angola for the entire time that the Schoons were in the country. On 16 February 1984, the apartheid state signed an agreement with the Angolan government to withdraw their troops. Nonetheless, the South Africans violated this agreement for many months to come. On 3 June 1984, the *Jornal de Angola* reported that 'Sul-Africanos Ainda Ocupam Parte do Território Nacional [The South Africans still occupy part of the national territory]'.[21]

By the time the Schoons arrived, the South African military presence in Angola had been ongoing since the very first days of independence. In 1975, as the Portuguese were departing, and before an independent government was able to take over, the apartheid state invaded Angola and attempted to march through the whole length of the country, aiming to capture the capital. The MPLA was able to repel the South Africans, and the SADF retreated in 1975. According to Marius, during this initial invasion 'the South Africans had captured Lubango, and Lubango was actually their headquarters. During that time, I think they had built up some form of underground structure.'[22] After the 1975 retreat, the war continued to varying degrees, straight through until nearly the final days of apartheid rule. In 1989, with the help of thousands of Cuban soldiers, the South Africans were forced to sign a treaty that not only ended the war, but also granted independence to occupied Namibia. Sadly, the war in Angola was far more complex, pernicious and relentless than simply having to deal with the apartheid military. War in Angola lasted for generations, from the early 1960s until the beginning of the twenty-first century. It was, in one sense, the quintessential Cold War conflict, with intervention from the Americans, the Cubans and the apartheid state. On the other hand, the framework of the 'Cold War' falls short of understanding the dynamics at play, since the conflict was never cold in Angola.

Even though the war in Angola had been going on for so long, Marius nonetheless claimed to be surprised by the fact that Lubango was a war zone:

> As always, when the ANC does things, we hadn't been adequately prepared for it ... We hadn't had one minute's Portuguese training ... [and] nobody had given us a briefing about what Lubango was actually like. It really wasn't a place to be taking two young kids. I've

said this to comrade Makghoti quite strongly, but it was actually craziness sending two young kids into the situation in Lubango.[23]

While this is an intriguing assertion and says something about the Schoons' state of mind about being deployed to Angola, it doesn't appear one hundred per cent factual. Multiple people have asserted that Marius received (extremely minimal) military training at an ANC camp in Angola *prior* to being deployed there in 1983. Furthermore, both Jenny and Marius were very literate, deeply engaged political actors, who would have had a basic knowledge of Angolan politics, especially given their interest in socialism, and the long duration of South Africa's invasion of the country.

Thus, it doesn't seem plausible that the Schoons were unaware that Lubango was at war. Nonetheless, it is very much believable that the extent of the warfare, and the level of devastation and deprivation that came with it, were shocking to witness. Patrick Fitzgerald's assumption is that Marius Schoon's previous deployment for military training in Luanda would have been his framework for imagining the deployment to Lubango:

> Angola was not necessarily a hardship posting. Luanda was so much more fun than Lusaka. It had that Mediterranean culture. It had brilliant restaurants along the sea … and the ANC were honoured guests in Angola. Everything was done for you by the Angolan authorities… Marius thought Lubango was going to be like Luanda. Luanda is like a crazy third world capital. Luanda is an eminently pleasant place; it's got lots of compensations. Lubango turned out to be a hardship posting, but he wouldn't have known that.[24]

It is very much believable that Lubango was far more inhospitable – especially for the children – than anything that they could have imagined or would have been told by their commanding officers.

## There was literally nothing to eat

> There was also nothing to eat. I mean, literally nothing to eat. We arrived just after new year, in '84. We didn't get ration cards until sometime in May … But, even when we got the ration cards, one could basically get bugger all

> on the ration cards. I mean, the whole time we were in Angola, we got a meat ration once, for the whole family, it was half a kilo of meat. That was the only fresh meat that we had in the house. There was nothing in the shops. Money was like Monopoly money. You actually couldn't spend it. It just wasn't a place to be sending kids, deliberately. I still rather resent having been asked to take the kids there.
>
> — Marius Schoon, audio interview by Hilda Bernstein

Marius Schoon is a passionate person. He speaks tersely, but forcefully. After listening to hours of a recorded interview with him, I am most struck by his description of the food shortages in Angola. It is heartbreaking to imagine the Schoons scraping together enough to eat, based on some combination of severely under-resourced state-run shops, a university canteen, bartering and gifts. All of this would have been difficult enough for Marius himself to bear, but he was also someone who was prepared to make sacrifices, especially for what he understood to be a just cause. Marius had spent 12 years in jail in South Africa. However, while Marius may have been conditioned to and prepared for deprivation, one can clearly hear how heavily it weighs on him to have put his children into such a situation. His voice quakes, and he virtually stutters as he says that he 'still rather resents having been asked to take the kids there'. For someone who lived and died inside of the anti-apartheid movement – and lost virtually everyone he loved (apart from Fritz and his other daughter, Jane) along the way – it is not a small thing to admit that you 'rather resent' an order given by the African National Congress. More than any other moment in Marius's narrative, this lingering regret hints at the possibility that the Schoons did not actually want to go to Angola; or, at least, in hindsight, questioned the wisdom of deploying small children into a war zone. It certainly seems appropriate for Marius Schoon to resent the fact that the ANC asked him to bring his two small children to Angola in 1984, especially in light of the fact that there had already been reason to fear for their safety while living in Botswana.[25] Furthermore, I was told by other ANC members that it was highly unusual for the ANC to encourage any of their members to go to Angola with children; in virtually all cases, the policy was to absolutely avoid sending children into war.[26]

Marius's depiction of the shocking paucity of food available in Angola was unanimously and emphatically affirmed, by absolutely everyone I spoke to, both South Africans who were in Angola around the same time, as well as all the Angolans I met. Everyone insisted that times were incredibly hard, and that to survive it was absolutely necessary for people to gift and trade whatever food they were able to buy through the rationing system, or to grow. The state-run grocery stores offered food and other household necessities erratically, and within a hierarchical system of rationing, whereby certain people had access to different stores, or slightly better supplies than others. People would make up for the frequent shortages of products by using supplies sparingly, and by bartering whenever they were able to access a glut of something. There is a lot that is frightening and exhausting about living in this way, but Angolans also spoke often of the ways in which a state of constantly not-enough created a sense of family, and community, where people provided for one another, however they were able. Marius absolutely emphasises the fact that 'colleagues and friends that we made in Lubango were very good to us',[27] by which he means, in fact, that the community at Lubango College quite literally kept his family alive. The school provided daily meals at a canteen (that served either 'rice with fish, or fish with rice')[28] and students and colleagues at Lubango College remember Katryn and Fritz often showing up to share in these meals.

Heinz Klug, who was sent to Angola for military training, explained that these shortages of food were endemic also within the ANC military camps stationed in Angola:

> I was in Angola from July 1982 until December '82; in the camps. Those conditions were just really rough, and I don't think that they got any better by the time Marius & Jeanette got there. They took us once into Luanda (we were out in Viana[29]) for like a fancy meal, a treat. It was literally a little cup of rice, and a sprinkle of sardine chips on the top. That was a special meal. This was at a hotel, in Luanda. Now, there may have been an elite that was living differently. But the ANC commanders who were part of that command believed that was a treat.[30]

In sharing this memory with me, I think Heinz imagines that perhaps conditions in Lubango were even worse than those he experienced. In fact, from Marius's account, and from the testimony of others who lived in Lubango, it seems that, in some ways, the Schoons were substantially better off than the soldiers in the camps, because they were embedded within a community of local people, who appreciated and supported them. The Schoons were also supported by comrades outside of Angola, who would regularly send them care packages with food.[31]

When I met with one ANC member, who had lived in Lubango in the latter half of the 1980s (after Jenny's death), I was surprised to hear him describe the economic system in Angola at the time as 'feudalism', rather than calling it 'socialism'.[32] However, to call it feudalism seems apt, because the combination of the sabotage caused by the fleeing colonial army, and the endless sabotage of civil war, created a state infrastructure that was barely functional and could not possibly meet people's needs. On 23 May 1984, the *Jornal de Angola* newspaper printed a front-page article with the headline 'Luanda Tera Carne Na Proxima Semana [Luanda Will Have Meat Next Week]'.[33] The article explained that beef was to be imported from Argentina and Zimbabwe, with chickens being brought in from Brazil. The need to import meat in this way, and the fact that such importation ought to be headline news, strikingly underlines the widespread, systemic shortages that all of Angola was struggling through during this period.

Of course, the problems related to decolonisation and war affected every aspect of daily life, not only the food that was available. In his memoir, Jack Curtis explains how his daughter's time living in Angola helped him to understand the full extent of these devastating conditions:

> From our letters from Jenny we were able to form some slight idea of the desolation that had been created in Angola ... In Luanda and other major towns, the [fleeing Portuguese] removed or destroyed all the plans covering the reticulation systems for power, light, fuel and water supplies and sanitation and other services; plans of new erections of buildings, townships, roads and industrial installations were similarly treated; key elements of generating and pumping equipment were removed and, short of actual physical destruction, everything possible was done to sabotage the operation of the infrastructure of the country.[34]

Marius also spoke at some length about the infrastructural problems that were a regular feature of daily life in Angola. This included the fact that their apartment building had intermittent electricity[35] and very rarely had running water (perhaps once a week), not to mention a functional elevator. Framing such severe infrastructural problems within the political context of a protracted struggle to end colonialism and build a socialist society might have provided some salve for the hardships of daily life. However, considering Marius's resentment towards his superiors, in the aftermath, it seems unlikely that revolutionary zeal was able to erase all of the suffering associated with living in Lubango.

## A Marxist education

> Set off against these bodily deprivations was the spirit of fulfilment which glowed through all of Jenny's letters. Confined as they had been in South Africa, harassed by the restrictions on communication with her fellow human beings, they reveled in the free interchange of thoughts and views with all with whom they came in contact.
>
> — John Francis Curtis, *South African Saga*

Despite their need for asylum from the relentless persecutions of the apartheid state, and despite the many daily difficulties, living in Angola may well have been for the Schoons an exciting opportunity to engage in revolutionary political work. As Marius put it, 'The reality of the recent revolution is apparent all the time in Angola.'[36] Unfortunately, in the Angolan case, the 'reality of the recent revolution' was often manifest in material deprivation and the desperate need to defend against the onslaught of counter-revolutionary war. On the other hand, there was also the very real work – no matter how fraught – of attempting to build new institutions, and the Schoons found themselves happily embedded within exactly such a project.

What was then called Lubango College, and is now called ISCED,[37] is very much a product of an independent Angola, aspiring towards socialism. The university was created after the colonial college collapsed, and the vast majority of the professors fled from the country. As a result, Lubango College – both by necessity and by design – sought the assistance of teachers from throughout the world, and particularly from socialist countries.

Both professors and textbooks flooded in to Lubango from throughout the Eastern bloc countries, as well as sympathetic African and Latin American countries (and, of course, Vietnam). In this context, Heinz Klug is exactly correct to assert that 'to teach at an Angolan university *was* a political commitment. Angola was the frontline of the struggle against apartheid. It's not about just teaching English, it's about being part of the broader struggle against the regime, but not being able to be in a forward area.'[38]

While Heinz understands the broader political impact of teaching at Lubango College, he perhaps underestimates the political content of *the pedagogy itself*. This much is not obvious when looking only at the surface level of teaching English as a second language. Furthermore, considering Marius's admission that the ANC provided 'not one minute' of Portuguese instruction before their arrival, it feels hard to imagine Jenny and Marius being very effective teachers. However, the students and colleagues from Lubango College whom I spoke with assured me that the Schoons were in charge of teaching advanced English and therefore it was possible to interact quite freely with students. Furthermore, those who had studied at Lubango College in the early 1980s sought to impress upon me that the curriculum was heavily influenced by Marxism, in many respects. One man even showed me a copy of his transcript, to demonstrate that even though he majored in psychology, he nonetheless took a number of Marxist classes, such as political economy, materialism: dialectical and historical, and scientific communism. In short, the Schoons were teaching a new generation of Angolan teachers, and they were teaching them alongside a cadre of international people, within a context that was explicitly Marxist.

Given the structure of their work at Lubango College it is understandable that 'Jenny's letters posted via the UK were invariably cheerful, with an underlying feeling that they were now making a positive contribution ...'[39] Everyone in Lubango who had known Jenny spoke of her warmly, as both a friendly person and a dedicated teacher. One student from Lubango College told me that she had no real desire to learn English, but she nonetheless sought out Jenny, since she admired Jenny as a person. As proof of this, I was offered an anecdote of one of Jenny's sandals breaking while walking up the stairs, and Jenny simply smiling, and walking up barefoot into her classroom.

From all accounts, Jenny took her teaching seriously, and was very much appreciated for her efforts. As for Marius's role at Lubango College, the accounts varied widely, with some affirming that he was also teaching English, to others insisting that he was often out of town, and at least one declaring that Marius was not a teacher at all. These conflicting memories of Marius's work as a teacher speak to a larger set of concerns regarding the other political work that Marius (and Jenny) were, or may have been, engaged in.

## Out of town, undercover

> I think Marius would have been thinking about, 'how can we connect?' I think to that degree, an acceptance to go to Angola might have offered a chance to be engaged with the troops in the camps, with people headed back to South Africa.
>
> — Heinz Klug, interview

Perhaps, rather than hoping to get away from danger, the Schoons were actually hoping to assist in the military campaign against apartheid South Africa.

Now, the line between political and military work in the ANC's exile structures is not always obvious and is disputed even among comrades within the organisation. Despite being an advocate for strict boundaries between military and political work, Heinz Klug gave a markedly complex assessment of the Schoons' role inside the ANC while in Angola. First of all, Klug speculated:

> If Marius had a reason to say, 'let's go to Angola,' it's because of the sense that it's still near the front. There was a sense that maybe you could work with education of MK guys, so maybe he imagined that he would play the kind of role that Jack Simons had played in the 1970s, which was to give education in the camps. I have no evidence that he ever got to do any of that.[40]

Having previously acknowledged that Marius may well have wanted to play a role in educating soldiers, Klug then quickly complicated things by insisting:

> Marius wasn't part of the war effort in any way in Angola. They weren't part of the ANC underground network in Angola. They

weren't part of the MK structures. So, they were *just* teaching English in Lubango.[41]

As he insisted, Heinz Klug could not provide concrete evidence, either to show that the Schoons did play a role in educating soldiers or to confirm that their role in Angola was strictly teaching English. Therefore, both statements are merely speculations. However, it is crucial to acknowledge that the two declarations cannot both be true.

Barry Gilder, who worked in the intelligence wing of the ANC[42] and received training in the military camps in Angola (but who did not know the Schoons as well as Klug did), presumes that the Schoons must have been involved with MK in Angola:

> I would assume that to be sent to Lubango as teachers was a cover for assisting MK in some way. I would assume. That's an educated assumption but not necessarily true.[43]

Gilder was careful to insist that he had no direct knowledge of what the Schoons were doing. Nonetheless, as a career operative within the ANC, as someone with very direct knowledge of the workings of the ANC military camps and the corresponding political education work, Gilder 'would assume' that the Schoons were 'assisting MK in some way'. This is significant. What Gilder is signalling (based on his expertise) is what is visible from a superficial look: in the main, the primary activity of the ANC in Angola was military work. Therefore, it's reasonable to assume that an ANC member going to Angola must have a military role. Imagining the specific role that the Schoons would have likely played, Gilder echoed Klug. Even though he began by stressing that 'I've never heard of Marius or Jenny participating in the teaching of MK trainees', Gilder nonetheless speculated that 'that might be a possibility; they might have been helping with curriculum'.[44] For those who insist that the Schoons were absolutely not involved in anything at all resembling military work, this is a problem. Two members of the same organisation, both white men, both intellectuals and socialists, both having received military training in Angola, both see it as a reasonable possibility that the Schoons worked on educating MK soldiers. The only thing odd about this is that one of them also insists that the Schoons were not involved in military work.

We know that Marius Schoon spent time in Luanda. He was there on the day that the bomb went off. He describes going to Luanda upon arriving in Angola, for at least a week. In between, either Marius or Jenny would make a trip up to Luanda from Lubango. Although Marius mentions these trips to Luanda in multiple interviews, he never describes the purpose of the trips in very much detail. On one occasion, Marius describes the trips to Luanda almost as if they were shopping trips, for food that was harder to access in Lubango. 'Then, one of us was going up once a month to Luanda, to do some work on our development projects around Luanda, with the chief rep. So, whenever anybody came back, they'd just bring tins of stuff.'[45] Now, in addition to bringing back 'tins of stuff', the other reason to be in Luanda was 'to do some work on our development projects'. What is a development project, in this context? What work did Jenny and Marius do? Jack Curtis provides a similarly vague, euphemistic description, but with slightly more detail:

> Jenny and Marius settled easily into their new routine, with Jenny or Marius coming up [to Luanda] from time to time to assist with the planning of a development centre for South African refugees located outside Luanda.[46]

Who were the 'South African refugees located outside Luanda'? Again, the vast majority of South African 'refugees' living in Angola at that time were soldiers. So, while the notion of a 'development center' is quite vague, it sounds most likely that it was a military centre, in one form or another. Only once, speaking just a few months after the assassination, did Marius say anything more specific about the 'development project' by explaining that 'we were establishing a vocational training school'.[47] Stanley Manong, who was an MK commander in Angola during this period, makes numerous references to a 'plot in Luanda where the ANC was building a vocational school sponsored by the United Nations and the Finn Solidarity Movement from Finland'.[48] Manong was even stationed at this location for some period. However, despite mentioning it on numerous occasions in his memoirs, Manong never provides any specific details regarding who the school was for or what kind of vocational training was provided. Given these hazy details, even the fact that an MK commander was stationed at the same vocational school that the Schoons were working on is not proof, by any stretch, that the Schoons were involved with military work. As Gilder would say, 'that's an educated assumption, but not necessarily true'.

It is not possible that the Schoons were both educating ANC soldiers *and* not involved in the military work of the ANC in any way? But then, what precisely does it mean to be 'involved' in military work for the ANC? As Patrick Fitzgerald explains, 'I did poetry writing workshops for MK camps in Angola. Does that make me a combatant?'[49] This is a critical point. Without having any specific evidence regarding the Schoons' potential role as educators of MK cadres, it would be quite a leap to presume that their role as educators could reasonably be characterised as 'military' work. Furthermore, having himself been a political educator for the ANC underground, Fitzgerald questions the basic premise that the Schoons would have eagerly taken on such a role. As he describes it, political education work for the ANC involved extensive engagement with books on both South African history and Marxist political theory. According to Fitzgerald:

> Political education wasn't really Marius' thing. His political education was like, 'Comrade, why do you not want to support the ANC? What is it you feel when you analyse the country that would not be accommodated by a broad front, led by the ANC?'[50]

Whatever the true nature of their work in Luanda, it is certainly the case that Marius, at least, developed a reputation among people in Lubango of being often away, with the presumption always being that his trips were on ANC business. In addition, the plaque commemorating the assassination of Jeanette Schoon in Lubango defines her as a *Militante Nacionalista* and whenever I attempted to suggest to those who knew her that she was 'just' a teacher, they all scoffed; she was a militant, of that there was no doubt. About Marius, the consensus was even more firm: he was a militant of the African National Congress, no question about it. Of course, none of these people could speak with any real confidence about the precise nature of the Schoons' work for the ANC in Angola. As a banned organisation operating in exile, the ANC developed a fairly secretive culture. The people whom I spoke with in Lubango repeatedly stressed that the Schoons lived a secluded life. Agnelo, one of the students at Lubango College at the time, remembers them as being open and friendly with the students, but very much not interested in the normal collegial activities.[51] The Schoons' neighbour at Simpor remembers them as very private people.[52]

One thing that adds to my impression that the Schoons *were* involved with something more than simply their teaching duties at ISCED (and potentially related to the armed struggle) is the fact that there were a number of other ANC comrades in Lubango, both during the time that the Schoons were there, and also in the years that followed. I was given the phone number of one ANC member who was in Lubango after the assassination. When I called him, I tried asking, 'Why did the ANC want you, and the Schoons, to be in Angola?' To this, he replied, 'Let's look at it superficially. It would be better to look at this on the surface, especially on the phone.' So we scheduled a time to meet. When we met in person, the man was jovial and friendly. He told many animated stories about his time living in Angola. When I tried another time, gently, to raise the topic of his work for the ANC, he answered, 'I made an oath never to speak about this; why would I tell you now?' In addition to this encounter, I also met with a man in Lubango who had been a close friend of the ANC person. Again, this Angolan man was warm and friendly, and spoke comfortably about many different topics, until I asked about what these ANC folks were doing in Lubango. To this, I was told, '*fue uma outra época* [it was a different epoch]' in which the MPLA and the ANC supported one another, within the context of the Cold War. That was all he was prepared to say. Clearly there is something in the story of this group living in Lubango in the 1980s that the ANC is simply *not* willing to speak about, even nearly forty years later.

## Tickets to Ireland

Perhaps the Schoons had absolutely no desire to be in Angola and instead hoped to find asylum in a safer place and just couldn't make it happen.

Marius Schoon says that, at the time of the assassination, their family's planned trip to Ireland was just a few weeks away:

> Jenny had gotten an Irish passport, because her grandfather was an Irish citizen. So, we had made arrangements that we were going to

> go over to Ireland during the university vacations, in the middle of the year. We were going to investigate the possibility of my getting an Irish passport, as well. She had seen the embassy in Harare. She hadn't had very much joy from them.[53]

If it is true that the Schoons would have preferred to live in Ireland (and, it seems, they had been working on this plan for roughly a year beforehand), then it appears that the move to Angola was always intended to be temporary, at best. Furthermore, if the Schoons were actively seeking Irish citizenship, it would be reasonable to conclude that they were not involved in the armed struggle and, rather, genuinely hoped for a safe place to live together as a family, to raise their children in peace. Once again, had the British government not intervened, it is quite possible that neither Jeanette nor Katryn would have died so young, and so brutally. While the extent to which the Schoons understood that the UK was not a possible option for them is not clear, what does seem clear is that they continued to seek asylum, in the ways that they knew how – even *after* moving to Angola.

As it turned out, after the assassination, Marius decided to head to Ireland, all the same, with Fritz in tow.

> As I've said earlier, we'd made the arrangements to come over to Ireland, before Jenny and Katryn were killed, and very wisely I had decided, in Angola, that in fact we were still going to come. My good friend Colin came over with us, to Ireland. Then we were joined in Ireland by my cousin, Tony. The two of them actually held me together and enabled me to get myself a little bit sorted out, during those three weeks in Ireland. It was very good.[54]

Sadly, along the way to Ireland, Marius and Fritz encountered further trouble from the British authorities. It is pitiful to imagine that, even after his wife and daughter had been murdered, the British government still essentially viewed Marius as a terrorist, and therefore made it difficult for him to feel at all welcome in the UK:

> It was very difficult to get into Britain. MPs eventually had to intervene to get us visas. So we only had a visa for a month. We stayed

for about three weeks, and then we went over to Ireland. We spent a month in the west of Ireland, then we went up to Dublin. Then, I had decided that I needed to be somewhere where I could get myself together. It was impossible to get another visa to get back into Britain. So, we decided we would stay in Ireland, which actually I think was very wise.[55]

Listening to Marius Schoon speaking with Hilda Bernstein in 1990, it is clear that his time in Ireland had served him well. Life in Ireland offered Marius an opportunity to be respected for his long career in the anti-apartheid struggle, and to live a peaceful and nonracial existence, which had never before been possible. In addition, Marius fell in love with Sherry McLean, an Irish supporter of the anti-apartheid movement. Sherry helped to raise Fritz and stayed with Marius until his death in February 1999. Sherry now continues to live in Johannesburg, where Fritz also resides.

## Mama Janeth and Little Katryn

Even in the midst of a gruelling civil war, the murder of a young woman in her 30s, and her curly-haired kindergartener, was a tragedy that the Angolan city of Lubango has carried close to their hearts for many years. The teacher's college built a memorial garden in honour of Jeanette Schoon, and as the community has gathered in recent years to remember the history of Lubango College, they sang together a song written to remember 'Mama Janeth'. It is remarkable to witness the ways in which a community that has been devastated by decades of warfare nonetheless engages with this one killing with such warmth, such deep compassion. I was repeatedly moved by the ways that people I met in Angola took on 'my' research work as if it were their own, contributing in all the ways that they could think of. Young academics helped to translate and set up meetings with people who might know something useful. Older teachers shared their memories of the early 1980s and drove me around town to see the different spaces that I was being told about.

One of the most moving moments was when the father of a girl who had gone to school with Katryn finally found – after days of searching – a copy of an old photo of Katryn and a group of her classmates. It is not surprising that everyone spoke warmly about Katryn. Children are lovely, and the death of a child always weighs more heavily on people's hearts. But I think there's more to it than this. I think also that Katryn was integrated into Angolan society in ways that her parents (and Fritz, who was quite young) could not have been. By necessity, Katryn learned to live in Portuguese, and therefore, perhaps, built deeper bonds with her peers. Jack Curtis portrays it this way:

> Katryn had adapted readily to her new environment and companions, and in addition to her knowledge of Setswana acquired in Botswana, she was now acquiring a working knowledge of Portuguese as spoken by her age group. It looked as though things were set fair for a stable and productive life.[56]

Sadly, Marius did not agree with this assessment of Katryn's life in Angola:

> The last six months of the little girl's life were unfortunately not happy for her. She found Angola very, very difficult. She had to cope with the language much more than we did ... but I think she felt very lonely, very isolated, whereas she'd felt very close to various people in Botswana, and I think she missed them enormously.[57]

Still, even if Katryn was lonely in certain respects (and it is certainly believable that she was happier in Botswana, where she lived longer, in more comfortable conditions) it is nonetheless notable that the Angolans viewed her as a welcome addition to their community.

What is significant about the ways that the community in Lubango speak of 'Mama Janeth' and her daughter is what they are also saying, by implication, about what it means to them to have hosted this family for a short period – and having been witness to the atrocious way in which they were killed. From my conversations, it seems clear that the Angolans knew and appreciated that the Schoons were fleeing a deeply racist and brutal society. From reading the daily editions of the *Jornal de Angola* from 1984, it is clear that the Angolans were acutely aware of the dangers of the apartheid state. The newspaper virtually never spoke of 'South Africa', but rather constantly contrasted between *o Povo Sul-Africano* [the South African people] and *as Racistas* [the racists, meaning the government]. In contrast, Angola is easily one of the least racist countries I have ever visited. Aside from mentioning Katryn's cute blonde curls, no one made any mention of the fact that the Schoons were white. Further, I can't imagine that the people of Lubango understood the killing of Jeanette and Katryn as the death of 'white people', in the sense of people with more privilege or power. I doubt that the assassination matters to Angolans 'more' than the deaths of the many thousands of Angolans who died during the war. Rather, I feel that their death was seen within the context of having attempted to provide refuge for people who wanted to end apartheid and who paid a gruesome price for that decision.

## Rumours of the real target

> There was a whole lot of nonsense where the innuendo was that I was actually responsible for Jenny's death. The same sort of innuendo has been made about Cde. Joe Slovo about Ruth's death – I don't think anybody takes that seriously. I don't think any progressive human being anywhere in the world takes that seriously, and in fact I don't even think that the majority of reactionary South Africans take that seriously ... that sort of stuff is just something that comes out of a poisoned mind.
>
> — Marius Schoon, interview by Julie Frederikse

A persistent theme, which dogs any attempt to make sense of the killing of Jeanette Schoon, is the declaration – or presumption – that Marius was the real target for this killing. Perhaps people mean no ill-will towards Jeanette when they make comments in this direction. Given Marius Schoon's decades-long engagement with the radical left, as both a communist and as a member of the ANC, it is certainly plausible that the state would view him as a threat. However, to view Jenny Curtis as therefore 'simply' an innocent victim would be a gross misunderstanding at best, and sexist slander at worst. Thankfully, Marius himself never tolerated this kind of demeaning characterisations of his wife and comrade; he always insisted that 'Jenny was not just an ordinary teacher. She was a teacher who had spent her whole adult life in opposition to the apartheid regime.'[58] By the time Jenny died – at the age of 35 – she had been a student activist, a trade union organiser, an archivist for the South African Institute of Race Relations and a member of the ANC's organisation in exile. Despite this, some people whom I spoke with in Lubango nonetheless said things like, 'Jeanette is the wife, only.' Beneath the blatant slander, this comment speaks to a pervasive, subtler slander, which validates what men like Marius do as definitely political work and is blind to the contributions that women like Jeanette make to radical struggle.

Of course, it is understandable why the apartheid state would argue that Marius Schoon was the intended target of the parcel bomb. This allows Williamson simultaneously to insist that the attack was strategically motivated, in that it was directed towards a known communist and ANC militant, and also a mistake, in that the wife and daughter died instead. Both of these lines of reasoning attempt to weasel out of taking full responsibility for killing a young woman and a little girl. Of course, none of the loved ones or comrades of the Schoons appreciated this weasel logic. Judy Seidman's feelings capture the mood of those who were close to Jenny and Marius:

> My own feeling is that I think both of them [Jenny and Marius] were targets.
>
> One of the things I have a very strong memory of is Marius talking about Katryn as 'this is our future'. To kill her was about the worst thing you could conceivably do to Marius. I don't think it was that targeted ... But I also don't think that it was against their values.[59]

The death of Katryn Schoon was obviously the most uncomfortable fact for the killers to try to weasel out of. Allegedly, when Williamson first heard that Katryn had died, he quipped, 'served them right,' and claimed that the Schoons deliberately used their own children to inspect packages, for fear of bombs. While Williamson may well be that sadistic a man, it was nonetheless not a position that the state could officially adopt. Williamson and others who killed in defence of apartheid needed to at least pretend that their actions had strategic aims, and no amount of rhetorical acrobatics could make the obliteration of a child sound that way.

Marius Schoon always spoke articulately and passionately about the assassination and was careful to place the tragedy that his family experienced within the broader context of apartheid atrocities.

> Jenny and Katryn are not the only opponents of apartheid who have been murdered by the South African regime. Joe Gqabi was shot down in the streets of Harare, Ruth First was blown up in Maputo. I think of the massacre in Maseru, the massacre in Matola. I think very particularly of the deaths in the detention cells in South Africa. Katryn, of course, is not the only child to be killed by the apartheid system. Thousands of our children are killed every year by the South African regime. These are the children that die in the so-called homelands of starvation. The South African government is the bringer of death in the whole of the Southern African sub-continent.[60]

Marius's words resonate powerfully, many years later, and help us to remember that in making sense of the death of one mother and her child we are also, by necessity, indicting an entire system.

## Conclusion

There are significant barriers to determining precisely why the Schoons went to Angola and what they did while they were there. Nonetheless, the stakes of answering these questions remain high. The lines between being a military combatant and a member of the political underground in Angola may well be blurry (and intentionally obscured) but still, this line was used as a key barometer for measuring whether men like Craig Williamson were entitled to amnesty. In other words, was Jeanette Schoon a 'legitimate target' for state-sponsored murder, merely an *unintended* target, or something else entirely?

Within the context of the TRC, there was little room for a nuanced answer to these questions, as the commission was obliged to either grant amnesty or deny it. However, the decision to grant Craig Williamson amnesty fell far short of adequately resolving these questions. As a result, for many people – particularly the Schoon family and those who knew them best – the killing of Jeanette and Katryn Schoon remains a lingering wound: without justice, and without recourse to justice.

# Epilogue | Amnesty and Justice, 1995–2007

IT IS HEREBY CERTIFIED:

That on 22 January 2007 at 12h00 at 96A PERCHERSON STREET, BEAULIEU, KYALAMI being the defendant's residential address, payment of the judgement debt in the amount of R325,000.00, my costs plus VAT was demanded from WILLIAMSON CRAIG MICHAEL ... declared that he has no money, moveable or disposable property wherewith to satisfy the said warrant...

It is further certified that WILLIAMSON CRAIG MICHAEL was requested to declare whether he owns any immovable property which is executable, on which the following reply was furnished, 'No.'

— J van den Heever, 'Return: Execution of Writ of Execution' to the High Court, Johannesburg

The attempts to bring Craig Williamson to justice for the murders of Jeanette and Katryn Schoon took many forms, spanning more than a decade. Even though Williamson confessed to his role in the murder and despite the tenacious persistence of the Schoon family to do everything in their power to stop Williamson from evading justice, their efforts ended with the limp, pathetic lie that Williamson gave to Deputy Sheriff Van den Heever.

To make sense of this remarkable travesty of justice, an entirely separate book could be written. There is neither time nor space to analyse all the twists and turns in Craig Williamson's path to amnesty and beyond.

However, it is necessary briefly to sketch the broad contours of this process, towards an assessment of the specific significance of this book to contemporary contestations around justice for the crimes of apartheid. In addition, tracing Williamson's successful evasion of justice offers important signposts for further research, which could build on this book and take it in new directions.

## Evading justice

Crucially, it was Marius Schoon who first sought justice for the murder of his wife and daughter by filing a civil suit against Craig Williamson, on 18 August 1995. Marius Schoon's case against Williamson came about in response to a televised confession by Williamson, who showed no shame for his role in the 1984 bombing of the Schoons' home in Angola. Citing over a decade of trauma endured by himself and young Fritz, Marius Schoon sued for R1 million,[1] with roughly a quarter designated in Williamson's 'personal capacity' and the rest in his 'representative capacity' as a servant of the police.[2] Far from desiring any form of reconciliation, Marius Schoon spent the last years of his life passionately insisting that Craig Williamson was a murderer, a man who ought to be denied amnesty and duly punished for his crimes. In fact, Schoon testified to the TRC that 'the only time he ever wished to see Williamson again was "across the sights of an AK47 rifle"'.[3]

In the following year (1996) Craig Williamson travelled to Angola, purportedly to do business. While in Angola, Williamson was arrested and detained for an extended period, while the Angolans attempted to ascertain precisely who Williamson was and whether he might have committed any crimes in Angola, which would allow them to indict him.[4] The Angolans interrogated Williamson extensively and compelled him to write out a full autobiography of sorts. Williamson's account about the ordeal of his detention is notable as much for what it says about his own self-image as for what it says about the conditions of an Angolan jail:

> That was a real Stasi/KGB interrogation. That's how they do it. Write, and write again. Look, it was very unpleasant but thinking back on it, it was really quite amusing. Because they were terrified

of me. I stopped eating and they were terrified that I was going to die, and the implications that would have. At the same time, they never physically abused me, because they were too scared to come near me. They had some image that I was some James Bond like character, and if they came too close to me, I would just kill a few of them and escape out the door. They approached me with two guys and then guys behind with AKs. They'd even come in my cell, the four guys with AKs. They'd make me stand with my hands against the wall.[5]

Contained within the 86 pages of Williamson's hand-written life story is a purely fabricated depiction of the murders of Jeanette and Katryn Schoon. While imprisoned in an Angolan jail, Williamson wrote:

I *suspect* although I have no direct information, that the explosion in the ANC house in Lubango in 1984 when Jeanette and her daughter Katryn were killed could have been carried out by S.A. military intelligence, working with UNITA.[6]

In other words, despite having confessed to his role in this killing over a year prior, Williamson was careful not to claim responsibility for an attack on Angolan soil while being detained by the Angolan police. In our recent interview, Williamson claims to have had no fear of being indicted for what he called 'the Schoon thing'.[7] According to Williamson, 'there's an amnesty around that, which was already in place. All acts of war during that period had a blanket amnesty.'[8] The amnesty that Williamson was referring to was the Lusaka Protocol, passed in 1994 with the intention of ending the civil war in Angola. While the peace accord provided amnesty for Angolan combatants in the civil war, it is not at all clear that a South African state-sponsored bombing inside an Angolan city would have been eligible for such a 'blanket amnesty'. In any case, if Williamson was as fearless about this risk as he now claims, why didn't he confess to his role in the murder?

According to Terry Bell, who now holds in his personal archives the documentation related to Williamson's detention in Angola, the Angolan authorities reached out to the ANC-run government in South Africa, seeking any additional information that they might have regarding Craig Williamson. Remarkably, given that Marius Schoon's civil lawsuit had been filed already in 1995 and given the relatively high-profile nature of the assassination of the Schoons, the ANC did not intervene to assist the Angolans in indicting Craig Williamson. According to Williamson, the Angolans notified the South Africans, "'I've got Craig Williamson". They said, "So?" He thought they would say, "oh, fantastic, thank you"'.[9] Without a confession from Williamson or support from the ANC, the Angolans were obliged to release Williamson and he was allowed to travel safely back to South Africa, rather than serve out a life sentence for murder in an Angolan prison. Worst of all, Williamson even claims that the South African government sent a jet plane to Angola to collect him.[10] 'That was a bit indiscreet, because that convinced people in Angola that I was still obviously involved in intelligence structures.'[11]

## Amnesty

Soon after his return to South Africa, on 14 January 1997, Craig Williamson applied for amnesty at the Truth and Reconciliation Commission. In addition to the assassinations of the Schoons, Williamson also applied for amnesty for the assassination of Ruth First and the bombing of the London office of the ANC. Many people have speculated that Williamson played a role in other apartheid killings, including the murder of Biko, the assassination of Swedish Prime Minister Olaf Palme, and the Cradock Four.[12] Nonetheless, his amnesty applications focused only on the three incidents that Williamson has willingly confessed to. The timing of Williamson's amnesty application was quite precise, as the civil suit brought by Marius Schoon was due to begin on 5 February 1997, just a couple of weeks later.[13] In his application for amnesty, Williamson offered the following justification for the Lubango parcel bomb:

> The Schoons had been the subject of intense SA intelligence scrutiny and were to my knowledge regarded as key ANC/SACP operatives and hence, in terms of the counter-revolutionary strategy of the time, as prime targets ... The fact that the Schoons moved to Lubango, Angola made me and other SA intelligence officers even

more convinced of the Schoons' important role in the ANC/SACP and therefore in the whole Soviet orchestrated onslaught.[14]

In other words, a central feature of Williamson's amnesty application was the claim that the Schoons were 'key ANC/SACP operatives' and therefore 'prime targets' for state-sponsored elimination.

Against the reasoning of Williamson and his legal team, the ANC representatives at the TRC insisted, emphatically and repeatedly, that the Schoons played no role in the military work of the ANC during their time in Angola. In making their case, the ANC acknowledged, or at least implied, that the Schoons had played a more important role for the organisation during their time in Botswana. However, once the Schoons moved to Angola, 'they were now completely uninvolved' in their earlier IPRD work, under the command of Mac Maharaj. As Mac Maharaj put it, the Schoons' role in Angola was 'just as a member who was living in Canada'.[15] The official ANC position was that the Schoons were sent to Lubango to teach *and only to teach* and that Lubango was far from any of the ANC's military camps in the country, so of course the Schoons were not involved in military work. Maharaj testified that 'it was physically not possible and not feasible, not practical'.[16] In response to assertions that it was either 'not practical' or 'not possible' that the Schoons were connected to the ANC's military structures, Williamson's lawyers asked – quite plausibly – if you admit that the Schoons' teaching work in Botswana was a cover for underground activities, what is to stop them from having used teaching as a cover on a second occasion?

The dispute about whether the Schoons were simply teachers, or involved in armed clandestine activities, was one of the most fundamental concerns of the TRC's judgement regarding Williamson's appeal for amnesty. If, as Williamson argued, the Schoons were involved in some form of military activity, then that makes them enemy combatants and therefore legitimate targets for a 'politically motivated' assassination. If, however, as the ANC argued, the Schoons were 'simply' teachers, then they ought to be regarded as non-combatant civilians and therefore innocents killed without justification.

Grounded in his legal expertise, Heinz Klug argued fiercely at the TRC against granting amnesty to Williamson and urged the commission to make a sharp distinction between political and military work. In Klug's framework, merely supporting armed revolutionary activity (ideologically, rhetorically) does not make someone an armed combatant. To be considered military, an individual needs to have received training as a soldier and needs to have taken concrete actions that support the military effort (for example, housing a soldier, at least). As Klug clarified to the TRC, 'many people in the frontline areas felt they were targeted, but I do not believe they were legitimate targets'.[17] In other words, the protocols for determining eligibility for amnesty that the TRC relied on were intended to be precise. It was not sufficient for members of the security police to simply argue that individuals were politically distasteful or simply part of the 'Soviet orchestrated onslaught'. To be eligible for amnesty for murder, Williamson needed to demonstrate that his decision to kill the Schoons had an explicit political goal. However, the complex realities related to the sustained military conflicts between the apartheid state and the MPLA, MK and SWAPO in Angola meant that the 'political' objectives for the apartheid state in Angola were necessarily *military* objectives of counter-insurgency warfare. Therefore, Klug argued that for Williamson to claim a political motive for the assassination, his decision would need to have been based on reasonable intelligence that the Schoons were directly involved in MK's Angolan operations. Williamson's legal team at the TRC never provided any concrete evidence to prove that this was the case.

As the final chapter of this book analysed in detail, the lines between the political and military wings of the ANC – particularly in the Angolan context – were not nearly as clean-cut as Klug would like us to believe. The TRC testimony of Puso Tladi, one of the Schoons' ANC comrades in Angola, provides a striking example of the inherent fuzziness of this whole discussion. Speaking to his own role within the ANC, Tladi explained that he 'was a trainee, I was being trained as a military man'. However, in addition to his military training, Tladi also 'became an instructor, political instructor'. So, which was it? Was Tladi playing a military role or a political one? 'I was instructing soldiers, MK soldiers.'[18] What is striking about Tladi's multi-layered depiction of his own work in Angola is that it precisely mirrors what Barry Gilder and (indeed) Heinz Klug suspected *may* have been the role of the Schoons – political instructors of MK soldiers. Furthermore, Tladi explicitly referenced in his testimony the fact that the

Schoons 'took interest in a little facility, a vocational facility that was just outside Luanda'.[19] However, beyond clarifying that this 'little facility' was funded by the Norwegians, Tladi offered no details as to the nature of instruction that took place at this facility. Given Tladi's complicated portrayal, it is understandable that the question of the Schoons' precise role in Angola was such a thorny issue for the TRC to address.

In his testimony to the TRC, Klug did more than simply insist that the Schoons did not have a military role while in Angola. Klug argued that Williamson's decision to send a bomb to the Schoons was grounded in personal animosity, rather than 'the counter-revolutionary strategy of the time'. This argument had two key components. First, Klug echoed Maharaj's insistence that being in Botswana constituted a 'forward area' for the ANC – close enough to South Africa to allow for underground, cross-border activity – but that the Schoons entirely left behind their earlier roles when they moved to Angola. Once again, according to Klug, the Schoons 'were not involved ... even [in] political activity at the time, let alone anything else'.[20] Therefore, the decision to attack the Schoons *after* their underground political work had ceased was not justifiable or proportional to the threat that the Schoons posed.

On a more fundamental level, Klug testified that Williamson had targeted the Schoons based on personal malice because he believed that he, himself, was also someone that was targeted by Craig Williamson. Klug believed that his cell of the ANC in Botswana (including the Schoons and Patrick Fitzgerald) played a critical role in exposing Karl Edwards and Craig Williamson as spies. This story is recounted in detail in chapter 5. However, in the context of the TRC, Klug used this story to attempt to prove that Williamson held a long-lasting grudge against everyone who played a role in blowing his 'cover'. In addition to the attack on the Schoons, Klug further testified that Craig Williamson 'was in the command centre' that orchestrated the 1985 SADF raid on the ANC in Gaborone, including the office of the Solidarity News Service (SNS). Heinz Klug – who barely escaped Botswana in time to survive the raid – speculated to the TRC that Williamson encouraged the SADF to attack the SNS precisely because the organisation 'had been taken away from him and had been turned against him, had been involved in his exposure, and therefore [he] was completing the job of destroying it'.[21]

Unsurprisingly, Craig Williamson emphatically rejects this whole line of reasoning by Heinz Klug.

> This bullshit story that Fitzgerald and Klug came up with at the TRC: that they were working with Marius, and they were investigating me, and they found out I was a spy, so I had a personal motive to kill Marius and Jeanette, because somehow I was so upset that I blew my cover ... I know why they were saying it ... But they lied.[22]

From Williamson's perspective, the whole idea that being exposed as a spy would lead him into a deadly rage simply doesn't make sense because, having one's cover blown as a spy is 'part of the game. It's not a personal thing.' Despite this refrain of calling the work of the security police a 'game', Williamson speaks ruthlessly about the calculations that went into deciding who to kill and who to merely surveil:

> It's not like, Oh my god, I feel so desperately angry with those particular people! Why did we never take out Mac Maharaj then? Because he was more useful alive than he would have ever been dead. Because we watched Mac for years and everywhere he went, we knew exactly what he was doing ... This intelligence business, at that level, has nothing to do with individual feelings. It's a very cold game.[23]

While Klug would surely not contest the intensely 'cold' nature of the apartheid state's murderous operations, he nonetheless insisted at the TRC that 'there seemed to be a concentration on a group of people who happened to have been involved with Sana at the time that we took it away from Williamson and used it to expose him'.[24] Perhaps Williamson was fully prepared for having his cover blown; he certainly landed firmly on his feet upon returning to South Africa, continuing on and even being promoted within the security police hierarchy. However, given Williamson's lifelong obsession with the ANC, Klug is correct to point to the fact that being exposed as a spy made it impossible for Williamson to successfully infiltrate the ANC.

Given Williamson's extensive campaign against the Schoons' network of radicals – which is documented extensively in this book – it is quite clear why Klug would testify that there was a particular 'concentration' on these individuals. It is entirely plausible that after a decade of surveilling Jeanette and Marius Schoon, Williamson simply despised them, for any number of reasons ... or for no reason whatsoever. However, there is a fatal flaw in Klug's insistence that this concentration was rooted in animosity rather than strategy. As Williamson correctly clarifies:

> The decision to take (how would one term it) 'executive action' against them, wasn't my decision. It was a decision made at a different level. My involvement was to pass on an order. I knew a lot of people within the ANC who were potential targets, but at the end of the day, it's a war. It's the same as the guy who tells the drone to go to those co-ordinates and then presses the button. You've got to accept that that's your role within the organisation. You're a soldier. You carry out your instructions.[25]

Craig Williamson's amnesty proceedings were profoundly influenced by the fact that his commanding officer, Brigadier Piet Goosen, was dead by the time the TRC took place. Therefore, Williamson was able safely to testify to his own role in various murderous activities, without putting Brigadier Goosen at risk and without offering any real opportunity for a truthful recounting of the actual decision-making apparatus of the apartheid state's security services. As Kevin O'Brien explains, there were remarkably few cases where commanding officers ever faced any kind of justice, even before the TRC:

> While more than 7,700 lower-level security force members ... applied for amnesty for a wide range of acts ... almost no senior apartheid political or security force leader applied for amnesty or testified to the TRC's hearings, by-and-large refusing to accept full responsibility ...[26]

We know from Williamson's applications that Goosen was the commanding officer for all the bombings that Williamson was involved in, including the murder of Ruth First and the attack on the ANC offices in London. Therefore, to say that all these attacks were carried out as a result of personal animus on Williamson's part assumes a different relationship between a brigadier and his major than police hierarchies generally tolerate. In addition, Warrant Officer Jerry Raven was included on all the amnesty applications, because he had the technical knowledge required to manufacture all the bombs used. In the case of the London bombing, four other police captains, including the infamous Eugene de Kock, were included in the amnesty application. In fact, all the officers involved in the London bombing had been 'awarded the Police Star for Excellent Service by Louis le Grange, the Minister of Police'.[27]

These operations relied on co-ordination with other members of the South African police or military intelligence in the UK, Botswana, Mozambique and Angola. It is even plausible to assume that individuals within the state apparatus *above* Brigadier Goosen played an important role, in terms of setting the priorities for 'executive actions', which Goosen then followed through on. To reduce this whole complex matrix of state-sponsored violence to mere hatred on Williamson's part would be grossly to understate the actual menace made manifest in moments such as the parcel bomb that arrived in Lubango on 28 June 1984.

The TRC ruled in favour of Craig Williamson and Jerry Raven, both of whom were granted amnesty for the killings of Ruth First and the Schoons, as well as for the terrorist attack on the London office of the ANC. In deciding to grant amnesty, Judge Andrew Wilson's amnesty committee acknowledged that all these acts took place outside of South Africa. Therefore, the amnesty ruling stressed that 'no parliament can legislate for foreign countries and no court or amnesty committee could bind foreign countries'.[28] This is a critical distinction, which means that it is at least theoretically possible for the authorities in Angola, Mozambique or the UK to press charges against Williamson and other security police officers involved in these attacks, regardless of the amnesty ruling. Peter Hain, a South African-born Labour MP in the British Parliament, 'assured *The Observer* in 1995 that [Williamson] would be prosecuted for the London bombing if he set foot in Britain'.[29] However, in the intervening 25 years, no attempt has been made to prosecute Williamson for his crimes outside South Africa – and inside the country the amnesty decision has remained binding.

At the core of the TRC's amnesty ruling was the determination that 'the offences were ... committed *bona fide* with the object of countering or resisting the struggle'.[30] In sum, the committee accepted Williamson's claims that these bombings were politically motivated and not rooted in personal malice. In deciding to rule out malice as a motive, the committee crucially declared: 'it is not disputed that Williamson's cover was broken as a result of the defection of a security police member who had documentary proof of Williamson's real activities.'[31] In other words, if the Schoons' cell in Botswana was not responsible for blowing Williamson's cover, 'the committee concludes that the motive was associated with a political objective'.[32] Beyond the question of how Williamson's cover was blown, the amnesty committee unfortunately accepted the crudest, nastiest framing of Williamson's 'political objective'. Judge Wilson's ruling essentially ignored the extensive arguments put forward by Williamson that the Schoons were 'key operatives' as well as the counter-arguments by ANC members, insisting that the Schoons did *not* have a prominent role within either the military or political underground of the ANC while in Angola. Rather, the amnesty committee settled on the vaguest possible framework and argued that the parcel bomb had the object of 'countering or resisting the struggle'. In articulating Williamson's political objectives so loosely, the committee essentially echoed the terroristic section of Williamson's amnesty application:

STATE POLITICAL OBJECTIVE SOUGHT TO BE ACHIEVED ...
ii) To psychologically destabilize and disrupt the ANC/SACP by causing confusion and fear in their ranks, especially through killing or injuring ANC/SACP personnel in a rear area regarded by them as 'safe'.[33]

The TRC's decision to accept the idea that widespread 'confusion and fear' or psychological 'destabilization' were legitimate 'political objectives' for the apartheid state sets a dangerous precedent for any efforts to bring those responsible for crimes against humanity to justice.

The amnesty committee further declared that the bombings were 'not disproportionate to their objectives'. That is,

The offences were meant to destabilize, demoralize and disadvantage the liberation forces. It might not have demoralized them, in fact it seems as though it had the opposite effect, but the deaths were a severe blow to the ANC and SACP and shocked many people. According to the evidence that is what they wanted to achieve.[34]

While this conclusion is logical, in so far as it correctly analyses the terroristic aims of Brigadier Goosen's unit of the security police, it nonetheless obliterates any specific consideration of the role that the Schoons played within 'the liberation forces'. By accepting that the aim of these parcel bombs was widespread destabilisation and demoralisation, the specific target of the attack diminished in importance. Most importantly, the amnesty committee chose to downplay the significance of Katryn Schoon's death. According to their ruling, 'she was killed in what has often in amnesty hearings been referred by applicants on either side of the political struggle as the crossfire'.[35] While the amnesty committee well understood that 'once a weapon such as a letterbomb is used ... it must be foreseen that innocent civilians could also be killed', they chose not to deny Williamson and Raven amnesty, despite the fact that murdering a six-year-old girl could not by any stretch be declared a 'bona fide' political act. The amnesty committee's key error in dealing with this issue was that they accepted as truthful Williamson's testimony that 'he didn't expect the Schoon children ... to be with their parents in a military zone. He thought they were left in London with Jeanette's sister because the security police were aware that she visited her sister shortly after leaving Botswana.'[36] It is profoundly problematic that the amnesty committee accepted this explanation because Williamson cannot simultaneously claim to have had excellent intelligence information regarding the Schoons *and* been so completely wrong about whether their children were living with them in Angola. If Williamson's intelligence regarding the children was faulty, then the amnesty committee should have assumed that his broader characterisation of the Schoons' role as 'key operatives' in Angola was also faulty.

## Appealing for justice

In the months following the granting of amnesty, the Schoon and Slovo families engaged in an extended dialogue about whether and how to oppose the ruling. Both families were traumatised by their experience at the TRC and felt deeply betrayed by the decision to grant amnesty. Gillian Slovo's depiction of the amnesty hearings provides a strikingly different perspective from the generally rosy accounts of the TRC in popular portrayals:

> The hearings were extremely traumatic and exhausting. My sisters and I were particularly disturbed by the attitude of [Williamson and Raven] ... their arrogance, vindictiveness and lack of remorse struck us deeply. We knew that remorse was not a requirement for amnesty but were nonetheless shocked by the total lack thereof. Their lies, too, surprised and angered us.[37]

Marius Schoon's wife Sherry McLean's description of the Schoon family's feelings echo Slovo's:

> When we heard of the decision to grant ... amnesty, Fritz and I were shocked and angry. We said at the time how upset Marius would have been to hear of the decision, were he still alive. Having sat through what seemed like the endless horrors of the hearings, and then to get the news that [Williamson and Raven] were now free, felt like yet another kick in the stomach.[38]

In November of 2000, the two families together filed a legal action to demand a review of the amnesty committee's decision by the high court, towards revoking amnesty. This was a momentous decision. The ANC was intensely invested in the success of the TRC process. Therefore, for two resolutely loyal ANC families formally to oppose a decision by the TRC was remarkable and rare.

According to Sherry McLean, 'Marius would have wished' for the amnesty to be appealed, 'so that our experience at the hearings was not in vain and that perhaps there may be a chance to see that justice is done'.[39] If the amnesty could be revoked, the Schoons planned to pursue the civil action that Marius had initiated in 1995, once again. McLean's affidavit to the high court declared that Judge Wilson's decision to grant amnesty 'infringes Fritz's constitutional right ... to administrative action that is lawful, reasonable and procedurally fair'. That is, the Schoons not only disagreed with the amnesty ruling, but they also believed that the amnesty committee's decision contained 'such material misdirections that the decision ought to be reviewed and set aside'.[40] In other words, in the parlance of criminal trials, this was an appeal for a mistrial. While the listing of 'material misdirections' contained in Sherry McLean and Gillian Slovo's affidavits are more extensive than can be neatly summarised, there are two key points that need to be stressed.

First, the appeal focused extensively on the amnesty committee's handling of the death of Katryn Schoon. McLean emphatically rejected the idea that Katryn was merely caught in the 'crossfire'.

> If the committee had properly and reasonably considered the evidence ... it would have concluded that [Williamson] dispatched the bomb either intending to kill Katryn and Fritz or, realizing that the children might be killed, reckless as to whether they were killed or not. I submit that Katryn's murder was motivated by personal malice, ill will or spite and that it was disproportionate to the political objective allegedly being pursued.[41]

From the perspective of Fritz Schoon and Sherry McLean, Katryn was not only an 'innocent civilian' but a person who was explicitly targeted by the apartheid state, either consciously or recklessly. That the amnesty committee treated Katryn as collateral damage is galling and is the result of taking Craig Williamson at his word, when he claimed that he believed the children were in London.

> If the committee had properly considered the evidence before it, it would have come to the conclusion that the probabilities were overwhelming that [Williamson] knew, or ought reasonably to have known, that Marius and Jeanette were living with their children in Lubango.[42]

The amnesty committee's willingness to believe Williamson regarding the whereabouts of the Schoon children was linked to another major problem with the proceedings. The conditions for amnesty required a full and honest disclosure from the amnesty applicants. Neither the Schoons nor the Slovos were persuaded that either Williamson or Raven were fully truthful in their testimony. As Gillian Slovo stated in her affidavit, 'the committee ought fairly and reasonably to have come to the conclusion that [Williamson] is a skilled deceiver and a calculating liar and that [Raven] has the ability to lie without exhibiting any signs of discomfort'.[43] For example, Williamson repeatedly changed his evidence to the committee:

> He first said that they had gone to Lubango to play 'an even more [high] profile role in the command structures of the ANC,' later that they 'were in fact specifically sent to Lubango to co-operate with the Cuban Forces that were very strongly there and that were assisting in the development of this air defense system in Angola,' and even later, under cross-examination, that he was the first to mention 'that it was believed that they were teaching English.'[44]

The amnesty committee's final decision did take note of one aspect of Williamson and Raven's testimony that troubled them, which was regarding what these men knew about the intended targets of the bombs. Neither officer was willing definitively to clarify whether Marius or Jeanette (or both at once), Joe Slovo or Ruth First (or both at once) were the intended targets of their bombs. By evading an authoritative answer to this question, both men obfuscated the committee's capacity to determine whether the choice of targets was 'legitimate' or rooted in malice. The most troubling testimony, in this aspect, came from Jerry Raven, who provided a convoluted and confused description of the elaborate lengths that he went to in the process of manufacturing the explosive device inside the packages, to *not* learn anything about who the packages would be sent to. McLean and Slovo both declared Raven's testimony to be 'absurd' and 'highly improbable' in multiple ways and they felt strongly that the committee had failed adequately to address these absurdities. Indeed, despite noting these inconsistencies in their final decision, nonetheless the committee was satisfied that the applicants had fully disclosed what they knew and therefore deserved amnesty.

During the ensuing appeals process, the Slovo family decided to withdraw from the suit and the Schoons decided to push on without them. In the end, a settlement was reached, which allowed the amnesty to hold but ordered Williamson to pay damages to Fritz Schoon, in the amount of R325 000 (roughly, US$50 000). Far from seeking personal gain through these proceedings, the Schoons planned to use these funds to establish a scholarship fund. However, as a final gruelling act of disdain, Williamson has cunningly evaded paying to this day.

Williamson denied that he had the money to pay the amount in damages that the courts had ordered him to pay the Schoon family. In response, Fritz Schoon filed a legal order to force Williamson into a state of 'sequestration' – formally insolvent, with his finances analysed by the high court. In filing this claim, Fritz Schoon argued that Williamson had 'operated for a long period in his life as a secretive and undercover agent. He is therefore capable of concealing assets.'[45] In addition, Schoon's legal team provided evidence that Williamson had a financial stake in five separate businesses. While the court agreed to sequester Williamson's assets, this did not succeed in compelling Williamson to pay anything at all in compensation to the Schoons. Rather than pay a single cent of this penalty, Williamson moved all his assets into his wife's name and thereby weaselled his way out, once again, of taking any responsibility for his crimes.

Craig Williamson continues to live a comfortable life – safe in his home in the suburbs of Johannesburg, driving his Land Rover with the licence plate 'CMW-001'.[46]

## Conclusion

Many people continue to believe that Jeanette and Katryn Schoon were murdered in cold blood and that Craig Williamson is a criminal – plain and simple.

As the years pass – indeed, the decades – for the family, friends and comrades of the Schoons, these crimes continue to feel unresolved, without any recourse for justice. Making sense of what happened on 28 June 1984 (and in the aftermath) has broader implications, beyond how Williamson and the Schoons are remembered. Embedded in the contestations between the Schoons and Williamson – at the TRC and in the courts – are several larger issues related to how the struggle against apartheid is understood.

How must we understand the contribution of women like Jeanette Schoon or Ruth First? Did they have a 'military' role in opposing apartheid?

If they did not, is it still possible to see their radical political commitment as threatening to the apartheid state?

Should men like Williamson be denied amnesty, *even if* their actions had a clear rationale within the logic of defending apartheid?

Furthermore, if Williamson's amnesty was unjustly granted, does this mean that many others who killed in defence of apartheid should not have been granted amnesty?

This book has begun to open up paths towards answering these questions.

In tracing the lives of Craig Williamson and the Schoons over a 12-year period – from the moment Williamson infiltrated the student movement in 1972 until the parcel bomb exploded in 1984 – this book has shown that the assassination of Jeanette and Katryn Schoon fits within a much larger, and multi-faceted, project of state repression. Analysing the assassination within this broader context, I have made every attempt to seek to understand the rational motivations behind the actions of Williamson and other operatives of the state.

Craig Williamson has gone to great lengths to present his career spent defending the undefendable in strictly rational terms. He has consistently insisted that he was motivated not by zealotry, but was simply following the cold calculus of protecting the state against a revolutionary onslaught. Then, for at least one moment, Williamson

> claimed in 1995 that the deaths of Jeanette and Katryn Schoon had 'disillusioned him.' He wrote an article in the *South African Journal of Criminal Law* in which he suggested that: 'using armed force against the civilian population symbolizes the end of civilian government, and that was the end of my career. I came to the conclusion that the war was lost ... the strategy that was being used was wrong. It was getting more and more military and less and less political, and it had to go the other way.'[47]

Despite this feigned display of disillusionment, Craig Williamson remains a murderer – and an unrepentant one, at that. As this book has demonstrated repeatedly, Williamson's key contribution to the security services was to help steer the anti-apartheid struggle towards an explicitly military conflict and therefore to attempt to justify the violence of the apartheid state. Therefore, among the myriad lies expressed by a man whose profession was deceit, the above declaration of remorse ought to be read as among the most egregious and pathetic of Williamson's attempts to deceive.

Seen within the full context of Williamson's campaign of infiltration, surveillance and sabotage, as outlined in this book, the conclusion is clear: the decision to grant Williamson amnesty was a travesty of justice. To declare Williamson a criminal – that he should have been indicted for his crimes and forced to stand trial – is not merely a moral argument. Evaluated solely within the narrow terms that were established by the TRC, there are profound reasons to doubt that Williamson met the basic minimum conditions for being granted amnesty.

1. It is not clear that Williamson was entirely truthful regarding his role within Brigadier Goosen's unit. Was Williamson really just following orders with these bombings, or did he advocate for them, actively?
2. It is not clear that Williamson was entirely truthful regarding the specifics of the actual bomb preparation and shipping. Did he really not know who the intended targets were?
3. In applying for amnesty, Williamson presented two articulations of his political motives – and these two motives are *entirely* different. In the first framing, the Schoons were described as 'key personnel'. In the second, the motive was simply to 'destabilize and disrupt' by killing *any* 'personnel'. The amnesty committee ought to have rejected the second framework entirely, as terrorist reasoning. Then, Williamson would have been compelled to prove that the Schoons were 'key personnel', which he was simply unable to prove.
4. Classifying Katryn Schoon as a 'casualty' of the parcel bomb was a horrendous error on the part of the amnesty committee. As the child of the so-called 'targets', Katryn (and, by extension, Fritz Schoon) was not simply a bystander, but was intimately connected to the crime at hand. Therefore, Katryn ought to have been considered one of the *principal* victims of the bombing, rather than a casualty. If Katryn's death had been treated as a crime in its own right, any claims regarding political motives would have immediately collapsed.

In sum, it seems clear that the amnesty committee should have denied Craig Williamson's amnesty application, as neither of the two core criteria – a truthful account, and a political motive – was sufficiently met in his case. Failing this, the decision ought to have been overturned once the Schoon and Slovo families bravely came forward with an appeal.

It is important to stress that it is possible to advocate for denying amnesty to Williamson *without* agreeing to all the arguments put forward by the ANC and family members during the TRC proceedings. The repeated attempts to insist that the Schoons were 'now completely uninvolved' in the ANC's underground structures in Angola was a line of argumentation forced upon them by the terms of the TRC. Clearly, the TRC forced the friends and family of the Schoons into a quite narrow (and, frankly, convoluted) framework for evaluating the 'political motive' for state-sponsored murder. As this book has repeatedly outlined, the contours of contradictions and void spaces are a serious barrier to any attempt definitively to define the Schoons' role within the ANC's exile structures. The fact that there is disagreement among the comrades of the Schoons at this point – forty years after the assassination – says something about human memory and about the nature of secrets in an organisation that is forced to develop a sophisticated, international underground. But the point of engaging with these different rememberings of the same story is not to clearly draw the line between 'political' and 'military' once and for all. The point is to show that such a line cannot be drawn. Whatever the intentions, whatever the rhetoric, the stories contained in this book quite clearly show that the actual operations of the ANC in exile necessarily resulted in a continual blurring of the lines between political work and military work.

At the same time, the point is that no matter what the Schoons' role was, Craig Williamson (in service to the apartheid state) saw them as threatening and set out to eliminate them. In starting the book before the Schoons went into exile, I have demonstrated that the apartheid state identified Jenny Curtis as among a 'leadership clique' of student activists and immediately began taking steps to repress her. It is critical to understand that the apartheid state was motivated to suppress Curtis's generation of student radicals, even as these young people were privileged, non-violent and unaffiliated with either the banned ANC or SACP. Therefore, more than a decade before the parcel bomb arrived in Lubango – before Jenny

Curtis had even contemplated joining the underground – the threat from the apartheid state was already lurking.

Throughout, I have shown that Craig Williamson played a critical role in *escalating* the conflict between the Schoons and the state. Williamson's campaign to push the IUEF to support the ANC was in hopes of funnelling the anti-apartheid struggle into a narrow, armed conflict. Williamson wanted war. He wanted war, and he wanted to prove that the ANC wanted war as well. Williamson's testimony at the trials of Barbara Hogan and others connected to the Schoons offered a public platform to cast the ANC as an inherently violent organisation. In refusing to acknowledge any form of political participation other than the armed struggle, Williamson sought to define every member of the ANC as armed combatants.

Craig Williamson's testimony against the ANC in Hogan's trial was essentially a pre-emptive attempt to rationalise and justify his own murderous role within the state apparatus. On 18 August 1982, the Slovo family was sifting through the rubble and the grief caused by Williamson's parcel bomb. Meanwhile, Williamson was on the witness stand, insisting that 'even giving a phonebook' to an ANC member counted as supporting the armed struggle. Given such a thorough and scathing obliteration of all distinction between politics and violence, how could it possibly matter whether Ruth First was writing books on African history or supporting her husband's work with Umkhonto we Sizwe, or both?

*

The question is, can we actually see rational thought embedded within the violence of the apartheid state? Or is there nothing but the violence?

By itself, violence is meaningless. I insist that the violence of apartheid becomes illegible if it is divorced from the ideologies and strategies that protected and directed it. I insist that we must grapple with the thinking of men like Craig Williamson, because his attacks on the anti-apartheid struggle spread far wider and were far more insidious than the most explosive moments in his career.

To be clear, there is a critical distinction to be made between acknowledging that an action – even an egregious act of extra-legal violence – has a rationale (a logic, a thought process behind it) and *rationalising* that same act.

Without a doubt, it must be said, simply and plainly: the murders of Jeanette and Katryn Schoon were crimes against humanity, unjustifiable by any metrics. Furthermore, if the trauma inflicted on Marius and Fritz, the Curtis family, the extended family of the ANC underground and the host community in Lubango could possibly be presented as a 'political motivation' for the bombing, then whoever says so is a psychopath, a terrorist.

No matter how much this book attempts to understand Craig Williamson, neither he nor the broader project he represented can ever be forgiven for their crimes.

Let us never forget.

*

There is no way to write a history of the anti-apartheid struggle without tragedy. Jeanette and Katryn Schoon deserve to be remembered for the tragedy of their loss.

And yet, how can we recover the story of these lost lives?

That is, how can we begin to imagine the life that Jeanette Schoon might have lived, if she had been able to live beyond her 30s, to die of old age in the democratic South Africa that she dedicated her life to creating? Who would Katryn Schoon have grown up to be, as a young woman born and raised in exile by two ardent communists and loyal members of the African National Congress? Raising these questions is not merely for curiosity's sake. We must do more than acknowledge the martyrs. We must strive, against the tremendous weight of what happened, to highlight what might have been.

The story we cannot tell is the one in which the Schoons survived the onslaught all around them and carved out a future for themselves and for their children. Without appreciation for the lives the Schoons might have led over the past forty years, we will not be able to understand the full extent of what was lost on 28 June 1984.

# Notes

## Preface
1 Liliesleaf has been closed to the public since September 2021, but may reopen managed by the Department of Public Works. Accessed 11 May 2024, https://www.news24.com/news24/southafrica/news/question-mark-over-future-of-historic-liliesleaf-farm-20220622.
2 For an in-depth account of this – known as the Wankie Campaign – see Stephen R Davis, *The ANC's War Against Apartheid: Umkhonto we Sizwe and the Liberation of South Africa* (Bloomington: Indiana University Press, 2018).
3 Janet Cherry, *Spear of the Nation (Umkhonto weSizwe): South Africa's Liberation Army, 1960s–1990* (Athens: Ohio University Press, 2012), 13.
4 Marius Schoon, interview by Julie Frederikse, Harare, 1986, for Julie Frederikse, *The Unbreakable Thread: Non-racialism in South Africa* (Johannesburg: Ravan Press, 1990). Interview transcript, South African History Archive, AL2460_A19.05.1, accessed 25 June 2024 https://www.saha.org.za/nonracialism/transcript_of_interview_with_marius_schoon.htm, 14–15. Note that the spelling of 'Jennie' has be changed to 'Jenny' in quotations from this transcript.
5 The Institutional Review Board is an arm of the university that approves interviews and other forms of research involving living subjects.
6 Black is capitalised when referring to Africans and people of African descent.

## Introduction
1 John Francis Curtis, *South African Saga: A Political Odyssey* (Braddon: TW Campbell, 2006).
2 Jonathan Ancer, *Spy: Uncovering Craig Williamson* (Johannesburg: Jacana Media, 2017).
3 Hilda Bernstein, *The Rift: The Exile Experience of South Africans* (London: Jonathan Cape, 1994).
4 Julie Frederikse, *The Unbreakable Thread: Non-racialism in South Africa* (Bloomington: Indiana University Press, 1990).
5 I have adopted the idea of 'unusable pasts' from: Hedley Twidle, 'Unusable Pasts: Life-writing, Literary Non-fiction, and the Case of Demetrios Tsafendas', *Research in African Literatures* 46, no. 3 (2015): 1–23.

6   Luisa Passerini, *Autobiography of a Generation: Italy, 1968* (Hanover: Wesleyan University Press, 1996); Robert Foster, *Vivid Faces: The Revolutionary Generation in Ireland, 1890–1923* (New York: WW Norton, 2015).
7   Glenn Moss, *The New Radicals: A Generational Memoir of the 1970s* (Johannesburg: Jacana Media, 2015).
8   Barry Gilder, *Songs and Secrets: South Africa from Liberation to Governance* (Johannesburg: Jacana Media, 2012).
9   Judy Seidman, *Drawn Lines: An Autobiography* (Scotts Valley: CreateSpace Independent Publishing Platform, 2017).
10  Rebecca Ginsburg, *At Home with Apartheid: The Hidden Landscapes of Domestic Service in Johannesburg* (Charlottesville: University of Virginia Press, 2011).
11  Raymond Suttner, *The ANC Underground in South Africa, 1950–1976* (Johannesburg: Jacana Media, 2008), 83.
12  I spent years researching the Schlebusch Commission, poring over the 1 200-page report, interviewing people who were subpoenaed to testify before the commission, even spending months tracking down a shopping cart full of dusty, deteriorating old books of evidence (primarily in Afrikaans) in the archives of the South African Library of Parliament.
13  Padraigh O'Malley, *Shades of Difference: Mac Maharaj and the Struggle for South Africa* (New York: Viking, 2007), 204.
14  O'Malley, *Shades of Difference*, 217.
15  O'Malley, *Shades of Difference*, 218.
16  Jacob Dlamini, *Askari: A Story of Collaboration and Betrayal in the Anti-apartheid Struggle* (Johannesburg: Jacana Media, 2014).
17  Neil Hooper, 'Our Man in Moscow', *Sunday Times*, 27 January 1980.
18  Denis Kuny, interview by Billy Keniston, 8 February 2019.
19  Kevin A O'Brien, *The South African Intelligence Services: From Apartheid to Democracy, 1948–2005* (Abingdon: Routledge, 2011), 76. Elsewhere (26), O'Brien clarifies that 'The relationship, however, came to an abrupt halt in 1976 when the British government directed the security services and Special Branch to "stop all liaison with South Africa except in matters specially identified as directly advantageous to Britain".' Therefore, the extensive involvement of the British FCO in the early 1980s is significant.
20  James Sanders, *Apartheid's Friends: The Rise and Fall of South Africa's Secret Service* (London: John Murray, 2006), 187.
21  Greg Nicolson, 'Barbara Hogan Tells Inquest of "Aggressive" and "Morbid" Aggett Interrogators', *Daily Maverick*, 30 January 2020.
22  Mark Heywood, 'Apartheid-era Crimes: A Commission of Inquiry is Needed to Establish the Truth', *Daily Maverick*, 21 June 2021. Accessed 11 May 2024. https://www.dailymaverick.co.za/article/2021-06-21-apartheid-era-crimes-a-commission-of-inquiry-is-needed-to-establish-the-truth/.

## Prologue: The Assassination, 1984

1   Luise White, *The Assassination of Herbert Chitepo: Texts and Politics in Zimbabwe* (Bloomington: Indiana University Press, 2003), 2.

2  White, *The Assassination of Herbert Chitepo*, 7.
3  White, *The Assassination of Herbert Chitepo*, 9.
4  Schoon, interview by Julie Frederikse, 43.
5  Schoon, interview by Julie Frederikse, 43.
6  Curtis, *South African Saga*, 140.
7  Judy Seidman, interview by Billy Keniston, 10 February 2019.
8  Curtis, *South African Saga*, 140–141.
9  Curtis, *South African Saga*, 141.
10 Curtis, *South African Saga*, 140. Despite this divergence, Jack Curtis does confirm the image that Marius related, with Jenny sitting at the table and Katryn playing nearby.
11 Based on notes from an informal meeting with a neighbour of the Schoons at Simpor who prefers to remain anonymous, June 2019.
12 Based on notes from an informal meeting with a neighbour.
13 Paula Dias, interview by Billy Keniston, 28 May 2019.
14 Dias, interview.
15 Marius Schoon, audio interview by Hilda Bernstein, 1990, Wits Historical Papers, ZA HPRA A3–299 B4.1.2.2.177.
16 Maritz Moolman and Sefako Nyaka in Johannesburg and Ian Hobbes in London, 'Britain Forecast Killings', *Rand Daily Mail*, 30 June 1984. The source is referred to as 'a Whitehall source'.
17 Schoon, audio interview by Hilda Bernstein.
18 Michael Wolfers, *Angola in the Frontline* (London: Zed Press, 1983); see also Lara Pawson, *In the Name of the People: Angola's Forgotten Massacre* (London: I.B. Tauris, 2014).
19 Schoon, audio interview by Hilda Bernstein.
20 Schoon, interview by Julie Frederikse, 41.
21 Schoon, audio interview by Hilda Bernstein.
22 Schoon, audio interview by Hilda Bernstein.
23 Schoon, audio interview by Hilda Bernstein. In the interview, Marius lists the 'various' people on the flight: 'representatives from the students' union, from the trade union, from the university administration, and the ANC comrade that was working with us there [in Lubango]'.
24 ANC archives, Fort Hare University, LUM/028/0020/25.
25 Schoon, interview by Julie Frederikse, 42.
26 Schoon, audio interview by Hilda Bernstein.
27 Angola Press Agency, 'Agentes de Pretória Assassinam Militante do ANC no Lubango', *Jornal de Angola*, 3 July 1984. Accessed at CIDAC archive, Lisbon.
28 Angola Press Agency, 'Marido de Jeanette Schoon Acusa Regime de Pretória,' *Jornal de Angola*, 6 July 1984.
29 Moolman, Nyaka and Hobbes, 'Britain Forecast Killings'.
30 Schoon, audio interview by Hilda Bernstein. 'Jack & Joyce on South African passports. No visas. Straight into the VIP lounge. They were treated as though they were really important visitors to the country.'
31 Curtis, *South African Saga*, 142.

32  Schoon, interview by Julie Frederikse, 40.
33  Curtis, *South African Saga*, 142.
34  The raid took place on 14 June 1985. For more on this, see Diana Wylie, *Art + Revolution: The Life and Death of Thami Mnyele, South African Artist* (Charlottesville: University of Virginia Press, 2008); Clive Kellner and Sergio-Albio González, *Thami Mnyele + Medu Art Ensemble Retrospective* (Johannesburg: Jacana Media, 2009).
35  Curtis, *South African Saga*, 142. According to Marius, the roses were flown in from Lisbon, as a result of a special effort put in by a comrade who worked at the hospital in Luanda.

## Chapter 1 Student Radicals

1  Some Nusas members had joined the African Resistance Movement (ARM), which had attempted property destruction and sabotage, and carried out the bombing of the Johannesburg train station in 1964, in which one person died and 23 were injured. John Harris was hanged for this action, and the ARM was entirely suppressed by the end of 1964. See Charles Jonathan (Jonty) Driver, *Elegy for a Revolutionary* (London: Faber & Faber, 1969) and Hugh Lewin, *Stones Against the Mirror* (Johannesburg: Umuzi, 2011).
2  Alwyn Schlebusch, Second Interim Report of the Commission of Inquiry into Certain Organisations (Pretoria: Government Printer, 1973), 16.
3  Alwyn Schlebusch, Fourth Interim Report of the Commission of Inquiry into Certain Organisations (Pretoria: Government Printer, 1974), 516.
4  Schlebusch, Second Interim Report, 31.
5  The wing of Nusas that was focused on social welfare projects.
6  Schlebusch, Second Interim Report, 9.
7  Schlebusch, Second Interim Report, 9.
8  Schlebusch, Second Interim Report, 17–18. It is instructive that, in stressing the need to take action against these individuals, the Schlebusch Commission was careful to underline the fact that all of them played a role in providing their own evidence.
9  Paul Pretorius, Philippe le Roux, Paula Ensor, Chris Wood and Neville Curtis were among the banned. Clive Keegan was the one other student who received a banning order. In addition, there were the two non-students, Sheila Lapinsky and Rick Turner.
10  Paula Ensor, Philippe le Roux, Chris Wood and Neville Curtis all lived with Jenny Curtis at 100 Belvedere Road, in the Claremont suburb of Cape Town. John Frankish was the only other member of the household who was not banned.
11  Renfrew Christie, Nicki Westcott and Barry Streek lived at 21 Milldene Avenue, also in Claremont, only 600 metres away from the house on Belvedere Road.
12  Clive Keegan, interview by Billy Keniston, 10 August 2017.
13  Charles Nupen, interview by Billy Keniston, 20 March 2019.
14  Nicki Westcott, interview by Billy Keniston, 9 May 2019.
15  Westcott, interview.

16 Nupen, interview.
17 Paula Ensor, interview by Billy Keniston, 23 January 2019.
18 Paul Pretorius, interview by Billy Keniston, 30 June 2016.
19 Roy Ainslee, letter to the Minister of Justice, 2 March 1973, Nusas collection (BC 586), Special Collections Archive, University of Cape Town.
20 Paul Pretorius, letter to the Minister of Justice, 6 May 1974, Department of Justice files related to Paul Pretorius, held in the South African National Archives.
21 WAJ van Zyl, Secretary for Justice, classified memo, 19 June 1974, Department of Justice files related to Paul Pretorius, held in the South African National Archives.
22 Pretorius, interview. According to email communication with Alan Fine, the store was also called 'Paul's Band' for a period.
23 Alliance for Radical Change election brochures, 1974, Hoover Institute, Stanford University. Notably, a similar election campaign was carried out by Peter Randall, one of the leaders of the Study Project on Christianity in an Apartheid Society (Spro-cas), which was also targeted by the Schlebusch Commission. Randall was not banned at the time, but nonetheless his attempt to run for office as a social democrat in the Von Brandis constituency was a provocative move.
24 Alliance for Radical Change election brochure, 1974.
25 Nusas was well aware of the presence of infiltrators on the campuses. Take, as one example, the fact that when Williamson was first elected to the Wits SRC, 'a quarter of that year's SRC was made up of spies. Of the 16 members, Williamson, Sarbutt, McGiven and Brune were agents'. See Ancer, *Spy*, 17.
26 Craig Williamson, interview by Billy Keniston, 29 March 2019.
27 Ancer, *Spy*, 24. Literally, the term means 'k--- brother' and translates into the US racist epithet, 'n--- lover'.
28 Patrick Fitzgerald, interview by Billy Keniston, 21 September 2021.
29 Ancer, *Spy*, 23.
30 Ancer, *Spy*, 23.
31 Williamson, interview.
32 Schlebusch, Fourth Interim Report, 515.
33 Michael Lobban, *White Man's Justice: South African Political Trials in the Black Consciousness Era* (Oxford: Clarendon Press, 1996), 83.
34 Williamson, interview.
35 Williamson, interview.
36 Williamson, interview.
37 Williamson, interview.

## Chapter 2 Post-student People
1 Barbara Hogan, interview by Billy Keniston, 24 April 2019.
2 Glenn Moss, interview by Billy Keniston, 9 March 2019.
3 Moss, interview.
4 Hogan, interview.
5 Hogan, interview.

6   Moss, interview.
7   Moss, interview.
8   According to the email communication with Alan Fine, Jenny Curtis lived in a couple of different situations during her years in Yeoville, always with leftists. Notably, Curtis lived with Janet Love, who later worked for the ANC underground, and then also lived in a house with a few different people, including Alan Fine, Ian Roberson and Merle Barsel, all of whom were connected to the ANC or SACP in some form. Barbara Hogan also lived in Yeoville during this same period.
9   Hogan, interview.
10  Hogan, interview.
11  Hogan, interview.
12  Moss, interview.
13  Alan Fine, email communication with Billy Keniston, June 2021.
14  Govan Mbeki was imprisoned on Robben Island at the time, and Thabo Mbeki was in the exiled ANC leadership.
15  Hogan, interview.
16  Moss, *The New Radicals*, 156–157.
17  Moss, *The New Radicals*, 157.
18  Moss, *The New Radicals*, 160.
19  Moss, *The New Radicals*, 160.
20  Moss, *The New Radicals*, 163.
21  Moss, *The New Radicals*, 175.
22  Moss, interview.
23  Hogan, interview.
24  Ensor, interview.
25  Moss, *The New Radicals*, 185.
26  Curtis, *South African Saga*, 117.
27  Curtis, *South African Saga*, 115.
28  Curtis, *South African Saga*, 120.
29  Curtis, *South African Saga*, 117.
30  Breyten Breytenbach, *The True Confessions of an Albino Terrorist* (London: Faber & Faber, 1984), 47.
31  Moss, interview.
32  Moss, interview. Moss adds: 'I've always suspected also that they were protecting one or two other people who were in our circles as reporting agents'.
33  Ancer, *Spy*, 33–34.
34  Curtis, *South African Saga*, 117.
35  Curtis, *South African Saga*, 118.
36  Moss, *The New Radicals*, 192.
37  Curtis, *South African Saga*, 119.
38  Hogan, interview.
39  Heinz Klug, interview by Billy Keniston, 22 September 2018.
40  Klug, interview.
41  Schoon, audio interview by Hilda Bernstein.
42  Hugh Lewin, *Bandiet: Seven Years in a South African Prison* (London: Penguin, 1976), 77–78.

# NOTES

43 Curtis, *South African Saga*, 122. Furthermore, 'Subsequently some of the messages were found in Breyten's possession and action was taken against him.'
44 Klug, interview. According to personal communication with Tom Lodge – a historian of the South African Communist Party – it is unlikely that Marius Schoon formally joined the party.
45 Commissioner of Prisons, classified memo to the Minister of Justice, August 1976, Classified documents related to Marius Schoon, South African National Archives. (Quotation in Afrikaans translated by Google Translate.)
46 Commissioner of Prisons, classified memo. (The memo is in English.)
47 Department of Justice, classified internal memo, 2 August 1976, Documents related to Marius Schoon, held at the South African National Archives. (Translated from Afrikaans by Google Translate.)
48 Department of Justice, classified internal memo.
49 Department of Justice, classified internal memo.
50 Department of Justice, classified internal memo.
51 Department of Justice, classified internal memo.
52 Department of Justice, classified internal memo.
53 Department of Justice, classified internal memo.
54 Moss, interview.
55 Hogan, interview.
56 Curtis, *South African Saga*, 122.
57 Schoon, audio interview by Hilda Bernstein.
58 Hogan, interview.
59 Schoon, audio interview by Hilda Bernstein.
60 Moss, interview.
61 Ensor, interview.
62 Hogan, interview.
63 Schoon, audio interview by Hilda Bernstein.
64 Hogan, interview.
65 Hogan, interview.
66 Devan Pillay, interview by Billy Keniston, 30 March 2019.
67 Pillay, interview.
68 Hogan, interview.
69 Ensor, interview.
70 Moss, interview.

## Chapter 3 Cover Stories

1 Alan Fine, interview by Billy Keniston, 15 February 2019.
2 Curtis, *South African Saga*, 122.
3 Curtis, *South African Saga*, 122.
4 Helen Suzman, note to Minister of Justice Kruger, 22 June 1977, Classified Department of Justice files related to Marius Schoon, held at the South African National Archives, obtained via a PAIA request.
5 Minister of Justice, classified internal memo, in response to letters from Schoon and Curtis on 29 March and 30 March 1977, Classified Department of Justice

6   Curtis, *South African Saga*, 122–123. Kotzé was a member of the Christian Institute and very politically sympathetic to the young banned couple.
7   Fine, interview.
8   Curtis, *South African Saga*, 123.
9   Curtis, *South African Saga*, 123.
10  Curtis, *South African Saga*, 123.
11  Michael Hubbard, email communication with Billy Keniston, January 2021. Hubbard says that the Schoons' compass was *not* in fact broken, and that he still has it in his possession.
12  Curtis, *South African Saga*, 123.
13  Headquarters of the Security Branch of the South African Police.
14  Minister of Justice, classified memo, 24 June 1977, Classified Department of Justice files related to Marius Schoon, held at the South African National Archives, obtained via a PAIA request.
15  Minister of Justice, classified memo.
16  Michael Hubbard, interview by Billy Keniston, 4 November 2018.
17  Hubbard, interview.
18  Hubbard, interview.
19  Hubbard, interview.
20  Hubbard, interview.
21  Commissioner of Police, letter to the Minister of Justice, 23 June 1977, Classified Department of Justice files related to Marius Schoon, held at the South African National Archives, obtained via a PAIA request. (Translated from Afrikaans by Google Translate.)
22  Judy Seidman, interview by Billy Keniston, 7 February 2019.
23  International University Exchange Fund (IUEF), Report of the Commission of Inquiry into the Espionage Activities of the South African Government in the International University Exchange Fund, 1980, AD 1757, Historical Papers Archive, University of the Witwatersrand, 11.
24  IUEF, file note on Discussions with Craig Williamson, 30 July 1976, Danish National Archives, IUEF Director's Office Files, 1974–1980, 10377, AI, Box 294.
25  IUEF, Report of the Commission of Inquiry, 12.
26  Lars-Gunnar Eriksson, memo on a 'special fund', 19 August 1976, Danish National Archives, IUEF Director's Office Files, 1974–1980, 10377, AI, Box 294.
27  Williamson, interview.
28  IUEF, Captain Craig Williamson biography, 8 February 1980, Danish National Archives, Administrative A/GF IUEF Geneva Executive, 12.04.1979–30.07.1981, Copenhagen, Denmark, 10377, Box 963.
29  IUEF, Report of the Commission of Inquiry, 12.
30  Lars-Gunnar Eriksson, memo to all staff, 27 June 1978, Danish National Archives, IUEF Directorate Papers, 1976–1980, 10377, AI, Box 767.
31  IUEF, Report of the Commission of Inquiry, 13. The ANC was, at various times, consulted by Eriksson regarding Williamson, but not in terms of his hiring or promotion.

32  IUEF, Report of the Commission of Inquiry, 13.
33  Based on notes from an informal meeting with Jeff Ramsay and Gary Wills, June 2019. It is worth noting that both Ramsay and Wills are white expatriate teachers from the UK and US. Villagers born and raised in Molepolole may well describe their community in quite different terms.
34  Ramsay and Wills notes.
35  Ramsay and Wills notes.
36  Based on notes from informal meetings with Salome and Wilheminah, June 2019.
37  Ramsay and Wills notes; Fitzgerald, interview.
38  Curtis, *South African Saga*, 135.
39  Ramsay and Wills notes. Close friends Patrick Fitzgerald and Judy Seidman both dispute the notion that Jenny and Marius provided 'nothing lavish', as they remember both of the Schoons as absolutely loving to cook.
40  Klug, interview.
41  Curtis, *South African Saga*, 135.
42  Klug, interview.
43  Billy Keniston, *Choosing to Be Free: The Life Story of Rick Turner* (Johannesburg: Jacana Media, 2013), 151.
44  Keniston, *Choosing to Be Free*, 150.
45  Keniston, *Choosing to Be Free*, 155.
46  Curtis, *South African Saga*, 136.
47  Curtis, *South African Saga*, 136.
48  Curtis, *South African Saga*, 136.
49  Klug, interview.
50  Klug, interview.
51  Barry Gilder, interview by Billy Keniston 1 June 2019.
52  Mike Kahn, interview by Billy Keniston, 21 January 2019.
53  Kahn, interview.
54  Kellner and González, *Thami Mnyele + Medu Art Ensemble Retrospective*, 76.
55  For a more complete listing of Medu's members, see Kellner and González, *Thami Mnyele + Medu Art Ensemble Retrospective*.
56  Kahn, interview.
57  Seidman, interview.
58  Klug, interview.
59  In addition to the individuals interviewed and discussed here, others who were connected to the Schoons included Patrick Fitzgerald, Petra Röhr-Rouendaal and Gordon Metz.
60  Kahn, interview.
61  Williams spent years as deputy police commissioner in post-apartheid South Africa.
62  Kahn, interview.
63  Seidman, interview.
64  Seidman, interview.
65  Seidman, interview.
66  Kellner and González, *Thami Mnyele + the Medu Art Ensemble Retrospective*, 162.

67  Kellner and González, *Thami Mnyele + the Medu Art Ensemble Retrospective*, 194.
68  Williamson, interview.
69  IUEF, Strictly Confidential memo, anonymous, n.d., Danish National Archives, IUEF Director's Office Files, 1974–1980, 10377, AI, Box 297.
70  IUEF, Strictly Confidential memo, anonymous, n.d.
71  IUEF, Clandestine Funds accounting sheet, n.d., Danish National Archives, IUEF Director's Office Files, 1974–1980, 10377, AI, Box 295.
72  Charles is almost certainly Karl Edwards. Paul is likely Paul Assmussen.
73  Williamson, interview.
74  Williamson, interview.
75  Craig Williamson, Strictly Confidential memo on means of illegally getting funds into South Africa, 17 May 1978, Danish National Archives, IUEF Director's Office Files, 1974–1980, 10377, AI, Box 295.
76  Georg Sehl (Amnesty International, West Germany), letter to the IUEF, 6 July 1977, Danish National Archives, IUEF Director's Office Files, 1974–1980, 10377, AI, Box 300.
77  Craig Williamson, letter to Georg Sehl, 15 July 1977, Danish National Archives, IUEF Director's Office Files, 1974–1980, 10377, AI, Box 300.
78  Craig Williamson, Strictly Confidential memo on means of illegally getting funds into South Africa. BPC stands for the Black People's Convention.
79  Lars-Gunnar Eriksson, memo, Re: Southern Futures Vaduz Transactions, 19 May 1978, Danish National Archives, IUEF Director's Office Files, 1974–1980, 10377, AI, Box 300.
80  Williamson, interview.
81  Williamson, interview.
82  Lars-Gunnar Eriksson, Strictly Confidential memo, 13 November 1978, Danish National Archives, IUEF Director's Office Files, 1974–1980, 10377, AI, Box 300.
83  Williamson, interview.
84  Williamson, interview.
85  According to Steen Christensen, Brandrup 'is in fact an interesting person in his own right. He was an exception in the antiapartheid solidarity work by being an outspoken and prominent member of the Conservative Party ... He came to be very close to Lars-Gunnar and was the lynchpin in the Danish member organizations' work with the IUEF.' From email communication with Billy Keniston, March 2021.
86  Williamson, interview. While Williamson and Brandrup clearly knew one another and while Brandrup definitely travelled to South Africa, the veracity of Williamson's story about bringing him to Daisy Farm is disputed by many people and for multiple reasons. Steen Christensen, for example, does not believe Williamson's version of this story, at all. Steen Christensen, email communication with Billy Keniston, March 2021.
87  Williamson, interview.
88  Williamson, interview.

89 South African Press Association, 'Policemen Had a Dungeon to Imprison Slovo, TRC Hears'. South African Department of Justice, 22 September 1998. Accessed 5 May 2020, https://www.justice.gov.za/trc/media/1998/9809/s980922b.htm.
90 Email communication with Henrik Thomsen, a Danish journalist who has written extensively about Williamson's exploits, March 2021.

## Chapter 4 Undercover Stories

1 Klug, interview.
2 Klug, interview.
3 Klug, interview.
4 Klug, interview.
5 Fitzgerald, interview.
6 Fitzgerald, interview.
7 Klug, interview.
8 Jacob Dlamini, *The Terrorist Album: Apartheid's Insurgents, Collaborators, and the Security Police* (Cambridge: Harvard University Press, 2020), 161.
9 Dlamini, *The Terrorist Album*, 162.
10 'Williamson and Edwards Background Information', no author, 5. Part of the documents for the legal defence for Barbara Hogan, Historical Papers, University of the Witwatersrand, ZA HPRA 2422, 11.
11 Dlamini, *The Terrorist Album*, 153.
12 Klug, interview.
13 Klug, interview.
14 Klug, interview.
15 Klug, interview.
16 Williamson, interview.
17 Craig Williamson, autobiography statement while in an Angolan jail, 10 October 1996, personal archives of Terry Bell, Muizenberg, South Africa.
18 Williamson, interview.
19 Craig Williamson autobiography statement.
20 Craig Williamson, letter to the ANC, 24 May 1977, London Mission Records, ANC archives, Fort Hare University, Box 0004.
21 Craig Williamson, letter to the ANC, 21 October 1978, London Mission Records, ANC archives, Fort Hare University, Box 0004.
22 ANC, letter of recommendation for Ingrid Williamson, 16 November 1978, London Mission Records, ANC archives, Fort Hare University, Box 0004.
23 Sanders, *Apartheid's Friends*, 139.
24 Craig Williamson, report on 'Discussions with friends in Gaborone', 10 February 1978, Danish National Archives, IUEF Director's Office Files, 1974–1980, 10377, AI, Box 298. According to Steen Christensen, Ranwedzi was 'a founding member of Saso and a prominent BCM representative … Together with Abram Tiro he escaped to Botswana and was in charge of the office of the BCM' in Gaborone. Steen Christensen, email communication with the author, March 2021.

25 See note 24 for information on the identify of Ranwedzi.
26 Craig Williamson, report on 'Discussions with friends in Gaborone'.
27 IUEF Board Meeting resolution, 19–21 June 1978, Danish National Archives, IUEF Stipendiater, 1977–1980, 10377, AI, Box 242.
28 Williamson, interview.
29 Williamson, interview.
30 Williamson, interview.
31 Williamson, interview.
32 Meeting between IUEF Secretariat and ANC, Geneva, 4 July 1979, Danish National Archives, IUEF Director's Office Files, 1974–1980, 10377, AI, Box 298.
33 Meeting between IUEF Secretariat and ANC, Geneva, 4 July 1979.
34 Klug, interview.
35 Kahn, interview.
36 Kahn, interview.
37 Gilder, interview.
38 Seidman, interview.
39 Klug, interview.
40 Kahn, interview.
41 Seidman, interview.
42 Seidman, interview.
43 Ensor, interview.
44 Ensor, interview.
45 Kahn, interview.
46 Klug, interview.
47 Fitzgerald, interview.
48 Moss, interview.
49 Hogan, interview.
50 Klug, interview.
51 Hogan, interview.
52 Cedric de Beer, affidavit in support of Barbara Hogan, Barbara Hogan vs. Officer Commanding New Johannesburg Prison and the Commissioner of Prisons, 1983–1984, Wits Historical Papers, ZA HPRA AK2442-C, 13.
53 Kahn, interview.
54 Gilder, interview.
55 Seidman, interview.
56 Seidman, interview.
57 Seidman, interview.
58 Fitzgerald, interview.
59 Fitzgerald, interview.
60 This is a true story. Someone was actually charged for having ANC symbolism on a mug.
61 Klug, interview.
62 Kahn, interview.
63 Kahn, interview.
64 The parastatal energy company.

65 Klug, interview.
66 Ensor, interview.
67 Klug, interview.
68 Seidman, interview.
69 Seidman, interview.

## Chapter 5 Exposing Craig Williamson

1 Moss, interview.
2 Hogan, interview.
3 While other police members of 'Operation Daisy' – as it was known by the security police – have not confessed in the same ways, there are a number of lower-level participants in the infiltration whose identity is fairly certain, such as Williamson's sister, Lisa, and the Assmussen brothers.
4 Moss, interview.
5 De Beer, affidavit, 6.
6 De Beer, affidavit, 12.
7 De Beer, affidavit, 12.
8 De Beer, affidavit, 12.
9 Fitzgerald, interview.
10 De Beer, affidavit, 14.
11 De Beer, affidavit, 10.
12 IUEF, Report of the Commission of Inquiry, 14.
13 IUEF, Report of the Commission of Inquiry, 15.
14 IUEF, Report of the Commission of Inquiry, 15.
15 IUEF, Report of the Commission of Inquiry, 20.
16 It is worth noting that Eriksson was a Swedish citizen, so it makes sense for the Swedes to contact him directly.
17 IUEF, Report of the Commission of Inquiry, 16.
18 IUEF, Report of the Commission of Inquiry, 19.
19 IUEF, Report of the Commission of Inquiry, 17.
20 IUEF, Report of the Commission of Inquiry, 23–24.
21 IUEF, Report of the Commission of Inquiry, 18.
22 IUEF, Report of the Commission of Inquiry, 21.
23 Klug, interview.
24 Moss, interview.
25 Klug, interview.
26 Klug, interview.
27 Klug, interview.
28 Klug, interview.
29 Klug, interview.
30 Seidman, interview.
31 Klug, interview.
32 'Williamson and Edwards Background Information', no author, 2.
33 Andrew Wilson, 'BOSS Agent Quits to Reveal Spy Secrets', *The Observer* (London), 30 December 1979.

34 IUEF, Report of the Commission of Inquiry, 44. This was later confirmed by McGiven's testimony to the IUEF Commission of Inquiry. McGiven claimed that refraining from stating Williamson's name in the newspaper was not only a decision taken to protect Williamson himself, but also 'that as long as Williamson remained outside South Africa, people would be safe and useful work could continue ...'. This is, to say the least, specious reasoning.
35 Andrew Wilson, 'The British "Targets" of BOSS', *The Observer* (London), 6 January 1980.
36 IUEF, Report of the Commission of Inquiry, 35.
37 IUEF, Report of the Commission of Inquiry, 35.
38 Lars-Gunnar Eriksson, 'Our Accounts Were Stolen', *The Observer* (London), 13 January 1980.
39 IUEF, Report of the Commission of Inquiry, 36.
40 IUEF, Report of the Commission of Inquiry, 36.
41 IUEF, Report of the Commission of Inquiry, 36.
42 IUEF, Report of the Commission of Inquiry, 41.
43 IUEF, Report of the Commission of Inquiry, 36.
44 IUEF, Report of the Commission of Inquiry, 37.
45 IUEF, Report of the Commission of Inquiry, 37.
46 IUEF, Report of the Commission of Inquiry, 38.
47 IUEF, Report of the Commission of Inquiry, 39.
48 IUEF, Report of the Commission of Inquiry, 39.
49 Hugh Lewin and Walter Schwarz, 'SA Spy Alleged in Relief Agency', *The Guardian* (London), 21 January 1980.
50 IUEF, Report of the Commission of Inquiry, 41.
51 IUEF, Report of the Commission of Inquiry, 25.
52 IUEF, Report of the Commission of Inquiry, 48.
53 IUEF, Report of the Commission of Inquiry, 49.
54 Lars-Gunnar Eriksson, resignation letter, 2 June 1980, Danish National Archives, Administrative A/GF, IUEF Geneva Executive, 12 April 1979–30 July 1981, 10377, AI, Box 963.
55 IUEF, Report of the Commission of Inquiry, 43.
56 IUEF, Report of the Commission of Inquiry, 45.
57 IUEF, Report of the Commission of Inquiry, 45.
58 IUEF, Report of the Commission of Inquiry, 45.
59 IUEF, Report of the Commission of Inquiry, 46.
60 And, not incidentally, one of the commissioners of the Schlebusch Commission.
61 Patrick Laurence, 'SA Minister Praises Spy's Role in Geneva', *The Guardian* (London), 25 January 1980.
62 As quoted in Patrick Laurence, 'SA Minister Praises Spy's Role in Geneva'.
63 Seidman, interview.

## Chapter 6 The Damage is Done
1 IUEF, Report of the Commission of Inquiry, 1.
2 IUEF, Report of the Commission of Inquiry, 1.

NOTES

3 IUEF, Report of the Commission of Inquiry, 77. Other ANC members were listed, but not as representatives of the ANC, such as Zanele Mbeki, Heinz Klug, Patrick Fitzgerald, and perhaps others.
4 IUEF, Report of the Commission of Inquiry, 2.
5 IUEF, Report of the Commission of Inquiry, 7. 'The organisation's funds come largely from the Governments of Sweden, Norway, Denmark, the Netherlands, Canada, Great Britain in the case of Zimbabwe, and, most recently, Finland. Funds have also been received from voluntary agencies in several countries and from some international bodies.'
6 IUEF, Report of the Commission of Inquiry, 3.
7 IUEF, Report of the Commission of Inquiry, 5.
8 IUEF, Report of the Commission of Inquiry, 6.
9 This is strikingly different from the International Defence and Aid Fund (IDAF). One notable moment of weakness within the IUEF was the early links to the CIA. According to the Commission of Inquiry, 'the IUEF's parent body, the ISC [International Student Conference] was dissolved in March 1969 after revelations that it had received funds from the CIA'. Report of the Commission of Inquiry, 6.
10 IUEF, Report of the Commission of Inquiry, 51.
11 IUEF, Report of the Commission of Inquiry, 53.
12 IUEF, Report of the Commission of Inquiry, 57.
13 IUEF, Report of the Commission of Inquiry, 29.
14 IUEF, Report of the Commission of Inquiry, 57.
15 IUEF, Report of the Commission of Inquiry, 56.
16 IUEF, Report of the Commission of Inquiry, 53.
17 IUEF, Report of the Commission of Inquiry, 70.
18 IUEF, Report of the Commission of Inquiry, 58.
19 IUEF, Report of the Commission of Inquiry, 59.
20 IUEF, Report of the Commission of Inquiry, 63.
21 IUEF, Report of the Commission of Inquiry, 13.
22 IUEF, Report of the Commission of Inquiry, 26.
23 IUEF, Report of the Commission of Inquiry, 27.
24 IUEF, Report of the Commission of Inquiry, 64.
25 IUEF, Report of the Commission of Inquiry, 22–23.
26 IUEF, Report of the Commission of Inquiry, 23.
27 IUEF, Report of the Commission of Inquiry, 24.
28 IUEF, Report of the Commission of Inquiry, 20.
29 IUEF, Report of the Commission of Inquiry, 21.
30 IUEF, Report of the Commission of Inquiry, 67.

## Chapter 7 Arrests and detention

1 Hogan, interview.
2 Pillay, interview.
3 Tim Jenkin was a computer programmer, who later played an important role in helping the ANC develop an encrypted means of communication, which was far more sophisticated than the coded communications described here.

4   Pillay, interview.
5   Pillay, interview.
6   Fine, interview.
7   Guy Berger, interview by Billy Keniston, 23 February 2019.
8   Janice Warman, *The Class of '79* (Johannesburg: Jacana Media, 2014), 53.
9   Devan Pillay similarly told me, 'Honestly, I wasn't doing a hell of lot, actually. They thought I was involved in a lot more than I was.'
10  Warman, *The Class of '79*, 73.
11  Kuny, interview.
12  Warman, *The Class of '79*, 61–62.
13  'Statement of Barbara Anne Hogan', Historical Papers, University of Witwatersrand, ZA HPRA AK2442-G, 1.
14  'Statement of Barbara Anne Hogan', 1–2.
15  'Statement of Barbara Anne Hogan', 2.
16  Hogan, interview.
17  Hogan, interview.
18  Hogan, interview.
19  Dlamini, *Askari*.
20  Hogan, interview.
21  Hogan, interview.
22  Fine, interview.
23  'Statement of Barbara Anne Hogan', 3.
24  'Statement of Barbara Anne Hogan', 7.
25  'Statement of Barbara Anne Hogan', 5.
26  'Statement of Barbara Anne Hogan', 6.
27  'Statement of Barbara Anne Hogan', 11.
28  'Statement of Barbara Anne Hogan', 11.
29  'Statement of Barbara Anne Hogan', 23.
30  'Statement of Barbara Anne Hogan', 13.
31  'Statement of Barbara Anne Hogan', 8.
32  'Statement of Barbara Anne Hogan', 9–10.
33  'Statement of Barbara Anne Hogan', 18.
34  'Statement of Barbara Anne Hogan', 12.
35  'Statement of Barbara Anne Hogan', 19.
36  'Statement of Barbara Anne Hogan', 19.
37  'Statement of Barbara Anne Hogan', 9. This could either be referring to Cedric de Beer or Cedric Mayson, both active within the white left.
38  Hogan, interview.
39  Auret van Heerden, affidavit in the inquest into the death of Neil Aggett, Historical Papers, University of the Witwatersrand, ZA HPRA AK2216, 9.
40  Auret van Heerden, affidavit, 10.
41  Auret van Heerden, affidavit, 10.
42  Auret van Heerden, affidavit, 1.
43  Auret van Heerden, affidavit, 2.
44  Auret van Heerden, affidavit, 5.

45 Auret van Heerden, affidavit, 5.
46 Auret van Heerden, affidavit, 10.
47 Warman, *The Class of '79*, 52.
48 Warman, *The Class of '79*, 52.
49 Warman, *The Class of '79*, 52. Pillay clarifies that he was made to stand on his tip-toes, with the drawing pins (tacks) underneath his heels. While this was immensely unpleasant, Pillay succeeded in not getting cut by the pins.
50 Pillay, interview.
51 It is important to note that, as Pillay also stresses, Aggett was the only white person to die in detention, out of 53 in the apartheid years before his death.
52 'Dr. Neil Aggett Inquest'. Wits Historical Papers, Johannesburg. ZA HPRA AK2216. Aggett's inquest was reopened in 2020 and concluded on 4 March 2022, with a ruling that Aggett's death was the result of police torture, rather than simple suicide. Accessed 12 May 2024, https://www.saflii.org/za/cases/ZAGPJHC/2022/110.html.
53 Slang for the National Party, the ruling party.
54 Hogan, interview.
55 Pillay, interview.
56 Pillay, interview.
57 Pillay, interview.
58 Berger, interview.
59 Pillay, interview.
60 Pillay, interview.
61 Lewin, *Bandiet*, 77. Notably, Marius Schoon was one of the white political prisoners that was detained alongside Lewin and stayed in jail until 1976.
62 According to email communication with Devan Pillay (June 2021), it is probable that white political prisoners were actually separated from 'common law' prisoners.

## Chapter 8 The Trials

1 Warman, *The Class of '79*, 60.
2 The State vs. G.J.E. Berger and D. Pillay, Historical Papers, University of the Witwatersrand, ZA HPRA AK2306-2, 114.
3 The State vs. Berger, 96.
4 The State vs. Berger, 100.
5 The State vs. Berger, 105.
6 The State vs. Berger, 87.
7 The State vs. Berger, 121.
8 'They are in the archives, I would assume, of our National Intelligence Service.' The State vs. Berger, 122.
9 The State vs. Berger, 120.
10 The State vs. Berger, 120.
11 Fine, interview.
12 The State vs. Berger, 143.

13 The State vs. Berger, 106.
14 The State vs. Berger, 115.
15 The State vs. Berger, 117.
16 The State vs. Berger, 117.
17 The State vs. Berger, 88. The South African Congress of Trade Unions was a union formation that had been explicitly aligned with the 'Congress Movement' in the early years of apartheid, before the ANC was officially banned, in the aftermath of the Sharpeville Massacre. Sactu was never declared an illegal organisation, but membership in Sactu did tend to imply a sympathy for, or membership of, the ANC.
18 Fine, interview.
19 Kuny, interview.
20 Kuny, interview.
21 Fine, interview.
22 The State vs. A.M. Fine; Craig Williamson's testimony from 2 August 1982, 71, Historical Papers, University of the Witwatersrand, ZA HPRA AK2306-4.
23 The State vs. Fine, 83.
24 The State vs. Fine, 105.
25 The State vs. Fine, 75.
26 Fine, interview.
27 Fine, interview.
28 Craig Williamson testimony at The State vs. Hogan, 8, Historical Papers, University of the Witwatersrand.
29 The State vs. Hogan, 9.
30 The State vs. Berger, 228.
31 The State vs. Hogan, 24.
32 A white communist, who had been a member of the sabotage organisation, the African Resistance Movement, and then left the country in 1964.
33 A white communist, and a member of ANC intelligence.
34 The State vs. Hogan, 16.
35 The State vs. Berger, 229.
36 The State vs. Berger, 200.
37 The State vs. Hogan, 24.
38 The State vs. Berger, 202–203.
39 The State vs. Berger, 205.
40 The State vs. Hogan, 34.
41 The State vs. Berger, 201–202.
42 The State vs. Berger, 208–209.
43 The State vs. Berger, 213. It is notable that Williamson, also, described Jeanette as 'a senior SACTU official in Gaborone', rather than as an ANC member.
44 The State vs. Berger, 212.
45 The State vs. Berger, 213.
46 Hogan, interview.
47 Hogan, interview.
48 Hogan, interview.

# NOTES

49 Hogan, interview.
50 The State vs. Hogan, 56.
51 The State vs. Hogan, 74.
52 The State vs. Hogan, 78.
53 The State vs. Hogan, 55.
54 The State vs. Hogan, 60.
55 The State vs. Hogan, 59.
56 The State vs. Hogan, 82.
57 The State vs. Hogan, 17.
58 The State vs. Hogan, 82.
59 The State vs. Berger, 181–182.
60 The State vs. Berger, 235.
61 Hogan, interview.
62 Hogan, interview.
63 The State vs. Hogan, 427.
64 The State vs. Hogan, 422.
65 The State vs. Hogan, 423.
66 Tom Lodge, memorandum (not to be used in court), Barbara Hogan Defence Files, 1.
67 Tom Lodge, memorandum, 1.
68 Stephen Ellis, *External Mission: The ANC in Exile, 1960–1990* (London: Hurst, 2012).
69 Tom Lodge, memorandum, 1.
70 Tom Lodge, memorandum, 2.
71 Tom Lodge, memorandum 2–3.
72 Tom Lodge, memorandum, 6–7.
73 The State vs. Hogan, 431.
74 The State vs. Hogan, 495.
75 Prior to 1979, while white workers and even, to a lesser extent, Coloured and Indian workers, had the right to organise into unions, the Black majority within the working class was heavily restricted in terms of the right to establish collective bargaining agreements with their employers, or to strike. Wages for Black workers were set industry wide, with representation only allowed in a minimal way, as if through a 'tribal' leader.
76 The State vs. Hogan, 484.
77 The State vs. Hogan, 493–494.
78 The State vs. Hogan, 497.
79 The State vs. Hogan, 491.
80 The State vs. Hogan, 500.
81 The State vs. Hogan, 501.
82 The State vs. Hogan, 501.
83 The State vs. Hogan, 504.
84 Personal communication with Tom Lodge, 7 October 2023. Lodge remembers Swanepoel as 'far and away the best prosecutor I ever encountered, having testified at roughly 20 trials during apartheid'.

85 The State vs. Hogan, 502.
86 The State vs. Hogan, 505.
87 Barbara Hogan Defence Files, 'Questions Arising out of Craig Williamson's Evidence', Historical Papers, University of the Witwatersrand, ZA HPRA, A3104-E-E4.
88 Barbara Hogan Defence Files, 'Questions Arising out of Craig Williamson's Evidence', 4.
89 The State vs. Hogan, 506.
90 The State vs. Hogan, 535.
91 The State vs. Hogan, 508.
92 The State vs. Hogan, 520.
93 The State vs. Hogan, 507.
94 Barbara Hogan Defence Files, 'Questions Arising out of Craig Williamson's Evidence'.
95 The State vs. Hogan, 48–49.
96 The State vs. Berger, 106.
97 The State vs. Hogan, 52.
98 Hogan, interview.
99 The State vs. Hogan, 41.
100 The State vs. Hogan, Sentencing, 44.
101 The State vs. Hogan, Sentencing, 45.
102 The United Democratic Front (UDF) was a mass organisation that engaged in widespread protests against apartheid, starting in 1983, and escalating heavily through the states of emergency in the middle of the decade. The organisation was not itself the ANC, but was grounded in the Freedom Charter, and therefore aligned itself quite consciously with the ANC. See Jeremy Seekings, *The UDF: A History of the United Democratic Front in South Africa, 1983–1991* (Cape Town: David Philip, 2000).
103 Hogan, interview.
104 The State vs. Hogan, Sentencing, 47.
105 The State vs. Hogan, Sentencing, 43–44.

## Chapter 9 No Asylum from Her Majesty

1 1971 to 1984.
2 Nigel Watt, interview by Billy Keniston, 15 March 2019.
3 Watt, interview.
4 Watt, interview.
5 Watt, interview.
6 Watt, interview.
7 Watt, interview. Watt further clarified in email communication with Billy Keniston, June 2021, that IVS volunteers were generally paid less than many other European NGO workers.
8 Watt, interview.
9 Watt, interview.
10 Watt, interview.

# NOTES

11  It is not possible to state the source definitively, as the sources are redacted in the FCO files, and the relevant files are closed for at least 40 years.
12  In fact, the great majority of the British FCO documents refer exclusively to Marius, not Jenny.
13  MPJ Lynch (of the British Council's Official Development Assistance), report, 2 February 1983, British National Archives, FCO 105.1161.
14  DA Newberry, Southern African Department, 5 January 1983, British National Archives, FCO 105.1161.
15  MPJ Lynch, report, 2 February 1983.
16  Watt, interview. It is worth nothing that when Nigel Watt was asked to speak about this hiring, he only remembers hiring Marius, not the couple working as co-directors.
17  Nigel Watt, *The First Communists in Fort Jameson: Recollections of Africa and Other Places 1955–2018* (London: Books of Africa, 2018), 152. In a follow-up email from Nigel Watt to the author, June 2021, Watt clarified that losing this amount of funds would have forced IVS to close all of their overseas programmes.
18  CW Squire, report, 21 February 1983, British National Archives, FCO 105.1161.
19  Nigel Watt, 23 January 1983, British National Archives, FCO 105.1161.
20  Nigel Watt, 23 January 1983.
21  A small handwritten note at the bottom of a file a few weeks later.
22  Watt, interview.
23  Lord Elwyn Jones, 17 March 1983, British National Archives, FCO 105.1161.
24  Lord Elwyn Jones, 17 March 1983.
25  For a book about the ANC, and different experiences of living in exile.
26  Schoon, audio interview by Hilda Bernstein.
27  RFR Deare, note on telephone call with Nigel Watt, 20 April 1983, British National Archives, FCO 105.1161.
28  Watt, interview.
29  Watt, interview.
30  RFR Deare, 20 April 1983, British National Archives, FCO 105.1161.
31  Lord Elwyn Jones, 28 April 1983, British National Archives, FCO 105.1161.
32  Lord Elwyn Jones, 28 April 1983.
33  Lord Elwyn Jones, 28 April 1983.
34  Mr Onslow to JR Vascoe, 4 May 1983, British National Archives, FCO 105.1161.
35  Watt, interview. Nigel Watt claimed that he was aware that Marius was doing ANC work in Botswana at the moment of hiring.
36  RFR Deare, Note on telephone call with Nigel Watt, 20 April 1983.
37  NJ Thorpe, 9 May 1983, British National Archives, FCO 105.1161.
38  Lord Elwyn Jones, 24 May 1983, British National Archives, FCO 105.1161.
39  Lord Elwyn Jones, 24 May 1983.
40  Lord Elwyn Jones, 3 June 1983, British National Archives, FCO 105.1161.
41  Lord Elwyn Jones, 3 June 1983.
42  Lord Elwyn Jones, 3 June 1983.
43  Lord Elwyn Jones, 3 June 1983.
44  Lord Elwyn Jones, 3 June 1983.

45  Mr Thorpe, 3 June 1983, British National Archives, FCO 105.1161.
46  Mr Thorpe, 3 June 1983.
47  Mr Thorpe, 3 June 1983.
48  Mr Thorpe, 3 June 1983.
49  Mr Thorpe, 3 June 1983.
50  Mr Thorpe, 3 June 1983.
51  Mr Thorpe, 3 June 1983.
52  Mr Thorpe, 3 June 1983.
53  NB Hudson, 8 June 1983, British National Archives, FCO 105.1161.
54  NB Hudson, 8 June 1983.
55  NB Hudson, 8 June 1983.
56  NB Hudson, 8 June 1983.
57  NB Hudson, 8 June 1983.
58  Foreign and Commonwealth Office (FCO), flash telegram to the British High Commission, Gaborone, 10 June 1983, British National Archives, FCO 105.1161.
59  FCO, flash telegram to the British High Commission, Gaborone.
60  FCO, flash telegram to the British High Commission, Gaborone.
61  FCO, flash telegram to the British High Commission, Gaborone.
62  Schoon, audio interview by Hilda Bernstein.
63  British High Commission, Gaborone, telegram to Foreign and Commonwealth Office, London, 10 June 1983, British National Archives, FCO 105.1161.
64  British High Commission, Gaborone, telegram to FCO, London.
65  British High Commission, Gaborone, telegram to FCO, London.
66  British High Commission, Gaborone, telegram to FCO, London.
67  Seidman, interview.
68  British High Commission, Gaborone, telegram to FCO, London.
69  British High Commission, Gaborone, telegram to FCO, London.
70  British High Commission, Gaborone, telegram to FCO, London.
71  I did place a formal request with the British National Archives seeking to access a further cache of FCO files that are currently blocked from public access. My request was denied.

## Chapter 10 A Kind of Asylum

1  Klug, interview. Heinz Klug told me that he asked permission of the ANC before marrying.
2  Marius Schoon, interview by Colin Buckley, 29 August 1984.
3  Schoon, audio interview by Hilda Bernstein.
4  Fitzgerald, interview.
5  Fitzgerald, interview.
6  This is based on a casual discussion with Macmillan. His book is: Hugh Macmillan, *The Lusaka Years: The ANC in Exile in Zambia, 1963–1994* (Johannesburg: Jacana Media, 2013).
7  Fitzgerald, interview.
8  Fitzgerald, interview. He clarifies that 'Jenny would have had the stiff upper lip; she went through every hardship without any complaint.'

## NOTES

9. This meeting was not part of an official interview, and the individual chose to remain anonymous.
10. Fitzgerald, interview.
11. Fitzgerald, interview.
12. Curtis, *South African Saga*, 138.
13. Schoon, audio interview by Hilda Bernstein.
14. Judy Seidman recollects the Schoons talking with her about the fact that they did *not* want to go to Tanzania, while they were living in Botswana. This information was shared in a telephone call with Billy Keniston, June 2021.
15. Seidman, personal communication, June 2021.
16. Klug, interview.
17. Fitzgerald, interview.
18. Fitzgerald, interview.
19. Schoon, audio interview by Hilda Bernstein.
20. Angola Press Agency. 'Bombardeamento Sul-Africano a 16KM da Cidade do Lubango', *Jornal de Angola*, 31 December 1983.
21. Angola Press Agency. 'Sul-Africanos Ainda Ocupam Parte do Território Nacional', *Jornal de Angola*, 3 July 1984.
22. Schoon, audio interview by Hilda Bernstein.
23. Schoon, audio interview by Hilda Bernstein.
24. Fitzgerald, interview.
25. Seidman, interview.
26. Klug, interview; Gilder, interview.
27. Schoon, audio interview by Hilda Bernstein.
28. Based on notes from an informal meeting with Margarida, June 2019. I was also told that alcohol was a controlled substance. That is, it could only be sold at restaurants, alongside a meal. Therefore, to get one beer, one would have to order a plate of rice and fish. Thus, the joke, 'another plate of rice and fish, please!' as the way to order a beer.
29. An industrial suburb of Luanda. In contemporary Angola, Viana is a largely expatriate community, with many well-apportioned middle- and upper-class housing developments.
30. Klug, interview.
31. Seidman, interview.
32. See note 9, this chapter.
33. Angola Press Agency, 'Luanda Tera Carne Na Proxima Semana', *Jornal de Angola*, 23 May 1984. Accessed at CIDAC, Lisbon, November 2018.
34. Curtis, *South African Saga*, 139.
35. When I was in Lubango in May 2019, electricity outages spanned from between 8 to 18 hours per day, every day! Petroleum is used to generate electricity, and even though Angola is a massive oil-producing country, they can refine only about 10 per cent of their needs, causing electricity shortages and extremely long queues for gasoline.
36. Schoon, interview by Julie Frederikse, 38.
37. Instituto Superior de Ciências da Educação (Higher Institutes of Education Sciences).

38  Klug, interview. A 'forward area' is a territory near to the border of South Africa.
39  Curtis, *South African Saga*, 140.
40  Klug, interview.
41  Klug, interview.
42  See Kevin O'Brien, *The South African Intelligence Services*, 77: 'The ANC and MK were left without a defensive – counter-intelligence – capability, which the apartheid intelligence apparatus exploited ruthlessly, and would continue to do so over the following decades. Therefore, a twinned focus on both penetrating South Africa's intelligence structures and counter-intelligence aimed at preventing the same being done to the ANC by the apartheid state would be the lasting legacy of NAT.'
43  Gilder, interview.
44  Gilder, interview.
45  Schoon, audio interview by Hilda Bernstein.
46  Curtis, *South African Saga*, 140.
47  Schoon, interview by Colin Buckley, 29 August 1984.
48  Stanley Manong, *If We Must Die: An Autobiography of a Former Commander of uMkhonto We Sizwe* (Cape Town: Nkululeko, 2015), 215.
49  Fitzgerald, interview.
50  Fitzgerald, interview.
51  Based on notes from an informal meeting with Agnelo Carrasco, June 2019.
52  Based on notes from an informal meeting with a neighbour of the Schoons at Simpor who prefers to remain anonymous, June 2019.
53  Schoon, audio interview by Hilda Bernstein.
54  Schoon, audio interview by Hilda Bernstein.
55  Schoon, audio interview by Hilda Bernstein.
56  Curtis, *South African Saga*, 140.
57  Schoon, interview by Julie Frederikse, 39.
58  Schoon, interview by Colin Buckley, 29 August 1984.
59  Seidman, interview.
60  Seidman, interview.

## Epilogue Amnesty and Justice, 1995–2007

1  More than US$300 000 at 1995 values.
2  Marius Schoon, Combined Summons filed against the Minister of Safety and Security and Craig Williamson, 18 August 1995. Obtained from the law office of Karien Norval, attorney for the Schoon family.
3  South African Press Association. 'Amnesty Judge Extends Condolences to Marius Schoon's Son' [coverage of the TRC], *SAPA*, 2 March 1999. Accessed 11 May 2024, https://www.justice.gov.za/trc/media/1999/9903/s990302a.htm.
4  Williamson, interview. Williamson claims that it was the Swedes that pushed the Angolans to arrest him, in connection with the murder of Olaf Palme.
5  Williamson, interview.
6  Craig Williamson, autobiography statement, 65–66.
7  Williamson, interview.
8  Williamson, interview.

## NOTES

9   Williamson, interview.
10  Williamson referred to a 'Citation', which is a make of private jet produced by Cessna. Williamson said that he did not wait for this plane to arrive and flew home on a regular flight.
11  Williamson, interview.
12  A former security policeman, Jaap van Jaarsveld, told the TRC in 1998 that 'during the middle of 1984, I received an order from Mr Craig Williamson to investigate whether it would be possible to take out Matthew Goniwe – that means kill'. Sanders, *Apartheid's Friends*, 210.
13  Sherry McLean, affidavit to appeal Williamson's amnesty, 3 November 2000, 4. McLean details how Williamson had attempted to gain a 'stay' in the trial, which Marius repeatedly opposed.
14  Craig Williamson, application for amnesty, 14 January 1997, 5. Obtained from the law office of Karien Norval, attorney for the Schoon family.
15  Mac Maharaj, testimony to the Truth and Reconciliation (TRC) Amnesty Hearing, 2 November 1998. Department of Justice. Accessed 11 May 2024, https://www.justice.gov.za/trc/amntrans/1998/98110206_pre_98112pta.htm.
16  Maharaj, testimony to the TRC.
17  Heinz Klug, testimony to the TRC, 23 February 1998. Department of Justice. Accessed 11 May 2024, https://www.justice.gov.za/trc/amntrans/1999/9902220304_pre_990223pt.htm.
18  Puso Tladi, testimony to the TRC, 23 February 1998. Department of Justice. Accessed 11 May 2024, https://www.justice.gov.za/trc/amntrans/1999/9902220304_pre_990223pt.htm.
19  Tladi, testimony to the TRC.
20  Klug, testimony to the TRC.
21  Klug, testimony to the TRC.
22  Williamson, interview.
23  Williamson, interview.
24  Klug, testimony to the TRC.
25  Williamson, interview.
26  O'Brien, *The South African Intelligence Services*, 221.
27  Sanders, *Apartheid's Friends*, 183.
28  TRC, Decision of the Amnesty Committee in response to applications of Craig Williamson and Roger Howard Leslie Raven, 30 May 2000, 18. Obtained from the law office of Karien Norval, attorney for the Schoon family.
29  Sanders, *Apartheid's Friends*, 190.
30  TRC, Decision of the Amnesty Committee, 18.
31  TRC, Decision of the Amnesty Committee, 19.
32  TRC, Decision of the Amnesty Committee, 19.
33  Craig Williamson, application for amnesty, 14 January 1997, 5. Obtained from the law office of Karien Norval, attorney for the Schoon family.
34  Williamson, application for amnesty, 5.
35  TRC, Decision of the Amnesty Committee, 18.
36  TRC, Decision of the Amnesty Committee, 18.

37 Gillian Slovo, affidavit to appeal Craig Williamson's amnesty, 6 November 2000, 3.
38 McLean, affidavit to appeal Craig Williamson's amnesty, 3 November 2000, 6.
39 McLean, affidavit, 7.
40 McLean, affidavit, 7.
41 McLean, affidavit, 9.
42 McLean, affidavit, 8.
43 Slovo, affidavit, 13.
44 McLean, affidavit, 10.
45 Herman Frederik Schoon, affidavit, October 2007. Obtained from the law office of Karien Norval, attorney for the Schoon family.
46 Herman Frederik Schoon, affidavit.
47 Sanders, *Apartheid's Friends*, 188.

# Bibliography

African National Congress and Marxist Workers' Tendency. *South Africa's Impending Socialist Revolution: Perspectives of the Marxist Workers' Tendency of the African National Congress.* London: Inqaba ya Basebenzi, 1982.

Albertyn, Catherine Hester. *A Critical Analysis of Political Trials in South Africa: 1948–1988.* Cambridge: University of Cambridge, 1991.

Ancer, Jonathan. *Spy: Uncovering Craig Williamson.* Johannesburg: Jacana Media, 2017.

Angola Press Agency. 'Bombardeamento Sul-Africano a 16KM da Cidade do Lubango'. *Jornal de Angola*, 31 December 1983.

Angola Press Agency. 'Luanda Tera Carne Na Proxima Semana'. *Jornal de Angola*, 24 May 1984.

Angola Press Agency. 'Sul-Africanos Ainda Ocupam Parte do Território Nacional'. *Jornal de Angola*, 3 June 1984.

Angola Press Agency. 'Agentes de Pretória Assassinam Militante do ANC no Lubango'. *Jornal de Angola*, 3 July 1984.

Angola Press Agency. 'Marido de Jeanette Schoon Acusa de Regime Pretória'. *Jornal de Angola*, 6 July 1984.

Bernstein, Hilda. *The World That Was Ours.* London: Heinemann, 1967.

Bernstein, Hilda. *The Rift: The Exile Experience of South Africans.* London: Jonathan Cape, 1994.

Biko, Steve. *I Write What I Like.* London: Bowerdean Press, 1996.

Breckenridge, Keith. *Biometric State: The Global Politics of Identification and Surveillance in South Africa, 1850 to the Present.* New York: Cambridge University Press, 2014.

Breytenbach, Breyten. *The True Confessions of an Albino Terrorist.* London: Faber & Faber, 1984.

Brownell, Josiah. 'The Hole in Rhodesia's Bucket: White Emigration and the End of Settler Rule'. *Journal of Southern African Studies* 34, no. 3 (2008): 591–610.

Burton, Mary. *The Black Sash.* Johannesburg: Jacana Media, 2016.

Callinicos, Luli. *A People's History of South Africa.* Johannesburg: Ravan Press, 1980.

Cell, John Whitson. *The Highest Stage of White Supremacy: The Origins of Segregation in South Africa and the American South.* Cambridge: Cambridge University Press, 1982.

Cherry, Janet. *Spear of the Nation (Umkhonto WeSizwe): South Africa's Freedom Fighters, 1960s–1980s* (Ohio Short Histories of Africa). Athens: Ohio University Press, 2012.

Clingman, Stephen. *Bram Fischer: Afrikaner Revolutionary.* Amherst: University of Massachusetts Press, 1998.

Coelho, João Paulo Borges. 'Memory, History, Fiction: A Note on the Politics of the Past in Mozambique'. Paper presented at Conference at École des Hautes Études en Sciences Sociales, 21–22 October 2010, Paris. Accessed 5 May 2024. https://www.ces.uc.pt/estilhacos_do_imperio/comprometidos/media/jp%20borges%20coelho%20text.pdf.

Couper, Scott. *Albert Luthuli: Bound by Faith*. Pietermaritzburg: University of KwaZulu-Natal Press, 2010.

Curtis, John Francis (Jack). *South African Saga: A Political Odyssey*. Braddon: TW Campbell, 2006.

Daniels, Eddie. *There and Back: Robben Island, 1964–1979*. Bellville: Mayibuye Books, 1998.

Davis, Stephen M. *Apartheid's Rebels: Inside South Africa's Hidden War*. New Haven: Yale University Press, 1987.

Davis, Stephen R. *The ANC's War Against Apartheid: Umkhonto we Sizwe and the Liberation of South Africa*. Bloomington: Indiana University Press, 2018.

Dick, Archie L. *The Hidden History of South Africa's Book and Reading Cultures*. Toronto: University of Toronto Press, 2012.

Dlamini, Jacob. *Askari: A Story of Collaboration and Betrayal in the Anti-Apartheid Struggle*. Johannesburg: Jacana Media, 2014.

Dlamini, Jacob. *The Terrorist Album: Apartheid's Insurgents, Collaborators, and the Security Police*. Cambridge: Harvard University Press, 2020.

Drew, Allison. *Discordant Comrades: Identities and Loyalties on the South African Left*. Aldershot: Ashgate, 2000.

Driver, Charles Jonathan (Jonty). *Elegy for a Revolutionary*. London: Faber & Faber, 1969.

Ellis, Stephen. *External Mission: The ANC in Exile, 1960–1990*. London: Hurst, 2012.

Eriksson, Lars-Gunnar. 'Our Accounts Were Stolen', *The Observer* (London), 13 January 1980.

Evans, Ivan Thomas. *Cultures of Violence: Lynching and Racial Killing in South Africa and the American South*. Manchester: Manchester University Press, 2009.

Field, Connie. *Have You Heard from Johannesburg?* Clarity Films, 2010.

First, Ruth. *117 Days*. New York: Stein and Day, 1965.

Foster, Robert. *Vivid Faces: The Revolutionary Generation in Ireland, 1890–1923*. New York: WW Norton, 2015.

Frankel, Glenn. *Rivonia's Children: Three Families and the Cost of Conscience in White South Africa*. Johannesburg: Jacana Media, 2011.

Frankel, Philip H. *An Ordinary Atrocity: Sharpeville and Its Massacre*. New Haven: Yale University Press, 2001.

Frederikse, Julie. *The Unbreakable Thread: Non-racialism in South Africa*. Bloomington: Indiana University Press, 1990.

Fredrickson, George M. *White Supremacy: A Comparative Study in American and South African History*. New York: Oxford University Press, 1981.

Gilder, Barry. *Songs and Secrets: South Africa from Liberation to Governance*. Johannesburg: Jacana Media, 2012.

Ginsburg, Rebecca. *At Home with Apartheid: The Hidden Landscapes of Domestic Service in Johannesburg*. Charlottesville: University of Virginia Press, 2011.

Grunebaum, Heidi. *Memorializing the Past: Everyday Life in South Africa After the Truth and Reconciliation Commission*. New York: Routledge, 2017.

Hanlon, Joseph. *Beggar Your Neighbours: Apartheid Power in Southern Africa*. London: Catholic Institute for International Relations in collaboration with James Currey, 1986.

Harris, Peter. *In a Different Time: The Inside Story of the Delmas Four*. Cape Town: Random House Struik, 2008.

Henriques, Joana Gorjão. *Racismo no País dos Brancos Costumes*. Lisbon: Tinta da China, 2018.

Heywood, Mark. 'Apartheid-era Crimes: A Commission of Inquiry is Needed to Establish the Truth'. *Daily Maverick*, 21 June 2021. Accessed 11 May 2024. https://www.dailymaverick.co.za/article/2021-06-21-apartheid-era-crimes-a-commission-of-inquiry-is-needed-to-establish-the-truth/

Hirson, Baruch. *A History of the Left in South Africa: Writings of Baruch Hirson*. London: I.B. Tauris, 2005.

Hooper, Neil. 'Our Man in Moscow', *Sunday Times*, 27 January 1980.

International University Exchange Fund. *Summary of the So-Called Schlebusch Committee's Final Report on the National Union of South African Students (NUSAS)*. Geneva: IUEF, 1975.

Israel, Paolo. 'A Loosening Grip: The Liberation Script in Mozambican History'. *Kronos*, no. 39 (2013): 10–19.

Jeffery, Anthea. *People's War: New Light on the Struggle for South Africa*. Johannesburg: Jonathan Ball, 2009.

Keitseng, Fish. *Comrade Fish: Memories of a Motswana in the ANC Underground*, edited by Barry Morton and Jeff Ramsay. Gaborone: Pula Press, 1999.

Kellner, Clive and Sergio-Albio González, eds. *Thami Mnyele + Medu Art Ensemble Retrospective*. Johannesburg: Jacana Media, 2009.

Keniston, Billy. *Choosing to be Free: The Life Story of Rick Turner*. Johannesburg: Jacana Media, 2013.

Klug, Heinz. Testimony to the TRC, 23 February 1998. Department of Justice. Accessed 11 May 2024. https://www.justice.gov.za/trc/amntrans/1999/9902220304_pre_990223pt.htm

La Guma, Alex. *In the Fog of the Season's End*. London: Heinemann, 1972.

Laurence, Patrick. 'SA Minister Praises Spy's Role in Geneva'. *The Guardian* (London), 25 January 1980.

Law, Kate. *Gendering the Settler State: White Women, Race, Liberalism and Empire in Rhodesia, 1950–1980*. New York: Routledge, 2016.

Legassick, Martin. *Armed Struggle and Democracy: The Case of South Africa*. Uppsala: Nordiska Afrikainstitutet, 2002.

Levy, Norman. *The Final Prize: My Life in the Anti-Apartheid Struggle*. Cape Town: South African History Online, 2011.

Lewin, Hugh. *Bandiet: Seven Years in a South African Prison*. London: Penguin Books, 1976.

Lewin, Hugh. *Stones Against the Mirror: Friendship in the Time of the South African Struggle*. Johannesburg: Umuzi, 2011.

Lewin, Hugh and Walter Schwarz 'SA Spy Alleged in Relief Agency', *The Guardian* (London), 21 January 1980.
Lewin, Hugh and Walter Schwarz. 'How Spy was "Blown"'. *The Guardian* (London), 23 January 1980.
Lobban, Michael. *White Man's Justice: South African Political Trials in the Black Consciousness Era*. Oxford: Clarendon Press, 1996.
Lodge, Tom. *Sharpeville: An Apartheid Massacre and Its Consequences*. Oxford: Oxford University Press, 2011.
Macmillan, Hugh. *The Lusaka Years: The ANC in Exile in Zambia, 1963–1994*. Johannesburg: Jacana Media, 2013.
Macmillan, Hugh, Stephen Ellis, Arianna Lissoni and Mariya Kurbak. 'Debating the ANC's External Links During the Struggle Against Apartheid'. *Africa* 85, no. 1 (2015): 154–162.
Macqueen, Ian Martin. 'Re-imagining South Africa: Black Consciousness, Radical Christianity and the New Left 1967–1977'. DPhil diss., Sussex University, 2011. Accessed 3 May 2024. https://sussex.figshare.com/articles/thesis/Re-imagining_South_Africa_Black_Consciousness_radical_Christianity_and_the_New_Left_1967_1977/23316536
Magaziner, Daniel R. *The Law and the Prophets: Black Consciousness in South Africa, 1968–1977*. Athens: Ohio University Press, 2010.
Maharaj, Mac. Testimony to the Truth and Reconciliation Amnesty Hearing, 2 November 1998. Department of Justice. Accessed 11 May 2024. https://www.justice.gov.za/trc/amntrans/1998/98110206_pre_98112pta.htm
Manong, Stanley. *If We Must Die: An Autobiography of a Former Commander of uMkhonto We Sizwe*. Cape Town: Nkululeko, 2015.
McDonald, Peter D. *The Literature Police: Apartheid Censorship and Its Cultural Consequences*. Oxford: Oxford University Press, 2009.
McLean, Sherry. Affidavit to appeal Craig Williamson's amnesty, 3 November 2000. Karien Norval Law Office.
Miller, Jamie. *An African Volk: The Apartheid Regime and Its Search for Survival*. New York: Oxford University Press, 2016.
Mngxitama, Andile, Amanda Alexander and Nigel Gibson, eds. *Biko Lives! Contesting the Legacies of Steve Biko*. New York: Palgrave Macmillan, 2008.
Moolman, Maritz, Sefako Nyaka and Ian Hobbes. 'Britain Forecast Killings'. *Rand Daily Mail*, 30 June 1984.
Moss, Glenn. *The New Radicals: A Generational Memoir of the 1970s*. Johannesburg: Jacana Media, 2014.
Nicolson, Greg. 'Barbara Hogan Tells Inquest of "Aggressive" and "Morbid" Aggett Interrogators'. *Daily Maverick*, 30 January 2020.
Nixon, Rob. *Homelands, Harlem, and Hollywood: South African Culture and the World Beyond*. New York: Routledge, 1994.
Nixon, Ron. *Selling Apartheid: South Africa's Global Propaganda War*. Johannesburg: Jacana Media, 2015.
O'Brien, Kevin A. *The South African Intelligence Services: From Apartheid to Democracy, 1948–2005*. Abingdon: Routledge, 2011.

O'Malley, Padraigh. *Shades of Difference: Mac Maharaj and the Struggle for South Africa*. New York: Viking, 2007.
Passerini, Luisa. *Autobiography of a Generation: Italy, 1968*. Hanover: Wesleyan University Press, 1996.
Pawson, Lara. *In the Name of the People: Angola's Forgotten Massacre*. London: I.B. Tauris, 2014.
Payne, Leigh. *Unsettling Accounts: Neither Truth nor Reconciliation in Confessions of State Violence*. Durham: Duke University Press, 2008.
Pinnock, Don. *Ruth First*. Pretoria: HSRC Press, 1997.
Podbrey, Pauline. *White Girl in Search of the Party*. Pietermaritzburg: Hadeda Books, 1993.
Randall, Peter. *A Taste of Power: The Final Co-ordinated Spro-cas Report*. Johannesburg: Study Project on Christianity in Apartheid Society, 1973.
Sanders, James. *Apartheid's Friends: The Rise and Fall of South Africa's Secret Service*. London: John Murray, 2006.
Saunders, Christopher. *The Making of the South African Past: Major Historians on Race and Class*. Cape Town: David Philip, 1988.
Schlebusch, Alwyn. Second Interim Report of the Commission of Inquiry into Certain Organisations. Pretoria: Government Printer, 1973.
Schlebusch, Alwyn. Fourth Interim Report of the Commission of Inquiry into Certain Organisations. Pretoria: Government Printer, 1974.
Schlebusch, Alwyn. Report of the Commission of Inquiry into Certain Organisations. Pretoria: Government Printer, 1974.
Schoon, Herman Frederik. Affidavit. Legal damages claim, October 2007. Karien Norval Law Office.
Schoon, Marius. Interview by Colin Buckley, 29 August 1984. Personal papers of Nigel Watt, interviewed by Billy Keniston 15 March 2019, London, England.
Schoon, Marius. Interview by Julie Frederikse, Harare, 1986, for Julie Frederikse, *The Unbreakable Thread: Non-racialism in South Africa*. Johannesburg: Ravan Press, 1990. Interview transcript, South African History Archive, AL2460_A19.05.1. Accessed 25 June 2024 https://www.saha.org.za/nonracialism/transcript_of_interview_with_marius_schoon.htm.
Schoon, Marius. Combined summons filed against the Minister of Safety and Security and Craig Williamson, 18 August 1995. Karien Norval Law Office.
Seekings, Jeremy. *The UDF: A History of the United Democratic Front in South Africa, 1983–1991*. Cape Town: David Philip, 2000.
Seidman, Judy Ann. *Drawn Lines: An Autobiography by Judy Seidman*. Scotts Valley: CreateSpace Independent Publishing Platform, 2017.
Shubin, Vladimir. *ANC: A View from Moscow*. Johannesburg: Jacana Media, 2008.
Simpson, Thula. *Umkhonto We Sizwe: The ANC's Armed Struggle*. Cape Town: Penguin Books, 2016.
Slovo, Gillian. *Every Secret Thing: My Family, My Country*. Boston: Little, Brown, 1997.
Slovo, Gillian. Affidavit to appeal Craig Williamson's amnesty, 6 November 2000. Karien Norval Law Office.

South African Press Association. 'Policemen had a Dungeon to Imprison Slovo, TRC Hears'. Department of Justice, 22 September 1998. Accessed 5 May 2020. https://www.justice.gov.za/trc/media/1998/9809/s980922b.htm.

South African Press Association. 'Amnesty Judge Extends Condolences to Marius Schoon's Son' [coverage of the TRC], *SAPA*, 2 March 1999. Accessed 11 May 2024. https://www.justice.gov.za/trc/media/1999/9903/s990302a.htm.

Study Project on Christianity in an Apartheid Society (Spro-cas). *Power, Privilege and Poverty*. Johannesburg: Spro-cas, 1972.

Study Project on Christianity in an Apartheid Society (Spro-cas). *White Liberation: A Collection of Essays*. Johannesburg: Spro-cas, 1972.

Suttner, Raymond. *The ANC Underground in South Africa, 1950–1976*. Johannesburg: Jacana Media, 2008.

Tladi, Puso. Testimony to the TRC, 23 February 1998. Department of Justice. Accessed 11 May 2024. https://www.justice.gov.za/trc/amntrans/1999/9902220304_pre_990223pt.htm.

Trewhela, Paul. *Inside Quatro: Uncovering the Exile History of the ANC and SWAPO*. Johannesburg: Jacana Media, 2010.

Truth and Reconciliation Commission. Decision of the Amnesty Committee in response to applications of Craig Williamson and Roger Howard Leslie Raven, 30 May 2000. Karien Norval Law Office.

Turok, Ben. *The ANC and the Turn to Armed Struggle, 1950–1970*. Johannesburg: Jacana Media, 2010.

Twidle, Hedley. 'Unusable Pasts: Life-writing, Literary Non-fiction, and the Case of Demetrios Tsafendas', *Research in African Literatures* 46, no. 3 (2015): 1–23.

Van den Heever, J. 'Return: Execution of Writ of Execution' to the High Court, Johannesburg, 23 January 2007. Karien Norval Law Office.

Vigne, Randolph. *Liberals Against Apartheid: A History of the Liberal Party of South Africa, 1953–68*. Basingstoke: Palgrave Macmillan, 1997.

Vinson, Robert Trent. *Albert Luthuli*. Athens: Ohio University Press, 2018.

Walshe, Peter. *Church Versus State in South Africa: The Case of the Christian Institute*. London: C Hurst, 1983.

Warman, Janice. *The Class of '79*. Johannesburg: Jacana Media, 2014.

Watt, Nigel. *The First Communists in Fort Jameson: Recollections of Africa and Other Places, 1955–2018*. London: Books of Africa, 2018.

White, Luise. *The Assassination of Herbert Chitepo: Texts and Politics in Zimbabwe*. Bloomington: Indiana University Press, 2003.

Wieder, Alan. *Ruth First and Joe Slovo in the War Against Apartheid*. New York: Monthly Review Press, 2013.

Williamson, Craig. Autobiography statement, 10 October 1996. Terry Bell personal archive.

Williamson, Craig. Application for amnesty, 14 January 1997. Karien Norval Law Office.

Willoughby-Herard, Tiffany. *Waste of a White Skin: The Carnegie Corporation and the Racial Logic of White Vulnerability*. Oakland: University of California Press, 2015.

Wilson, Andrew. 'BOSS Agent Quits to Reveal Spy Secrets'. *The Observer* (London), 30 December 1979.
Wilson, Andrew. 'The British "Targets" of BOSS', *The Observer* (London), 6 January 1980.
Wolfers, Michael. *Angola in the Frontline*. London: Zed Press, 1983.
Wylie, Diana. *Art + Revolution: The Life and Death of Thami Mnyele, South African Artist*. Charlottesville: University of Virginia Press, 2008.

## Interviews by Billy Keniston

Guy Berger, 23 February 2019, telephone interview
Geoff Budlender, 31 July 2017, Cape Town, South Africa
Cedric de Beer, 1 July 2016, Johannesburg, South Africa
Paula Dias, 28 May 2019, Luanda, Angola
Paula Ensor, 23 January 2019, Cape Town, South Africa
Alan Fine, 15 February 2019, Johannesburg, South Africa
Patrick Fitzgerald, 21 September 2021, online interview
Barry Gilder, 1 June 2019, Johannesburg, South Africa
Barbara Hogan, 24 April 2019, Johannesburg, South Africa
Michael Hubbard, 4 November 2018, Birmingham, England
Mike Kahn, 21 January 2019, Cape Town, South Africa
Clive Keegan, 10 August 2017, Cape Town, South Africa
Horst Kleinschmidt, 24 June 2016, Cape Town, South Africa
Heinz Klug, 22 September 2018, Madison, Wisconsin, USA
Denis Kuny, 8 February 2019, Johannesburg, South Africa
Glenn Moss, 10 June 2016 and 9 March 2019, Cape Town, South Africa
Clive Nettleton, 16 August 2017, London, England
Charles Nupen, 20 March 2019, Johannesburg, South Africa
Devan Pillay, 30 March 2019, Johannesburg, South Africa
Paul Pretorius, 30 June 2016, Johannesburg, South Africa
Michael Savage, 14 June 2016, Cape Town, South Africa
Judy Seidman, 7 and 10 February 2019, Johannesburg, South Africa
Nigel Watt, 15 March 2019, London, England
Nicki Westcott, 9 May 2019, Cape Town, South Africa
Craig Williamson, 29 March 2019, Johannesburg, South Africa

## Archives consulted

African National Congress Archives, University of Fort Hare, Alice, South Africa
Associação Tchiweka de Documentação, Luanda, Angola
Botswana National Archives, Gaborone, Botswana
British National Archives, London, England
British National Library, London, England
Centro de Intervenção Para o Desenvolvimento Amílcar Cabral, Lisbon, Portugal
Danish National Archives, Copenhagen, Denmark

Historical Papers, University of the Witwatersrand, Johannesburg, South Africa
Hull History Centre, Hull, England
Law office of Karien Norval, attorney for the Schoon family
Nelson Mandela Foundation, Johannesburg, South Africa
South African History Archive, Johannesburg, South Africa
South African Library of Parliament, Cape Town, South Africa
South African National Archives, Pretoria, South Africa
Special Collections, University of Cape Town, South Africa

# Index

**A**

Abraham, Eric
  security police harassment of 93, 113–115
African National Congress *see* ANC
African Resistance Movement (ARM) 10, 296n1
Aggett, Neil 19, 25, 185, 309n51
Alexander (Simons), Ray 102, 200–201
Alliance for Radical Change (ARC) 56
Amnesty International 106–107
ANC 58, 62
  banning (and unbanning) of 18, 65, 100, 124, 220, 246
  Jenny Curtis's connection with 62–63, 65, 72, 79–80
  non-violent 'above ground' organising of 7, 21, 211–212
  *see also* armed struggle: relationship/distinction between political work and; non-violent resistance
ANC in exile 2, 10, 13, 15, 62, 100, 142
  bombing of London offices 19, 25, 280
  intelligence wing of 260, 316n42
  response to warnings about Williamson 16–17, 113, 142–144
  Williamson's 'Moscow line' on 116–117
  *see also* ANC Lusaka; Tanzania
ANC Lusaka 102, 116, 147–148, 159, 201–202
  decision to remove Schoons from Botwana 239–240, 242
  deployment of Schoons to Angola 24–25, 245–247, 250, 253–254
  institutional culture of 247–248
  IPRD project 13–14, 128, 200, 275
  Mazimbu College 249

  Schoons in 24, 246–247
  utilisation of Williamson by 143–145
ANC underground 26, 78, 83
  cover/undercover stories within 2, 7–8, 14, 91, 95, 100, 102–103, 123
  fragility of 8–10
  military hierarchy of 245–246
  support for AIS of 65, 67–68
  secrecy as dominant mode of 15, 123–124, 127, 262–263
  Williamson on modus operandi of 7, 197, 203
  *see also* Fitzgerald, Patrick: Botswana cover/undercover story of; Klug, Heinz: Botswana cover/undercover story of; Schoon, Marius: undercover in Angola
Ancer, Jonathan 1, 57
Angola 266–267
  arrest and detention of Williamson in 272–274, 317n10
  Schoons' undercover work in 259–263, 276–277, 289
  *see also* armed struggle: Angola as critical location for; Luanda, Angola; MK: Angolan operations; Schoons in exile, Lubango
Angolan civil war 22, 24, 35, 42–43, 245
  Lusaka Protocol 273
  Marius's description of war zone 251–253
  devastating impact of 253–254, 256–258, 315n35
  *see also* South African Defence Force: 1975 invasion of Angola

anti-apartheid movement 7, 17, 20, 115
  British special branch spying on 22–23, 228–229
  criticisms of London 249
  impact of Williamson's espionage activities on 6, 153, 166–167, 290
  shifting landscape of 82, 104, 117, 120–121
  security police campaign against 6–8, 15, 109–110
anti-apartheid struggle 1, 9, 26, 99
  'above ground' position 7
  Black-led 2–4
  Cold War lines of 7, 116, 244, 252, 263
  Schoons' non-violent engagement with 7, 22, 65, 76
  see also armed struggle; white radicals: contribution to anti-apartheid struggle
apartheid state
  Affected Organisations Act (1974) 58, 104
  privileging of white radicals under 3–4
  repression of student leaders by 10–11, 44, 49–52, 56, 289
  tensions between violence and rationality within 4–6, 19, 50–51, 185, 207, 288, 290
  see also non-violent resistance: apartheid state criminalisation of; Schlebusch Commission; security police
armed struggle 1, 4, 7, 20, 26, 50, 120, 210
  Angola as critical location for 23–24, 255–256, 263
  development of exile infrastructure 77–78
  Marxist Workers' Tendency critique of 126, 134
  relationship/distinction between political work and 15–17, 21, 130, 132–135, 205–206, 212, 222, 276, 289
  training of volunteers for 82, 92
  Williamson's views on 121–122, 205–206, 290
  see also ANC underground; MK; non-violent resistance
assassination of Jeanette and Katryn Schoon 5, 8, 22, 24–25, 52, 126, 201, 246, 264–265
  different takes on 27–30, 32
  difficulties in researching 35–36
  as lingering wound 270, 286, 291
  Marius on 30–31, 38–42, 126, 269

Paula Dias on 37–38
  rumours about real target 267–269
  Williamson's motivation for 9, 28, 268, 273–276, 278, 281, 284, 287–289, 291
  see also Schoon, Fritz; Schoon, Marius: on burial of Jeanette and Katryn

B
Barrett, Linde (née Schoon) 75–76, 87
Berger, Guy 18, 172, 175
  arrest and interrogation of 173–174, 184
  see also under political trials of Schoon network
Bergerol, Jane 39–40, 45
Bernstein, Hilda 1, 38, 79, 231, 239, 248, 251, 254, 265
Berold, Robert 140–141
Biko, Steve 120, 166, 210, 274
Bizos, George 210, 218–221 see also Hogan's trial: legal defence team in
Black Consciousness Movement (BCM) 63, 78, 150, 164, 172, 220, 303n24
  assassinations of leadership of 33
  critique of white liberalism of 3, 10–11, 67
  role in setting up Medu Arts Ensemble 101, 103
  shift away from 82
  support of white radicals for 3, 12, 16, 61, 66, 80–81
  Williamson's views on 116–117, 121–122
  see also 1976 Soweto uprising: as product of BCM
Botswana 8
  assassination attempt on Schoons in 241–242
  Schoons' application for asylum in 91, 98
  Schoons' illegal crossing into 88–90
  strategic role in war against apartheid 91, 99–100
  teaching as Schoons' cover story in 14–15, 95
  see also Schoons' exile structures in Botswana
Botswana special branch 236
  Adolf Hirschfeld as head of 235, 239–240
Brandrup, Poul 109, 302n85&86
Breytenbach, Breyten 18, 73–74, 87, 299n43
  Okhela group 11, 68–69

# INDEX

British High Commissioner, Botswana *see* Jones, Lord Elwyn
British intelligence services 43–44
   collaboration between South African and 23, 228–229, 235, 239–241, 244, 294n19
   *see also* Foreign and Commonwealth Office
Bureau for State Security (BOSS) 142, 149–152, 159

## C

Campbell, Piers 150–155, 162–163
Christie, Renfrew 52, 166, 296n11
Claremont communes 61, 71
   Belvedere Road house 52–54, 90, 296n10
   Milldene Avenue house 52–53, 65, 296n11
Coetzee, Brigadier 152, 155–156
Commission of Inquiry into espionage activities in IUEF 14, 149, 153–155, 306n34
   and concerns about death of Steve Biko 166
   criticism of Eriksson by 141–145, 162, 165
   on Williamson's devastating impact on IUEF 142, 160–166
   principle function of 159–160
   *see also* Williamson's infiltration of IUEF
communism 19–20, 55, 62, 207, 214, 268, 291
   ANC position on 216, 218
   scientific 258
Communist Party 248 *see also* South African Communist Party
Cronwright Major (security police) 175, 179
Curtis, Jack (John Francis) 1, 27, 73, 96, 249
   on burial of daughter and granddaughter 44–45
   on detention of Jenny 68–71
   harassment by security police of 98
   on Jenny's time in Angola 256–257, 261, 266
   on killing of Jeanette and Katryn 32–35
   on relationship and marriage of Marius and Jenny 78, 87
   on Schoons' escape to Botswana 89
Curtis, Jeanette (Jenny)
   banning order against 11, 71–72, 78, 87
   detention of 11, 68–71
   political transformation of 11
   relationship with Marius 78–79
   role in Sactu 7
   *see also* Nusas: Jenny Curtis as student activist in; Schoon, Jeanette; South African Institute of Race Relations: Jenny's work as archivist at
Curtis, Joyce 44, 71, 78, 88, 98
Curtis, Neville 11, 44, 51, 61–62
   banning of 52–53

## D

de Beer, Cedric 105, 130, 138–141
Dlamini, Jacob 16, 113

## E

Edwards, Karl 21, 157, 167, 173, 198, 201, 277, 302n72
   as 'courier' for Schoons' Botswana network 13, 15, 21, 137–139, 146, 192–193, 201–202
   EDA as front for 15, 105, 140–141, 163–164
   exposure of 17, 145–147, 277
   infiltration of Nusas by 56, 70, 138, 192, 198, 287
   suspicions about 16–17, 112–113, 115, 138–141, 193
   *see also* political trials: testimony of Karl Edwards in; Sana: Karl Edwards involvement with
Ensor, Paula 51, 53–54, 56, 61, 82, 134–135
   banning of 296n10
   on Black Consciousness Movement 67, 80–81
   relationship with Jenny Curtis 55, 126–128
Environmental and Development Agency (EDA) *see* Edwards, Karl: EDA as front for
Eriksson, Lars-Gunnar 14, 91, 104, 118, 120, 122, 165, 305n16
   collapse of relationship with Williamson 150–156
   failure to respond to warnings about Williamson by 16, 141–145, 151
   rapport with Williamson 92–94, 108, 114, 161
   top-down decision making of 161

Eriksson, Lars-Gunnar (*continued*)
  *see also* Campbell, Piers; Commission of Inquiry into espionage activities in IUEF: criticism of Eriksson; IUEF, Geneva; Southern Futures Vaduz

**F**
Fine, Alan 63, 199, 208, 213, 234
  arrest of 173, 177–178
  connection to Schoons in exile 129–130, 173, 178, 192–193, 195–197
  on marriage of Marius and Jenny 88
  *see also under* political trials of Schoon network
First, Ruth 1, 174, 290
  assassination of 19, 25, 33, 43, 207, 235, 267, 269
  *see also* TRC amnesty hearings: Slovo and Schoon families' appeals against rulings of
Fischer, Bram 74, 210
Fisher, Foszia 97–98
Fitzgerald, Patrick 57, 111, 140, 277–278, 301n39
  Botswana cover/undercover story of 112–113, 115
  role in exposure of Edwards 146–147
  on role of Schoons in Botswana 128, 132, 247
  on Schoons in Angola 248–251, 253, 262, 314n8
  *see also* Sana; SNS
Foreign and Commonwealth Office (FCO) 228–229, 236, 239, 294n19
  concerns about Marius's politics 231–232, 234, 240–241, 264
  opposition to asylum for Schoons 22–23, 233, 237–238, 242–244, 248, 264
  *see also* IVS: FCO's role in forcing Schoons out of; Jones, Lord Elwyn
Frankish, John 51, 296n10
Frederikse, Julie 1, 30, 267
Freedom Charter 121, 219, 312n102
Freire, Paulo 64, 174
Friedman, Steve 64–65

**G**
Gilder, Barry 2, 99, 103, 124, 131, 260, 262, 276
Goosen, Brigadier Piet 279–280, 282, 288

Gqabi, Joe 43, 269
Gxanyana, Mandla 172–173, 186

**H**
Harris, Lindy 172, 174
Hogan, Barbara 61, 81, 133, 171
  arrest and detention of 175, 177–178, 185
  on detainees support committees 203–205
  doubts about Schoons' network 137–138
  involvement in trade union movement of 64, 129, 138, 181
  on Jenny Curtis 62–63, 66, 71, 79–80
  on Neil Aggett's death 185
  security police surveillance of 176–177
  security police torture of 179–184
  views on MK/armed struggle 129–130, 208, 212–213, 219–220
Hogan's trial 18–21, 198–200, 204, 207, 222, 229
  legal defence team in 207–208, 210, 213–214, 216–221
  Peter Swanepoel's prosecution of 201, 209–210, 213–217, 311n84
  political significance of 208–209
  significance of Judge Van Dyk's ruling in 220–222
  Williamson's testimony at 18, 207, 210–212, 215, 218, 290
  *see also* Bizos, George; Lodge, Tom; Webster, Eddie
Hubbard, Michael 90, 98, 100, 300n11

**I**
Industrial Aid Society (IAS)
  Jenny as founder member of 11, 64–68
International University Exchange Fund *see* IUEF
International Voluntary Service *see* IVS
Ireland 25, 249
  Marius's life in 263–265
IUEF, Geneva
  effectiveness of organisation 160–161
  failure to apprehend Williamson by 150, 153–155
  financial deterioration of 161–162, 307n5
  theft of documents from 150–151, 162
  switch of support from BCM to ANC of 16, 117–120, 122, 150, 164–165

*see also* Commission of Inquiry into espionage activities in IUEF; Williamson's infiltration of IUEF
IVS 233, 242–243, 312n7, 313n17
  overseas programme 225–226
  Schoons as co-directors of Botswana branch 225, 227–228, 231–232
  support of volunteers for Schoons 234
  FCO's role in forcing Schoons out of 22–23, 228–232, 234, 236–239
  *see also* ANC Lusaka: decision to remove Schoons from Botwana; Watt, Nigel

**J**
Jenkin, Tim 172, 307n3
John Vorster Square 68, 175, 204
Jones, Lord Elwyn 240, 242–243
  meeting with Nigel Watt 231
  pressure on IVS to remove Schoons by 233, 235–238
  warning to Marius 239–240

**K**
Kahn, Carol 100, 123
Kahn, Mike 99–102, 123, 125–127, 131, 133
Kasrils, Ronnie 145, 199
Keegan, Clive 53, 296n9
Klug, Heinz 94, 101, 314n1
  on ANC underground in Botswana 123, 125, 128
  on armed struggle and MK 130, 132–134, 255
  Botswana cover/undercover story of 111–113, 115–116
  friendship with Marius 72–74
  on Schoons in exile in Botswana 95–97, 99
  on exposure of Williamson and Edwards 145–148
  speculation about Marius's role in Angola 250, 258–260
  TRC testimony of 275–279
  *see also* Sana; SNS
Kotzé, Theo 88, 300n6
Kuny, Denis 20, 174, 207–208, 210, 214
  defence of Alan Fine 196–198, 208, 213
  defence of Berger and Pillay 187, 191–192, 194
  *see also* Hogan's trial: legal defence team in; political trials, Williamson's testimony: Kuny's tactics to undermine

**L**
Lewin, Hugh 149, 151, 153, 188, 309n61
  *Bandiet* 71, 73
Liliesleaf 10, 293n1
Lobban, Michael
  *White Man's Justice* 58–59
Lodge, Tom 210–212, 216–218, 299n4
  on socialism 214–215
Luanda, Angola 29, 39–42, 245, 251, 253, 255–256, 277
  Alto Das Cruxes cemetery in 45–46
  development centre for SA refugees in 261–262
  Marius' military training in 253
  Seguranza do Estado (State Security Police) in 35
  Viana 255, 315n29
Lubango College (now ISCED) 29, 34, 37, 42, 249
  Marxist pedagogy of 24, 258
  memorial garden for 'Mama Janeth' at 265–266
  Schoons as teachers at 24, 29, 32, 255, 257–259, 263
  Simpor teachers' accommodation 29, 36, 263

**M**
Maharaj, Mac 13–15, 122, 131, 137, 145, 159, 200–201
  on Schoons' role in Angola 275
  security police surveillance of 277–278
Makghoti, Henry 96, 113, 200, 246, 248, 250, 253
Mandela, Nelson 174, 209–210, 218
Manong, Stanley 261–262
Marxism 66–67, 82, 171
  'homespun' 10, 62, 64, 78, 140, 177
  *see also* Lubango College: Marxist pedagogy of; New Left radicalism
Mayibuye 172, 174, 215
Mbeki, Govan 63, 298n14
Mbeki, Thabo 63, 159, 298n14
McGiven, Arthur 149–150, 159, 297n25
McLean, Sherry 265, 283–285, 317n13
Medu Art Ensemble 13, 15, 100–101, 103
  'Culture and Resistance' festival 102–103
Mfeti, Pindile 63–64
MK 17, 63, 91, 115–116, 129, 133–134, 175–178, 198, 228, 290, 316n42

MK (*continued*)
   Angolan operations 24, 28, 130–132, 198, 248, 259–262, 276
   culture of silence within 14
   recruitment/training 68, 113, 121, 127, 131, 133, 200
Molepolole, Botswana 301n33
   as space of asylum for Schoons 94–97
Molepolole Secondary School
   Schoons as teachers at 94–95, 125
Moss, Glen 2, 71, 145
   concept of 'homespun' Marxism 10, 62
   on risks of Schoon network 129, 137–138
   detention and interrogation of 68–70
   as IAS director 64–65
   opinions about Marius 77, 80, 83
Movimento Popular de Libertação de (MPLA) Angola 65, 97, 180, 202, 276
   support for Marius of 40–43
   underground structure, Lubango 252, 263
   *see also* armed struggle: Angola as critical location for

## N
Naidoo, Indres 63
Namibia 91, 252
National Intelligence Services (N.I.S.) 191–192, 194
National Prosecuting Authority (NPA)
   reopening of TRC cases 25
National Union of South African Students
   *see* Nusas
New Left radicalism 2, 78
   and shift towards ANC 10, 79–80, 82–83, 177–178
   *see also* Marxism: 'homespun'
Nkobi, Thomas 122, 143, 159, 200
nonracialism 1
   transition to ideology of 82, 95, 101
non-violent resistance 7, 21, 50, 210–212, 216
   apartheid state criminalisation of 18, 21, 166, 186, 196, 204–206, 289–290
   *see also* armed struggle: relationship/distinction between political work and; political trials, Williamson's testimony: as indictment of ANC ideology

Nusas 99
   Charles Nupen as president of 53
   radical rupture within 50
   Release Mandela Campaign 59
   Jenny Curtis as student activist in 10–11, 49, 51–52, 61, 90, 289
   security police infiltration of 9, 56–57, 138–139, 192, 297n25
   Wages Commission 64, 67, 90
   *see also* apartheid state: repression of student leaders; Claremont communes; Williamson, Craig: infiltration of Nusas by
Nusas bannings 10–11, 51–55
   leadership vacuum as result of 56

## O
Okhela group *see under* Breytenbach, Breyten
O'Malley, Padraig 13–14

## P
Pahad, Aziz 145, 192, 201
Palme, Olaf 118, 274
Pan-Africanist Congress (PAC) 156
   banning of 50
   IUEF support for 144
Pillay, Devan 18, 171, 173–175, 309n49
   detention and torture of 172, 184
   interaction with Mandla Gxanyana 172–173
   on shift away from Black Consciousness 82
   *see also under* political trials of Schoon network
political prisoners
   political enrichment of 10, 73–74, 187–189
   racialised experiences of 184, 188–189, 309n62
   *see also* Prisoners Support Trust
political trials of Schoon network 17–18, 20, 171
   Alan Fine 18, 20–21, 195–197, 204
   Devan Pillay 21, 175, 186–188, 191, 197–198, 201–202
   Guy Berger 20–21, 175, 186–187, 191–193, 197–199, 201–202, 310n17
   solidarity among comrades during 186–187
   as state mechanism 19, 21

testimony of Karl Edwards in 21, 191–194, 198
*see also* Kuny, Denis; Hogan's trial; Webster, Eddie
political trials, Williamson's testimony
as indictment of ANC ideology 17–18, 21, 186, 196, 203–208, 210–212, 290
Kuny's tactics to undermine 196–198, 207–208, 210
on personal connection to Schoons 196, 199–202
as weaponisation of undercover work 9
*see also* Hogan's trial: Williamson's testimony at 18, 207, 210–212, 215
Pretoria Central Prison 71, 151
incarceration of Marius Schoon in 10–11, 72–76, 78, 87
Pretorius, Paul 52, 54–55, 296n10
Prisoners Support Trust (PST) 106–107, 163

# R
racism 1, 57, 95, 173, 266–267
Ramsay, Jeff 94–95, 301n33
*Rand Daily Mail* 39, 43
Ranwedzi 92, 120, 303n24
Raven, Jerry 27–28, 31–32, 280, 282–283, 285
Rhodes University 171–172, 187, 192
Richer, Pete 175, 199
Rivonia trials 10, 177
Robben Island 63, 68, 96, 107, 188

# S
Sactu 64–65, 68, 201, 206, 208, 234, 310n17
links between ANC and 195–196
Sana 15, 93, 112–114, 116, 278
IUEF involvement in 115, 163
Karl Edwards involvement with 112–113, 115, 145, 163
plan to expose Edwards 146–147
*see also* SNS
Sanders, James 22, 119
Schlebusch Commission of Inquiry 6, 294n12, 296n8, 297n23, 306n60
link between infiltration of student movement and 56, 58–59
and Nusas leadership 10–11, 49–52
*see also* Nusas bannings

Schoon, Fritz 29, 32, 126–127, 241, 254–255, 272, 288
in Ireland 264–266
post-assassination trauma of 41–42, 291
response to amnesty ruling 283–284, 286
whereabouts during assassination 29, 36–39
*see also* TRC amnesty hearings: Slovo and Schoon families' appeals against rulings of
Schoon (née Curtis), Jeanette 1–2, 7
contribution to radical struggle 267–268, 286–287, 291
*see also* assassination of Jeanette and Katryn Schoon; Curtis, Jeanette; Schoons in exile, Lubango; Schoons' exile structures in Botswana
Schoon, Katryn 97–99, 125, 127, 273, 286–287, 291
life in Angola 265–266
TRC downplaying of death of 282, 284, 188, 288
Williamson's response to death of 268–269
*see also* assassination of Jeanette and Katryn Schoon
Schoon, Marius 1–2, 5
banning order 77–79, 87
on burial of Jeanette and Katryn 42–45
civil suit against Williamson 272, 274, 283
lifelong commitment to ANC 7, 10, 23, 28, 79–81, 83, 123, 125, 127, 129, 227–228, 231, 246
marriage to Jenny Curtis 87–88
old-style Communist views of 74–76, 78, 299n44
possible contact with MK 130–132
role in Medu 101
role in Sactu 7, 195–196
*see also* Pretoria Central Prison: incarceration of Marius Schoon in
Schoons in exile, Lubango 22–24, 27–28, 33, 35, 124, 245–246, 250–251
impact of food shortages on family 25, 253–255
support of local community for 255–257
*see also* Angola: Schoons' undercover work in; Lubango College

Schoons' exile structures in Botswana 12,
	21–23, 123–125, 200
  Internal Political Reconstruction
	Programme (IRPD) 13–14, 128, 200
  and links with white radical networks 13,
	128–130, 137, 146, 157, 173
  Williamson's sabotaging of 8, 16, 93,
	114–115, 137–138, 173, 198–199, 201,
	279, 288
	*see also* Edwards, Karl: infiltration of
	Schoons' Botswana network by; IVS
Schwarz, Walter 149, 153
*Sechaba* 211, 215, 218
Security Branch *see* security police
security police 91
  assassinations carried out by 25, 27,
	32–33, 43
  Compol House 69, 76, 89
  exaggeration of effectiveness of 156–157,
	164, 166
  faux ANC cell of 192–193, 197–199
  harassment of Schoons in Botswana by
	98–99
  infiltration of radical underground by 3,
	5–7, 278
  'Operation Daisy' 109–110, 167, 302n86
  'railroad' 13, 93, 104, 110, 115
  use of 'front' organisations by 15–17
  *see also* Bureau for State Security; Nusas:
	security police infiltration of
Sehl, George 106–107
Seidman, Judy 2, 33, 91, 135, 157, 241, 268,
	301n39, 315n14
  on culture of secrecy 124
  as member of Medu 100–102
  on Schoons in Botswana 125–127,
	131–132, 148
Sharpeville 106, 210, 310n17
Simons, Jack 101, 200–201, 259
Slovo family 282, 289–290
  Gillian 283–285
  Joe 1, 110, 267
  *see also* First, Ruth; TRC amnesty hearings.
	Slovo and Schoon families' appeals
	against rulings of
SNS 15, 115–116, 129, 133, 277
socialism/socialists 24, 29, 40, 73, 76, 102
  democratic 118
  nonracial 82

Williamson on 59
  *see also* Lodge, Tom: on socialism;
	Williamson, Craig: virulent
	anti-communism of
Socialist International 150–151
Solidarity News Service *see* SNS
South African Communist Party (SACP) 7,
	10–11, 58, 66, 78, 156, 198, 206, 215, 218
  banning of 50, 289
  Jenny Curtis' connnections with 62–63
South African Congress of Trade Unions
	*see* Sactu
South African Defence Force (SADF)
  1975 invasion of Angola 99, 252
  attack on SNS 116
  counter-insurgency manual 175
  Gaborone raid 44–45, 277
  opposition to conscription of white
	soldiers into 99, 111–112, 199
  Pretoria bombing 235
South African Institute of Race Relations
  Jenny's work as archivist at 11, 62–64, 268
South African News Agency *see* Sana
South African Police (SAP) 74
  extra-legal abuses of 20
  Williamson's first years in 57
  *see also* security police
South African Students Organisation (Saso)
	66, 167, 303n24
Southern Futures Vaduz (SFV)
  Williamson's control of 15, 107–109,
	161–163
  *see also* Eriksson, Lars-Gunnar
Soviet Union 62, 90, 117–118, 134
1976 Soweto uprising 92, 99, 103, 120
  as product of BCM 81–82, 121–122
Suttner, Raymond 9
Suzman, Helen 70, 87, 185, 299n4

T

Tanzania
  Marius' views on 249–250, 315n14
*The African Communist* 175, 201, 215
Tladi, Puso 276–277
torture in detention 5, 17, 19–20, 83, 167, 189
  complicity of doctors in 179–180
  deaths associated with 269
  and interplay between violence and 'rule
	of law' 19, 178

# INDEX

*see also* Aggett, Neil; Hogan, Barbara: security police torture of; van Heerden, Auret: systematic torture of
Thorpe, NJ (Southern Africa Department, FCO) 234, 236–237
Tip, Karel 92, 142
trade unions
    Wiehahn Commission 213, 311n75
    Williamson's views on 206–207
    white leftists involvement in 67, 129, 195–197, 213
    *see also* Hogan, Barbara: involvement in trade union movement of; Sactu
TRC amnesty hearings
    Slovo and Schoon families' appeals against rulings of 282–286
    ruling on Williamson's case 6, 27–28, 269–270, 280–282, 287–289
    security police 'Soviet orchestrated onslaught' argument at 275–276
    testimony against Williamson at 275–277
    Williamson's application to 9, 271–272, 274–275, 281
    Williamson's testimony at 31, 110, 273, 278–279
    *see also* Raven, Jerry
Truth and Reconciliation Commission (TRC) *see* TRC amnesty hearings
Turner, Rick 52, 90, 97, 111, 296n9

## U
UCT 52–53
Umkhonto we Sizwe *see* MK
United Democratic Front (UDF) 121, 312n102
University of the Witwatersrand SRC
    Williamson as undercover agent at 8, 56–57, 297n25

## V
van Heerden, Auret 18, 141, 177
    systematic torture of 182–184

## W
Watt, Nigel 225, 227, 231, 234, 236–239, 313n16
    anti-apartheid position of 226, 230
    erasure of Jenny's role in IVS by 227–228
    UK job offer to Schoons by 232–233
    *see also* IVS; Jones, Lord Elwyn

Webster, Eddie
    testimony at Fine's trial 197
    testimony at Hogan's trial 213–214, 216, 218
Weinberg, Eli 65–66
Westcott, Nicki 52–53, 296n11
Western Cape Workers' Advice Bureau
    Jenny Curtis at 55, 67, 126
white liberalism 3, 11, 61, 67, 90
White, Luise 27–28
white radicals 8, 58
    arrests and detentions of 18, 167
    contribution to anti-apartheid struggle 1–3
    leftist debates among 11, 79–82
    and realities of race and class 3, 19, 52–53
    political trials against 17–18
    student 9, 52–53, 58–59, 61–65, 111
    Williamson's campaign against 18
    *see also* Claremont communes; New Left radicalism; political trials of Schoon network; Schoons' exile structures in Botswana: and links with white radical networks
Williams, Tim 101
Williamson, Craig 1
    ANC exile leadership's trust of 16, 113
    delusions about own importance 156–157, 164, 166, 174, 202–203
    escape cover story of 92–93, 111
    evasion of justice by 270–272, 286
    ideological role in apartheid project 6–7, 287–288, 290
    infiltration of Nusas by 9, 16, 56–60, 70, 138, 192, 198
    interconnection between Schoons and 6, 12–13, 18, 114
    weaponisation of undercover surveillance 9, 12
    wife Ingrid 119, 150–151
    virulent anti-communism of 6, 18, 116–117, 152, 165, 206
    *see also under* Schoons' exile structures in Botswana
Williamson's exposure as spy 14, 17–18, 83, 147–152, 277–278, 281
    mounting concerns/suspicions leading to 9, 16, 106, 112–113, 115, 138, 142–143, 145, 193, 201
    SA government response to 155–157

Williamson's infiltration of IUEF 6, 12–14, 91–94, 112, 198
  and campaign for support of ANC 16, 116–122, 143, 165
  use of funds for security police projects 104–107, 109–110, 140, 147, 161, 163
  impact on white activist networks of 167
  warnings to IUEF about 16, 141–143
  *see also* Commission of Inquiry into espionage activities in IUEF; EDA; Prisoners Support Trust; Sana: IUEF involvement in; Southern Futures Vaduz

Wills, Gary 94–95, 301n33
Wilson, Andrew 280–281, 283
Wood, Chris 51, 56, 61, 90
  banning of 52, 296n10
working-class movement
  as ANC tradition 67, 80

**Z**

Zambia 91, 102, 159, 247 *see also* Lusaka, ANC in
Zimbabwe 91, 256
Zimbabwe African National Union (Zanu) 118, 142–143, 159
Zurich 152–156

Printed and bound by CPI Group (UK) Ltd, Croydon, CR0 4YY
01/04/2025
14651529-0005